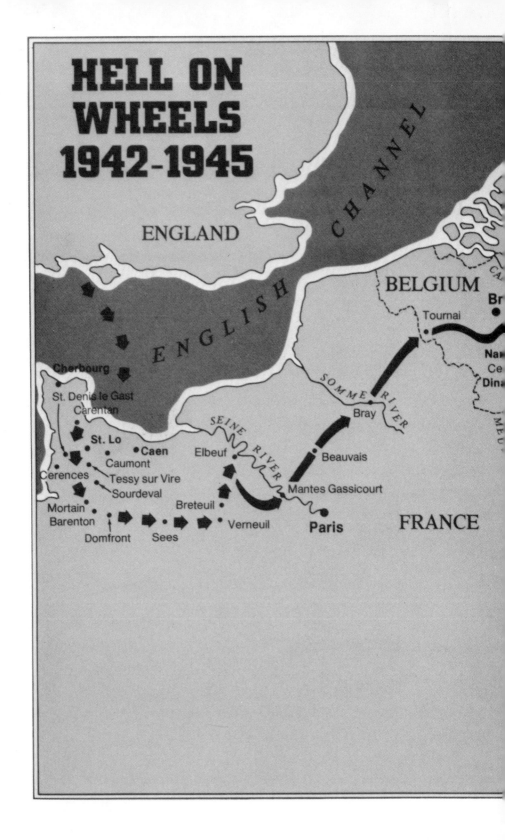

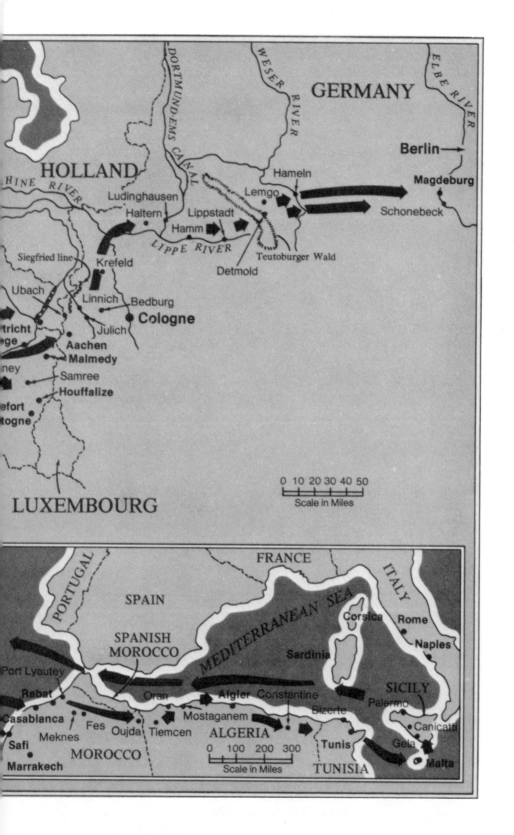

★ ★ ★

HELL ON WHEELS

THE 2D ARMORED DIVISION

by Donald E. Houston

PRESIDIO

Library of Congress Cataloging-in-Publication Data

Houston, Donald Eugene, 1938–
    Hell on wheels.

    Bibliography: p. 441
    1. World War, 1939–1945—Regimental histories—United States. 2. United States. Army. Armored Division. 2nd—History. I. Title.
[D769.30532nd.H67 1986]   940.54'12'73   86-4929
ISBN 0-89141-273-5 (pbk.)

Printed in the United States of America

to Guyla and Donny

CONTENTS

ILLUSTRATIONS

Photographs

Figures

Foreword

No greater privilege can occur in the career of any soldier than to be given the command of troops in combat. This is always true and applies to any organizational echelon, from squad to field army. But the most satisfying command slot is the one with the double X on the map symbol, the division. Moreover, when you add the old tank tread to the symbol to designate one of the army's few armored divisions, you have the greatest of all commands. At least, this was my thought when I first took over the Hell on Wheels division, the 2d Armored, on July 31, 1942.

By this time the division had come a long way from its activation with the 1st Armored on July 15, 1940. The army planned to organize twenty of these new divisions but had only formed sixteen by the end of the war. Located at Fort Benning, Georgia, the 2d Armored had fewer interruptions in its organization and training than did the 1st Division which was supporting the Armored Force School at Fort Knox, Kentucky. The 2d Division also was blessed with good commanders. Among these I would like to mention especially Charles Scott, George Patton, Willis Crittenberger and Edward Brooks.

Scott was a true pioneer in armor development, including its tactics and organization. He had the good luck to serve as an observer with the British Eighth Army in its battles with Rommel's Afrika Corps and therefore was able to bring back many lessons learned the hard way. He was able to overcome army branch prejudice against effective employment of the new Armored Force and obtain acceptance of the concept within the army's highest echelons.

George Patton followed Scott, giving the division dash, coupled with an aggressive attitude and the ultimate in fighting spirit—qualities never lost by its soldiers. Crittenberger added pride in organization and appearance, while Brooks, the artilleryman, taught the units how to coordinate the fire of basic weapons of tanks, infantry and artillery.

I like to think that I added to overall combat efficiency, because in Morocco we were able to conduct highly realistic battle training, maneuvering under live ammunition in the wide open spaces available there but not in America. We stressed the need for our tanks to lead the attack, never permitting our infantry or artillery to be overrun by enemy armor. We insisted that the infantry arrive on the objective with the absolute minimum of casualties. We devoted much time and effort to disciplined marching by all units, a quality absolutely essential to armor's battle efficiency. These efforts paid off for our task force which landed in Safi, Morocco, when we moved rapidly through about 100 miles of enemy territory to assist in the capture of Casablanca.

We received our motto after breaking out of the Normandy hedgerow country, outflanking and destroying German armor in the process. So rapid was our progress against the German Fifteenth Army, that the Belgians dubbed us, ''La Division Fue-en-Roue,'' loosely translated as ''Hell on Wheels.'' The motto implied both speed and shock action, but coupled with it was an unstated resolve to take on any mission. When asked by the army commander if we could operate north of the Albert Canal in rather low country, I replied that if the Germans could maneuver there, we sure as hell could too. That summed up our aggressive attitude.

The German forces, which opposed us in our crossing of the Meuse, our penetration of the Siegfried line and our advance to the Roer River, were surprised to see us turn up again 100 miles to the south during the Battle of the Bulge. Here we were at our best as a battle-trained division. With only four hours' notice we marched in complete combat order ready for battle. We moved in blackout conditions, with radio silence, over sleet-covered roads in unknown territory, losing only seventeen vehicles en route. Combat Command B surrounded and destroyed the 2d Panzer Division, while Combat Command A and the Reserve battled elements of the 9th, 15th and Panzer-Lehr Divisions which were trying to rescue the 2d Panzer. We defeated them, driving them several miles south to Rochefort, thus protecting the right flank of VII Corps. The division then regrouped to cut off the salient and eat the Christmas dinner which had been delayed by our all-out attack on Christmas Day. In this immense operation in the snow and sleet we had more casualties from frozen feet than German bullets.

The division later crossed the Rhine to meet the Russians on the Elbe and was proud to serve as the honor guard for President Truman when he attended the Potsdam Conference after the war.

It was my great honor to have commanded this great 2d Armored Division on two separate occasions in combat. During our war experience and after, the division's officers and men always displayed a warmth and affection toward me which I deeply appreciate but can never repay.

One thing I do know is that we could lick anyone of reasonably relative size or larger, given tank terrain on which to operate.

Ernest N. Harmon
Major General, USA (Ret)
Sarasota, Florida
December 13, 1976

Acknowledgements

This book had its beginnings in 1959 while I was a cadet at the Reserve Officers Training Corps summer camp at Fort Hood, Texas, home of Hell on Wheels. The next summer as a newly commissioned second lieutenant and while awaiting artillery school at Fort Sill, Oklahoma, I was briefly assigned to the 1st Howitzer Battalion, 14th Field Artillery, 2d Armored Division. Following my tour of duty, I left the army for the education profession.

While in the army and as a teacher, I became interested in military history, primarily in the early history of armor and in Gen. George S. Patton, Jr. In graduate school I became aware that there was not a detailed account of the 2d Armored Division. This was disappointing because of the division's brilliant battle record and because it had been commanded by Patton, that colorful and controversial master of armored warfare, in North Africa and Sicily. After many letters to and from former members of the division, and assured of their help, I decided to undertake the effort to write the Hell on Wheels story.

No one has ever written a history without incurring debts. This is especially true of this effort. I am particularly indebted to the 2d Armored Division Association, which for many years was under the able leadership of Colonel R. F. Perry and is now in the capable hands of Albert M. Jordan. Both announced the project in the association's bulletin which elicited valuable responses from the membership. Members of Hell on Wheels agreed to be interviewed and spent many hours recounting their experiences. Especially helpful in providing an overview were Gen. Jacob L. Devers, former chief of the Armored Force, and Gen. William H. Simpson, former commanding general of the Ninth Army.

Archivists of various research centers often anticipated my needs: Dr. Richard Sommers of the United States Army Military History Research Collection, Carlisle, Pennsylvania; Timothy Nenninger, Charles Phillips and Gloria Wheeler of the National Archives, Washington, D.C.; Ann Turner, reference librarian at the Henry Prescott Chaplin Memorial Library, Norwich University, North Field, Vermont; and Josh H. Stroman, John Dana, Heather MacAlpine Lloyd and especially the late Marguerite Howland of the Oklahoma State University.

In military circles, the Office of the Chief of Military History provided much assistance through its collection of unpublished materials. Mary Lee Stubbs and Stanley Russell Conner of the unit history section provided guidance on the formation of the 2d Armored Division. Detmar Finke and Hannah Zeidlik of the reference section opened their collection to me and uncovered important sources. The deputy chief historian, Charles B. MacDonald was most helpful. As the author of several volumes in the *United States Army in World War II* series, he was more than familiar with the role of the 2d Armored Division in Europe. He loaned me the manuscript of *The Last Offensive,* which covers the conclusion of the European phase of the war. The United States Armor School Library at Fort Knox, Kentucky, under the supervision of Brig. Gen. Robert W. Galloway and his successor, Brig. Gen. George S. Patton, loaned me studies done by advanced course students. *Armor* and its two able editors, Col. O. W. Martin, Jr., and Maj. Robert E. Kelso, lent materials and scheduled appointments with several of the interviewees.

Several friends, LeRoy H. Fischer, Homer L. Knight, Harold V. Sare, Douglas D. Hale, H. James Henderson, John A. Sylvester and Maj. William K. Emerson, have read the manuscript and offered invaluable suggestions. John and Carole Albright provided a home away from home while I was in Washington, D.C. John led me through the mazes at the Office of the Chief of Military History and introduced me to those who aided my search for materials.

Finally, I owe much to the two people who have lived with this work for several years. My wife, Guyla, edited, typed, critiqued and generally supervised the project. My son, Donny, though not always understanding why I did not have time to play with him or why loud noises and concentration do not mix, gave me the love and understanding that only a son can give.

In spite of the valuable assistance, advice and aid along the way, this is my work; I alone assume responsibility for any errors in fact or interpretation.

Introduction

Hell on Wheels is a direct descendent of the World War I American Tank Corps. In 1916, with the European battlefield stalemated, some means had to be found to force a conclusion to the war. Armor was the answer. In the U.S. Army, command of the new weapon went to George S. Patton, Jr., whose name later became synonymous with tank warfare.

When the war ended, the Tank Corps came to the United States, and for a while it appeared that the corps might become part of the regular army. However, Congress agreed with General of the Armies John J. Pershing that tanks had been an infantry support weapon and should remain as such. Congress thereby initiated a conflict which dominated military thought, debate and writing for two decades.

In the 1920s and 30s, while the infantry and cavalry branches argued about the merits and employment of armored vehicles, a small band of far-sighted officers began to experiment with and write about new ways of using tanks. To escape censure from their superiors, many included in their articles a disclaimer saying that the article was based only on theory or materials on hand. A few officers were able to take tanks into the field for tests to develop new tactics. While some of these experiments were reported in professional journals, branch dogma remained unchanged until the late 1920s.

The first change came with Secretary of War Dwight F. Davis's directive that the United States develop an armored force. He had witnessed the British Mechanized Force's public display for foreign dignitaries. With that directive, the War Department began what was to be a four-step process of creating an armored force. The first step was the creation of an experimental force, followed by the conversion of an existent cavalry regiment to a mechanized one. Then, the mechanized cavalry regiment was enlarged to a brigade. Finally in 1940 the creation of the Armored Force was complete. The evolution of armor was much too slow for some and much too rapid for others.

During the 1920–1930 era, the officers and noncommissioned officers who would lead the armored force were being trained. Also, during the two developmental decades, tactics and techniques were studied. In the end, both infantry and cavalry arguments proved correct. More importantly, the methods for employing a combined arms team were formulated. When the Armored Force was created in 1940, the men and tactics were ready.

The 2d Armored Division was activated on July 15, 1940, at Fort Benning, Georgia. Some of the new units in Hell on Wheels had been on continuous active duty: the 66th, 67th and 68th Armored Regiments, the 14th Artillery and the 78th Field Artillery Battalion. Other units were transferred from other commands: the 17th Engineer Battalion and the 17th Ordnance Company. Several units were created for the 2d Armored Division: the 48th Signal Company, the 2d Reconnaissance Battalion, the 14th Quartermaster Battalion and the 48th Medical Battalion.

The division was ordered to be ready for combat just a few months after its activation. With its commander's attention turned to necessary administrative details, training soon fell on the willing, able shoulders of the brigade commander, Col. George S. Patton, Jr. He quickly stamped his personality on the division and the men. When the division commander, Maj. Gen. Charles L. Scott, became the I Armored Corps commander, Patton assumed command of the division.

Following training at Fort Benning, Hell on Wheels made its first tactical public debut in the Tennessee maneuvers of 1941. It impressed friend and foe alike. In the Louisiana and Carolina maneuvers of the same year, the division learned to be part of a team, while infantry units learned to work with armor. Patton cautioned the division that time for training was growing short, for soon the United States would probably enter the war. His prediction came true with the Japanese attack on Pearl Harbor.

In the summer and early fall of 1942, the division began preparations for one of the most dangerous of all wartime experiences—the invasion of a foreign country. On November 8 the men and tanks went ashore in North Africa. Three days later, the French ended hostilities. While the 2d Armored Division did not take part in the desert campaigns, it had to reequip the 1st Armored Division after its disastrous defeat at Kasserine

Pass and also armed the 2d French Armored Division. At the same time, the division was preparing for its second amphibious landing, this time in Sicily. After twelve combat days (though the Sicilian campaign lasted thirty-eight days), the division scored a major victory with its capture of Palermo. Assuming occupation duty but ever-ready to move to the fighting front, the Hell-on-Wheelers performed the tasks of military governors with the same excellence that had earned them combat fame.

In late 1943, the division was ordered to England where it prepared for the cross-channel attack against Europe. While not making the combat landing, Hell on Wheels was the first armored division thrown into the battle to stop a German counterattack. With workmanlike precision, the tankers repulsed the assaults and earned the grudging respect of the German military and political leaders. In July, though the division was originally assigned a secondary role in the breakout at St. Lo, it quickly had to take over the primary attack. Success or failure rode on the turrets of the division; it opened the hole through which the Third Army and Gen. George Patton roared. German resistance stiffened, and the tankers labored to reach Tessy sur Vire and Vire, where they were to pivot northeastward.

Hitler ordered a major attempt to retake Avranches, which would cut a gap between the First and Third Armies. At Barenton and Mortain, Hell on Wheels struck the German flanks, defeating every effort to move forward. Finally after several days of extremely heavy fighting, the Germans pulled back. In a full-scale armored pursuit, the tankers attacked round the clock, driving the Germans to the Seine River and through Belgium. Finally gasoline shortages forced the Americans to take a few days' rest. That gave the enemy time to regroup and man defenses in the Siegfried line.

In the four-month period from October, 1944, through January, 1945, the division faced the heaviest fighting of its career. Attacking through the Siegfried line, it drew German armor as though it were a magnet. For two grueling months, Hell on Wheels struggled to advance about twelve miles. Finally having reached the Roer River, the division was making plans to cross it when it was alerted for use in the Battles of the Bulge. The 2d Armored Division halted the spearhead of the German army just three miles short of the Meuse River. In January, 1945, against debilitating weather, determined enemy resistance and extreme fatigue, the division reduced the German salient in the Ardennes.

Following the Bulge, the Hell-on-Wheelers attacked across the Roer

River and almost scored one of the major successes of the war: it came within a hairsbreadth of capturing a bridge across the Rhine. As the infantrymen prepared to charge across the bridge, it was destroyed—literally in their faces. Finally, crossing the river, Hell on Wheels attacked eastward, with Berlin as its goal. Reaching the Elbe River, the division had almost set up a bridge when German artillery fire destroyed it and prevented any success. However, part of the division pushed across the river at Barby and retained their position. As a reward for its tremendous battle record, the 2d Armored Division was selected to be the first American force to occupy Berlin.

In late 1945 and early 1946, the division returned to the United States and, except for the three-year period 1951–1954, has not left America. Although it supplied men and units for both the Korean and Vietnam Wars, the division itself did not participate in those conflicts.

It is easy to write about a great division, its combat commands, regiments, battalions, companies, platoons, squads and individual tanks. One too often forgets that the division is not an impersonal, faceless mass but rather an organization of men. When the tanks attacked, the artillery fired, the infantry charged and the other units supported the attacks, it was men, not machines, doing the fighting. And it was the men who were killed, wounded or maimed.

The men had complex thoughts and emotions all along—from the first day the new recruits and draftees dismounted the trucks at Fort Benning to face the officers and old-time sergeants, through the training era, and then in combat and occupation duty. Some of their stories are humorous; others are tragic; some are simply the stories of men doing their jobs. The history of the 2d Armored Division is not about the hardware of war; it is a story of brave men and their activities.

HELL ON WHEELS

Chapter 1

CREATING AN IDEA

On February 28, 1945, the 2d Armored Division crossed the Roer River, attacking northeastward toward the bridge over the Rhine River at Krefeld-Uerdingen, Germany. Flying above the green cabbage fields in a Piper Cub, Sidney Olson, a correspondent for *Time* magazine watched the action below. First came a long row of tanks followed at a suitable distance by a greater number of tanks and tank destroyers. Following the assaulting wave, half-tracks and truck-borne infantry maneuvered to clear stubbornly defended strongpoints. Shells from field artillery to the rear were clearing openings for the attacking troops. The ground action was under an air umbrella from which Thunderbolts and P-47s strafed and bombed any enemy activity. It was a beautiful demonstration of the combined arms team in combat motion.

In this classic armored attack, the correspondent did not see the many years of thinking, training and rehearsal that led to the assault. Before anyone obtained this powerful war machine, armored doctrine slowly evolved from 1917 to 1940. Nor did he mention two pioneers in

1

armor warfare, Maj. Gen. I. D. White and Brig. Gen. Sidney R. Hinds, who were leading the very attack he was watching.

The tank came into existence because of military necessity in World War I. The European battlefields had become stalemated as machine guns, barbed wire and massed artillery eliminated maneuver from the battleground. The only possible attacks were costly frontal assaults against well-prepared defensive positions. These attacks usually followed massive artillery barrages intended to overcome defensive positions but more often tore up the ground in no-man's-land which slowed the assaulting force.

A British lieutenant colonel, Ernest D. Swinton, conceived the idea of an early model tank after seeing a tractor in France. He recommended that the vehicle be armor covered, armed with guns and used in combat. Winston S. Churchill, first lord of the Admiralty, liked the idea and urged its adoption. Because of his encouragement, naval terms such as hull, turret, deck and ports are used today to describe various parts of the tank. Tanks were first used in combat on September 15, 1916, at the Battle of the Somme and were considered a failure, despite limited success. An extremely ardent tank enthusiast, Nathan A. Smith, later explained that these tanks were employed over unsuitable terrain, in small numbers and without the element of surprise. The attack was a failure not because of mechanical problems or tactical usage, but because of leadership. Smith said that generals trained under an ultraconservative system were too hidebound, their minds too inelastic to grasp the possibilities of the new weapon or to see the similarity with the past. All they could see were mechanical failures. It was better to suffer defeat while obeying ancient tactical customs than to win by the use of a radical idea.

In the Battle of Cambrai, where tanks were next engaged on November 20, 1917, some of the earlier problems had been overcome. Tanks were used en masse, achieved surprise, and local reserves were provided. While some tanks were assigned distant objectives, others were detailed to help the infantry forward. The basic idea was to go as far and as fast as possible to attack reserve and rear area positions. Cambrai, while a tactical success, was a strategic failure, again because of poor generalship. The British commanders did not think the tanks could achieve surprise, failed to provide sufficient reserves and neglected to exploit the breakthrough or to hold the ground won. The Germans launched a vicious counterattack, regaining their lost territory.

Following the Somme battle, the American military mission in

France submitted a report on the use of tanks. Maj. Gen. John J. Pershing, commander of the American Expeditionary Force, approved the report and decided that tanks would be a useful addition to the American army. Pershing had his staff study the tank question. When they determined that between 375 and 600 heavy tanks and 1,200 to 1,500 light tanks would be needed, he asked the War Department to secure the tanks for him.

The American Tank Corps, which came into existence because of the Battle of the Somme and the subsequent report by the American military mission, had two beginnings: in France in 1917, and in the United States in 1918. In a letter of application for a command in the Tank Corps in France, Capt. George S. Patton, Jr., compared the mission of light tanks to that of light cavalry. His application approved, Patton organized and trained the first American tank troops.

While training his command, Patton stressed that tanks must aid the infantry's advance. To do this, the tanks would cut barbed wire not destroyed by artillery, stop enemy infantry's manning the trenches when artillery barrages lifted, prevent enemy machine guns and cannon from firing on friendly infantry, help mop up positions, neutralize strongpoints or blind them with smoke, patrol to prevent counterattacks and pursue the enemy after friendly forces had consolidated the positions. Equally important, he stressed coordination between tanks and infantry. While readying his command, Patton urged ending preparatory artillery fire because of terrain damage. As an alternative, he proposed using smoke to blind antitank guns and urged using airplanes to maintain radio contact between artillery and tanks.

On August 27, 1918, the headquarters of the First Army ordered tactical tank employment, and the later official infantry branch policy, in a memorandum, "Combat Instructions for Troops of First Army." The first mission of tanks was to clear gaps through wire. Their second role was to drive the enemy into shelter to prevent their manning machine guns and cannons against friendly infantry. Infantrymen were instructed to follow their assigned routes regardless of the direction of the tanks; they were not to place themselves between tanks, as that would prevent the tanks from firing to the flanks. The infantry was to remain closer to the tanks to take advantage of the shock action of the attack and to point out targets. Finally, engineers were to be near enough to help tanks over rough ground. Artillery was instructed to fire smoke shells to impair the vision of antitank defenders.

Lecturing at the tank school, Patton stressed that tanks and other "auxiliary arms are but a means of aiding infantry." In his final report of operations, he emphasized in capital letters the dictum that "Tanks Must Stay With the Infantry." Patton and the First Army memorandum set the tone and doctrine that would govern armored usage for the next two decades. In 1921, while visiting the tank school, Brig. Gen. Samuel D. Rockenback stated that there was no such thing as an independent tank attack. Tanks were an infantry auxiliary and, as such, their tactics had to conform to those of the infantry. Tanks might proceed, follow or accompany foot soldiers but would be controlled by the infantry commander.

The second beginning for tanks was the creation of the Tank Service of the National Army, authorized by the War Department on January 16, 1918. On that date the chief of engineers, Maj. Gen. William M. Black, raised the first unit under this authorization. The 65th Engineer Regiment was composed of two light tank battalions and two heavy battalions: the 1st Separate Battalion, Heavy Tank Service, and 2d Battalion, Heavy Tank Service. Most units raised under this authorization stayed in the United States.

The Tank Service merged with the Tank Corps in 1919, but remained a separate and distinct organization because of funding in the Army Appropriation Act of June 19, 1919. This law permitted the continuance of the Tank Corps until June 30, 1920. This may have led to optimism for the tankers, who possibly foresaw their status as a separate arm. On June 3, 1920, the National Defense Act transferred the tanks, "lock, stock, and monkey wrenches," as Brig. Gen. Sidney R. Hinds put it, to the infantry. The force was divided between Fort Benning, Georgia, and Franklin Cantonment, Camp Meade, Maryland. Later, the infantry divided the tank battalions into companies, deactivated some and assigned the remainder to infantry divisions.

The National Defense Act of 1920 was a crucial step in armor development. Probably because of tank usage as an auxiliary of infantry during World War I, and perhaps because of the lack of mechanical reliability and speed, the infantry assignment was logical at the time. An independent tank corps was probably doomed by Pershing's testimony before the House Committee on Military Affairs on October 31, 1919, in which he said that the tank was a valuable weapon for use with infantry and that its development should be encouraged. He then stated what would be the death knell of a separate tanks corps. "The Tank Corps should not be a large organization; only of sufficient numbers, I should say, to carry on investigations and conduct training with the infantry, and

I would place it under the Chief of Infantry as an adjunct of that arm.'' In his final report as chief of the Tank Corps, Rockenback correctly observed that "the successful development and value of the arm in the future depends upon the sympathy and support it is given." Infantry gave it very little of either during the next two decades.

Capt. Dwight D. Eisenhower in a 1920 article, "A Tank Discussion," observed that it was incumbent upon the infantry to study tanks to determine their capabilities, limitations and future usage. After considering the question for two decades, the infantry's answer was to maintain the tank as a support weapon to aid the foot soldiers' advance. Because of that decision, tanks lost their independence of action and were relegated to the pace of infantry: about 2½ miles per hour.

Infantry thinking was influenced by several factors during the 1920s and 1930s. There was a tendency to embrace the successful tactics of the past with little or no thought of change for future wars. This attempt to establish absolute methods and procedures based on past experiences was an effort to reduce the constantly evolving complexities of war to static methods. This attitude fostered a belief that the next war would be the same as the last and encouraged rigidity and dogma, neither of which proved serviceable in warfare.

The early tanks were either mechanically unreliable or, when functioning properly, moved forward quickly and left the infantry behind. In either case, the foot soldier had no tank support. The view that tanks were unreliable failed to consider that mechanical devices could be improved; apparently no thought was given to speeding up the infantry. The tank was originally developed to solve a particular problem—impenetrable defenses. This might not occur in a future war. Why, the infantrymen asked, should tanks be developed? This view contradicted the idea that success in war would influence future thinking. If tanks were successful in breaching the static defenses of 1917 and 1918, would they not be similarly successful in the future? If the next war was not along static defense lines, then it would be one of maneuver. In that case, the tank would be most useful in escorting the infantryman while he maneuvered to an advantageous position.

In the late 1920s, thinking began to change slowly and imperceptibly. The chief of infantry stated that the tank, essentially an offensive weapon, should be used to support the unit delivering the decisive attack. These ideas came from the old Tank Corps, but any idea that light tanks could be used in exploiting a successful attack was new to the infantry. In this new role, tanks could be assigned the task of moving forward quickly to deliver the blow which might turn the enemy's defeat into a rout, attacking the tails of retreating columns, crushing wagons and artillery. They might even race the enemy to bridges and railroad centers, attempting to prevent their escape. They could do that even if mechanized cavalry was available. The risk involved, including the possibility of being out of range of supporting infantry or artillery, was justified when there was a reasonable chance of decisive results. A decade later, in the 1938–1939 era, infantry tanks were restricted to exploiting breakthroughs or chasing a defeated enemy. While the latter was a slight retreat from the former position, both gave tanks a mission similar to cavalry—to pursue, attack and destroy.

While the official infantry position was that tanks were auxiliary weapons to aid the foot soldiers' advance, a few people foresaw mobile war. These spokesmen argued that tanks would be a principal weapon used with supporting infantry, artillery and engineers. The unit would be organized, trained and function as a team, an independent striking force attacking deep into enemy territory. This view caused rivalry and branch jealousy. The proposal transgressed the traditional roles of infantry and cavalry. Neither branch could tolerate the idea of being subordinate to tanks, a problem not encountered by the artillery and engineer branches, which had traditionally been support units.

There was little tank activity in the 1920s, when the tanks belonged to the infantry and were subordinate to it. Articles occasionally appeared in professional military journals and some experimental problems were conducted by tank enthusiasts. But at the same time, an emphasis on mobility began to spread throughout the army, and by the end of the 1930s a few military leaders were in positions to implement this new idea.

In 1922, the infantry conducted tests in the Panama Canal Zone to determine if tanks could be used there. Col. John W. Heavey, commanding officer of the 33d Infantry Regiment, had the World War I vintage tanks removed from storage so that his men could experience working with and against armored vehicles. In each instance, when battalions were maneuvering against each other, the tank-supported unit won. The tanks, commanded by Capt. Sereno E. Brett, one of Patton's battalion commanders in World War I, maneuvered over the rugged, wooded terrain. When the test concluded there was little doubt that tanks could operate anywhere in the Canal Zone—anywhere artillery could go and almost anywhere that mountain units could go. It was thought that the experiment would lead to some modifications about using tanks in jungles, but apparently that did not happen.

Although the Canal Zone experiment was reported in the *Cavalry Journal,* the largest single factor in the dissemination of the mobility concept was the Tank School at Camp Meade, Maryland. Brig. Gen. Sidney R. Hinds, while a first classman at the United States Military Academy, had his introduction to tank warfare in a lecture by Brigadier General Rockenback. After graduation in 1920, Hinds attended the infantry officers' school at Fort Benning, Georgia, where he received about a week's instruction in tanks. The class was taught by Captain Brett, who emphasized that in this gasoline-powered age the days of the 2½-miles-per-hour infantryman was over. Brett challenged the young officers to attend the full-year's course at the Tank School. Hinds was among those who attended in 1928 and 1929.

The Tank School faced several problems, including lack of funds, lack of War Department interest and lack of a library, as well as outmoded World War I tanks and official infantry doctrine. Some instructors such as Lt. Cols. Allen F. Kingman, Sereno E. Brett, Alvin C. Gillem, Jr., and Capt. Walter McAdams resisted official doctrine and challenged students to find a better way. The students spent two weeks on map reading, reconnaissance and road sketching; three weeks on weapon maintenance and firing; seven weeks on all phases of vehicular maintenance; three weeks on driving and convoy routing; a week on history and organization; and two weeks on tactics, including night problems. The final examination was unusual. After completing the course, the student was assigned to the ordnance shop for two or three weeks during which time he had to repair a tank and drive it out of the shop under its own power. The student was then assigned to a tank unit at Camp Meade.

After completing the Tank School program, First Lieutenant Hinds was assigned to the 1st Tank Regiment at Camp Meade and settled into the routine of garrison life. He recalled that after necessary work details and other distractions only two or three men were available for training. The tanks were mechanically unreliable, and during training one tank was often kept in reserve as a retriever if the first broke down or got stuck.

While at Camp Meade, Hinds uttered the most serious heresy conceivable for an infantryman: he suggested that tankers should be trained in cavalry tactics. He was quickly reminded that tanks were infantry support weapons and would continue in that role. Admittedly, he reflected at a later time, the equipment of the 1920s and 1930s would not realistically

have supported wide envelopments, breakthroughs or distant and powerful pursuit, all maneuvers in which Hinds would participate while commanding the 41st Armored Infantry Regiment and later Combat Command B, 2d Armored Division in World War II. In spite of inadequate
equipment, thoughts still turned to finding a better way to fight a war. The
mobility concept was germinating, and only when the vehicles to fertilize
it became available did it come to full fruition.

In 1931, Hinds was transferred to Schofield Barracks in the
Hawaiian Islands and was assigned to the 11th Tank Company, which
supported the Hawaiian Division. There tanks were used according to
standard doctrine: one tank platoon attached to an infantry battalion for
offensive action. Tanks were not massed for exploiting a breakthrough of
enemy lines. In defense, especially against an invasion, tanks were to be
dug in and used as armored pillboxes. The tank company officers urged
that this concept be abandoned and that the tank company be held in
reserve to counterattack against any landing force. To do this required
complete reconnaissance of trails and roads on the islands. Hinds drove
the motorcycle and 2d Lt. Ralph W. Zwicker, later a general involved in
Sen. Joseph McCarthy's demagoguery, sat on the rear holding a stick
slightly longer than the width of a tank. Thus where the motorcycle and
stick could go, tanks could go also. In a later exercise, the concept of
tanks in counterattack proved valid, and the tank plans were changed
accordingly. Though a small change, it was a deviation from accepted
infantry doctrine.

From 1920 to 1928, there was little development in tanks or doctrine. One man, however, came to the front—Maj. Bradford G.
Chynoweth was described by a former editor of *Armor* as the leading tank
philosopher in the 1920s and 1930s. In the period from 1920 to 1940,
there were generally three attitudes toward the tank. First was praise from
former tankers who had fought successfully in the vehicles. Next was
sarcasm and condemnation from those who had served in tanks which
failed to accomplish their mission. Last came a more balanced, objective
evaluation from those who had arrived at independent conclusions.
Chynoweth was one of the latter group.

In an article, "Tank Infantry," Chynoweth reviewed the reasons for
adopting tanks, concluding that in a mechanical age the army had to
prepare for mechanized warfare. He carried the argument further in
"Cavalry Tanks," stating that future tanks would have greater speed (25
to 35 m.p.h.) and increased vision. Tanks afforded speed, shock, fire-

power and protection, but their use raised a fundamental question in the author's mind: would tanks be controlled by a separate arm? Chynoweth delivered a stinging attack when he said that the army was clinging to old concepts of organization, refusing to create a new branch whose existence contradicted accepted tactical principles, simply because the tank had supported infantry in World War I.

Cavalry tanks would, in Chynoweth's opinion, be better than infantry tanks, for cavalry was the maneuvering element of an army. The mobile arm could be concentrated for an attack and dispersed for reconnaissance and security missions. Many cavalry functions could be carried out with a slight change of equipment, and, the author reasoned, tanks afforded increased firepower and mobility. He concluded that a tank was only an iron horse and did not detract from real horses. Such a comment did not win the author friends in either the infantry or cavalry and may have been one of the many factors which led to branch jealousies for the next two decades.

Chynoweth sent the "Cavalry Tank" article to Maj. George S. Patton, Jr., for comment; the reply was printed immediately following the article. Patton argued that the United States needed neither infantry nor cavalry tanks, but an independent tank corps, as they were special, technical and vastly powerful weapons. Cavalry, Patton argued, had to advance by enveloping movements or await a tank breakthrough; it could not batter itself against a stone wall. Fulfilling other cavalry missions such as screens, raids and long turning movements would make the tanks more a handicap than a help. Cavalry lived off the land; tanks were dependent on long supply lines. Patton saw further that there were places where tanks could not function, such as in Philippine rice paddies, in the mountains of Mexico, in the forests of Canada, in the hills and gullied plains of Texas, or in the face of competent artillery fire. Patton then predicted that an overseas force would not give up that priceless commodity, deck space, to large shipments of tanks.

During the 1920–1930s a war of words was fought in the professional journals. Apparently the chiefs of cavalry and infantry ordered their respective branch officers to hew to the orthodox line. After leaving the White House in 1961, Dwight D. Eisenhower recalled in *At Ease: Stories That I Tell to Friends* that he and Patton, while stationed at Camp Meade, experimented with tanks, machine guns and tactics to improve their efficiency. Since their printed ideas conflicted with accepted doctrine, Eisenhower was called before the chief of infantry, Maj. Gen.

Charles F. Farnsworth, who told him to desist, as his ideas were not only wrong but dangerous, and to keep any deviant opinions to himself. Furthermore, if the young infantry captain could not comply with accepted doctrine, he would be court-martialed. Eisenhower also thought that Patton received the same message from the chief of cavalry, Maj. Gen. Williard A. Holbrook. Such admonitions only strengthened their resolve to improve tank usage.

If the first success of tanks was their transfer to the infantry in 1920 rather than outright abolition, then their second success came in 1928. That year, Secretary of War Dwight F. Davis visited the British armor demonstration at Andershot, England, and was impressed. Upon returning home he expressed a desire that the United States develop a similar force. The War Department had, up to that time, not given any thought to such a force, its possible role, mission or organization.

While the War Department was debating whether to create a mechanized force, the first nontank armored unit came into existence. General Order Number 5, issued by Headquarters, Third Army Corps, in February 1928, created a provisional platoon, the 1st Armored Car Troop of one officer and twenty-three enlisted men. The platoon had studied at the Motor Transport School and was stationed at Fort Holabird, Maryland. In May the platoon marched to Fort Benning, Georgia, a distance of 875 miles, in three and one-half days. They returned to Fort Holabird by way of Fort Bragg, North Carolina, a distance of 925 miles, in five days. On July 10, 1928, the Third Army Corps issued General Order Number 19, which changed the platoon to the 1st Armored Car Troop, with a strength of two officers and forty-seven enlisted men. This platoon later became part of the mechanized force.

In 1928, the War Department authorized an Experimental Mechanized Force to be assembled at Fort Leonard Wood, now Fort George G. Meade, Maryland. The force, organized in June 1928, was to be a completely mechanized, self-contained unit of great mobility and striking power, but of limited holding power. It was to be considered a special offensive unit, since armored divisions were not envisioned at the time. The tank was to be the principal attack element and all other components were to assist. Tactics were to be built around this tank concept as well as the rapid consolidation, securing and exploiting successes achieved by the tanks. Tactics should insure surprise, speed and deep penetrations; members of the command were to be imbued with an attitude of using speed to the maximum advantage. Finally, the force was to be considered a tactical unit as well as a tactical laboratory.

The Experimental Mechanized Force, dubbed the ''Gasoline Brigade,'' was activated July 1, 1928. It contained an infantry battalion from the 34th Infantry Regiment, 1st Armored Car Troop, 2d Battalion of the 6th Artillery, a company of engineers, a signal company, a chemical warfare platoon armed with 4.2-inch smoke mortars, an antiaircraft artillery battery, the 16th Tank Battalion (light tanks), the 17th Tank Battalion (medium tanks) and the 2d Platoon, 4th Tank Company (light tanks). It was a balanced force patterned after the British: a striking force (tanks), a holding and mopping-up group (infantry), fire support (field artillery), chemical mortars, antiaircraft artillery, support troops (engineers and transporters) and supply trains.

In the early summer of 1928, the Experimental Mechanized Force, commanded by Col. Oliver S. Eskridge, and the G-3, operations and training officer, Maj. Douglas T. Greene, later commanding officer of the 67th Armored Regiment, 2d Armored Division, supervised the organization and training of the individual units. They conducted essentially strategic or pre-engagement road marches to Upper Maroboro, Maryland, Gettysburg and Toby Hanna, Pennsylvania. The exercises showed that most of the equipment was obsolete, a fact previously known to the men, and that vehicular convoy marching was slower than individual vehicular speed. The positive side was the demonstration that convoy movements of seventy-five miles a day were normal; this was three to five times faster than foot troops could march. Distance and speed permitted a larger radius of action and increased capacity for achieving surprise. In late summer, the units started combat training to determine the best tactical use of such a force. All elements of the command took part, but only the tracked vehicles underwent combat exercises. Overall these were of limited value, for only the newer vehicles could attain a speed over seven miles per hour, but several valuable lessons were learned in the areas of supply methods, command and control, and procedures for conducting night operations.

In the concluding exercise, three tanks and two cargo carriers marched from Camp Meade to Gettysburg and returned under their own power. The route was seventy-two miles. Going to Gettysburg the force averaged six miles per hour; using all vehicles, wheeled and tracked, the force averaged 7½ per hour. The conclusion was that while tracked vehicles were not significantly slower than a mixed vehicular column, tanks should not move long distances under their own power because of short track and vehicular life. This march was evidence of the army's technical advancement and a major factor in bringing about mechanization.

The Experimental Mechanized Force learned valuable lessons from these maneuvers, which it passed on to the War Department for study and evaluation. A need for uniformity in the speed and characteristics of armored vehicles was evident. Also, the personnel needed to be intelligent and highly trained to operate the equipment. In the combat phase of training, the force showed that it had enormous firepower compared to a nonmechanized force. The importance of chemical warfare was established, especially the use of smoke; airplanes also proved to be vital for all aspects of mechanized operations.

The two main problems were communications and armored infantry carriers. For want of improved radios, a force should be highly trained so that it could respond automatically to various types of situations. For infantry carriers, full-tracked vehicles should be developed that would carry between one-half and a full squad with weapons.

The 1928 experiment proved or disproved various positions previously adopted and was a failure or success depending on who was evaluating it. Critics usually emphasized that mechanical problems justified their contentions about static warfare for the future. Supporters countered by pointing out that mechanical reliability would improve. Most importantly, the Experimental Mechanized Force showed that different branches could work together as a team. Especially promising was the fact that motorized infantry could keep pace with tanks. One positive effect was the start of a lively literary battle, for now writers had a positive example from which to work and not merely theory. One editor saw the experiment as an effort to emulate Europe. He cautioned: ''Let not the glamour of the great armies of Europe be a cause for mechanization which may result in war material unsuited for physical conditions in possible theaters of operations.''

The War Department created a Mechanized Board to study the results. It concluded that a new mechanized force should be created, consisting of a combined arms team of regimental size, serving as a laboratory to test weapons and tactics for future wars; it would be a separate branch under a general officer. This recommendation was a major step forward in the tanks' battle for life.

From 1929 to 1931, the army, which has always enjoyed a jargon all its own, became involved with semantics, including some hair-splitting distinctions. One such distinction, however, was essential if any other branch was to work with tanks. General Charles P. Summerall, army chief of staff, in his 1929 annual report, urged the army to mechanize and motorize. *Mechanization* was the application of mechanics to combat soldiers on the battlefield with a view to increasing their mobility, protection and striking power. *Motorization* was the replacement of animal-drawn vehicles by motor-powered vehicles and the use of motor trucks for rapid movement of large bodies of troops from one part of a theater of operations to another. These definitions suggested that mechanization was of tactical value, while motorization was of strategic importance.

Before General Summerall left the War Department in 1930, he issued a memorandum to "assemble that mechanized force now, station it at Fort Eustis, Virginia. Make it permanent, not temporary." The same year, Congress authorized $284,000 to implement mechanization plans in spite of the Mechanization Board's recommendation of $4 million over a four-year period.

In October, 1930, the new mechanized force began assembling at the location selected by Summerall. It was commanded by a cavalryman, Col. Daniel Van Voorhis; the executive officer was Maj. Sereno E. Brett. The force included representatives from all arms and some services. The selection of Van Voorhis was desirable in spite of his having no mechanical background. He firmly believed that there was a need to develop a better cavalry mount, because a mounted soldier fought better than one on foot, especially if the mount was maneuverable and afforded a good base of fire. Van Voorhis saw his mission as giving the mounted soldier a decisive role on the battlefield.

The new mechanized force was a self-contained unit designed to fulfill particular missions on the battlefield. For reconnaissance it had Troop A, 2d Armored Car Squadron. Its striking element was Company A, 1st Light Tank Regiment, supported by Battery A, 6th Field Artillery. The holding and mopping-up element was Company H, 34th Infantry Regiment. Company C, 13th Engineer Regiment would provide engineer support, while the 19th Ordnance Company and a quartermaster mobile repair shop would keep the vehicles running. A platoon from Battery E, 69th Coast Artillery was added for antiaircraft protection. A detachment from the 1st Chemical Warfare Service, equipped with 4.2-inch mortars, was to provide that support. The force assembled at Fort Eustis comprised

Above: Capt. Sereno E. Brett, pioneer in armor theory.
Right: Lt. Gen. Daniel Van Voorhis, commanding officer of the first permanent mechanized force.

190 officers, 2,900 enlisted men and 845 vehicles, including 230 tanks, 50 self-propelled guns and mortars, 90 half tracks, and 19 armored cars. While this mechanized force was a composite of all branches, Van Voorhis, a tough disciplinarian, instituted a traditional cavalry policy. Before the men left the motor park, the vehicles were maintained, washed and fueled for the next day's training. This became standard procedure ten years later in the armored force.

The unit began its training by taking part in extended maneuvers. Many times the main body marched seventy-five miles a day while the reconnaissance elements often went 200 miles ahead. Night marches and maneuvers were conducted without lights and used all vehicles. The unit learned to fight under all conditions. While training in field maneuvers, command post exercises and road marches, officers soon realized that the primary use for such an organization would be offensive in nature. Its main value was mobility; success would depend on shock gained by speed, armor and firepower from its many automatic weapons. Training stressed operations against entrenched infantry or other mechanized forces. Attacks included wide turning movements, seizure of crucial terrain features, covering larger units, counterattacks, exploitation of breakthroughs and flank and rear guards—all traditional cavalry-type missions.

While undergoing field training, the mechanized force was being studied closely by the chiefs of infantry and cavalry. Rumors began circulating about the possibility of the mechanized force becoming a separate arm; this alarmed the infantry, which feared that the cavalry was attempting to break the infantry's tank monopoly. Infantry's greatest dread was that the mechanized force was trying to acquire infantrymen; this the infantry branch would not tolerate.

In late 1931, the experimental force ran out of funds and was disbanded. Some troops returned to their parent units, while the headquarters, armored car troops, ordnance, quartermaster unit and signal corps elements went to Camp Knox, Kentucky, to create the cadre for a mechanized cavalry regiment. In spite of complaints about obsolete equipment, members of the force made sound and valid recommendations that would be heeded in the future. Maj. Robert W. Grow, later the first G-3 of the 2d Armored Division, noted in his diary that members of the command had to begin thinking in minutes, not miles, and that each vehicle should have an antiaircraft weapon; the .50 caliber machine gun was such a weapon. Grow talked with Capt. George C. Kenney, Army

Air Corps, who recommended that the vehicles be spread seventy-five to one hundred yards apart on road marches. The consolidated report that Grow helped write emphasized that a mechanized force was for the execution of mobile warfare. He stated that the present force was not suitably organized, equipped or of adequate strength to carry out the War Department's directive that all arms be mechanized. Such a force needed all its components if it were to train and develop the tactics necessary for success on the battlefield. The report concluded with the recommendation that a mechanized brigade be organized.

In 1931, Army Chief of Staff Gen. Douglas MacArthur ordered all arms and services to adapt mechanization to their traditional roles. For cavalry this meant substituting vehicles for horses. The chief of staff recognized that the first step would be to mechanize one regiment. He also realized there might be a need to keep some horse units. He felt that modern weapons had eliminated the horse as a source of power, and except for infantry, the horse was the slowest means of transportation. He envisioned columns of mechanized cavalry, units from the Tank Corps and motorized infantry all moving at a uniform speed and all supported by artillery. Either he failed to realize that tanks could traverse the same terrain as horses, or he was making concessions to cavalry; perhaps both.

In laying down guidelines for mechanization, MacArthur recognized that tanks had improved mechanically and therefore could be given missions beyond the normal infantry support role. Cavalry was to develop combat vehicles capable of performing reconnaissance, counterreconnaissance, flank actions, pursuit and similar operations. At the same time infantry was to develop tanks to increase its striking power against strongly held positions. He recognized that tanks were assault weapons and would probably be used only a short time during any action. In developing tanks, stress had to be placed on strategic mobility even though their primary use would be as a tactical weapon. With improved performance, tanks would probably be assigned to the corps or to the army and used where needed. To evade the provisions of the 1920 National Defense Act, and recognizing that infantry and cavalry would probably develop similar vehicles, MacArthur said that "tanks" would be the term applied to infantry vehicles, while "combat cars" would refer to cavalry vehicles.

MacArthur recommended that the army mechanize a cavalry brigade, two infantry tank regiments, seven separate armored car troops (three for the regular army, four for the National Guard), thirteen scout car platoons for regular cavalry regiments and seven tank companies for use with regular infantry divisions. Though a bit visionary for the time, it was a step toward developing a mechanized force. The cavalry phase was assigned to Maj. Gen. Guy V. Henry, chief of cavalry. Henry acted slowly for reasons not entirely his fault: limited resources, the reluctance of ordnance to accept ideas from the automotive industry and the protracted debate over mechanization. This slowness only added to the conviction of Van Voorhis and Adna Chaffee that mechanization would not make much progress unless it was a separate branch or under the War Department itself.

The War Department assigned the mechanized force to the cavalry in 1931, with directions to organize a cavalry regiment in order to develop the organization and equipment necessary to perform cavalry missions. That same year, 15 officers and 159 enlisted men were sent to Camp Knox, Kentucky (which became Fort Knox in 1934), forming the cadre for the mechanized cavalry regiment. In 1933, the 1st Cavalry Regiment, without its horses, was transferred to Camp Knox to become the 1st Cavalry Regiment (Mechanized). In developing the unit, the first objectives were always organization and equipment. New developments were the result of constant experimentation, using a wide range of thoughts and ideas.

Traditionally, cavalry had been the branch of mobility and shock. While retaining both strategic and tactical mobility, firepower gradually took the place of shock. Before World War I horse cavalry attacked mounted, but afterwards it maneuvered mounted and attacked dismounted. Gradually the fixed defensive doctrine adopted by the army during World War I began to change in favor of a new trend to restore movement to the battlefield. Mechanized cavalry was a natural response to this required mobility, since it could attack sensitive enemy positions some distance from the front, especially if roads were available. This new breed of cavalry could make maximum use of the firepower of the fast light tanks or combat cars.

In February, 1932, Van Voorhis, Chaffee, Grow and Brig. Gen. Julian R. Lindsey, the commanding general of Camp Knox, discussed the organization of a mechanized regiment and brigade, along with the necessary attachments—artillery, chemical, ordnance and quartermaster. Grow was ordered to draw up a table of organization for a mechanized brigade. He was not optimistic, for such a proposal had been turned down before, and the chief of cavalry mandated that cavalry officers had to be thoroughly indoctrinated into horse cavalry before being assigned to the mechanized regiment.

In the early phase, the cadre for the mechanized cavalry regiment conducted motor maintenance schools which all members were required to attend, and later there were specialty schools. During the summer it gave demonstrations for the Officer Reserve Corps, the Reserve Officers Training Corps, the Citizens Military Training Camps and the National Guard. These demonstrations provided another means to test principles and techniques. It required a salesman's job to sell mechanization, but the end result was to make the officers and enlisted men try harder.

During the demonstrations, good and bad points about the equipment appeared. One proposal was to substitute the .50 caliber machine gun for the .30 caliber weapon. After the demonstrations, the units began range firing and discovered that the telescopic sight for the 37mm main tank gun was inadequate when the vehicle was moving. While trying to develop tactics and techniques, the cavalry school published a memorandum on the employment of mechanized cavalry. Grow noted that it proposed to break up the mechanized regiment and use the parts to assist horse troops forward. Van Voorhis complained about uninformed people writing regulations.

In attempting to determine equipment and organization, Van Voorhis thought that the regiment should have fewer but bigger tanks, while Grow held the opposite view. Grow maintained that in combat tank life would be short and therefore large reserves would be needed. Organizationally it was thought necessary to have a separate armored car troop under the regimental commander for reconnaissance purposes. A service troop should assume control of the supply vehicles from the combat troops. The regiment was to have a striking squadron and a holding squadron, a carry-over from the mechanized force. On July 1, 1932, the name of the unit was changed from Detachment for Mechanized Cavalry Regiment to Detachment, 1st Cavalry (Mechanized). This signified that the army was converting an existent regiment from horses to combat cars.

The 1st Cavalry Regiment was stationed at Fort D. A. Russell, Marfa, Texas. Van Voorhis left Camp Knox on December 17, 1932, making the round trip of 3,240 miles in thirty-one days. Considering that the trip was made on icy roads, through much snow and in below freezing weather, and with the loss of only one vehicle, it was a success. No officer of the 1st Cavalry Regiment was to stay with the regiment. Grow noted that in his conversations with officers at Fort D. A. Russell that many realized that cavalry had reached a turning point. When the men arrived at Camp Knox on January 15, 1933, they became the 1st Cavalry Regiment (Mechanized), a force of 52 officers and 747 enlisted men. This first mechanized regiment in the American army was commanded by Col. Bruce Palmer; assisting the regimental commander was Maj. Robert W. Grow, executive officer and acting S-3, and 1st Lt. I. D. White, aide to Brig. Gen. Julian R. Lindsey. The regiment had two combat car squadrons of two troops each, a headquarters troop, a platoon of six mortars, a service troop, a machine gun troop and an armored car troop. Each combat vehicle carried three or four machine guns, as well as radios.

Once the 1st Cavalry Regiment had been mechanized, training resumed in earnest in progressive steps. After the men were introduced to the equipment and had learned to handle it, they began tactical training. During the firing and maneuvering exercises problems emerged. Grow noted that combat cars tended to stop in exposed positions to fire rather than to move forward continually, firing at targets as they appeared. He saw that if the vehicle must stop, it should do so in a defilade position or at least under cover to lessen its chances of being destroyed by antitank guns. Map reading was stressed, especially after the advanced guard became lost on a maneuver. Other tasks included segregating baggage trucks from the combat elements, adjusting the distance between the advanced guard and the main body, having the kitchens carry more food, maintaining outposts and guards and improving radios.

Some problems were apparently solved, for in 1934 the 1st Cavalry Regiment (Mechanized) marched to Fort Riley, Kansas, to participate in maneuvers against horse cavalry units. One of the primary purposes was to assess the progress of the cavalry in mechanization, motorization and the introduction of new weapons. Prior to these exercises, opinion was sharply divided on the question of whether horse and mechanized units could, or should, work together. But after the maneuvers, most calvarymen believed that it was certainly possible to work in harmony with the tanks. In fact, the consensus among all observers was that tanks were here to stay and that horses were on the way out, for in most of the exercises the mechanized regiments had run circles around the mounted units. But it would be 1942 before the horses were finally turned out to pasture.

One of the important lessons concerned the mechanized cavalry units' sensitivity to terrain. Rough, broken ground or water delayed or detoured the mechanized force. Demolitions, it was thought, would assume a greater role in warfare. Supply routes over extended distances had

L to R: Maj. Gen. Adna R. Chaffee, commanding general, Armored Force; Maj. Gen. Charles L. Scott, first commanding general, 2d Armored Division.

to be planned and protected. Another conclusion was that mechanized forces would need infantry support for protection at night or else pull back from their advanced positions. Most important, the "iron horse" had performed cavalry missions. Grow thought that the problems had been honestly drawn so as not to favor either participant. Despite some weaknesses in the tanks' performance, all but the most shortsighted horsemen saw that the future of the cavalry lay in mechanization. Grow was convinced that as a result of the maneuvers, mechanized cavalry established itself as a permanent part of the army in 1934.

The most immediate result of the maneuvers was a training directive published by the War Department entitled "Defense Against Mechanized Units." As a result of the directive, the cavalry started issuing .50 caliber machine guns and 37mm antitank guns to its horse units. During the demonstrations of its weapons, the mechanized cavalrymen fired their .50 caliber machine guns at armor plate, penetrating one-half inch at 1,100 yards and three-quarter inch at 600 yards. Since no vehicle carried more than one-half inch of armor, the .50 caliber machine gun could destroy any known vehicle. The directive instructed artillery to be used in an antitank role along with antitank guns of the infantry or cavalry regiments. Tanks would be kept concentrated for an attack or for use in a counterattack. Apparently no one in the War Department foresaw using a tank or combat car in an antitank role.

The antitank weapons debate added one more problem for the mechanized force. Mechanized warfare was seen as a struggle between tanks and tanks or between tanks and antitank guns. Strictly speaking, an antitank gun is a defensive weapon, while the tank is offensive in character. To develop antitank weapons, the army had two possible choices. The first was to make the weapons tactically mobile, as heavily armed as the tank, and attempt to obtain first-round disabling hits through superior training and skill. The second was to make the weapon a stationary gun platform, using concealment and extreme accuracy to give an edge to the antitank gun. The army chose to do both, using the tank as an additional antitank weapon.

The 13th Cavalry Regiment, commanded by Col. Charles L. Scott, later the first commanding general of the 2d Armored Division, arrived at Fort Knox on September 5, 1936. It joined with the 1st Cavalry Regiment (Mechanized) to form the 7th Cavalry Brigade (Mechanized), a force of 150 officers, 2,500 enlisted men and more than 500 vehicles. Composed of two mechanized cavalry regiments, an artillery battalion of sixteen guns, an engineer troop, a maintenance troop, a medical troop, and the 12th Observation Squadron, it was a modest mechanized force. Besides being a laboratory to develop new equipment and doctrine, it was a tactical unit that could take the field if necessary. While radio was the primary means of communications, the force did have 109 motorcycle messengers. It was the second step in cavalry mechanization, and the next to last step in creating the Armored Force.

In discussing the 7th Cavalry Brigade (Mechanized), Van Voorhis stated that it retained cavalry-type missions, while rejecting the use of large antitank weapons and increasing armor thicknesses because the added weight would decrease mobility. It also resisted introducing a holding force (infantry) because the mission of cavalry was not to hold objectives. If the brigade was given such an assignment, infantry could be attached by general headquarters. Looking to the future, he stated that if the mechanized force expanded, his brigade would provide the basis for that growth. One question concerning expansion was the number of fighting vehicles that a single commander could control. Based on Van Voorhis's experience, the number was between 500 and 600, or two regiments. Any larger force would strain the commander.

In 1936, Col. Bruce Palmer, commanding officer of the 7th Cavalry Brigade (Mechanized), led his men into the Second Army maneuvers. Attached to the 7th Cavalry Brigade was the 12th Infantry Brigade composed of the 2d and 6th Infantry Regiments. Also attached were artillery and observation aircraft. Preparing for the maneuvers, Palmer conducted active and simulated exercises, using both real and theoretical unit attachments. The purpose was to determine how best to use such augmentations as infantry, horse cavalry, motorized artillery and observation aircraft. These preparations had four goals: to develop the men's professional skills; to make the 7th Cavalry Brigade an efficient combat force; to develop the tactics best suited to the brigade; and to build a smooth functional staff and communications system. Combined, these were to conserve manpower and to bring vehicles and equipment up to maximum efficiency. To achieve the greatest surprise, night marches were thought to be the rule and not the exception. Using speed and surprise, Palmer hoped to avoid prepared enemy defenses. This training was conducted under the supervision of the brigade's S-3, Lt. Col. Willis D. Crittenberger, later commanding general of the 2d Armored Brigade and the 2d Armored Division.

Palmer viewed the mechanized unit as just another part of the army team, a tool which could be appreciated and understood only if trained with other parts of the team. During the maneuvers, the 7th Cavalry Brigade (Mechanized) operated against forces several times its size. By attacking flanks and rears, it caused disruptions. To reach these attack positions, it had to make long night marches, which it did successfully, justifying its previous training. Tactically, the brigade tried to place its elements in positions to allow several choices of action against the enemy. Repeatedly the brigade's speed and ability to move to the necessary place at the proper time confirmed the belief that these were two of the most important principles of mechanized warfare.

The combat cars had shown that they could perform under trying conditions, but the attached units even more forcefully impressed the 7th Cavalry Brigade (Mechanized) commander and observers. The accuracy of the artillery had visitors shaking their heads in amazement. This was achieved by attaching artillery forward observers to all elements of the brigade and by using air corps and observation aircraft. In addition to firing high-explosive shells, the artillery and mortars in the mortar platoon of regimental headquarters fired more smoke shells in attempting to neutralize antitank guns. The premise, proved valid during World War II, was that if the aim of the antitank guns could be disrupted the advance would be easier. In maneuvers, no attack was initiated without first firing a simulated smoke screen. Several valuable lessons, later implemented, came from the use of indirect fire weapons. Artillery and mortars should be integral parts of a mechanized force. Ideally a battalion of artillery should be attached to each mechanized regiment, and a mortar platoon should be in the regimental headquarters company.

Infantry had been attached to the brigade. For two years Fort Knox had been experimenting with and urging adoption of the concept of infantry as an organic part of the mechanized force. The brigade definitely needed infantry to protect artillery once it was in position, to patrol and serve outpost duty, to relieve mechanized forces once they had seized a position, to delay attacking enemy infantry and to take part in coordinated combat car and infantry attacks. A rifle troop could be combined with the machine gun troop to create a fire support squadron. Colonel Palmer believed that motorized infantry was useful, placing only two restrictions on its use. First, infantry should be able to move into position without special protection; second, the infantry truck column should not interfere with the tactical mobility of the mechanized elements. Maneuvers showed that combat cars and infantry could move and attack over unknown terrain.

The maneuvers were successful from the mechanized cavalry point of view. Usually the mechanized regiment operated as a part of a larger force, but it could also operate independently as a rapidly moving strike force. The maneuvers were a real test for the light tanks or combat cars. Attacks were made over unreconnoitered, rugged ground which would have previously been considered unsuitable terrain. Long, sustained operations showed that the light tank was mechanically sound and could take prolonged rough usage. One article summed up the feeling of the mechanized force in the assertion that "dobbin is making his last stand."

One result of the 1936 maneuvers was the recommendation that observation aircraft be attached to the brigade. The following year, the 12th Observation Squadron was attached to the 7th Cavalry Brigade (Mechanized). During training exercises, technique and communication problems were solved, enabling the aircraft to support ground troops both in reconnaissance and combat. This was the beginning of close air-ground coordination that typified combat in Europe during World War II.

The War Department took a special interest in mechanization. In 1938, it published "Policies Governing Mechanization" and "Tactical Employment of Mechanized Units." Mechanization was viewed not as a new arm but as a new weapon to enable the combat arms to do their job. Combined arms (infantry, artillery and cavalry) were essential to success. The basic considerations for combat were movement, surprise and the objective. The attacking force was to be supported by artillery, aviation and antitank weapons. Mechanized cavalry could take an objective, but could not hold it for a prolonged period without support from infantry or horse cavalry.

The War Department directive divided mechanized employment into cavalry and infantry sections. Cavalry mechanization developed along lines that increased mobility, firepower, radius of operation and strategic mobility beyond that of horse cavalry. The great value of mechanized cavalry, as seen by the War Department, was its ability to conduct distant reconnaissance and create initial successes which could form the basis for further action by higher commands. It could have a special role in pursuit and delaying actions because of its mobility and firepower. The mechanized cavalry was especially adept in envelopment, turning movements or exploiting breakthroughs. To execute these missions, the cavalry needed to be a self-contained force capable of independent action. Its scout and combat cars formed the main mechanized elements. Some limitations were placed on the mechanized force which was thought to be sensitive to obstacles, terrain, enemy air attacks and antitank defenses. To overcome these limitations, there was a need for complete ground reconnaissance, a fact already known to the mechanized force.

For infantry, mechanization moved along lines that would increase the foot soldiers' ability to overcome strongly organized resistance. Infantry tanks were not to be committed to action until a clearly defined objective had been located. Most tanks were to be used at that portion of the front where the decisive effort was to be made. While tanks would not normally operate beyond the effective range of artillery, they would not necessarily be tied to the speed of foot troops. This was the first major change in official policy, and from the main desire of infantry to keep the tanks as a close support weapon. The infantry believed that attacks would be in succeeding waves. The first wave of medium tanks would closely follow the artillery barrage, eliminating antitank defenses. The second wave, light tanks, would then move forward to eliminate machine guns.

In neither case, however, were tanks given a separate and equal role. Their use was restrictively defined and controlled by higher headquarters. In both cases, and perhaps accidently, the War Department stressed that combat cars and tanks might need support from artillery, aviation and engineers; this officially stated the combat team concept, which cavalrymen had stressed since 1928. One bright spot that emerged was that, if given the opportunity, mechanized cavalry could pursue, subject to some limitations.

In 1938, the 7th Cavalry Brigade (Mechanized) moved to Fort Riley, Kansas, to take part in maneuvers. In the force were 100 officers, 2,000 enlisted men and 638 vehicles. The 700-mile march required forty-one hours, including halts. Each night seventeen refueling vehicles, with a capacity of 300 to 1,200 gallons each, took approximately 2½ hours to fuel the command. The force averaged 16.07 miles per hour, considerably faster than horse cavalry or infantry. It arrived ready for action, the most important consideration in any troop movement.

In these maneuvers and later, Brig. Gen. Van Voorhis commanded the brigade from the air. He used radio communications to direct his two regiments to the proper place at the appointed time. While on a road march to Georgia, the force again demonstrated its resourcefulness. Previous reconnaissance had shown that the bridge over the Cumberland

River at Burnside, Kentucky, could support the weight of a combat car. When the 13th Cavalry Regiment (Mechanized) arrived, it was told that it could not use the bridge. Telephone calls to state and local officials were to no avail. Discovering a ferry nearby, Colonel Scott loaded his combat car on it and crossed the 280-foot-wide river. The regiment followed.

Certain cavalry officers began to assert that the mechanized force should be expanded to a division and be considered equal to cavalry and infantry. For the cavalry in 1938, however, an unsurmountable stone wall was erected: Maj. Gen. John K. Herr became the chief of cavalry. A devoted horseman all his life, this last chief of cavalry declared that he would accept mechanization, but "not at the expense of converting any horse units." Such a position assured the limitation of mechanized cavalry. Congress established the size of the army at an average strength of 165,000 enlisted men and 14,659 officers in fiscal year 1938. Due to budgetary restraints, officer strength was limited to 12,250, while enlisted strength averaged about 162,000. Thus Herr was safe in insisting that any increase in the mechanized force not be raised from existing units.

Major General Herr spoke to the students at the Army War College on the evolution and use of cavalry. He stated that the cavalry had adopted mechanization, developed it tactically and technically and learned to appreciate its value in relationship to the horse. Combat cars had been kept light and fast to enable them to carry out cavalry missions and not compete with infantry tanks. Mechanized cavalry was faster than horse units over favorable terrain and had greater firepower, but was difficult to control on the battlefield. To Herr, that was "a real problem." Because of supply and maintenance difficulties, it did not have the capacity for sustained operations or the flexibility of horse cavalry. Herr desired a mechanized cavalry division and eventually a cavalry corps of three horse and one mechanized division. He saw the possibility of a war, perhaps one of movement. If he were correct, then cavalry would be extensively used. He concluded by urging the students to study history and watch cavalry maneuvers. Ironically, his final comment was that "there are none so blind as those who will not see." Herr adopted a position, maintained it against advice and earned the distinction of being the biggest obstacle to mechanized cavalry expansion.

In 1939, Lt. Col. Robert W. Grow visited Fort Knox, where Brigadier General Chaffee demanded a division, even if the men had to come from horse units. He intended to have Gen. George C. Marshall, chief of staff designate, visit Fort Knox after the Plattsburg maneuvers in August and "go to the mat with him." On September 29, 1939, Chaffee, addressing the students of the Army War College, stated that the concept of infantry tanks to support the infantry and mechanized cavalry to aid the cavalry was sound and should be continued. While studying and using armored vehicles, the mechanized force had evolved the fundamental principle that tanks should not be used independently. They were noisy, blind and incapable of a prolonged defense, but they could serve as the backbone of a mobile force.

In terms which probably made the chiefs of cavalry and infantry furious, he stated that "mechanized cavalry was the newest fighting service in the army." He argued that the brigade was not the largest force that one person could control. It could be increased without changing the size of the supply and support echelons. He recommended the creation of a brigade reconnaissance force with additional infantry, an increase in the artillery from sixteen to twenty-four guns per mechanized regiment, an increase in the mechanized regiment from two to three squadrons each and an engineer unit. While making these recommendations, he noted that the brigade had never waited for men or equipment, but trained and fitted replacements into the organization when they arrived.

Chaffee reached the major thrust of his speech. To this point he had detailed the history, organization and tactical usage of mechanized cavalry without transgressing traditional lines. He advocated the creation of four mechanized divisions, an expansion of the mechanized force by 800 percent. In explaining his plan for recruiting men, he struck a very sensitive nerve: he wanted cavalry and field artillery officers who had demonstrated command ability to be reassigned from existing units. These vacancies could be filled by reserve officers on extended active duty. He recognized that some officers and enlisted personnel would have to be supplied at the expense of the horse cavalry and possibly infantry, especially if the increase could not be gained by enlarging the regular army. Such a position was heresy, but traditionally speeches to the Army War College have been expressions of individual views intended to stimulate student thinking, not army policy.

Comparing the German Panzer Division to the proposed mechanized cavalry division, Chaffee noted that each German division had sixty medium tanks which protected the artillery and supported the infantry components. These tanks, he concluded, might well be considered part of the supporting echelon. Based on the German experience in Poland, well-trained, boldly led mechanized forces left no doubt as to their value in a war of movement. Such forces could not be defeated by infantry or horse cavalry, no matter how gallant the defenders. The best defense against mechanized cavalry was a like force. In spite of continual urging since 1936, the activation or creation of a mechanized division or a similar force would not occur until 1940.

During the 1930s several groups of German officers visited Fort Knox. A visit by Maj. Hans von Greiffenberg revealed that the philosophies of the United States and Germany were similar. On this visit the Germans saw the equipment, except the .50 machine guns, and rode in the vehicles. Maj. Robert W. Grow concluded then, as later events confirmed, that the United States was more advanced than Germany with respect to the employment of mechanized forces. However, Germany was ahead in vehicular development, a conclusion later verified by the 2d Armored Division's study, "German versus American Equipment."

In the summer of 1937, Col. Adolph von Schnell, who was in charge of German auto, truck and tank production during World War II, visited Fort Knox to study American mechanized doctrine and equipment. He told the Americans that he had ridden in the tanks of each European country and was of the opinion that the American cavalry combat car (light tank) had more speed and power and rode easier than any in Europe. Scott, Chaffee and Schnell discussed the basis of German armor development. The Germans believed that an armored division had to use the combined-arms concept in battle; tanks had to be used in mass to achieve sustained driving power. The vehicles had to be simple, rugged and mass producible; all elements of the division had to be mobile, which permitted unity of action in all phases of the operation. There had to be 100% replacement of tanks and crews during long operations.

All these beliefs, later incorporated into United States armor doctrine, had already been expounded by Van Voorhis and Chaffee. As mechanized cavalryman Lt. Col. Alexander D. Surles stated, in actual performance Europe was ahead of the United States. In theory and its limited use the United States was about five years ahead of Britain by putting light tanks in the cavalry. Scott said that German and American armor developed along similar lines, but "we haven't blindly copied the German setup." The United States had been busy with its own development for several years, and Germany's success in Poland proved to Scott the soundness of American ideas.

During the 1939 First Army maneuvers at Plattsburg, New York, a team of German observers paid close attention to the equipment and its use. Suddenly the Germans officers departed and in a few days the reason was apparent: Germany had invaded Poland. During the first phase of the maneuvers, the 7th Cavalry Brigade (Mechanized) was fragmented and assigned to guard the flanks and rears of various infantry brigades, leaving only a small part of the mechanized cavalry to function as it should. Later the brigade was consolidated and employed as a unit. It cut supply and communication lines and raised havoc with the infantry units. Two invaluable lessons emerged. First, the mechanized brigade was a special weapon, and troops supporting it had to be thoroughly familiar with its tactics, strengths and limitations. Second, the brigade should be kept complete as a unit. It was a mistake to use the regiments separately, but a bigger mistake was to divide the regiments into task forces. The brigade should be given missions that were deemed most important.

In 1934, Maj. Gen. Edward Croft, chief of infantry, had transferred the Tank School to Fort Benning, Georgia, placing it directly under the Infantry School commandant. Tank school support troops were transferred to Benning and renamed. The 1st Tank Regiment became the 66th Infantry Regiment (light tanks), while the 2d Tank Regiment became the 67th Infantry Regiment (medium tanks). In 1940 these two regiments became part of the 2d Armored Division.

The following year the army chief of staff, Gen. Malin Craig, issued a directive stating that recent developments in motorization and mechanization may have created a need for new thinking in infantry, especially about organization and tactics. He further suggested that study groups consider keeping horses for artillery. The assistant commandant appointed a board of officers headed by Lt. Col. Alvin C. Gillem to study infantry and mechanization and to make recommendations on how infantry could improve itself and fight in a mechanized war. Gillem and his fellow board members, Maj. Earl Landreth, Maj. John N. Robinson and Capt. Floyd L. Parks, issued their report, "Reorganization of the Brigade, Division, and Higher Units of the Army," on December 6, 1935. It advocated eliminating all horses in infantry units, substituting motor transports. It also urged that infantry divisions be trained to defend against wide envelopments, because part of the enveloping force might include mechanized units. It further recommended that the division's light tank company be eliminated and a regiment of light tanks be concentrated at corps level. If needed, a battalion of light tanks could then be available to each of the corps's infantry divisions. The corps would also have a mechanized unit for offensive or defensive combat.

At the field army level, the board recommended eliminating one horse cavalry regiment and replacing it with a mechanized brigade. A mechanized force was thought to be of great value against enemy flanks and rears, and lines of communication, in exploiting breakthroughs, in pursuits and in seizing critical terrain features. The board recommended keeping one horse division for close-in protection and because some terrain might be unsuitable for a mechanized force. The mechanized brigade would have two mechanized cavalry regiments, a field artillery battalion, three battalions of 75mm guns, an engineer troop, a maintenance troop and a mechanized medical troop. Probably the army made very little, if any, use of the board's report. Whether it helped to influence the two-regiment concept for the 7th Cavalry Brigade (Mechanized) is doubtful, except the second regiment (the 13th) did not join the brigade until nine months after the report was submitted.

By 1940, cavalry had made giant strides in mechanization, but infantry had changed very little, if any. Lt. Col. Bradford G. Chynoweth, after completing military attaché duties in England, was assigned to the First Battalion, 66th Infantry Regiment (light tanks), stationed at Fort Benning. He remembered that his brother-in-law, Maj. Gen. George A. Lynch, chief of infantry, was determined to keep tanks in their proper place as close support weapons for the foot soldier. If any infantryman mentioned cavalry tactics or deviated from accepted doctrine, he was penalized. Chynoweth stressed mobility in exercises. He gave orders while moving and worked out hand signals for various maneuvers; meanwhile he received cold, icy stares from his superiors. He finally realized the tanks would continue to be infantry support weapons until somebody changed the system.

Probably unknown except within the War Department, the change so long awaited was about to occur. In the summer of 1940, the War Department decided to use the 7th Cavalry Brigade (Mechanized) and a provisional tank brigade of infantry tanks from Fort Benning in the Louisiana maneuvers of that year. These maneuvers were to test both horse and mechanized cavalry, mobile concepts of war and the new three-regiment triangular infantry divisions (instead of the older square division of four regiments in two brigades). In addition, observers would get a close look at command, supply, administration, maintenance and the use of aviation over a prolonged period.

Preparing for the maneuvers, Chaffee used his influence to have attachments made to the mechanized brigade, including an engineer troop and a medical troop, but most importantly the 6th Infantry Regiment (Motorized). For the infantry's part, a provisional tank brigade was created from the 66th and 68th Infantry Regiments (light tanks) and a battalion of the 67th Infantry Regiment (medium tanks), commanded by Brig. Gen. Bruce Magruder, the first commanding general of the 1st Armored Division. Several times during the maneuvers, the mechanized and tank brigades acted together as a provisional division; it impressed the observers. The chief of cavalry, Maj. Gen. John K. Herr, said that as a result of this experiment two mechanized cavalry regiments, the 1st and the 13th, were lost to cavalry.

Historians of armor stress that in the two decades following World War I, petty branch jealousies and conservative, almost reactionary leadership in infantry and cavalry prevented the creation of a mechanized or armored force prior to 1940. They further argue that military leadership continued to think in the terms that had won the previous war, with a rigid mentality and a reluctance to change philosophy or means. All this is true, but it fails to consider that men in positions of responsibility are men. They are no more able to foretell the future than anyone else. They were exercising their best judgement at the time, considering their biases, experience and the conflicting advice they received. What most historians have failed to see (partly because of their concentration on the negative aspects of the period) is that during those two decades armor tactics and techniques were evolving and, more importantly, the Armored Force leaders were training.

Often the men chose tanks at personal sacrifices. For example, Lt. Gen. Willis D. Crittenberger asked to go to the 7th Cavalry Brigade (Mechanized) in 1935 and was told that if he did he could no longer expect any help from the chief of cavalry's office. Chynoweth was assigned to an infantry regiment to get him away from tanks and as a result spent the war in a Japanese prisoner-of-war camp.

The American experience was successful. Gen. I. D. White said, "The 7th Cavalry Brigade (Mechanized) served as a model for the Germans to copy. The soundness of American tactical doctrine was proven in Poland, the Low Countries and France. As a result the Germans got ahead in technical development of armored vehicles but never surpassed Americans in tactics." This was a statement by an early pioneer in mechanized cavalry whose World War II experience included commanding a reconnaissance battalion, a tank regiment, a combat command and finally the 2d Armored Division during its race to Berlin in April 1945.

Chapter 2

THE FORT BENNING ERA:
Activating and Training
an Armored Division

The army chief of staff, Gen. George C. Marshall, testifying before the Military Affairs Committee on February 23, 1940, indicated that the War Department was considering expanding the 7th Cavalry Brigade (Mechanized) into a division and increasing the infantry's tank strength to two light and one medium tank regiments. About three weeks later the chief of cavalry, Maj. Gen. John K. Herr, told a subcommittee of the House Appropriations Committee that the cavalry had adopted mechanization and was considering a mechanized division. He still wished to maintain horses. While the Congress considered the military appropriations for fiscal 1941, the army gathered most of its armored vehicles for the 1940 Louisiana maneuvers. The most important lesson learned from these exercises was that there was a definite need for an armored force.

On May 25, 1940, immediately prior to the final critique of the Louisiana maneuvers, tank-minded officers of the infantry and cavalry met with the War Department assistant chief of staff G-3, Brig. Gen. Frank M. Andrews, in the basement of the Alexandria, Louisiana, high school. This group, including Brig. Gens. Adna R. Chaffee and Bruce Magruder and Col. George S. Patton, Jr., concluded that an armored force was needed at once. The far-ranging discussion concluded that the present infantry-cavalry mechanization concept was inadequate, that time to correct the situation was short and that tankers had so far received second-class treatment. The unanimous opinion of the basement group was that an armored force would have to be taken out of the hands of the chiefs of cavalry and infantry. It was decided that Brigadier Generals Chaffee and Andrews should take that message to Washington. The group recommended that two armored divisions be activated, using the 7th Cavalry Brigade (Mechanized) and the infantry Provisional Tank Brigade as a basis. One division should be stationed at Fort Knox, Kentucky, and one at Fort Benning, Georgia.

Chaffee saw Herr and presented the plans and recommendations of the basement group. Herr procrastinated and was not willing to sacrifice horses for tanks. Maj. Gen. Robert W. Grow noted that "he lost mechanization for the cavalry and . . . cavalry . . . lost a prestige that it can never regain."

General Marshall was more receptive to the recommendations of the armor advocates. Andrews presented written plans for the organization and tactical usage of the two proposed armored divisions. The ideas were presented to other staff sections and to the service chiefs for their comments. Lt. Col. Jonathan W. Anderson, War Plans Division, agreed with the armored concept and suggested that one division be completely organized from the 7th Cavalry Brigade immediately. Maj. Gen. Julian L. Schley, chief of engineers, argued that because of Germany's use of engineers, the engineer battalion should be increased from 281 men to approximately 400 to 500 men. He and his branch wanted to be part of an armored division and thought their contribution would be greater with an enlarged battalion. Predictably, major objections to the proposed force came from the chief of infantry, Maj. Gen. George A. Lynch, and the chief of cavalry, Maj. Gen. John K. Herr.

Word began to leak from the War Department that changes were imminent. Lt. Col. Robert W. Grow and his family arrived in San Francisco to sail for duty in the Philippines. Because of ship problems, his departure was delayed a few days. On June 26, 1940, he sent telegrams to the Adjutant General's Office and to Maj. Gilbert X. Cheves to explain the situation. In his reply the same afternoon, Cheves told Grow that he would probably be reassigned to mechanization headquarters at Fort

Knox or Fort Benning. He added, "very confidential, [it] looks like the Mech[anization] Force boys have won the day." When Grow and his family returned to Fort Knox, he found that he would be the G-3 of the division stationed at Fort Benning. He started studying organizational charts, concluding that the most difficult part of his job would be to "get the push into infantry tank regiments but that will be largely (Colonel) George Patton's job."

From late June until mid-July, the War Department set a rapid pace. On June 30, 1940, it selected Brig. Gen. Charles L. Scott, a cavalryman, to command the 2d Armored Division at Fort Benning; Brig. Gen. Bruce Magruder, an infantryman, was to command the 1st Armored Division at Fort Knox; and Brig. Gen. Adna R. Chaffee was to command the I Armored Corps and be chief of the Armored Force, headquartered at Fort Knox. The stationing of Scott and Magruder was apparently an attempt to alleviate bitter branch feelings.

The 2d Armored Division was activated on July 15, 1940, at Fort Benning, Georgia. At the first formation, there were about 99 officers and 2,202 enlisted men, mostly from the 66th Armored Regiment (Light), and a few cadremen of other divisional units. That same day Scott issued General Order 1, assuming command of the division. Since the division at full strength was to have 530 officers and 9,329 enlisted personnel, this initial formation represented only a skeleton force. To help alleviate the officer shortage, many reserve officers were ordered to active duty. Other officers and enlisted men were transferred from active duty units. The proposed draft law of 1940 was being introduced in Congress and if it were passed, then the men would be available.

The 2d Armored Division and its components were grouped into five functional echelons. Command rested with the division commander, his staff and special staff. Reconnaissance was the duty of the 2d Reconnaissance Battalion (Armored), which was to move in front of the division, gaining information about the enemy and terrain. Working with the ground reconnaissance force were to be observation aircraft. The battalion was armored and could fight, if necessary, to gain information. The third echelon was the strike force built around the 2d Armored Brigade, the three tank regiments and the artillery regiment. Assisting this group was the support echelon made up of the infantry regiment (known as the division troubleshooters), the engineers and the artillery battalion. Last was the service echelon, whose duty was to keep the men in good health and the machines repaired and supplied. To carry out this scheme, the division had about 700 armored vehicles, over 300 guns and howitzers, and more than 6,500 automatic and semiautomatic weapons. When moving, the Armored Brigade took up more than forty-one miles of road space, necessitating multiple columns. This may well have been a factor in creating combat teams.

Brigadier General Scott expressed his concept of armored warfare to Brig. Gen. Robert C. Foy. An armored division, he said, was similar to a cavalry division, except that the men rode in armored vehicles instead of on horses. In an orientation address to new officers in the division, Scott developed this theme. An armored division finds weak spots in enemy defenses, penetrates to the rear and then spreads out to cut communications and supply lines. It endeavors to drive the adversary into a holding force. Tanks are helped through enemy opposition by support units which quickly follow, taking advantage of the shock generated by the tank attack. A standing operating procedure, attempting to cover every situation that an enemy or terrain could present, should not be developed. To do so, Scott thought, would result in mental rigidity. Cooperation between tanks and all other divisional units would overcome enemy opposition; teamwork had to be practiced on all occasions. Coordination between the assault and support groups was essential.

An armored division, Scott maintained, was an offensive, aggressive weapon. Its most valuable attribute—surprise—was achieved by speed, direction of attack and continual forward movement. It used mobility to choose the best direction to attack and to reach the enemy's rear areas. All combat elements of the division had one common factor: when meeting the enemy, a base or pivot of fire was to be established while other divisional elements maneuvered to strike the flanks or rear of the adversary's position. The maneuver could be a single or double envelopment or penetration, depending on the enemy and the terrain, but fire superiority was to be established when the advance guard was unable to move forward. The procedure Scott described, pivot of fire and maneuver, is the same that Patton called ''grabbing the enemy by the nose and kicking him in the pants.'' Repeatedly during World War II the 2d Armored Division employed this device successfully.

A pressing problem for the 2d Armored was finding quarters for the men. Fort Benning was the home of the Infantry School and its support units and the home post of the 4th Infantry Division. Permanent buildings were at a premium because of the army's rapid expansion. The 2d Armored's headquarters was initially located in a red brick mess hall which

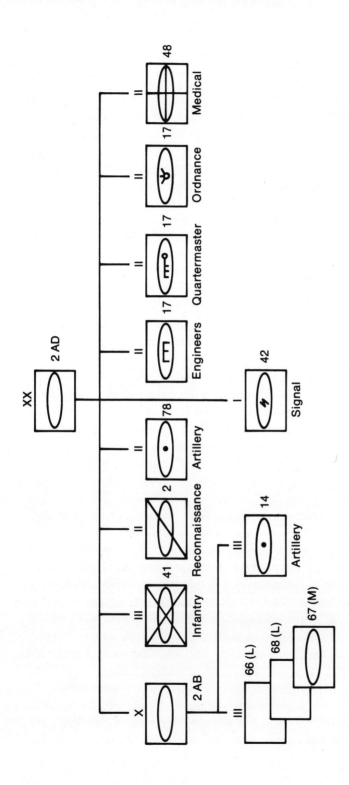

Figure 1. An Armored Division, 1940.

had been condemned several years before; its roof was so weak, it had to be propped up. Elements of the division, living in tents, were scattered from Harmony Church to Lawson Field, a distance of about eight miles. The men of the 66th Armored Regiment lived in brick barracks almost the size of a city block. When additional men began to arrive at Fort Benning, some soldiers, including Lt. Norris H. Perkins's platoon, had to live in tents inside the quadrangle formed by the barracks. While inspecting possible tent sites for the various units, Grow picked a suitable cantonment area for permanent buildings. Grow observed that new problems were arising all the time, but some progress was being made. It would take some time to make the division a fighting force.

The most serious problem facing the division—training—was complicated by many factors beyond anyone's control. The division was short of personnel, equipment, clothing, quarters and maintenance areas. A directive from the commanding general of I Armored Corps stated that the division would be ready for battle, with whatever men and equipment it had, by October 1, 1940—a mere 3½ months to convert an untried organization into a combat-ready force. To help solve part of the problem, the two armored divisions enjoyed a semiautonomous status, responsible to the chief of the Armored Force, who being also the Armored Corps commander could work directly with General Marshall and the War Department.

Col. George S. Patton, Jr., arrived at Fort Benning on July 27, 1940, to command the 2d Armored Brigade. As far as the division G-3 was concerned, Patton was responsible for brigade training. The problems which faced the brigade commander were inadequate material and morale. The troops were not motivated, and some officers looked on their assignments as chores, rather than as challenges. These early days tested the ingenuity and patience of both the officers and the men. There were no precedents for organizing an armored division, and insufficient time to learn by trial and error.

Scott told Chaffee that it was impossible to train properly because of equipment shortages. He reported that the division was short 4,297 pistols, 495 M-1 rifles and 1,381 submachine guns. Commercial revolvers could be substituted for pistols, but no proper substitutes could be found for the other weapons. In crew-served weapons, the division needed 120 machine gun mounts for the scout cars but had none; it also required eighty .30 caliber machine guns and had only twenty-two; it needed forty .50 caliber machine guns but had only seventeen. Since the 120 machine guns were to go in scout cars which had no gun mounts, the guns on hand were of limited use. Finally, Scott said he needed ninety-eight 37mm guns for the M2A4 (light) tanks but had only eighty-six. In the early phase the division trained with wooden guns.

In spite of shortages in material and lack of permanent housing, recruits, mostly from the southern states, began arriving in August 1940, and training began in earnest. The armored division also drew visitors. Gen. George C. Marshall arrived on August 14, refusing to say if any more armored divisions would be activated. Two days later, Maj. Gen. Adna R. Chaffee received the first formal escort, by the Machine Gun Company, 66th Armored Regiment, which the division conducted. Chaffee was optimistic that the division would have its equipment by fall, except for medium tanks, which would probably be available some time in 1941. He noted that recruiting parties were reporting that interest was high because the armored divisions offered opportunities for specialized training. The officers of the 2d Armored Division reported to Chaffee that the recruits were quick to learn.

Trying to get materials, housing, training manuals and firing ranges was extremely difficult and caused a constant flow of letters between Fort Benning and Fort Knox. About three weeks after activation, Scott received technical manuals on marching, advance guard, combat car drill, doctrine for small elements and schools. Clothing created other problems. Originally the men were issued four shirts and three pairs of trousers each, but they had to be reduced to two shirts and two pairs of trousers. They were forced to use overalls in almost all their work because of the clothing shortage. Scott informed Chaffee that if this situation continued, it could cause problems, because the men would not have uniforms to go on pass. Scott also sought $570,000 to build maintenance shops, pave roads and build parking sheds for his vehicles, especially those with radios. In October 1940, Lt. Col. Ernest N. Harmon, Armored Force G-4 and a future commander of the 2d Armored, told Scott that he had approval to spend $32,000 to build arms and radio storage buildings. The division also needed ranges and was able to arrange priorities with the post headquarters. Scott told the commandant of the Infantry School that he would need a moving vehicle range, moving target range, tank combat range, infantry combat range and an antiaircraft range.

Another problem faced by the division was the temporary loan of personnel to the Armor School at Fort Knox. In October the division sent 773 men and 100 vehicles to Fort Knox for three months of schooling in radio maintenance, gunnery and automotive maintenance. These men represented a cross section of recruits and veterans. The drive to Fort Knox was used to give the drivers experience in convoy operations and as a test of the equipment. In mid-February 1941, the division had to supply seventy-two enlisted men to be instructors at the Armor School; at the same time it sent 176 more students there for training. In January, 1941, thirty lieutenants had returned from a four-week gunnery school where they had learned to use all the weapons of the division. Now their mission was to train their units. On February 21, the officers began a three-week aerial observer course, an indication of the importance the division placed on such observation.

The division agreed with Major General Chaffee that an emergency existed. Scott and Patton stressed unit training and divisional maneuvers. The men received squad, platoon, company and battalion training and were required to display their skills in regimental, brigade and divisional exercises. The soldiers, receiving simultaneous training at both small and large unit level, hopefully would learn their assignments in a minimum of time. Scott instituted a division officer school where the tactics, methods, strengths and limitations of each unit were discussed. In addition, it served as a forum for division and brigade commanders to express their views about dress, military courtesy, care of men and social diseases.

In November, 1940, about the time that Patton assumed command of the division, the officer school was changed to a tactical school for unit commanders and their staffs. As a result of these officer schools, Patton acquired the famous nickname, Blood and Guts. He had repeatedly told the young officers that soon they would be ''up to their necks in blood and guts.'' One Monday evening, while drinking beer in the bachelor officers' quarters, Lt. Al Kirchner looked at his watch and said that it was about time to go hear old Blood and Guts. His remark was greeted with a burst of laughter. To that time Patton had been called the Green Hornet because of the tanker suit he had designed and because of his propensity for roaring around the training area in his light tank with its siren blaring.

As the division started training, its first major objective was to examine and eliminate the mistakes made in the 1940 Louisiana maneuvers. Apparently scout cars had been used as tanks but these vehicles had only a minimum of armor and should fight only when forced. Patton cautioned the reconnaissance elements that binoculars should be used to scout ahead and that before crossing a ridge or moving around a curve a foot reconnaissance should be conducted. The scout should be protected by the weapons of the reconnaissance force. When approaching crossroads, they were to stop the vehicles on the friendly side and proceed on foot. This could prevent the enemy from cutting an escape route. Every element should put out flank guards when halted; some units had not done this in Louisiana and had been surprised. If a column were attacked by aircraft, it should fire back; if not seen, it should hide and keep quiet. When any part of the command was hiding, it should be well off the road, with all glass, such as windshields and lights, covered, and it should use fresh camouflage materials. Vehicles should be refueled at every opportunity or each halt.

The first driving lesson, especially for tanks, was to familiarize the student with the controls and let him drive the vehicle. In the second lesson, he had to drive the tank with the ports closed ("buttoned up," in tank slang). After the third lesson, the driver had to maneuver in platoon formation, obeying flag signals. 1st Sgt. Victor S. Prawdzik, B Company, 2d Reconnaissance Battalion (Armored), took an active part in training the new men to drive tanks and other vehicles of the battalion. One of his students was the seventeen-year-old George S. Patton III, who thirty-five years later would command the 2d Armored Division. The tankers fired all vehicular weapons during the first month of training. To instill a spirit of fire and maneuver, the men were taught that they fired *to move,* not that they fired *or moved.* On all marches and maneuvers, combat vehicles were to move in battle order, with all weapons and ammunition racks mounted and all pistol ports closed.

Patton began to stamp his personality on the 2d Armored Brigade. He told his subordinates to "remember that your command is not only yours, but it is you." Training Memorandum Number 7 detailed the tactical training program and the objectives. The division was to be ready to take the field by October 1, 1940, and at the same time it was to train a 25 percent increase in personnel by the same date. The 1st and 2d Armored Divisions were to provide cadres for the projected activation of the 3d and 4th Armored Divisions. Training would be concurrent, it would conform to existing field manuals, and there would be frequent tactical exercises for all available personnel, equipment and vehicles. Tactical training was to include antiaircraft defenses, offensive and defensive operations against other armored forces, night operations, defenses of bivouac areas and protection of the supply and maintenance columns. Also included were reconnaissance and security, communications (both by radio and motorcycle messenger) and maintenance and camouflage training. The teaching was intended to instill a will to fight.

The first division exercise was simple and designed to acquaint all

personnel with the size of the division. The scenario envisioned a mythical enemy attacking Fort Benning. The 2d Armored Division was to move
to assembly areas preparatory to attacking the adversary. The move, led
by Major I. D. White's 2d Reconnaissance Battalion (Armored), was
followed by the three armored regiments, supported by the 17th Engineer
Battalion (Armored) and the 14th Field Artillery Regiment (Armored).
The 41st Infantry Regiment (Armored) and the 78th Field Artillery Battalion (Armored) were to follow the tank regiments and consolidate the
captured positions. The division moved out and halted on three roads so
that Scott could inspect their formations and dispositions. After inspection, the troops advanced and established their assembly areas, which
were also inspected; then the units returned to the post.

The exercise, which had involved about 350 vehicles, including 200
tanks, was considered a success. Especially pleasing to Lieutenant Colonel Grow was the performance of the 66th Armored Regiment (Light)
and the two artillery units, but he felt that the 41st Infantry Regiment
(Armored) had the poorest march disposition and discipline. There was
only one major problem: the division headquarters' radio had failed.
Patton was pleased with his brigade's overall appearance and remarked
that the deficiencies were "conspicuous due to rarity." His complaints
concerned officers and men who sat in vehicles in an unsoldierly manner,
some with their feet outside the vehicles. Some men had been smoking in
the vehicles; some vehicles did not have their tops down; and the distances
between vehicles (50 yards), as well as the interval between companies
and battalions (150 yards), was not always maintained.

On September 18, 1940, the division conducted its first dismounted
review with its 8,000 men assembled together for the first time. Patton
commanded the parade, while Scott, the reviewing officer, trooped the
line in a scout car. It was a spectacular scene. Grow observed that the
uniforms looked better than expected and that the units in cavalry boots
looked better than those without them. Later that remark caused many
hard feelings, especially among the infantry officers. Lt. Norris Perkins
wrote his parents that the infantry officers were disgusted with the cavalry
"brass hat big shots." The Armored Force had decided that the infantrymen in light tank units would wear the crossed sabres and yellow cavalry
patches instead of the infantry crossed rifles and blue patches. He considered it an insult because it was the infantry that had developed tanks,
while the cavalry was noted for its spit-and-shine, impractical and sense-
less practices based on tradition. Perkins thought that they would have

put saddles on the tanks if they could have gotten away with it. He complained that many thousands of dollars had been wasted earlier because the tankers had to wear boots and britches in the tanks. The order was later rescinded when the outfit proved impractical.

Scott reported later to Chaffee that while the units looked and marched well, the 2d Armored was still not receiving sufficient clothing. This shortage and a soldierly appearance were also concerns of Colonel Patton. In a training memorandum, unusual because it was over his own signature, rather than the brigade S-3's, Patton stated that many soldiers had been seen in downtown Columbus, wearing dirty uniforms, drunk, hitchhiking or in the colored people's part of town. While none of these men were members of the 2d Armored Brigade, he pointed out that an "ignorant recruit could cause problems." He then stated what was to become one of the division's hallmarks: the foundation of military perfection is soldierly pride in the dress and behavior of every officer and man. Once this state of mind is attained, organizational excellence follows naturally and easily. The meaning was clear and did not need to be repeated.

Early in September, the division was alerted to be prepared to receive some foreign delegations the following month and to conduct a demonstration of an armored division's attack. The division's response was Combat Exercise A, which became the standard exercise. Conducted in stages, it began with artillery concentrations on the initial objectives, followed by machine gun, mortar and bombing attacks. With the first objective under fire, the reconnaissance battalion was to advance, followed by the three tank regiments, then the supporting infantry was to follow to mop up and consolidate the positions. On October 1, when the division had conducted three rehearsals, it concluded that the area was too small for all units to be properly deployed, but considering the number of men and the amount of equipment the exercises had been satisfactory.

October 3 was an extremely busy day for the division. In the morning a hastily called ceremony with salute guns congratulated Scott and Patton on their promotions. Scott received his second star and Patton his first. According to division legend, Scott turned to Patton and said, "Well, George, they just promoted the two most profane men in the army."

Neither had much time to rest on their laurels, for twenty South American visitors arrived that afternoon. For this group, the division staged a review of two light tank battalions, a medium tank company, two field artillery batteries, two infantry companies and a motorcycle platoon, followed by a reception at the officers' club. The next day the division went through Combat Exercise A. Lieutenant Perkins wrote his parents about the exercise, concluding that the division generally messed up several of the miles of forests, brush and hilltops over which they were attacking. While to the untrained eye all went well, the commanders noted that the tanks were sluggish and failed to perform as combat cars, but the infantry, engineers and artillery did a good job.

Two weeks later, on October 17, the division again went through its exercises for more foreign visitors, and the tanks made a better showing. A month later, in the demonstration for Secretary of War Henry L. Stimson and retired Maj. Gens. Paul B. Malone and Harold B. B. Fike, the timing was off and the tanks attacked before the bombers flew over. During this exercise, Lt. J. P. Whitehurst of the 66th Armored Regiment was standing in the commander's hatch with his camera trained on one bomber. As it flew over the target, a bomb detonated either in the bomb bay or just under the airplane. He saw a flash and got the picture; when the film was developed, someone had substituted a wedding picture for it. Perkins, who sat out the exercise, saw the bomber go into a dive. Apparently the entire crew was lost, as he saw no parachutes. Later in the same month, at a demonstration for newsmen, rain grounded the bombers, but the other elements of the division gave an excellent performance.

In December and January, more demonstrations for a National Guard general officers class were conducted. The December exercise was an excellent show, but the January one was superior because of improved communications with the 27th Bomb Group. Lieutenant Colonel Grow probably echoed the thoughts of other cavalrymen in saying that the more he saw of Combat Exercise A, the more it appeared "that this division has a cavalry role and we should be cavalry, not a separate arm." While the demonstrations permitted the division to show its collective skills and impressed the inexperienced eye, unit training continued in order to smooth the rough spots.

The desire to have the division, or the available elements, combat ready by October 1, 1940, was a worthy but unrealistic goal. Col. Alvin C. Gillem, Jr., commanding officer of the 66th Armored Regiment, conducted a regimental officers conference on October 17. Discussing the organization of the Armored Brigade, he noted that the 66th had a regimental headquarters company and three light tank battalions, the 68th had two battalions organized from individual companies and platoons, and the 67th had a headquarters company and two medium tank companies.

Neither the 67th nor 68th had any personnel allocated for headquarters. While the 66th had six tank battalions, it had no maintenance or service companies to support them. The 66th regimental headquarters had become the provisional brigade headquarters and was working directly with the battalions.

Colonel Gillem was convinced that tank regiments should have the same strength in war or peace. He stated that the division's training was retarded by a lack of directives from the War Department, with the guidance for training coming from Patton's brigade headquarters. Later the Armored Force learned that the War Department had deliberately done this, forcing the men on the spot to think and act for themselves. Gillem pointed out that when problems had arisen, solutions had been found. Methods had been developed to pass tanks through ground troops and to use supporting fire while other tanks or infantry attacked. Having tank and other units training together was especially valuable. All men were to be skilled in reconnaissance, combat, intelligence, map and aerial photo reading, driving, shop and field maintenance, radio and basic tank communications, gas training, camouflage, tank tactics and platoon, company and battalion day and night operations. Here Gillem was stressing another trademark of the division: every man in a unit could perform the job of anyone else. The insistence placed on that ideal was to have immeasurable results during combat.

To the regimental commander of the 66th Armored Regiment, maintenance was a serious problem. The division hoped to have one type of light tank by January 1, 1941, but actually had three. In addition, there were seven types of engines, both gasoline and diesel, six types of generators, five different starters and three sorts of voltage regulators. The tanks were prime candidates for the junkyard; repair parts were unavailable through normal supply channels. An unconfirmed but often repeated story is that Patton heard a soldier say that back home, when needing some repair part, he ordered it from Sears, Roebuck and Company. The commander supposedly ordered the needed parts and paid for them himself.

In December, 1940, after Scott became commanding general of the I Armored Corps, and Patton had assumed command of the division, he told Patton that he had just stopped a news story that American tanks were junk, that ordnance was not trying to solve the maintenance problem and that the Armored Force was the army's stepchild. Some of the allegations, Scott said, were half-truths; others were totally false. In the future, he warned, the I Armored Corps commander would be the spokesman for armor, and anyone else who was critical would be disciplined. The officers of the Armored Force were to accept the issued equipment, learn to use it properly and teach their men to have confidence in it, or "we become a rabble."

Patton began his tenure as division commander with plans for a 600-mile road march to either Panama City or Valparaiso, Florida, in December. Lt. Col. George L. King, assistant G-3, and Maj. Redding F. Perry, division G-4, made an inspection trip and recommended Panama City because it offered better facilities and accessibility. King recommended that the march be undertaken December 12–17, regardless of limitations and shortages. He felt that the advantages of practice in marching, camping and resupply far outweighed the disadvantages; it would provide a nucleus around which to build. He estimated that 22 officers and 1,035 enlisted men would be left behind because of schools and other duties. Patton approved the plan and sent a convoy to Fort Knox to return some trucks that had just taken students to the Armor School. Next, priorities for personnel were established. Emphasis was placed on officers who had not made such a march, noncommissioned officers, prospective noncommissioned officers, drivers, maintenance and communications specialists. To make room for the maximum number of troops, personal baggage was limited.

Training Memorandum Number 37, issued on December 6, 1940, stated that the purpose of the march was to perfect march discipline, formations and procedures; bivouacs; ground and air reconnaissance; security, control and communications; and supply and field maintenance. To do this, the division was to move in two columns of approximately equal strength, with tanks in both columns. The 2d Reconnaissance Battalion (Armored) and the 16th Observation Squadron of the Air Corps were to furnish route reconnaissance. Gasoline and diesel fuel were to be furnished by commercial firms. On December 12, 1940, the division made its first public appearance in the march from Fort Benning, Georgia, to Panama City, Florida. In the convoys were 392 officers, 6,079 enlisted men, 101 light and 74 medium tanks, and approximately 1,000 other vehicles. The march went smoothly until about 3:00 P.M. when it started to rain. This gave the men the opportunity to learn to stay dry in the field. One plane crashed and the division had to provide a guard and rush the pilot back to Fort Benning for medical treatment. Apparently no other problems were encountered as the division pulled into Abbeville,

Alabama, and Blakely, Georgia, to refuel and spend the night. The 2d Reconnaissance Battalion (Armored) continued to scout ahead to determine if the route were feasible.

The next morning the east column resumed moving at 6:00 A.M., the west at 7:00 A.M., and they had no difficulty reaching Panama City that evening, after 114 and 156 miles respectively. Grow passed the column several times, checking march discipline, which he judged to be excellent. Patton was pleased with the appearance of the soldiers and the discipline displayed on the march. The division spent two days at Panama City, resting, maintaining vehicles and preparing to return on December 16. During a lull in activities, some men enjoyed deep-sea fishing in the Gulf of Mexico. Because of the rough seas, many became seasick.

On the return trip the Armored Brigade, the engineer and ordnance battalions, and detachments of the quartermaster and medical battalions constituted the west (Alabama) column. The east (Georgia) column had primarily wheeled vehicles, which could traverse lighter bridges. The columns left Panama City for Blakely, Georgia, and Abbeville, Alabama, at 6:00 A.M. in pouring rain and arrived late that afternoon. Grow expected Patton to order a surprise night march; and, as a good G-3 should, he planned ahead and drafted orders for such a move in case they were needed. The division did indeed order a night march. The call to arms came at midnight, with the advance guard to leave at 1:35 A.M., while the main column (east) was to move out at 2:00 and the brigade (west) at 7:45. The division could possibly have made twenty-four miles per hour in full moonlight without vehicle lights. Moving the final eighty-three miles in three hours and forty-five minutes, the division concluded its march with an attack on Fort Benning. Scott told Chaffee that the division had an exceptionally good march and that the maintenance was extremely pleasing because they had had to tow only one tank into Fort Benning.

The final report on the Panama City march was issued in late January 1941 and was generally laudatory. The units displayed very high standards in individual and unit training. While the weather had prevented extensive use of aircraft, each column was attacked, giving the men training in warning and reactions to such surprises. The reconnaissance battalion and regimental reconnaissance companies received extensive training in scouting routes in unknown territory and reporting that information to headquarters. While each column used security detachments and practiced control, more drill was necessary. All elements of the division had received valuable training in supply and maintenance. A night march with vehicle lights could cover about the same distance as daylight marching. The division also found that it could not rely on commercial agencies to supply gasoline but that the quartermaster battalion should have that assignment. It was decided that tanks needed to carry enough gasoline for 130 miles, while other vehicles should carry enough for 150 miles.

Before and after the Panama City march, each type of platoon in the division conducted demonstrations. These were not to be school solutions, but a means of stimulating discussion and solution finding. The 41st Infantry Regiment's (Armored) Platoon Problem A was an assault against prepared defenses. Mortars, assault guns and machine guns would begin firing on the objective, attempting to keep the defenders in their foxholes, then the mortars would fire smoke to blind the defenders. The indirect fire weapons would continue their shelling until the infantry platoon leaders requested that the fire be lifted, then the platoon would launch its final assault to capture the objective. The demonstration of 17th Engineer Battalion (Armored) involved obstacles that could stop tanks. Grow thought that railroad rails driven deeply into the ground would be effective. While a student at the three-month tank maintenance course at Fort Knox, Lieutenant Perkins had seen a demonstration of tanks overcoming particular obstacles. The engineers had driven piles into the ground. While the medium tanks could crush them, the light tanks would either drive them into the ground or literally be catapulted over the piles. The only obstacles which could delay tanks were deep, wide pits, but then the tanks simply hoisted each other out. Perkins observed that the engineers were crestfallen at this. The tanks were also used to show that when rolling over prepared positions, such as foxholes and machine gun nests, the occupant could escape injury if he stayed down, even when the machine gun nests were seven feet in diameter.

Company exercises were conducted at the same time. The first series of exercises was designed to teach the men how to react in certain situations. Each company was to make a blind approach to the enemy. The men were to be brought under antitank fire to learn what to do to avoid it and to suppress antitank weapons. Once the enemy had been located, the company was to make an approach using covering tank fire to help them reach the objective. Once on the objective, the men had to consolidate it, prepare for counterattacks and be ready to resume their own attack.

The reconnaissance and machine gun companies were to give similar demonstrations. The regimental reconnaissance companies were to show

how they moved when not in close proximity to the enemy and when the enemy was nearby. Finally, it was to demonstrate how to overcome a defended roadblock that could hold up the column's advance. The machine gun company was part of the advance guard and showed how it would react if the advance guard had to be deployed. It had to show how to cover a tank battalion attack, to give supporting fire, to protect an assembly area and to consolidate and hold a captured position. While the Machine Gun Company, 66th Armored Regiment, gave the best demonstration the division had had, the future of the machine gun companies was under consideration. On two problems the units had been totally destroyed (theoretically), and it was found that the armored cars were faulty, even the new ones.

The units began to train utilizing the capabilities of other divisional elements. River crossings, one of the most difficult exercises, involved getting a protective force to the opposite bank, enlarging the bridgehead, building a ferry to get light tanks across and then building a bridge so the whole division could cross. The Reconnaissance Company, 41st Infantry Regiment (Armored), devised a means to get its light vehicles across; it used the canvas of a large truck to make a raft and pushed the vehicle across the river. In December the infantry and engineer units gave a "splendid demonstration" of an assault crossing of the Uaptoi River. Grow later noted, while watching an infantry tank team serving as the advance guard, that it was odd to see infantry acting like mechanized cavalry and rated the 41st Armored Infantry Regiment as a good outfit.

Col. Paul W. Newgarden and Maj. Sidney R. Hinds, commander and S-3 respectively of the 41st Infantry Regiment (Armored), were long-time tankers who realized that the armored infantrymen had to be in peak physical condition. They created a physical training program more rigorous than today's airborne requirements. Before the regiment would classify anyone as a soldier, officers and enlisted men alike had to be able to drop to a prone position and fire an aimed shot in less than three seconds. Within eight seconds, he had to rush forty yards and drop to a prone position. The infantryman had to be able to chin himself six times or three times with his rifle slung over his shoulder. He had to jump an eight-foot ditch and march five miles within an hour.

Late in October, 1940, the 2d Armored Division was informed that it was to receive about 2,100 recruits and give them basic training. Then the recruits would be sent to the qualification ranges and learn to drive all the vehicles of the Armored Brigade. In addition, the division was to receive

133 newly commissioned officers and reserve officers called to active duty and would have to run a replacement depot for them. Scott told Chaffee that he would need to quarter the officers in tents, but he did not think it advisable to put the trainees in tents, especially when he found that the men would not arrive until January 1941. He also said that he would need $37,500 to establish the replacement center.

The first groups of trainees—draftees under provision of the Burke-Wadsworth Act of 1940—arrived from Chicago. In the first group of draftees was Joe Ravolli, better known as Italian Joe. When he dismounted from the truck, he spotted an officer but not knowing ranks or insignias he approached him and asked, "Where is the bathroom?" The officer, somewhat taken aback, asked if the new recruit saw his uniform. Ravolli answered, "Yes, it doesn't fit either; now where is the bathroom?"

Thomas M. Strickland was one of the first men called in the draft. He was inducted at Atlanta, Georgia, and sent to Fort Benning. The recruits were sent to the 2d Armored Division's replacement center where they were fed, clothed and assigned to barracks. At that time the division was still suffering from a shortage of uniforms. Strickland remembers that he was issued a shirt and a pair of trousers at Atlanta, which he had to wear for thirty-two days before he had a change of clothing. While he admits that he did not smell too bad because it was winter, it had the advantage of keeping him off KP because of fear that he would dirty the one uniform.

In one platoon at the replacement center, there were men from eight countries—the United States, Britain, Germany, Puerto Rico, Mexico, Italy, Czechoslovakia, Armenia—and from the city of Danzig. Included in this group was a former officer in the Italian army and one soldier of fortune. A newspaperman, John P. McDermott, who had a regular column, "Inside the Outpost at Fort Benning," wrote a humorous item about recruiting for the division. It seemed that at an interview, a potential recruit admitted that he had no special skills or abilities for any unit in the army: "Officer (unnamed): What was your occupation? Recruit: I was a merry-go-round operator. Officer: Fine. You're just the kind of man we want. You'll feel right at home with the 2d Armored Division." Lt. Norris Perkins, in typical junior officer fashion, saw the entire situation at Fort Benning as a merry-go-round. He told his parents that the division was having to send cadres to the Armor School, to the division's own replacement center, while training cadres for the 3d Armored Division. Officers and noncommissioned officers were being sent to specialty

Above: Elements of the 7th Cavalry Brigade (Mechanized) passing in review.
Below: First mounted review of Hell on Wheels, February 1941, Fort Benning.

schools all over the east coast. No one, he said, knew where he would go next.

For Perkins the next stop was the replacement center, where he became a platoon leader in a basic training company. While admitting that he first feared that he might miss some opportunity, he later realized that it might be a haven for those who did not want to train recruits at Fort Knox for the next five years or be sent to activate the 3d Armored Division. The recruits were to get twelve weeks of training; the first six would involve intensive basic; the second six, intensive training according to job assignment. After twelve weeks, the men were to be assigned to training companies for intensive individual and small unit (squad, platoon and company) tactical training. Later Perkins admitted that he appreciated the experience with the selectees. After only three days his platoon was chosen as the best drilled. The men, he thought, were serious, intelligent and willing. It was too bad that they would be split up and assigned to different units of the division. All the men of the division realized that in the current international situation war was a distinct possibility. The training was demanding but appreciated.

The two existing armored divisions, the 1st and 2d, became the parents of the Armored Force by providing trained cadres for the activation of the 3d and 4th Armored Divisions. During the training period, estimates as to how many officers and men would be lost varied from 600 to 900 officers and from 3,000 to 4,000 enlisted men. In April 1941, Brig. Gen. Alvin C. Gillem, Jr., with 687 officers and 4,875 enlisted men, went to Fort Polk, Louisiana, to activate the 3d Armored Division.

Patton protested the loss of men. He told Scott that cadres for the replacement centers were taking a heavy toll of potential noncommissioned officer material and he foresaw making corporals of men with less than five months of service. Patton wanted to know the ratio of officers to noncommissioned officers that would be put into the cadre for the 3d Armored Division. He recommended 30–70 percent. If it were 50–50, then he thought the combat effectiveness of the 2d Armored would suffer without making a "justifiable advantage" for the 3d.

Scott, in a blistering reply to Patton's inquiry, stated that he was familiar with the problems. He knew the 2d Armored had lost men to create new units, but the commanders had surplus qualified persons when compared to the World War I situation. The War Department wanted to expand the Armored Force as quickly as possible, by training as many men as it could. These objectives could not be attained if all the trained personnel were kept in one unit, leaving the newer ones with nothing. It was absurd, he reasoned, to think that division commanders could have fully trained units and expand at the same time. He then hit Patton sharply by asking, "How many experienced men did you have in your tank center overseas?"

To help solve potential noncommissioned officer problems, Scott recommended that incoming personnel be screened to determine if any had had Citizens Military Training Camp or military school experience, some of which might be better noncommissioned officer material than persons serving their second or third enlistments. Reserve officers, he thought, were better than their World War I counterparts and in "many instances are better than some of the old crocks that have been floating around the regular army for the past 25–30 years." Scott was insistent that the newer divisions get their fair share of trained personnel. The I Armored Corps commander was considering moving the old division, brigade and regimental commanders to the new divisions and turning over the older units to newer appointees. He declined to do that but ordered Patton and Magruder to pick the cadremen as if they were to command the new divisions themselves.

In January 1941 the 2d Armored Division began intensive range and combat firing, combat exercises and reconnaissance training. The 2d Reconnaissance Battalion (Armored) and the reconnaissance companies in the armored infantry regiment and the engineer battalion were to coordinate their efforts. Patton directed Maj. I. D. White, commanding officer, 2d Reconnaissance Battalion (Armored), to devise and conduct tests for all the reconnaissance companies. The purpose was to test their reaction to conditions that they might encounter on the battlefield. It involved the reconnaissance of towns, routes, defiles, fords and bridges, terrain for use by combat elements, observation of hostile units, hostile encounters, establishing bridgeheads, guiding troops, self-maintenance when operating alone, and above all reporting the information so that it could be used. The 24-hour test required gasoline for 150 miles and had twelve phases from the reception of the warning order to the execution of the mission.

The tests revealed what many had thought: all personnel needed more training in scouting and patrolling. Foot patrolling, vital at times, slowed the units, but speed could be made up between critical areas. Proper reconnaissance could only be accomplished if the reconnaissance unit were given a sufficient lead time. It could not be done from fast moving vehicles. All men had to be completely informed about a mission. During the test, one platoon leader, 1st Lt. John Tyler of the 66th Armored Regiment, was injured and could not continue. His platoon sergeant assumed command of the platoon, finished the test and scored the highest of any unit.

Shortly after the division was activated, Scott noted that the ground and air forces needed coordinated training with both observation and combat aircraft. He recommended that observation aircraft be attached to the division for use by the commanding general and the brigade commander and their staffs. In February, 1941, the 4th Infantry Division (Motorized), the 501st Parachute Battalion and the 2d Armored Division tried to work out several problems: minimum bomb distances, minimum altitude for attacks, communications, signaling the end of an air attack, calling for an air attack and proper target designations. Some method had to be found to differentiate friendly troops and aircraft from those of the enemy. How could the two coordinate an air-ground attack and what kind of targets would be proper for an air attack? How much lead time was needed and who would control the aircraft? These were questions that needed answering.

The first test in February 1941 had the 2d Armored Brigade attacking the 41st Infantry Regiment (Armored). The bomb group that was to support the brigade was stationed in Atlanta. The infantry regiment stopped the tanks, who in turn sent out a call for air support. The bombers were in the air in ten minutes and attacked fifty minutes after getting the call. The communications between the ground and the airplanes worked beautifully, but the airmen hit the wrong target. However, they did hit the enemy artillery about two miles away. Later the bombers accurately attacked a second target and needed only five minutes. The moral of this as Grow saw it was that these procedures needed practice: "You can't do them by theory." Air control was a recognized problem, and both the Air Corps and ground forces were working to find the solution. Scott told Patton that both had a lot to learn and probably would not get very far until the Air Corps worked with the ground troops every day. The best answer had apparently not occured to either branch. Hinds recalled that air-ground work improved when the Air Corps put a pilot in a tank who went into combat with the ground forces, but that was in 1944.

Patton wanted another exercise, stressing that an armored division did not attack strong points if it could find a weak spot or get on the enemy's flank. The operational theory behind an armored division was changing; instead of being a weapon for the reduction of strong points, it now avoided strongly held positions if possible. The armored division was not a great rushing mass of tanks, but a spear thrust through weak spots, then fanning out behind the enemy, trying to cut supply and communications lines and attacking reserve areas and command posts. It operated alone or in conjunction with other forces. The armored division was a powerful instrument but had limitations, for it was thought to be sensitive to terrain, and its utility could be reduced in mountains and in marshy areas; also, it was weak in holding power.

The division began extensive field work in April and May 1941, preparing for the summer and fall maneuvers of that year. The first of a long series of problems was held on April 2–3 when the division went on a march to a concealed bivouac and practiced supply and servicing under blackout conditions. With so many new men, the march out was ragged and sloppy, but the bivouac and resupply problem went well. The next morning after breakfast the division rolled into post for a mounted review in driving rain. Patton told the assembled division, about 14,000 men in 2,500 vehicles, that "armored and air warfare makes higher demands on courage and discipline than have ever before been experienced by the fighting men of our race." The review went fairly well, except that when passing the reviewing stand the columns were ragged and a traffic jam occurred because the men did not follow instructions.

Later in April, the division put on the same problem for Major General Chaffee. Grow, while checking the columns from the air, had to drop messages to them because his radio failed. After the exercise, Chaffee addressed the officers, pointing out that the vehicles were not displaying the proper identification panels for aircraft and that some drivers were negotiating corners too fast. He cautioned the officers to expect war soon. Division headquarters was aware that it had to solve some serious problems: the improper use or even nonuse of liaison officers and the vexation of brigade attachments. These questions had to be solved before the division participated in large-scale maneuvers.

In May, Patton issued a memorandum stressing that training would be progressive, from small unit to division. The division would move to the field in multiple columns while the 2d Reconnaissance Battalion (Armored) was to practice locating the division and if possible delay its movement. Regimental reconnaissance companies were to cover the movement to the maneuvers area. During the training, constant practice against ground and air attack was to be carried out, with alarms sounded, antiaircraft weapons manned and bivouacs blacked out. The commanders were cautioned about overcommanding and instructed to maximize radio usage; no written orders were to be given, but rather oral commands or fragmentary orders in conference were to be used.

The troops marched out on the afternoon of May 6, to go into night bivouacs and to prepare for a predawn assault river crossing. On this problem, Perkins almost became one of the division's casualties. His driver panicked and froze on the throttle. The tank roared through underbrush, crisscrossed the road, knocked down trees and finally became enmeshed in a big bramble patch. While the driver would not stop, he responded to kick signals to turn. During this wild ride, he hit a pine tree which snapped and fell over the commander's hatch where moments before Perkins had had his head. During the night, rain started. Patton had instructed the men that three long blasts of an air horn meant an air raid attack. The men were just beginning to fall asleep when the quiet was shattered by a long blast of a horn, followed by another, then a short blast. It was not an air raid warning, so the men attempted to go back to sleep, only to have the procedure repeated. The antiaircraft weapons were manned and ready for use when the horn sounded again. It turned out not to be a signal, but a horn on a scout car which had shorted. Its wires were disconnected and the men slept. The next morning the 41st Infantry Regiment (Armored), supported by artillery, seized a bridgehead over the Uaptoi River. The engineers built the bridge, and the division crossed to continue its attack. The problems were the nearest thing to actual combat, but with real bullets and bombs it would have been much worse. The division suffered four dead: three in accidents, while one could not stand the strain and committed suicide. In addition there were some twenty-one broken bones caused by accidents.

The week of May 19–26 was spent in the field following the directives Patton had given two weeks earlier. The division moved out in multiple columns and the 2d Reconnaissance Battalion (Armored) was again given the aggressor role of delaying the columns. The 66th Armored Regiment (Light) was delayed but reached its bivouac area. The next day the division practiced platoon and company problems. Major General Scott and Lt. Col. Hugh J. Gaffey, Allen F. Kingman and John M. Devine, all future commanders of the 2d Armored Division, were pleased when they viewed the problems and saw how the units functioned. The battalion problems went well, and the men prepared for the combined 2d Armored and 4th Infantry Division (Motorized) exercises.

The 2d Armored Division helped to devise the tests for the 4th Infantry Division (Motorized). In the final problem the 4th Infantry was to relieve the armored troops, who were to pull back, regroup and attack through the infantry division. There had been some good-natured rivalry displayed between the two divisions and the 4th Infantry supposedly intended to "show those high and mighty bastards something." The 2d Armored made a night attack stopped by officials for a critique at 11:45. During the maneuvers, much of the publicity centered around the 2d Armored Division because it was a new type of division, and tanks were drawing much print about their use in Europe. A messenger, Pvt. Ralph C. Radtke, Headquarters Company, 2d Armored Division, was given the mission of taking news releases to post headquarters for distribution. Taking a shortcut, Radtke was captured by men of B Company, 101st Antitank Battalion. The battalion adjutant, Capt. Keith F. Driseale, wrote a note to accompany Radtke, explaining how he had been captured, and had the private embarrassingly marched into post headquarters under guard. When the division returned to its post, it had a showdown inspection on the review field. Scott said that it was the first time that he had seen a showdown inspection, and he believed it to be the first time ever at the end of maneuvers. Many items were in short supply, but he believed that the division could fight if necessary.

In the critique, Maj. Gen. Lesley J. McNair, commanding general, Army Ground Forces, stated that the 2d Armored and the 4th Infantry Divisions were among the most ready for battle. He cautioned the officers that he did not say they were ready, but "that you are more ready than the rest." Patton observed that all the maneuvers had demonstrated that an armored division must be given "an assignment of mission rather than a definite assignment of method." Patton was arguing for the basic tenet of armored warfare that would be demonstrated repeatedly in Europe. When given an assignment of method, armored divisions were usually slowed down and suffered casualties far in excess of those suffered when executing the assignment of mission-type orders.

Scott noted that the division was ready for field duty and, referring to the forthcoming Tennessee maneuvers, warned the men that they had to get the most from the maneuvers—"Who knows? It may be the last chance you have to practice." A few days later, Scott told Lt. Col. Ernest N. Harmon that the division was in fine shape and that the small units were exceedingly well trained. Scott was very pleased at the way the companies and reinforced battalions worked against antitank guns and roadblocks.

While at Fort Benning, the division started two traditions which are still followed. General Order Number 7 specified how and when the division patch was to be worn. All men would wear it over the left breast on the field jacket, and officers would wear it over the left breast on their coveralls. Today every member of the division wears the patch over the left breast on the fatigue uniforms. The divisional motto, Hell on Wheels, originated at Fort Benning and was applied to the 2d Armored prior to the Tennessee maneuvers, though division legend holds that the nickname came from these exercises. On April 6, 1941, the *Columbus Ledger* stated that the man who first used the phrase must have foreseen American armored divisions. Two weeks later the paper carried a picture of the patch, saying that "it means Hell on Wheels." Between April 6 and May 23, the *Columbus Ledger* used that phrase no less than nine different times in referring to the 2d Armored Division. On May 2, a columnist, Allen Thomason, who replaced McDermott as the author of "Inside the Outpost at Fort Benning," wrote of activities of four officers from the "Second Armored 'Hell on Wheels' Division." By the time of the Tennessee maneuvers, the phrase clearly meant the 2d Armored Division; the Tennessee maneuvers only confirmed its appropriateness.

Chapter 3

THE TENNESSEE
MANEUVERS

The Armored Force was left undisturbed to develop its doctrines. After a year of training, the 2d Armored Division was to take part in large-scale field maneuvers. In February, 1941, Major General Scott, commanding general of the I Armored Corps, informed the War Department that he wanted to use the Fort Benning tankers in four exercises. Participating troops, he argued, would receive invaluable training in the concepts of deployment and defense against armored units. Young officers saw the maneuvers as a test of the division's great mobility and a means to determine its real value and employment.

Reorganization of the 2d Armored Division had been considered at the time of its activation. The division organization had been hastily drawn. The large brigade was too unwieldly; the division commander needed several combat teams. In September 1940, the I Armored Corps called the division G-3s together, suggesting a reorganization into two brigades, one of two light tank regiments and the other of medium tank and infantry regiments. Apparently this proposal was turned down. Finally in May 1941 Scott told the 2d Armored officers to experiment with

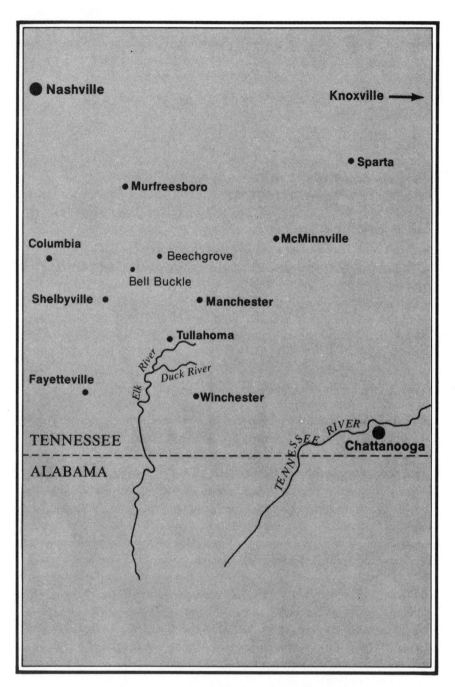

Figure 2. The Tennessee Maneuvers, 1941.

organizational changes in Tennessee. He wanted three battalions in the infantry regiment, three battalions in the medium tank regiment, three artillery battalions commanded by a division artillery commander and an additional bridge company in the engineer battalion.

In March, 1941, the War Department had selected the Camp Forrest, Tennessee, area for the Second Army maneuvers. The main features of this south central Tennessee terrain are the Duck River, which is twenty to fifty yards wide, and the Tennessee Cumberland Divide. There were concrete and light load carrying bridges, the river banks were generally steep and the bottoms rocky, but there were vehicle fords. This mountainous and forested region was thought to be unsuitable for tank warfare. A series of opening maneuvers seemed, to some members of the 2d Armored Division, to be specifically designed to limit or perhaps embarrass the division. The first disagreement concerned the amount of time the division would spend in Tennessee. Army general headquarters, commanded by Lt. Gen. Lesley J. McNair, made the division available for the entire maneuver period of June 2–28, 1941. The Second Army, commanded by Lt. Gen. Ben "Yoo Hoo" Lear, wanted the division for only part of that time, to which McNair agreed. The division chief of staff, Lt. Col. Geoffrey Keyes, told Lt. Col. Ernest N. Harmon that hopefully the situation would be settled to everyone's satisfaction.

A second problem arose concerning the division's use of the 87th Engineer Battalion (Heavy Pontoon). The Second Army had authorized the use of the complete battalion. General headquarters changed the authorization, alleging that inadequate motor transportation would permit using only one company. Two weeks prior to the maneuvers the Second Army consented to use the entire battalion. The division needed the engineers. Patton told Scott that he had driven around the Camp Forrest area and in his opinion any success would depend on the division's ability to make bridgeheads and force river crossings. The most severe blow came when the division learned that it would have to furnish fifty-one umpires for the maneuvers. Scott wrote Chaffee, protesting bitterly that the 2d Armored needed its officers to make a good showing; he recommended that the umpires be taken from the 1st and 3d Armored Divisions. Scott saw that this would be advantageous to all three divisions. The 2d Armored had recently furnished the cadre for the 3d Armored and was short of experienced officers and men. If the other divisions could furnish umpires, the 2d Armored officers could stay with their units. The division would not have to use noncommissioned officers to command units nor-

Left: Lt. Gen. Ben Lear and Maj. Harry A. Flint (who was killed in action in France, 1944). Note division patch above Flint's left pocket.
Below: Tankers halt for fuel. Note crewman with fire extinguisher at the ready.

mally commanded by officers. To accomplish this, however, would require additional funds. Scott was able to persuade Chaffee to make forty officers available from other armored divisions.

Scott assembled and addressed the maneuver umpires. He pointed out that both the Second Army and army general headquarters wanted to stress the proper usage of small units. The umpires were to see that small units received due credit for their good performances as well as citations for errors. He cautioned the umpires that they were neither to command nor instruct and should not reveal information gained through umpire activities. However, they were required to convey those things normally seen, heard or known in battle. In situations not covered by the umpire's manual, they were to use common sense. The higher-unit umpires working on the battalion, regiment, brigade and division levels were responsible for informing the lower-level umpires of situations and for moving them to places where they could best oversee the critical points and situations.

The most anticipated time in the maneuvers was the entry of the 2d Armored Division and its colorful commander, Major General Patton. Patton would try to move his division into the maneuver area undetected; however, the VII Army Corps commander, Maj. Gen. Frederic H. Smith, was determined to find the Hell on Wheels division. To add a little spice to the determination of both sides, Smith offered a $25.00 reward to the man who captured Patton. Not to be outdone, Patton placed a $50.00 bounty on Smith's head. The maneuvers opened on a note of high expectation.

The division left Fort Benning at 5 A.M. on July 14, 1941, in two columns, each about sixty miles long. All units were in the bivouac area by 6 P.M. on the evening of June 15. The next morning, the division moved to concealed bivouac areas, unloaded their tanks and half-tracks that had been sent by rail and prepared to enter the exercise. Patton was permitted to send reconnaissance units anywhere to gain information while the remainder of the division protected the detraining point. Scott thought that the enemy VII Army Corps might attempt to disrupt the unloading. Patton had been instructed that the problem opened tactically when he met Maj. Gen. Joseph M. Cummins, commanding general of the 5th Infantry Division.

The first problem was relatively simple. A Blue enemy force (27th and 30th Infantry Divisions) was attempting to push the friendly Red force out of the area. The Red 5th Infantry Division and the 153d Infantry

Regiment were to hold a defensive line until they could be reinforced by the 2d Armored Division. Then it was to attack, pushing the Blue troops west of Bell Buckle, Tennessee. The opening move was to be a practical demonstration of the nose-and-seat-of-the-pants theory. The 2d Armored Brigade was to attack the west rear of the Blue forces, while the 41st Infantry (minus one battalion) was to attack on the north flank. A composite force resembling the tank-infantry teams of World War II, led by Lt. Col. Sidney R. Hinds, attacked on the south flank. The holding job was to be handled by the 5th Infantry Division. While the Blue force was preoccupied on its flanks, the 67th Armored Regiment was to deliver the knockout blow from the east. At 8 P.M. on June 15, the plans were made, the columns were organized, and the division moved to its attack positions without lights and under radio silence. Umpires with the tankers called the road march the most magnificent ever made by tanks. Later Lieutenant Perkins and Pvt. Samuel W. Tackitt, C Battery, 14th Armored Artillery, were told that if they had been able to see the cliffs and chasms they would have been scared. Pvt. Thomas M. Strickland, B Company, 41st Armored Infantry Regiment, drove his half-track into a bivouac area at night. The next morning he found that he had parked only about six feet from a 300-foot sheer drop. By 4 A.M. the next morning the division was in position to launch the attack after its columns had moved from 70 to 130 miles.

The attack was coordinated by the column commanders. The 2d Armored Division entered the battle at about 6 A.M. on June 17. The enemy VII Army Corps (Blue) was forced to abandon its offensive and to assume a defensive posture. The tankers launched a swarming attack, hitting the enemy force from four directions. The 68th Armored and the 41st Armored Infantry Regiments captured Hoover's Gap about two and one-half hours after the exercise opened. The 67th Armored Regiment, attacking astride Highway 41, was slowed by strong antitank defenses. Every time a tank exposed itself, it was fired on. The main problem was the lack of infantry to eliminate the guns and to facilitate the tanks' advance. Maj. John P. Kidwell, commanding officer of the 2d Battalion, 67th Armored Regiment, led his thirty-one tanks over one extremely rugged mountain trail. He then sent Pvt. Francis Cutrupi to scout ahead but he was captured. Kidwell's tank was destroyed, but he was not a casualty. He returned with more tanks to challenge the 37mm antitank guns, only to have the umpires rule that he suffered three more losses. His battalion could not penetrate the antitank gun defenses.

In spite of the tenacious antitank defense, the 2d Armored Division drove the Blue forces to positions west of Bell Buckle, surrounded them and cut them off. While moving through Bell Buckle, one tank of I Company, 66th Armored Regiment, crashed through the town hall. Pvt. V. A. Esposito said the accident was caused because the tank driver swerved to avoid hitting a civilian truck. As the front of the building fell, it filled the inside of the tanks with bricks. The rescuers had to dig the tank commander out of the wreckage, but no one was injured. When reporters asked Patton about it, he replied that no one could blame the tank crew because the damn city hall was not on the map. The umpires terminated the exercise at 11:40 A.M. on June 17, about five and one-half hours after Patton and the tanks had entered the battle. The Blue forces were defeated but not destroyed. The 2d Armored Division was in position to deliver the final attack, even though Blue tanks threatened the flank of one column. The umpires ruled that Hell on Wheels had lost approximately 135 tanks, many other vehicles and many men. In the end, both sides claimed victory.

Both certainly learned from the experience. Maj. Gen. Samuel T. Lawton, commanding general of the 33d Infantry Division, had arranged his antitank guns into a new type of battalion, had dug them in, and positioned them on the flanks and in the rear. He explained that armored troops did not attack on as broad a front as the old system of antitank defense. Instead, they picked a weak spot and hit fast. The key was to get the defense into those weak spots before the tanks arrived. In a news conference Patton told reporters that fear of the unknown was the armored division's best weapon: the opposition did not know where the division was or where it would strike. As the exercise had unfolded, it was not uncommon for Blue soldiers to lay aside their weapons and grab their cameras as the tanks approached, for they were still an object of curiosity. A former correspondent for the *Memphis Commercial Appeal* noted that the great Confederate cavalryman, Nathan Bedford Forrest, did not believe in attacking enemy strong points, and neither did the 2d Armored Division. Forrest's motto, "Get 'em skerred and keep 'em skerred," well suited the Hell on Wheels division.

In the next exercise, the 2d Armored Division became part of the Blue army at midnight on June 19. Patton was permitted to start planning with the VII Corps before then, and the corps ordered him to dispatch the division's reconnaissance elements at 5:00 A.M. on June 19 to locate the Red army's positions. Grow flew to Lynchburg to talk with Major I. D.

White. On the return flight, when the plane was about fifty feet off the ground, it crashed. However, neither Grow nor the pilot was injured. When Grow returned to the division headquarters, he had to change the attack orders because of the conference between Patton and Smith. Patton had agreed to exploit a breakthrough made by the 28th and 30th Infantry Divisions. The 67th Armored Regiment, at Smith's insistence, was detached from the division and in effect became a general headquarters tank battalion to be used at the discretion of the corps commander.

On the second move a tank in H Company, 66th Armored Regiment, hit a bridge railing at forty-five miles per hour under blackout conditions. The wreck totally destroyed the tank and turned it on its side. A few feet further to the right was a forty-foot canyon. Lt. Norris Perkins arrived on the scene as the medics were loading the driver. He was usually the maintenance officer of H Company, but for the exercise was the commander of 3d Battalion, 66th Armored Regiment, Trains. He used a tank to pull the damaged tank out of one lane and got the column started again. By this time the regiment was some twenty miles ahead. The commander of H Company came to investigate and then took it upon himself to speed up the column. He succeeded only in stringing out the column. Perkins raced ahead to stop or slow down the captain. From the rear, the captain's tank, highlighted by the blue blackout lights of the only vehicle to stay with him, was a phosphorescent monstrosity. The tracks, weighing some 1,600 pounds each, were undulating wickedly like glowing eels from the *Ancient Mariner*. Red and blue fire from the exhausts completed the picture. Perkins finally caught him, and the unit joined the regiment before it launched its attack the next morning.

By dusk on June 19, the Blue infantry forces had made small gains, but at 7:00 A.M. on June 20, the 2d Armored added its weight to the assault. The 67th Armored Regiment attacked through the 30th Infantry Division along Highway 41 and was two miles from its objective, Manchester, by 8:45 A.M. Meanwhile, the bulk of the division was making a three-pronged advance toward Manchester from Lynchburg. Patton was out front fighting with his scout car and leading the division in his traditional manner. They had to cross many fords and had some close fights with the enemy. The division commander was in the midst of the action, cursing men and urging them on to Manchester. At about 9:00, three members of the 67th had observed an airplane drop a message near them and correctly reasoned that a headquarters lay nearby. The tankers attacked the infantrymen, who defended with rifles and machine guns, and captured Brig. Gen. Cortlandt Parker, commanding general, 5th Infantry Division, and his staff. For their initiative, a 2d Armored hallmark, the men received twenty-five dollars from a jubilant Patton. At 11:00, four hours after the 2d Armored Division entered the battle, the umpires ended the exercise.

In the third problem, the 2d Armored Division was still part of the Blue force. The 5th Infantry Division (Red) was occupying a defensive line from Tullahoma to Hillsboro. The Blue force mission was to rout the enemy to prevent his linking with additional Red forces to the northeast. The division planned to use the nose-and-seat-of-the-pants idea again. As events transpired, the posterior elements were in position and doing their jobs before the nasal units got started. While the 66th Armored Regiment was moving into position, one tank fell eight feet off a wooden bridge and became wedged tightly against the bridge pillars. While waiting for wreckers to pull the tank out, one farmer offered his mules and another man wanted to pull the tank out with his Model A Ford. The tank commander, 2d Lt. Joe Moore, had to eat one meal of emergency rations. During their meal, a woman treated the crew with a platter of biscuits, butter, honey and a pot of coffee. After three wreckers extracted the tank, Moore and his crew moved sixty miles, leading the tank through towns on foot, over a mountain pass and, unknowingly, through an enemy camp.

The 66th Armored Regiment, supported by the 1st Battalion, 78th Armored Artillery, a company of engineers and the 41st Infantry Regiment (less two battalions), was to attack the Red's east flank at 11:00. The 8th Bombardment Squadron was ordered to bomb Prairie Plains, 5th Infantry Division headquarters. The attack took place at 11:15 just ahead of leading 66th Armored elements. The attack was so successful that the 66th Armored Regiment reached the Elk River, the restraining line, by 12:15. The second flanking element was a composite force of the 82d Reconnaissance Battalion, the 3d Battalion of the 41st Armored Infantry Regiment, the 2d Battalion of the 78th Artillery and a company of engineers. This force reached Winchester by 10:00, proceeded to block the crossings of the Elk River and attacked the Red force in the rear. The bulk of the 2d Armored Brigade constituted the ''nose'' force. The brigade was ordered to attack the center of the Red line at 1:30; it did, passed through and started exploiting its success towards the Elk River. The attacks were so successful that the exercise was terminated at 2:10, forty minutes after the bulk of the 2d Armored Division entered the attack.

Observers had only praise for the tankers. For a problem thought to require twenty-four hours, the 2d Armored Division had needed only three. The division had used a ''trick play.'' A message was dropped to an armored car, later captured, which said that the main effort would be made from the west at 1:30. Actually it came from the northeast at 1:00. A second factor may have been press reports concerning the two earlier exercises, which indicated that the tankers were pulling their punches. In this third exercise, according to Strickland and Tackitt, the tanks and half-tracks roared through forests and over fences and fields. Previously, the vehicles had largely stayed on the roads, causing little damage. Capt. Harry B. Koon, Sr., chaplain of the 105th Quartermaster Regiment, 30th Infantry Division, was on his way to pick up his unit's mail. His vehicle was not flying the white administrative flag, so it was fair game. The vehicle and its occupants were captured by the chaplain's son, Pvt. Harry B. Koon, Jr., of the 2d Armored Division.

In the final exercise, the 2d Armored Division rejoined the 5th Infantry Division to constitute the Red force. The Blue forces were defending the area between the Duck and Elk Rivers. Red's mission was to push the Blue forces back and capture Tullahoma, with the problem to begin at 5 A.M. on June 26, 1941. The division started moving at about 3:00 to envelop the north flank of the Blue forces, while the 5th Infantry Division held the Blues in the line and enveloped the south flank. By 7 A.M. the 82d Reconnaissance Battalion had secured two crossings over the Duck River and turned them over to the 41st Armored Infantry Regiment to defend. The main body started crossing the river, and by 12:30 it had reached its assembly areas, regrouped and was launching attacks against Tullahoma. The problem ended at 1:20 with the capture of the town and the destruction of the enemy force—six and one-half hours after the 2d Armored Division had entered the fight. One Cub airplane being tested as an artillery observer and liaison aircraft signaled the end of the exercise. When the plane's signal was not understood, it landed, taxied down the road and overtook one tank to give its occupants the word.

The chief umpire noted that the 2d Armored Division's actions were rapid, coordinated and decisively effective. However, the division was criticized for inadequate reconnaissance, which resulted in unnecessarily high tank losses. The 41st Armored Infantry Regiment was credited with superior action. Self-criticism is probably the most valid. Lieutenant Colonel Grow noted that about half of the tanks of the 2d Armored Division were late getting across the Duck River, everything was committed piecemeal, and as a result the units were scrambled. The main reason for the debacle, according to Grow, was that the command and staff functioned very poorly. He thought that division headquarters was terrible and control was nonexistent because of personality differences. Grow observed that the men of the division were fine, but the unit got progressively worse up the organizational ladder.

The division returned to Fort Benning and began preparing for the Louisiana maneuvers, to be held in about six weeks. As Patton told reporters, the division no longer charged an opponent but probed for weak points through which to attack the flanks and rear. The Tennessee maneuvers tested the division's theory and training. During the exercises, the division ran roughshod over its opposition.

On July 7, 2d Armored Division headquarters issued General Order 28, which was both congratulatory and advisory in tone. The present state of training had been attained despite shortages of equipment and losses of experienced personnel to other units. Since equipment had begun arriving and personnel losses were due to slow down, the division was now to concentrate on training. The next day the division assembled at the 2d Armored Division Bowl at Sand Hill, and Patton critiqued the maneuvers. He noted the division's mistakes, saying that "if there were not mistakes, there would be no need for maneuvers." He complimented the men on their courtesy, dress and favorable impressions they had made on senior commanders and the secretary of war. He observed that if the men continued improving, "you will make your shoulder patch something that will cause as much dread to the enemies of your country as it causes pride among your friends."

The division commander thought that the men had carried out every mission with efficiency and timeliness. The division had earned a favorable reputation because of its performance and high standards. To continue to lead, the division could not be content with its accomplishments, but would have to continue to improve, avoiding errors such as those committed in Tennessee. Turning to the mistakes, Patton stated that the tanks' vulnerability must be recognized. It was folly to think of charging antitank guns with the intention of crushing them beneath their tracks, as the tank was only a squad with a large amount of firepower. Once through antitank defenses, their armor and speed permitted them to attack rear positions with a high degree of safety because rear area soldiers had no antitank defenses. To help overcome antitank guns, new sets of formations would soon be given to companies and battalions. Since antitank guns were towed and had to stay on or near roads, Patton ordered the tankers to get off the road when they came within 1,000 yards of an antitank gun. Since antitank guns were almost always at crossroads, the men were to flank them from one or both sides. In addition, if the force had artillery or mortars, these should be fired at the antitank guns or their suspected position.

Patton said that the division, especially the reconnaissance elements, was suffering a disease associated with the motorized age—"waffle ass." It was contracted by people who sat too much. More specifically, he told the reconnaissance elements that when approaching points that might contain mines and antitank guns they should get off the road and walk or crawl, using binoculars to investigate. This would be hard work, but it was better than getting killed. After securing information, they were to send it back to headquarters in the most expeditious manner possible, so that it could be used.

Teamwork was vital for success in an armored division. Patton thought that there was still too often a tendency for each unit to be a one-handed puncher: the rifleman wanted to shoot, the fellow with the mortar to burp, and so on. This was not the way to win a war. Each weapon, like each instrument in an orchestra, must support the others. He told the "musicians of Mars" not to wait for the leader to signal when to enter the battle but to use their own initiative and to be at the proper place at the proper time. Initiative was another topic of instruction. Patton told of an unnamed reconnaissance sergeant and crew who were the survivors of a platoon. When an umpire asked the man what he was doing, the sergeant told him the mission, what had been accomplished and what remained to be done. He then proceeded to complete the mission. That sergeant earned the congratulations of his division commander. But, Patton noted, since almost all members of the division had been in school for about a year, the division had acquired a "student complex"—a tendency to wait for instructions. That malady was particularly manifest in lieutenants, captains and noncommissioned officers. To overcome this he suggested that a very safe rule to follow was in case of doubt to "push on just a little further and then keep on pushing." Tackitt was near Mrs. Patton and overheard someone ask her about the general's language. She replied that she had heard him say worse.

The division was a victim of its own successes and the army's ignorance about armor warfare. It received little or no credit for its performance. In three attacks the division surrounded the enemy and was in position to destroy him, but the umpires and maneuver directors ruled against the division. In the third exercise, the division penetrated the enemy line, but the enemy escaped. Yet this was considered a major victory for the 2d Armored Division. This situation pointed out that major commanders must know armor tactics. The 2d Armored changed the tempo of battle. Each exercise ended the same day that the division entered it, usually twelve to twenty-four hours before the problem was scheduled to end. The maneuvers demonstrated that a fundamental change in philosophy had to occur. Instead of pushing the enemy back, emphasis should be placed on rapidly destroying him in place. Scott, commander of the I Armored Corps and an observer at the maneuvers, told Maj. Gen. Adna R. Chaffee, chief of the Armored Force, that the 2d Armored Division did an excellent job in Tennessee despite shortages. He noted that the division had less than 60 percent of its combat vehicles and 14 percent of its radio equipment, while 40 percent of its personnel had about four months of duty with tanks.

Scott raised three basic questions. First, if an antitank battalion were sent to stop an armored division, what would keep artillery and infantry from pinning the battalion down, thus permitting the division to go around it? Second, if enough antitank guns were available to establish a perimeter defense, what was to prevent the tanks' punching a hole in the enemy line, and then fanning out behind the guns, thus avoiding most of the antitank guns? Last, he asked, if the tanks penetrated enemy lines by either method, what was to protect rear installations? Adding a bit of humor, and perhaps because of Brigadier General Parker's capture, he wanted to know if rear area defenders would rush forward with rifles and light machine guns to try to stop the tanks.

Chapter 4

THE LOUISIANA MANEUVERS, 1941

The Louisiana maneuvers were the second large-scale exercise in which the 2d Armored Division participated in 1941. Lt. Gen. Lesley J. Mc-Nair, commanding general of the army ground forces, wanted the maneuvers to be realistic, as he wanted a crack officer corps. The exercises hopefully would reveal officers' strengths and weaknesses. Gen. George C. Marshall, army chief of staff, was looking for promotable colonels and lieutenant colonels. Most of the divisions were National Guard units, and the exercises were to acquaint them with the advantages and disadvantages of armor, its tactics and theory. The Armored Force would experiment with new concepts. Maj. Gen. Charles L. Scott, commanding general, I Armored Corps, told McNair that while the Armored Force had not studied the possibility of following armored divisions with motorized infantry and support units, the Louisiana exercise or the Carolina maneuvers scheduled for November would be a good time to consider it.

The maneuver area was bounded by Shreveport on the north, by Lake Charles on the south, by the Sabine River on the west and by the Red

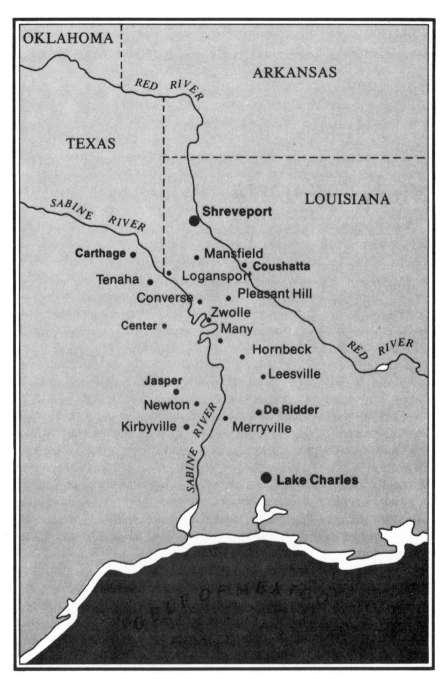

Figure 3. The Louisiana Maneuvers, 1941.

River on the east, an area which covered more than 13 million acres. Covered with rice fields, stagnant water, swamps and thick forests, it was not considered tank country. For the Louisiana maneuvers, the division's organizational structure was altered to that used in the Tennessee maneuvers. During the maneuvers, Lt. Col. Robert W. Grow, division G-3, was assigned to the 5th Armored Division. He was replaced by Maj. Howard L. Peckham, commanding officer of the 17th Armored Engineer Battalion.

The maneuvers were built around two mythical countries. KOTMK (Kansas, Oklahoma, Texas, Missouri and Kentucky) was the Red invaded nation. ALMAT (Alabama, Louisiana, Mississippi, Arkansas and Tennessee) was the Blue aggressor nation. Lt. Gen. Ben "Yoo-Hoo" Lear commanded the Red Second Army while Lt. Gen. Walter Krueger commanded the Blue Third Army.

The first problem had the Red Army V Corps landing at Lake Charles, then moving north to seize the Pleasant Hill-Noble-Mansfield oil field. For this, V Corps had the 32d, 34th, 37th, and 38th Infantry Divisions, the 1st Cavalry Division, and the 1st Tank Group. Defending, the Blue VIII Corps had the 2d Armored Division, 2d, 36th and 45th Infantry Divisions, 18th Artillery Brigade and the 56th Cavalry Brigade. Its mission was to attack southward, destroying the enemy and pushing the Red forces back into the Gulf of Mexico.

Maj. Gen. George V. Strong, commanding general of the VIII Corps, planned to attack southward, seizing the Peason Ridge area as a road net, then to continue southward, seizing Leesville. Hell on Wheels was to spearhead the VIII Corps movement, moving south to break through or envelop hostile resistance, seize Peason Ridge and continue southeast, with an infantry division on each flank mopping up bypassed resistance. The armored spearhead was supported by a 155mm howitzer regiment from the 18th Artillery Brigade. The 82d Armored Reconnaissance Battalion, commanded by Major I. D. White, assembled the afternoon of August 16, and White cautioned his battalion that their job was to gain information and to find the 1st Cavalry Division and the 1st Tank Group. They were not to worry about small groups, but only about the bulk of enemy forces. He stressed the need for teamwork: "We are not going to win the war all by ourselves as we did in Tennessee." The 2d Armored Division was organized into three columns, each having light and medium tanks, artillery, infantry and engineer support. The division waited for the order which would send them into the exercises. For control purposes, both corps would attack on Third Army's order, which was given at 2:00 A.M. on August 17, 1941. The reconnaissance battalion moved out about 4:00, while the division attacked about two hours later.

The exercise, which started in rain, soon ran into dust and trouble. In Tennessee, the division specialized in long marches and wide turning movements. In the initial move here, it was forced to operate in narrow corridors between large boggy areas. Poor roads and ridge lines perpendicular to the attack route made it difficult to advance against enemy antitank guns. Initial enemy contact was along the Anacoco-Kurthwood-Hornbeck line. The reconnaissance battalion was delayed about 1½ hours south of Kurthwood by a destroyed bridge, while the left column was held up for thirty-five minutes by a Red scout car south of Anacoco. After these delays, a platoon of tanks was placed in the lead and encountered little resistance until they met the 32d Infantry Division in a defile north of Rosepine.

From Kurthwood to Leesville, the 82d Reconnaissance Battalion ran into numerous 1st Cavalry Division antitank guns, which forced it to scout ahead on foot. The soldiers managed to work themselves around the guns and arrived at Leesville at 4:00 P.M. They continued south to a point two miles north of Pickering, while the leading elements of the three columns were at Anacoco, Kurthwood and Slagle by 4:30. North of Pickering, the reconnaissance battalion made contact with the 66th Armored Regiment, which was facing stiff opposition. White used B Company and 2d Battalion, 78th Armored Artillery, in an attempt to help them. The 66th Armored Regiment attacked repeatedly but could not dislodge the enemy from the defile north of Rosepine, losing an estimated forty to fifty tanks in the meantime. Late in the afternoon, the regiment broke contact, circled to the east and got on the flank of the 32d Infantry Division. By 8:00 P.M. part of the 66th Armored Regiment had managed to get into Rosepine. The first day ended with the 2d Armored Division making good progress. The 66th was about thirty miles ahead of the remainder of the division. The VIII Corps failure to follow the spearheading tankers with sufficient infantry to consolidate and exploit the tankers' gains caused serious problems for the 66th, the lead element of the main body of the division.

The power drive technique yielded to flanking attacks. The VIII Corps ordered the attack resumed at 5:00 A.M. on August 18. The plan was to envelop the enemy right flank and push the Red corps to the southeast. The 2d Armored Division was to make the main effort. The west column, 66th Armored Regiment (minus a battalion), started moving to the south of Pickering, but it was halted by hostile antitank guns four miles south of the town. It had the 144th Regimental Combat Team attached, but the infantry was unable to overcome the enemy's antitank guns. The west column was split and there was no chance of relieving it. The center column, 2d Armored Brigade, was heavily engaged near Slagle, but managed to reach Sugartown that night. The east column, 68th Armored Regiment, cleared Pitkin, took Sugartown by 1:45 P.M. and managed to work its way into Rosepine by 2:30. Darkness found the east column almost entirely surrounded by the 1st Cavalry Division and an infantry division. At 6:45, the VIII Corps ordered the division to disengage and to assemble near Craven, Pitkin, Leander and LeCamp. The next morning it was to attack towards DeRidder, break through and destroy those forces opposing the friendly 2d and 36th Infantry Divisions. The major effort was to be made by the 2d Armored and 45th Infantry Divisions. There was no hope of relieving the west column. It was left in place to attack southward the following day.

The attack resumed at 5:00 A.M. The center column made good progress below Pitkin; the east column pushed the enemy back and progressed toward Craven. The west column was impeded by the 32d Infantry Division all day. Finally, after a feint and by effective use of their artillery, the 66th Armored Regiment was able to advance some ten miles, capturing towns, enemy supply trains and many prisoners. The prisoners were turned over to the friendly motorized infantry, who had been rescued from a prisoner-of-war camp. In an enveloping attack, the 45th Infantry surrounded the 1st Cavalry, and the 2d Armored was almost to DeRidder. The reconnaissance battalion moved on south; one of its companies was at Lake Charles. The 3d Battalion, 66th Armored Regiment, escaped by destroying several batteries of 75mm guns. After the infantry set out smoke pots to hide a tank company's attack around the flank and while the tank company was scaring the artillerymen, a tank platoon attacked from the rear and destroyed the artillery. The regiment began to move into the Lake Charles area. The exercise ended at 3:00 P.M., with the units bivouacked in place keeping all roads open. During the lull, the men first did the necessary maintenance, fighting chiggers, mosquitoes and snakes. Some troopers found time to swim in the Sabine River. Perkins and Tackitt were surprised at the realism. Some men had died in accidents, others from snake bites. Nonetheless, morale was high; Patton's tankers were awaiting the next problem.

Above: Members of 41st Armored Infantry Regiment during Louisiana maneuvers.
Below: Members of Company F, 66th Armored Regiment, participating in Louisiana maneuvers.

For the second exercise, the 2d Armored Division was assigned to the V Corps (Red) and moved to assembly areas southeast of DeRidder on August 23. During this administrative move, the division practiced maintaining tactical distances during marches. In bivouac at DeRidder, the men received instructions to be sure that the tanks were correctly marked. In the first exercise some tanks had not been marked, while others carried Red organizational bands when the division was a member of the Blue forces. General Krueger wanted this confusion stopped.

In the theoretical situation, the Red forces had invaded Louisiana from the Gulf of Mexico and were trying to capture oil fields in the Mansfield area. Blue attacked south and was stopped along the Hemphill-Hornbeck-Kisatchie line. The Red mission was to drive the Blue defenders south of the Many-Robeline line and capture the oil fields in the Mansfield area. Grow formulated three plans. One was to make a wide envelopment into Texas and attack the Blue forces from the north (their rear). Regardless of whether the division got much of its force across the Sabine River, he thought the Red Corps would win the war. The second plan was to move a small force across the Sabine, as in the first plan, while the bulk of the division awaited an infantry breakthrough. The third plan was to wait for an infantry breakthrough, but he thought this would cause heavy casualties. The first plan was adopted. According to Field Order 6, the 2d Armored Division was to cross the Sabine, move north, seize crossings over the Sabine between Converse and U.S. Highway 59, cross the river and attack the Mansfield area. In the corps effort, the infantry divisions were to be the nose-holding elements while the 2d Armored kicked the Blue force from the west and the 1st Cavalry Division enveloped the east flank and did the same there.

The 2d Armored Division crossed the Sabine River the afternoon of August 24 and established bivouac in the Jasper-Burkeville, Texas, area. Using three columns, the division moved north on a 186-mile march, starting about 5:00 A.M. on August 25. The left, or west column, protecting that flank, went as far as Lufkin. The right, or east flank, column which protected the main body of the division moved through river bottoms, swamps, semijungles and along countless side roads. It marched at a fast pace to keep up with the main body which was moving by highway. It was a feat never before attempted or thought possible. The left flank column turned east, found and captured a useable bridge at Carthage, and Grow, who was with the column, asked Patton to put an armored regiment across. Patton failed to do so, and the 2d Armored Brigade had a more difficult experience because of his decision. The east and center columns turned northeast. Arriving at Logansport, they found the bridge there damaged but not protected by artillery or small arms fire. A heavy pontoon engineer battalion built 500 feet of bridge, while the 17th Engineer Battalion repaired the highway bridge. The lighter elements of the division began fording operations about noon, while the engineers worked, and by late afternoon, the division was across and behind Blue lines. Major General Strong, VIII Corps commander, noted that the limited drive by the tank brigade was an excellent attack, conducted to the satisfaction of all concerned except headquarters of the 125th Infantry Regiment, 32nd Infantry Division. It seemed that the infantrymen were "peeved to find tanks running over their mess kits."

The Blue force shifted most of its troops northward, intending to attack and cut off the 2d Armored Division from its supply trains and to open a route into the Mansfield area. The division resumed the attack on August 26 with its mission to advance to the Many-Robeline line, defeating the enemy wherever met. On this march, the engineers outdid themselves. They built river fords, bridges and corduroy roads to get the combat elements to the battle areas. The support trains were left to shift for themselves. The tracked vehicles had torn up the roads, making the trains' progress more difficult. The men cut trees and brush to fill the holes left by the tanks, but the solid-looking earth often broke, dropping trucks into three feet of muck. By winching, digging and dragging, Perkins was able to get all his supply vehicles to their proper destination without a single loss.

The 82d Reconnaissance Battalion moved southward, finding many antitank guns and blown bridges. It arrived at Fort Jessup about noon, only to discover that the town was already captured by one of its own units, a platoon from B Company. Apparently, the enemy did not counterattack because it thought a larger force occupied the town than the three scout cars actually there. Later in the evening, the enemy did attack and the umpires ruled that the reconnaissance troops would have to pull back, which was a fair decision. Armored vehicles are vulnerable at night.

During the day, most of which was spent detouring blown or burned bridges rather than fighting, the tankers showed their ingenuity. As one tank company traveled down a road, two infantry battalions of the 37th Infantry Division moved out on the road to see them. The infantrymen climbed on, and the tankers turned their guns on the foot soldiers. Umpires ruled the two battalions out of the battle. First Lieutenant D. A.

Kelley gained information by renting a boat, removing his clothing and pretending to fish. He rowed back and forth listening to the enemy talk. Returning to his side, he dressed and told his company commander what he had discovered. That night, a scout section of the 82d Reconnaissance Battalion, having only a scout car, smoke pots and a rifle, decided to ignite the smoke pots and fire the rifle as fast as possible at the enemy. The Blue force thought the battle was beginning and returned the fire. Messengers rushed away carrying the news of the attack and leading reinforcements to the ''battle.'' As a result, the local Blue forces got very little sleep that night.

Orders were issued to continue the attack at 5:00 the next morning, to complete the destruction. During the night of August 26, White had sent A and D Companies, 82d Reconnaissance Battalion, to block the Blue retreat to crossing points along the Red River. When these companies linked with the 1st Cavalry Division, Lieutenant General Krueger ruled that the last escape routes were closed and ended the battle at eight o'clock.

In the critique, Major General Strong, the losing Blue commander, noted that the Logansport bridge was guarded and had a written statement of damages. The chief umpire later reestablished partial damages, which the division had to repair, using 100 man-hours. Strong simply remarked, ''Some engineering.'' The bridge debate was the crucial issue, because by repairing and using the bridge the 2d Armored Division had been able to position itself behind Blue lines. Apparently, Strong felt that had the proper damages been observed he would have been able to shift his antitank units to counter the threat. The VIII Corps commander ended his remarks with scorn and sarcasm. He extended his compliments to the Fort Benning tankers for their new equipment—kangaroo tanks. These vehicles permitted the tankers to travel undamaged over demolitions emplaced by engineers and properly posted and flagged. After being critical of the 1st Cavalry Division, he cautioned that ''hell will have an awful stench of the burning of hair and flesh when these two divisions are called to their final reward.''

Exercises 3 and 4 opened on September 5 as a single problem, slated to terminate on the tenth. Rain from a hurricane turned the lowland into traps and threatened to take the blitz out of the maneuvers. Louisiana was becoming a tough proving ground. The exercise was built around two tactical concepts. The Red force was to occupy and defend the crossings over the Calcasieu River while the Blue force, of which the 2d Armored was a part, was to pursue and destroy the enemy. The division, assigned to the Third Army, initially was in reserve, positioned on the flank of VIII Corps to help either VIII or V Corps or to execute a wide flanking movement if the situation permitted. Patton led his men to bivouac areas near Leesville and was ordered to attack the afternoon of September 5. The division moved north in two columns to the Kisatchie-Kurthwood area to relieve pressure on VIII Corps's flank. One column met strong resistance from the 1st Cavalry Division, while the other column met resistance from Red infantry and armor. Plans were made to resume the offensive at 5:00 the next morning.

The Red threat against the VIII Corps flank was serious. The 2d Armored Division resumed the attack, meeting strong, determined opposition from the 1st Cavalry Division. The tankers captured Brig. Gen. Charles H. Gerhardt, commanding general, 2d Brigade, 1st Cavalry Division, as he led his brigade against the Third Army flank. Pushing through the Kisatchie National Forest in spite of land mines, antitank guns and inclement weather, the division encircled the enemy and was in position to start the systematic defeat of the Red force when the exercise ended at 7:00 A.M.

The men rested but were alerted to resume their attack at dark on September 7. The division was to move in two columns, bridge the Red River in the Montgomery area and cross the river to the Red forces on the east bank. Each column was to have rubber assault boats to make the crossing. The left column, commanded by Col. James R. N. Weaver, commanding officer, 68th Armored Regiment, was to feign an attack four miles northeast of Natchitoches to cover bridgehead operations west of Montgomery.

The right column, led by Brig. Gen. Willis D. Crittenberger, was to establish a bridgehead west of Montgomery and to cover it by a feint five miles northeast of Clouterville. The division marched from its bivouac area and met stiff resistance from the 1st Cavalry Division. The 82d Reconnaissance Battalion, leading the 2d Armored Brigade, captured most of the cavalry division's service elements. Upon reaching the Red River, the combat organization of the division was modified, but its mission remained unchanged. Crittenberger was to cross the Red River on a pontoon bridge to be built by the 87th Engineer Battalion, while the 68th Armored group protected the bridgehead. The 67th Armored group, commanded by Col. Douglas T. Greene, was to attack and destroy the 1st Cavalry Division and Corps medium artillery and to help the 68th Armored's defense.

Bridging operations began the next morning but were delayed about an hour by air attacks. The Air Corps was extremely active, diving at the tankers and causing some fear that the planes would crash into them. After diving, one plane was pulling up to make a second run when it sawed the tail off another aircraft. One pilot jumped to safety, but the second plane hit the riverbank and instantly burst into flames. Fortunately, it missed the bridge and its approaches, which were crowded with tanks. While the 87th Engineers built the pontoon bridge, the 17th Armored Engineer Battalion began ferrying tanks across the Red River. Patton had ordered that the bridge be completed by 9:00 P.M., which was achieved with two minutes to spare. The first vehicle crossed at 9:01. While the tankers were crossing, the 1st Armored Division came upon the rear of the 2d Armored. A realistic firefight followed, with both sides giving a good account of themselves. While the umpires assessed the casualties, the 1st Armored seemed to have the advantage. Then, word was received that it was all a mistake—the two divisions were in different maneuvers and had only accidently met in Montgomery. The 2d Armored crossed the Red River, turned south and entrapped the Red forces. The 67th Armored Regiment remained on the west bank repelling attacks by the 1st Cavalry Division. Finally Lieutenant General Krueger ended the problem about twenty hours ahead of schedule.

In the critique, Krueger complimented the 2d Armored Division's work, saying that it had completed its mission in an excellent manner. However, he was disturbed because certain elements were not ready for battle. Thirty-one vehicles from the 66th Armored Reconnaissance Company, 82d Reconnaissance Battalion, and 78th Armored Field Artillery had stumbled into an ambush. That itself did not anger Krueger, but the lead half-track had had its machine guns covered, a platoon of howitzers was covered, and the men in the vehicles did not have their individual weapons or were not wearing their ammunition belts. The Third Army commander wanted this situation corrected.

The last two exercises were to be large scale: Second Army versus Third Army. The first one opened at 5:30 A.M. on September 15. Krueger's Blue Third Army had invaded southern Louisiana. Its mission was to attack up the Mississippi River Valley, cutting the United States in half. Lt. Gen. Ben Lear's Red Second Army was given the mission of repelling the invaders. The 2d Armored Division, part of I Armored Corps, was to move after dark on September 14, cross the Red River at daylight and seize the Fort Jessup-Many line extending to the Sabine River. Once the line was taken, reconnaissance was to be pushed southward. Because of the experience of Patton's men, they were told to be prepared to do more than the 1st Armored Division. Lear opened the battle by sending his armored divisions south across the Red River. The columns were strafed by Air Corps and Navy aircraft. By early afternoon the division had taken its objectives and held its position against increasing enemy opposition until September 18. After preparing his defenses, Patton alerted the division to be ready to attack southward in two columns. The 82d Reconnaissance Battalion extended itself to Mt. Carmel in the early afternoon.

On the second day, a strong enemy force attacked Mt. Carmel, forcing the 2d Armored Division defenders out of the village. This junction of five roads was of paramount tactical importance. The 2d Armored counterattack was launched amid mass confusion. The men realized that a serious fight was about to occur. Many observer cars, press cars, commercial radio vehicles and newsreel cameramen's vehicles were headed for the village. With all these spectators, the element of surprise was lost. Maj. Leonard H. "Steamer" Nason, executive officer, 3d Battalion, 66th Armored Regiment, wanted to attack in the dust of the VIPs. However, the umpires ruled that out of order. The first attack was by one tank and one half-track, immediately ruled to be casualties, but this attack revealed the positions of four antitank guns. Finally the umpires permitted the attack to resume. Lt. Norris Perkins, who was the temporary commander of H Company, 66th Armored Regiment, led the attack on Mt. Carmel and a nest of 75mm antitank guns. One gun was directly in Perkin's path. Not wanting to lose any shock action and believing that the gun had been ruled out of action, he charged the gun. The gun crew, uncertain whether they were out of action, fired at Perkins at about 200 yards. The blank shell misfired as the tank drew closer. At about twenty yards, it fired. In Perkins's words, "it darn near blew us out of the tank." The blank hit the driver full in the face; only his goggles saved him from permanent eye injury. The tank crew was furious because they thought that the round had been fired intentionally. Perkins let his driver charge the gun, running over the trails and leaving it pointed at a useless angle. Perkins had to restrain his driver from chasing the artillery crew. The others in the company promptly dubbed the driver "Killer." Perkins later commented that the picture of those "pale, bug-eyed artillerymen still does wonders for H Company morale."

Two companies came out of the woods on the south to attack the defenders' rear. The umpires stopped the attack to assess damages and casualties. H Company, 66th Armored Regiment, lost three-fourths of its tanks. During the intermission, when aircraft bombed the neutral vehicles, both the Red and Blue forces wanted the umpire and other vehicles ruled out of action. Later the umpires decided that the 2d Armored Division had retaken the town. When attempting to drive the Blue force out of positions north of town, the tankers had to stop, "ambushed by umpires," because of safety considerations. All three sides argued about which combatant had the firepower and force necessary to win the battle. Patton's men finally won the round.

Patton was ordered to attack southward toward the Peason area to drive the Blue forces from that position. He warned the men that the Third Army had covered roads by antitank guns. The Blue force raced the 2d Armored Division to the Hornbeck area, won and controlled the hard-surfaced roads to the Third Army area. After the 2d Armored Division's defeat, two infantry divisions, the 2d and 45th, threatened to encircle the Red tankers, cutting off their escape routes. The terrain and antitank defenses had stopped the tankers. More crucial was the threat posed by the 1st Cavalry Division to the division's gasoline supply dumps and supply lines. The division was ordered to withdraw during the night of September 18 and then attack northwestward toward Zwolle to assist the 2d Cavalry Division in repelling the enemy 1st Cavalry Division. The 1st Cavalry captured the gasoline supply and earned its moment of glory. Without gas, the tankers could do nothing, and the exercises ended. For the first time, the 2d Armored Division was on the losing side.

The fight lasted five days and the Second Army had been defeated. The Blue forces had turned the Red's flank and destroyed bridges; the terrain was unsuited for armor. The tankers tried to break through at various points with some success, but they were captured or destroyed by Third Army's hunter-killer antitank units. The question of whether a smaller unit, using tanks (Second Army), could hold off a nonarmored force three times its size was answered negatively for the time being. However, the tankers pointed out that had the maneuvers been elsewhere the results would have been different. Patton's men grumbled, "Wait 'til the next time." Feeling that they had been denied the opportunity to use their speed and power properly, they were anxious to show what they could do.

Third Army was puzzled by the absence of armored strength on its front. The tanks had been pulled to the flank to soften the center for their infantry divisions. The early mission was commensurate with the mobility and firepower of the 2d Armored Division, but any advantage gained was lost by the imposed delay. Armor's flexibility had been shown by its ability to withdraw from action, regroup and then attack thirty miles in the opposite direction. The division also demonstrated that it could breach antitank gun defenses and make advances, but it lacked sufficient infantry strength to hold open the gaps. When the tanks passed through, the enemy infantry closed in behind the tankers and armored infantry, and they had to fight their way out. Lt. Col. Sidney R. Hinds and his 2d Battalion, 41st Armored Infantry Regiment, had been behind the Blue lines for the entire exercise. During the week, he and his men overran enemy positions, established ambushes and generally wreaked havoc. One morning after routing an infantry regimental combat team, Lt. Gen. Walter Krueger gave Hinds some "personal attention" for being "unrealistic." Even though the umpires supported the battalion commander, he had to comb the countryside, rounding up the routed enemy.

The final exercise, again Second Army versus Third Army, was the most spectacular and is most often referred to in connection with the 1941 Louisiana maneuvers or Patton. In this problem, the 2d Armored Division was part of Krueger's Third Army. Its mission was to advance on and capture Shreveport. The exercise began in the rain; roads were almost impassable and the creeks, bayous and rivers were flooded. In addition, Lieutenant General McNair wanted the armored attack and the antitank guns to be the focus of the exercise. However, it proved to be a battle of bridges. Given the terrain and weather, every move depended on destroying bridges and building pontoon bridges as replacements. Every strategic move hinged on the Red or Sabine Rivers. The defending Second Army had the advantage.

The battle for Shreveport opened on September 24; it was scheduled to end five days later. For this exercise the I Armored Corps consisted of the 2d Armored Division and the 2d Infantry Division (Motorized). It was a new type organization, one with which Major General Scott had indicated a desire to experiment. The infantry division could now keep pace with the tankers. Their mission would be to find and fix the enemy in positions. The tankers would attack through them. The 2d Infantry would follow, clearing enemy resistance overlooked or bypassed by the armor unit.

The division was held in reserve for two days. Given the mission to pass through the gap created by the 2d Infantry Division, cross the Sabine River and operate against the enemy's flank and rear, Patton issued orders for the envelopment of Shreveport. The division was divided into two columns. The west column, composed of wheeled vehicles permitted to use their lights, was made up of the 2d Battalion, 41st Armored Infantry Regiment, the 78th Armored Artillery, and C and D Companies of the 82d Reconnaissance Battalion. The east column was the remainder of the division. On September 25, the reconnaissance elements departed at 8:30 P.M., while the main body of the west column followed at 10:00. Crossing the Sabine at Orange, the west column moved through Beaumont, turned north through Woodville, Nacogdoches, Henderson, Gladwater, Jefferson and Belcher, Louisiana, ready to attack Shreveport on the 28th.

The east column crossed the Sabine at Merryville and moved north through Jasper, San Augustine, Taneha and Carthage. If successful, the tankers would be in position to launch attacks against Shreveport from the west, southwest or south. The tankers encountered blown and defended bridges. Col. William H. H. Morris, commanding officer, 66th Armored Regiment, found a ford, drove off the defenders in a two-hour battle (in reality it took that long to get an umpire to the scene), only to find the river had risen eight feet in twenty hours. He called for engineers to put in a pontoon bridge. Perkins was leading his company across a bridge when his tank broke through a sixteen-foot span. His driver managed to teeter the tank onto the next span. Now in enemy territory while the remainder of the battalion was not, Perkins was not able to detour because of either weak or blown bridges. Immediately the third battalion broke out their pioneer tools and began to build a span for the bridge. They had to float large trees to the site, past several water moccasins, one of which Perkins stomped to death. Anchored at one end and with enough length to allow for sagging, the bridge was ready, and H Company crossed in spite of the sagging and swaying. The other company commanders, after seeing the bridge, refused to cross and took a twelve-hour detour. Elements of the 68th Armored Regiment had crossed the Sabine and had moved to within about fifteen miles of Shreveport. But the conclusion of the exercise found most of the tanks at or near the river waiting to cross to the east bank.

The Shreveport campaign was ended not by the tank threat, but by the wheeled column that came upon Shreveport from the rear. The column came under stiff antitank gun fire from units that had been shifted to counter the threat. Led by Lieutenant Colonel Hinds, the 2d Battalion, 41st Armored Infantry Regiment, captured the water works on the city's western edge and then proceeded to capture the city airport and business district. While this was in progress, two platoons of B Company,

82d Reconnaissance Battalion, captured the operations office at Barksdale Field, preventing the Air Corps from sending out any more planes that day. In this maneuver, the 2d Armored Division had whip-lashed around Lear's flank and attacked him from the rear, forcing the Second Army commander to abandon defensive positions. He was pre-paring to retreat when the exercise ended at 4:45 P.M. on September 28, twenty-four hours ahead of schedule. The opinion that Patton had "little more than a nuisance grip" on the city hardly seems justified. McNair threw a bouquet to the tankers for their Sabine River crossing near the battle's end. Hinds and his men were called "damn nuisances," which they considered to be their first battle commendation.

The destruction of the Bon Weir Bridge caused the 2d Armored Division to take a 350- to 400-mile detour, completely out of the ma-nuever area. Captured quartermaster records revealed that, to make the move, the division had paid cash for a great quantity of fuel from local dealers. While not entirely illegal, this action required a liberal interpreta-tion of a VIII Corps memorandum for its justification. On August 11, VIII Corps said that gas and oil could be purchased for individual vehicles only on courtesy cards issued by the quartermaster of the home station. It did not permit authorization for motor parts. There was grumbling in some circles at the War Department that Patton did not play the game according to the rules of war. The only question, of course, is: whose rules? The ferocity of the 2d Armored Division was more than playacting.

Lieutenant General Krueger wrote Patton to congratulate him and the division on their performance. The Third Army commander was "constantly impressed by the high morale, technical proficiency and devotion to duty by personnel of 2d Armored Division." He wanted the men thanked for their "loyal, tireless, cheerful and efficient service." Several weaknesses, however, had been revealed. Maj. Gen. Jacob L. Devers noted that not all the junior officers knew their jobs and that there was faulty staff work at the higher command levels. March discipline, bivouacs, maintenance and reconnaissance should be stressed in the up-coming Carolina maneuvers.

Chapter 5

THE CAROLINA MANEUVERS

The Carolina maneuvers of November 1941 were the last large-scale peacetime exercises in which the 2d Armored Division participated. In Tennessee, the division discovered that it was a large organization; in Louisiana, it sharpened its offensive skills. The Carolina maneuvers honed its skills and helped the division to correct defects noted in both of the earlier maneuvers, while preparing it for a war that it hoped the United States could avoid. The maneuvers sought answers to two questions: how could the Armored Force be used to prevent or destroy an enemy invasion, and what was the most effective means to kill tanks.

In early October, 1941, Maj. Gen. Charles L. Scott, commanding general, I Armored Corps, addressed the 2d Armored Division officers about defects in training. Sandwiched between the laudatory opening and closing remarks was a recitation of errors that would have to be corrected if the Armored Force were to succeed in battle. He felt that column commanders did not use all their weapons when confronted by certain situations. Some officers displayed a lack of leadership by not being well

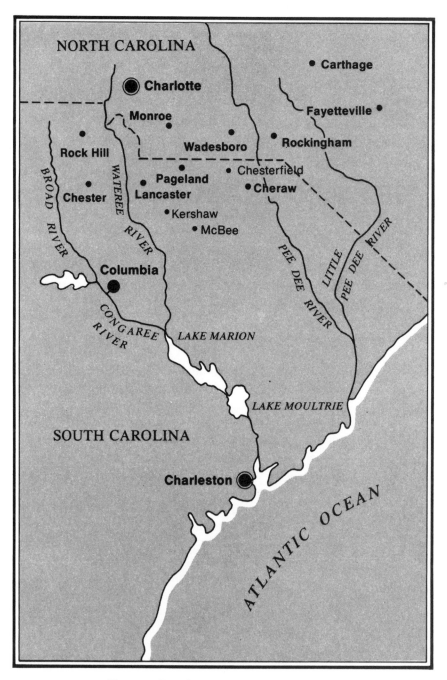

Figure 4. The Carolina Maneuvers, 1941.

forward in their columns or at the scene of problems. There were failures by some column commanders to arrange the various elements so that different units could be properly and quickly employed to their best advantage. He noted specifically that one officer was given a mission to force a river crossing and had his engineers and artillery to aid him. Since he had placed these units well to the rear of his column, crucial time was lost bringing them forward, where they should have been in the first place.

To eliminate some of the complaints, Patton issued instructions that drivers, platoon leaders and all commanders check their vehicles for defective lights, horns and brakes, both at the end of the day and prior to the next day's usage. To keep the troops informed and to disseminate orders, a point that Scott had stressed, messengers and couriers were ordered to stop at all command posts and report the situation to the command personnel. In addition, a daily order stated that sweat shirts were not authorized outer garments, especially the ones lettered "Hell on Wheels."

While preparing for the Carolina maneuvers, the division received 231 replacements for the more than 600 men who were discharged as overage. More equipment was arriving, such as 112 half-tracked personnel carriers and artillery prime movers, 32 M-3 medium tanks and 43 M-3 light tanks. Thirteen of the new light tanks, equipped with radial Guiberson diesel engines, went to H Company, 66th Armored Regiment. Lt. Norris Perkins, who was now the company commander, recalled that the engines had a high power-to-weight ratio, but they were tricky to maintain and hard to start in cold weather. On the eve of the Carolina exercises, the men felt that in spite of lacking about 2 percent of their equipment, primarily medium tanks, they were "fit for and capable of immediate and decisive combat in the event of a national emergency."

Bounded by Columbia, South Carolina, on the southwest and Salisbury-Sanford, North Carolina, on the northeast, the maneuver area would challenge the tankers, as had the Tennessee and Louisiana areas. Posing difficulties were the Broad, Catawba, Wateree, Black, Lynches, Great Pee Dee and Little Pee Dee Rivers. Again the division faced a battle for bridges. It would have to either seize them intact or build pontoons to get the vehicles and men across the watery barriers.

Movement orders were issued on October 27; the 2d Armored Division was to move in two columns to positions near Chester, South Carolina. Again the tracks were sent by rail, but for the first time the

L to R: Maj. Gen. George S. Patton, Jr., commanding general, 2d Armored Division; Brig. Gen. Willis D. Crittenberger, commanding general, 2d Armored Brigade; 1st Lt. Richard N. Jensen, aide to Patton.

half-tracks of the infantry and artillery were to take part in the road march. Column commanders were instructed to check march discipline, including the rate of march and the distance between vehicles. The 17th Engineer Battalion was dispatched three days ahead of the division to do some necessary work, while the tanks were sent by train. As in Tennessee and Louisiana, the division underwent the same reorganization.

In the first exercise, a hostile Blue army had landed at Savannah, Georgia, captured Columbia, South Carolina, and then attacked northward to protect its beachhead area for additional landings. The 2d Armored Division, part of the Red IV Corps, was to move south from Chester to attack and destroy the enemy force wherever found between the Broad River and Highway 21. The 31st Infantry Division was on the left flank of the tankers and the 4th Infantry Division (Motorized) was held in Corps Reserve. The Red army mission was the capture of Columbia, South Carolina, and its communications facilities.

During the evening of November 4, the 2d Armored Division was organized into three columns and moved to the restraining lines. The reconnaissance battalion and the advance guards moved further south, protecting the roads to the division's bivouac area. Preparations were made to attack anytime after 6:00 A.M. on November 5. When the attack order was received at 6:30 the men started moving south immediately. Initially, the division made satisfactory progress, destroying most of the 3d Cavalry Regiment. The center and east columns were slowed by enemy artillery, infantry, cavalry and antitank weapons. The west column continued to make excellent progress and the following day was in position to deliver a strong flanking attack to assist the advance of the center column. Company C, 82d Reconnaissance Battalion, captured the 179th Field Artillery Regiment (155mm howitzers) while they were moving down a road.

After the attack resumed on November 6, the 2d Armored Brigade reported capturing thirty truckloads of infantrymen of the 112th Infantry Regiment, 28th Infantry Division, while Company D, 82d Reconnaissance Battalion, captured the 1st Battalion, 103d Infantry Regiment, 43d Infantry Division. Headquarters IV Corps decided to commit the 4th Infantry Division (Motorized) to the battle on the 2d Armored Division's right flank, between the Broad River and U.S. Highway 215. This required that the 2d Armored shift the axis of its attack eastward. This maneuver had been practiced at Fort Benning. The 4th Infantry Division (Motorized) had passed through the 2d Armored Division's lines and

Above: Tankers circumventing a "destroyed bridge."
Below: "Motorized" 4th Infantry Division passes the new M-3 Grant tank of Capt. Norris H. Perkins.

taken over the attack, while the tankers pulled back, regrouped and attacked along a new front or around the enemy flanks.

Patton halted the division for the evening and resumed the offensive at 6:00 A.M. the following morning. With the 4th Infantry Division (Motorized) attacking southwest, the 2d Armored Division was to attack southeast and east, capturing Columbia and trapping the enemy troops east of the city. The center column advanced so quickly and with such surprise that it captured the commanding general of the 85th Infantry Brigade, along with 1,041 other officers and men. Meanwhile, elements of the 82d Reconnaissance Battalion reached Columbia about 9:00. The roads leading into the city were clear of enemy opposition and the 2d Armored and 4th Infantry Divisions were ready to launch their attack on the objective when the exercise was halted at 9:00. The first exercise was a partial repeat of the Tennessee and Louisiana maneuvers. The tankers had moved quickly through a zone, while having their attack corridor held open by an infantry division on each flank. The introduction of the 4th Infantry Division permitted the tankers to swing wide around the east flank of the city, once again performing a nose-and-seat-of-the-pants operation.

The second corps exercise matched the I Armored Corps (Blue) against the IV Corps (Red). This was the first time that the two trained armored divisions would participate in a maneuver together. The Red and Blue armies were fighting in northwestern Carolina. Both had large forces east of the Broad River, attempting to envelop the flank of the other. Movement west of the Broad River was permitted. A neutral state existed east of the Catawba River and both belligerents were pledged to respect its neutrality.

The I Armored Corps, camped north of Columbia, South Carolina, was to attack, seizing Chester, the railroad and its facilities and then prepare to attack the rear of the Red army. To accomplish this mission, Major General Scott decided to attack with three divisions abreast—the 1st Armored on the east, the 2d Armored on the west, and the 4th Infantry (Motorized) in the center. The route was the same as in the first exercise, except that the units would be moving north, not south.

The 2d Armored would attack north in three columns. The force commander had been verbally instructed to send reconnaissance and advance guard elements to the restraining line but not to cross it until ordered to do so by the division commander. At 11:30 P.M. on November 9, Field Order Number 6 was issued, alerting the division for possible employment any time after 6:00 P.M. that day. The column commanders were instructed to leave infantry detachments to guard bridges in order to relieve the 82d Reconnaissance Battalion of the task. The Armored Corps issued its attack order at 6:30 A.M. on November 10, but the message was delayed, not reaching the division headquarters until thirty-five minutes later. Initially, the two armored divisions were to lead the attack, but because of the lack of roads there was a change in plans and they were instructed to screen the 4th Infantry Division's zone until the 2d Armored passed through Lebanon and the 4th Infantry joined the attack.

The 2d Armored Division started northward, meeting initial opposition about 7:25 A.M., but progressed steadily, despite harrassment from the retreating Blue forces. One Blue combat team caused a traffic jam at a bridge over Salem Creek and was attacked by the Red bombers. By 12:15 P.M., the division was north of Lebanon and was ordered to clear the roads so that the 4th Infantry could enter the battle. When the infantrymen did join the fight, it freed one tank column to rejoin the division as its reserve. In the late afternoon the 107th Cavalry Regiment (Blue) attacked the division train (noncombat elements of the division), only to be driven off with the loss of two troops (companies). During the night of November 10–11, the division formed two combat columns instead of three, and the attack resumed at 6:30 the following morning. The enemy was retreating with no organized defenses. If the commanding general had correctly estimated the situation, the division's attack should gain speed and perhaps end the exercise ahead of schedule.

When the attack resumed, B Company, 41st Armored Infantry Regiment, stumbled onto a motor park containing cargo trucks, kitchen and other miscellaneous vehicles belonging to a Blue artillery regiment. One squad captured the motor park guards. A Blue artillery sergeant blew his whistle to rouse his men, and as they came out of their tents carrying their mess gear they were promptly captured. The division attack gained momentum, and by noon the 2d Armored had captured its objective, twenty-four hours ahead of schedule. Patton was pleased. He issued a general order congratulating the men for their tireless work and then observed that the "2d Armored Division is prepared to acquit itself in the final maneuvers with the First Army so as to maintain indisputably its well-earned position as 'Second to None.' "

While the sides were taking a short break in the action, the 17th Armored Engineer Battalion received the newest pontoon bridge equipment. The new 500-foot bridge was four times the length of the older and more bulky bridge. It was carried on its own trucks which had a crane for lifting the pontoon boats and steel treadway. Capt. J. V. Hagan, executive officer of the 17th Armored Engineers, explained that the advantages of the new bridge were rapid installation and greater practicality. Additionally, the bridge could be divided and used in three columns. The treadways could be used in some instances where the rubber floats were not practical. During this short interlude, the maneuver rules were altered. These changes, whether or not intentionally designed to handicap the armored force, had that effect. The changes permitted the destruction of tanks with hand grenades, but mortar fire could not destroy antitank guns; also smoke could not be used by the Armored Force to cover its advance. To counter these changes, Scott ordered the two armored division commanders to use their full firepower and to tell the umpires of the amount and types of weapons fired. The tank forces were to move cross-country, avoiding mines, hand grenades and antitank guns. On November 11, Maj. Gen. Oscar W. Griswold called a five-minute halt to the activities of IV Corps. In his message to all units he said, "It is most fitting that we of the IV Army Corps are preparing ourselves to take over the unfinished duties left to us."

The last phase of the maneuvers directed by general headquarters promised to be the most satisfying for Patton personally. The I Armored Corps was attached to IV Corps, commanded by Major General Griswold. The First Army was to be the opposition. It was commanded by Lt. Gen. Hugh A. Drum, a longtime enemy of Patton's. If either man could publicly embarrass the other, he would do so with pleasure.

In the problem, the Wateree River formed the boundary between two states, with Red on the west bank and Blue on the east bank. The Blue First Army was reportedly concentrating east of the Pee Dee River, getting ready to invade Red territory. They had established a bridgehead at Rockingham. To eliminate this threat, the Red I Armored Corps was ordered to attack, defeat all enemy forces, and cut Blue lines of communications west of the Pee Dee River. The 2d Armored Division was to attack, capturing the west bank of the Pee Dee between Cheraw and Morven. After dark on November 15, the division's three combat columns moved to concealed bivouac areas west of Great Falls and Camden, ready to attack the following morning. The 82d Reconnaissance Battalion and the advance guard elements crossed the Wateree River shortly after 6:30 A.M., while the main body waited for the 1st Armored Division to cross. By noon, all elements of the 2d Armored were on the east bank of the Wateree, hurrying to join the advanced guard.

The attack began with one spectacular action. Capt. John H. Huckins, commanding officer of D Company, 82d Reconnaissance Battalion, led a patrol to positions east of the Pee Dee River looking for "big game." General Drum had been watching his troops cross the Pee Dee River, and was returning to his headquarters when he came upon a roadblock. His vehicle stopped, and the young captain greeted him with "Good morning, general. Will you join me?" McNair was notified that his army commander had been captured; the umpires ordered the general released because he could not be returned to Red country.

After fighting all day, one column had reached Cheraw. Part of the 41st Armored Infantry Regiment became separated from the attacking column by a strong enemy attack from the direction of Society Hill. For the next forty hours a small force of light tanks, an infantry platoon and an artillery battery defended itself and the 2d Armored's flank from repeated attacks. That evening, Patton issued orders to withdraw to a line west of Pageland-Bethune and prepared to resume the attack either to the east or the south on the following morning.

After the Cheraw bridgehead had been reduced, the 4th Infantry Division (Motorized) took over the defensive area. This permitted the tankers to pull back to refuel and regroup. About midnight, Patton issued verbal orders to attack the next morning against Drum's left (south) flank and cut the supply and communication lines and escape routes. If they were successful, the Blue army would be trapped and ready to be reduced. In the first hours of the attack, a brigade command post, including a brigadier general and two regimental commanders and their staffs, was captured. By noon the town of Cheraw had been surrounded and within eight hours the town and the water and power plants had been captured and prepared for destruction. The main bridge over the Pee Dee River had been destroyed two hours earlier. After receiving orders to pull back to defensible positions at 8:00 P.M., supplies and utilities were destroyed.

On November 19, after a day of maintenance and rest, the attack resumed against the same south flank. The tankers made good progress until noon, when resistance began to stiffen near Chesterfield and Ruby. The 62d Infantry Regimental Combat Team attacked to relieve the pressure on the division but had to pull back in the face of a forest fire. In the late afternoon the division was again ordered to pull back to the area that it had occupied the previous evening. The attack continued on the morning of November 20. The main area was shifted to the region between Pageland and Monroe in order to relieve Blue pressure on the 1st Armored Division. Patton directed that the attack begin at 9:00 A.M., but difficulties caused by the night withdrawal delayed one column's attack almost three hours. The second column attacked on schedule, only to encounter massed antitank guns which slowed their attack. More embarrassingly, the 4th Infantry Division attacked straight into the spearhead of the 2d Armored Division, causing considerable confusion on both sides. Action was halted at 3:15 P.M. and the units were directed to pull back and regroup and attack the following morning at 6:00. Two and one-half hours later, at 8:40 A.M. on November 21, the exercise was ended.

The umpires' manual gave the antitank guns victory over the tanks primarily because the gun was a small, concealable weapon. If the guns were not concealed or were surprised by a tank, then the tank should be the victor. Antitank guns could also be neutralized by artillery fire or captured by infantry. The tankers were unhappy with the rules and one was heard to say, "Why goddamnit we'd go so fast in a real war we'd squash those gunners before they could fire." Most tankers agreed with the Armored Force commander, Maj. Gen. Jacob L. Devers, who said, "We were licked by a set of umpires' rules."

During a lull in the action, the 2d Armored Division demonstrated its new radios for the press. The old radios required that the operator know Morse code. The new radios, modeled after police radios, permitted commanders to have voice contact with their units. Lieutenant Perkins conducted the demonstration. He had his company moving along the road in column, then change to a battle line, then to a platoon V formation, then back to the column. He sent it into a simulated attack, then recalled the company from about a mile away—about the maximum distance for low power. At high power, the radios had about a 15–20 mile range.

The final phase of the maneuvers took place November 25–28. Again, the 2d Armored was assigned to the Red I Armored Corps, controlled by the Red IV Corps. The Blue forces were concentrated at Greensboro, North Carolina. The Red army was to defend actively its bridgehead over the Wateree River at Camden. To protect this bridgehead, the 2d Armored was to seize and hold the line from Monroe to Wadesboro along U.S. Highway 74.

The division assembled five miles south of Ruby, South Carolina, organized its three columns, and prepared to move north on order. The problem started at 6:30 A.M. on November 25. As the columns moved north they encountered light but increasing resistance. By noon, when the division was almost to its objective, it discovered that it was opposing the II Corps advance. The 2d Armored's advance was stymied; at one point D

Company, 82d Reconnaissance Battalion, found itself defending against an attack by a tank and an infantry battalion. The other divisional units were also facing the same type of increased pressure.

Patton issued verbal orders to start withdrawing during the night. The movement continued throughout the day against increasing Blue pressure. One column, F-2, was overrun and forced out of its positions. On the right flank, a gap occurred between F-2 and an infantry regiment, but division artillery fire prevented Blue from penetrating the gap. By nightfall, the division had pulled back to positions south of Black Creek, about the same location from which it had started the attack the day before. The day's action had been costly. The 1st Battalion, 41st Armored Infantry Regiment, had been surrounded and when the 3d Battalion, 67th Armored Regiment, was sent to rescue them, it was ruled to have 100 percent loss of tanks.

During the night of November 26, columns F-2 and F-3 were combined into one (F-2) under the 2d Armored Brigade, commanded by Brig. Gen. Willis D. Crittenberger. Orders were issued to F-1 to attack north through Pageland, while F-2 was to move further west and then north through Tradesville. This was an attempt to get on the flank and into the rear areas of the Blue force, causing disruption to supply and communications lines and to turn the Blue force around and make them counterattack northward. Before F-1 could reach its line of departure at 6:00 A.M., it was assaulted by Blue infantry and had to counterattack. However, by 9:00 F-1 had reached and secured Pageland against stiff resistance. It extended its forces northwest in time to break up an enemy attack so successfully that the enemy had to retreat. F-2 was making progress on the left flank, but by noon Patton had to issue verbal withdrawal orders because the 1st Armored Division had encountered very stiff resistance and could not keep pace with the 2d Armored Division.

The 2d Armored was pulled out of the line and ordered to assemble north of Kershaw. It was to be under corps control and was not to attack unless ordered by the Armored Corps. The 4th Infantry Division (Motorized) was to cover the division's withdrawal. However, because both the 4th Infantry and the 1st Armored were engaged in a heavy struggle and could not pull back on time, Patton had to cover the corps front during the night of November 27. The division continued to withdraw to positions just north of Camden on November 28. In McNair's judgement, the problem had been carried to completion, and he ended the exercise at 4:28 P.M.

In his final critique, McNair spoke of the men. Their training progressed from the individual, through various units and finally to army level. Noting that during World War I training had gone no further than division level, he felt that the soldier of the 1940s had improved his chances for survival and had improved the "prospect of American success." The training had also physically conditioned the men, so that in the director's opinion they could march as far and as fast as the German foot soldier. He was preparing to answer a question that reporters had repeatedly asked during the problem: "Are these troops ready for war?" McNair provided an answer: "It is my judgement that, given complete equipment, they certainly could fight effectively. But it is to be added with emphasis that the losses would be unduly heavy, and the results of action against an adversary such as the Germans might not be all that could be desired." He directed that the units return to their home stations to resume training and to attempt to raise the high standards even higher.

Major General Griswald was more concerned that armor learn to cooperate effectively as a team member and cease to operate independent of the rest of the corps. He thought that tanks and infantry should work more closely to reduce antitank defenses. These maneuvers convinced the IV Corps commander that the tank, in addition to being an offensive weapon, could be valuable in defense or in fighting a delaying action. The presence of tanks guaranteed caution and delay even before they were committed to action.

The division returned to Fort Benning. Patton and his men had spent sixteen weeks in the field and were probably the most maneuvered unit in the army. Paying tribute to Hell on Wheels, Patton issued General Order Number 67:

> *You have completed six months of active field training under severe conditions. Through Tennessee, Louisiana, and Carolina maneuvers, you have acquitted yourselves individually and by units as soldiers. You were commended by the highest and most experienced officers in the Army for your appearance, your discipline, your soldierly deportment, and your combat efficiency. By every test short of war you are veterans. Protect your record.*

Patton used words such as "soldier" and "veteran" sparingly and only in a most complimentary fashion. Ironically, his order was dated December 6, 1941, one day before the Japanese attack on Pearl Harbor.

Chapter 6

PREPARATION FOR WAR

The 2d Armored Division was one of the best trained units in the American army as a result of its participation in the three large-scale exercises of 1941. Many thought that the division was ready for war. However, Lieutenant General L. J. McNair observed that the army might suffer heavy losses and that the results might not match American expectations. When the Japanese bombed Pearl Harbor and Germany declared war on the United States, the prospects of combat became a reality. Whether the army was ready or not, the United States was now actively in the conflict. The division commanders were faced with the task of readying their men for battle.

The Japanese attack on Pearl Harbor was a stunning blow to the Americans. Pfc. Samuel Tackitt recalls that he was walking down the battery street when someone ran out and told him of the attack. He, like most of the men, spent the remainder of the day and night listening to the radio. Since he had turned down a fifteen-day leave in October 1941, because he did not want to go home to Arkansas during harvest time, it now seemed that he would not get to go home at Christmas as he had

Maj. Gen. Willis D. Crittenberger, commanding general, 2d Armored Division, and visiting Russian officers observe armored demonstration.

planned. 1st Lt. Norris Perkins recalled that within a week the first shocks began to fade. They were replaced with the courage-testing realities of the situation. He admitted that he had to fight a wave of sadness and a feeling of loss, because of the thoughts of not being able to study medicine, get married or raise a family. As time progressed, Perkins described the happier, more confident mood which was beginning to prevail among the men. This was stimulated by the knowledge of what was expected of the division, the sound of the national anthem, stories of heroism in the Pacific and the flowing surge of power across the country.

Part of Perkins's despondency was due to his meeting Miss Katharine Heath, sister of a fellow officer in the 66th Armored Regiment. On December 11, he escorted her to the 66th Armored Regimental Ball. General Patton danced with her and asked if she planned to marry Perkins, not knowing that it was only their second date. He commented that he would like all his officers to be married before going into combat. Later that same night, Perkins proposed; Miss Heath accepted and they were married in April 1942.

After returning from Carolina, the 2d Armored Division underwent a fundamental reorganization. In December the Armored Force directed that a tank destroyer battalion be activated at Fort Benning and that the men and equipment be furnished by the 2d Armored Division. Battery D, 78th Armored Artillery, was deactivated; the men and equipment were used to create the 702d Tank Destroyer Battalion. The War Department also ordered name changes, probably for uniformity, and General Order Number 3, from the 2d Armored Division, complied. For a year and a half, the units had been designated by the word "Armor" in parentheses following the numerical and branch designation. Now, the word "Armor" was to follow the number and come before the branch identification. The order also directed that the 66th and 67th Armored Regiments drop the words "Light" and "Medium" from their names. An indication of the thinking was the designation of the 14th Field Artillery (Armored) as the 14th Armored Field Artillery Battalion, 105mm Howitzer, changing it from a regiment to a battalion. The 92d Armored Artillery Battalion was activated on January 8, 1942, its men coming from the 14th and 78th Armored Artillery Battalions. Deactivated that same day was the 68th Armored Regiment (Light). The War Department directed that the personnel, equipment and property were to be disposed of as the 2d Armored Division commander directed. Most of the men and equipment were transferred to the 66th and 67th Armored Regiments. The same day,

General Orders Numbers 4 and 5 directed that the 14th Quartermaster Battalion and the 17th Ordnance Battalions be deactivated and the personnel transferred to a newly created Maintenance Battalion, 2d Armored Divison. To supervise this unit, the Headquarters and Headquarters Company, 2d Armored Brigade, was deactivated and the men used to form the Trains Headquarters Company, a new unit that would oversee divisional supply and maintenance.

The maneuvers indicated that a reorganization was needed at brigade level. During each exercise, attachments were made to the brigade; at no time had it fought as a brigade, but rather had been divided into combat teams. No one man could control the teams; the brigade was eliminated and two combat commands were substituted for it. These were tactical headquarters that had only headquarters personnel permanently attached. In combat, the division commander would be able to assign it the troops that he thought necessary. This assignment authority permitted the division and combat commanders to shape the command to the mission. By intention or by accident, the War Department and the Armored Force had created the main characteristic of armor—flexibility.

By the end of January 1942, the 2d Armored Division had taken its new shape. There were five major headquarters: Division, Combat Command A, Combat Command B, Division Artillery and Division Trains. In the tank regiments were two medium tank battalions and one light tank battalion. The infantry regiment of the division had three battalions, and the three division artillery battalions each had three firing batteries for a total of fifty-four howitzers. The division reconnaissance battalion lost its infantry company, but it had three reconnaissance companies and a light tank company. The engineer battalion had four companies and a treadway bridge company. Altogether the division numbered 14,618 officers and men.

During the maneuvers the 2d Armored Division had experimented with methods of employing the Air Corps in direct support. A Bomber Demand Unit (modern day Forward Air Controller) had always been attached to the 82d Reconnaissance Battalion and to each of the mission forces in the maneuvers. However, too much time was required from the time that air support was requested until the planes were over the target, ranging from twenty minutes to three hours. The problems were technological: the best type of communications was telephone or teletype, both unsuitable for armor. The solution, in the tankers' opinion, would be radio, which was later adopted.

While the division was undergoing reorganization, it was also getting a new commanding general. Maj. Gen. George S. Patton, Jr., was assigned to command the I Armored Corps. Replacing him was Brig. Gen. Willis D. Crittenberger. Patton had planned to depart without fanfare, but the men heard that he was leaving. They lined the streets, waving and cheering; some saw tears in Patton's eyes. Perhaps because it was the first and only division which he commanded, perhaps because of the send-off, or possibly because of later accomplishments, the 2d Armored Division was always Patton's favorite heavy armored division.

After the reorganization period, the division settled into a routine of squad and platoon tactics. Company and battalion commanders tried to include every conceivable type of situation that could be encountered on the battlefield. The men realized the urgency; earlier in 1941, after returning from the Carolina exercises, Patton had told the men that "this is the last time you will fight with blank ammunition. The next time we meet like this the bullets will be real." On one overnight exercise, the new division commander, Maj. Gen. Willis D. Crittenberger, was testing the perimeter defenses of the various units. One company commander, Capt. John K. Waters, received a note: "Captain Waters: For the purpose of training, I have directed Captain (Lindsey) Harkness to enter your camp by stealth and hand you this note." It was signed by Crittenberger. Waters said that after that night, his perimeter defenses improved. The same happened to Lt. Col. John H. Collier, commanding officer, 3d Battalion, 66th Armored Regiment. One "spy saboteur" entered his tent but was captured before he could do any damage.

In March 1942, while H Company, 66th Armored Regiment, was training in their new medium tanks they accidently began to take part in a live fire exercise. The problem was based on a platoon attack to eliminate an antitank gun. Four tanks gave covering fire while the fifth was maneuvering to rush and crush the gun. During the third time the troops did the problem, the tankers giving covering fire impulsively rained machine gun fire on the assaulting tank. The advancing crew added to the fun by zigzagging and dodging. Since the tanks were only firing machine guns and since the vision devices and gun sights were periscopic, there was little danger to the crew.

In mid-1942, events were taking place which would test the division and the men. In June, the Germans pushed the British back from El Alamein and there was a desperate need for reinforcements in Egypt. For a time, General Marshall considered sending the 2d Armored Division to

North Africa, either alone or as part of a larger force. This idea was abandoned in favor of sending every tank and self-propelled artillery piece from the division. The men were out in the field, testing the new M-4 medium tanks (Shermans) and the M-7, 105mm self-propelled howitzers, when Major General Devers called, directing the division to return to Fort Benning and prepare the tanks and the self-propelled howitzers for shipment to North Africa. Crittenberger did as directed, but at the same time sent a message to Marshall requesting that the men be allowed to follow the equipment. This request was disapproved, mainly because the division was to have a part in Operation TORCH, the Western Task Force invasion of North Africa. However, the men did not know it at the time.

In addition to the equipment, Generals Marshall and Devers wanted to send some trained mechanics to maintain it. These mechanics were directed to send each part that needed replacement back to the United States to determine the reasons for its failure. Heading the maintenance and advisory group was Maj. Gen. Charles L. Scott, former commanding general, 2d Armored Division. Since the 1st Armored Division had already sailed to Ireland, most of the men came from the 2d Armored Division. Devers sent Maj. Henry Cabot Lodge, Jr., who, with Lt. Col. Robert Murphey (an associate justice of the Supreme Court), had trained in H Company, 66th Armored Regiment, along with the group as his personal representative. During the Battle of Libya, former 2d Armored Division personnel, led by Major Lodge and Capt. Charles Stelling, manned some of the American tanks and destroyed nine German tanks in perhaps the first real battle in which 2d Armored personnel participated. The American vehicles were hit several times but not damaged, as the battle raged from 3,000 to 700 yards. Sergeant John Dinan of H Company, 66th Armored Regiment, was among the enlisted men sent to North Africa. He recalled later that the Germans lured the British close to their 88mm dual purpose guns and destroyed them. Dinan's squadron lost ten of their twelve tanks. He admitted that the Germans had many tricks, but hard experience had taught the British that they could defeat the Germans. He was confident that with proper equipment the British would chase the Germans all the way to Tripoli. In September, 1942, Dinan predicted what would happen in the following year. Following the battle, the General Sherman tank was rated the best in the desert.

The second major reason for having the Americans in the desert with the British was to study the tactical aspects of the war. Scott, who was less confident than Sergeant Dinan, told Maj. Gen. Ernest N. Harmon that the

British policy was to stop their movement when the Germans came into sight and to open fire. Since the German weapons had a longer range, the British were outgunned, wasted ammunition and suffered a heavier loss of vehicles. The solution, as Scott saw it, was to continue movement toward the enemy, reaching the effective range before firing.

Although the British were trying to improve, their maintenance was weak. Officers tended to delegate responsibility to the enlisted men and noncommissioned officers. However, officers led in battle and appeared to die gallantly. The British apparently had no concept of air-ground training—all they did was maneuver and fire. They were adding antitank guns and artillery to their armored brigades and increasing the number of antitank guns and artillery in the infantry brigades of their infantry divisions. Unfortunately, with these additions there was little or no training between the new elements and the units that they were to support. Tank commanders were heard to boast of how they were going to stop and shoot it out, even with dug-in antitank guns. If that happened, Scott predicted, the British would suffer even higher losses. His comments were factual and tainted with pessimism. However, he found nothing to warrant any major changes in American organization, equipment, tactics or techniques.

Scott continued to observe and to comment on what he saw. The British did not use their tanks, infantry, artillery, air and antitank guns in any coordinated manner. This was a major failure and violated the basic training doctrines of American armor. The American equipment, contrary to press and radio reports, was superior to that of the Germans. Therefore, according to Scott, the British situation had to be explained in different terms. Tactically, the Germans were superior to the British. Most of the British tank losses were due to the 88mm antitank-antiaircraft gun and the British habit of fighting tank-versus-tank. The Germans avoided such battles whenever possible, using their tanks to go around flanks to attack nerve centers and to reach decisive objectives.

Scott, however, was optimistic about American equipment and organization. The antiaircraft armaments were similar to the German arrangement and superior to the British. The Americans needed to strengthen their organization by adding dual purpose .50 caliber and 37mm antitank-antiaircraft guns. He believed that the American divisions should have two antitank battalions attached to them as priority units. They should have three-inch, self-propelled weapons. In addition, neither the Germans nor the British had armored personnel carriers for their infantry or artillery. The Germans lacked self-propelled 88mm antiaircraft weapons. Neither combatant had armored maintenance vehicles and no assault guns in their tank or infantry battalions. The American light tank was rated the most mechanically reliable and the fastest in the desert.

To correct any possible deficiencies in maintenance, Scott recommended that the 2d Armored Division's Ordnance Battalion have nine reserve tanks to support the regiments when necessary. The ordnance personnel should be divided so as to be able to give the maximum support to the regiments. He thought that any vehicle that had to go to the rear should not be the division's responsibility. There should also be nine reserve tanks in the regimental maintenance section. Each maintenance company in the regiments should have some type of rescue vehicle, which should be armored and on a medium tank or self-propelled artillery chassis.

The desert experience disproved the theory that a combat crew can fight all day and perform maintenance all night. Rather, the first echelon (crew) maintenance should be done by the company maintenance sections, which should not have any rescue vehicles and should not be required to evacuate any vehicles to battalion or regiment. That should be the duty of the higher headquarters. Scott, in passing along his observations, stressed those items which he thought might need improvement, so that the Americans could stay alive.

After sending its vehicles and a detachment of men to North Africa, the division received replacements. Even before the Japanese attack at Pearl Harbor, the division was training cadres for future armored divisions and separate tank battalions and sending instructors to the Armor School. They were doing this while understrength. During the time they were receiving replacements and trying to train them, rumors began to circulate about the division's use in a combat zone. Some even thought that the division would be sent to the Malay Peninsula; others speculated that it might go to Europe or Africa. On June 20, 1942, the Armored Force issued instructions that any armored unit might expect overseas orders and that they must ''be prepared to execute these orders expeditiously and efficiently.'' The directive then stated that the units should inventory their equipment, especially small items, tool kits and spare parts. Training was secondary. The units were to load their vehicles with the equipment assigned to it. Since the 2d Armored Division was the most experienced division and the 1st Armored Division was in Ireland, the alert could only mean that the division was slated for deployment somewhere overseas.

The 2d Armored Division was to take part in its last large-scale maneuvers—the Carolina maneuvers of 1942. The division would return to the area where it had been in 1941. Still, speculation on the possibility of overseas movement increased when Crittenberger issued Special Order 160 on June 29, 1942, which stated that the division and the 702d Tank Destroyer Battalion would depart for the main maneuver area July 7 or 8; at the termination of the exercise, neither unit would return to Fort Benning. The new permanent station would be announced later. Just before moving to the Carolinas, the division conducted Combat Exercise A for some 300 general officers. For the first time supporting aircraft and tanks used real ammunition. Mrs. Norris Perkins, who witnessed the demonstration, recalled that it was the greatest mechanized demonstration ever given in this country. Her husband felt the blast of bombs and artillery on his face. It was a graphic presentation of the tremendous striking power of an armored division.

The division went to the maneuver area and for a month raced back and forth across the Pee Dee River, testing ideas that were being sent back from the desert. Two essential improvements emerged from the exercises. First, communications were perfected, for along with the new M-4 medium tanks came better radios. In addition, the division constructed wire lines to its bridgehead force, putting those units in direct and secure contact with the division. Second, it was the first time that the division had received large quantities of materials under field conditions. It proved the wisdom of the division emphasis on maintenance and supply procedures.

During the Carolina maneuvers, Major General Crittenberger was transferred to command the III Armored Corps; Brig. Gen. Ernest N. Harmon assumed command of the 2d Armored Division. Despite the work of his three excellent predecessors, Harmon knew that he could not lead the division into battle unless the men could do their jobs. He had questions that had to be answered: could the artillery fire accurately and rapidly; could the tanks support each other; and could the infantry move with the tanks? He indicated his thinking to the division. Although noting President Franklin D. Roosevelt's praise of the division, Harmon asked the men to be realistic: "What in hell does the president of the United States know about the 2d Armored?" With Harmon's coming to the division, morale began to improve. Up to his time, many officers and men had been transferred to form new armored units. Additionally, the division was now receiving new tanks.

Following the maneuvers, the 2d Armored Division was assigned to

Fort Bragg, North Carolina, and began training for a secret assignment. When the men moved into their new area, they suffered an epidemic of dysentery so severe that it jeopardized the combat effectiveness of the division. At one time it was highly uncertain whether it would take part in the North African operation, although at that time very few in command knew that the operation was in the planning stage. The men suffered drastically with dysentery, and nearly every day the battalion aid stations were overflowing with patients. Once, when Technician Fifth Class (T5) Donald D. Dimock in the Medical Detachment, 67th Armored Regiment, was on duty a soldier came in complaining of stomach problems. The man's answers to the doctor's questions indicated another case of diarrhea. As the doctor was pouring a dose of medicine, he asked the man how many times he had to go to the latrine the previous evening. The man replied none; he had not had a bowel movement for eight days. There was a momentary silence; the doctor, almost dropping the medicine, began cursing and the men in the aid station began moaning. The reason or reasons for the epidemic are unknown.

The division stayed in one bivouac area for an extended period during the height of the fly season, and there were few, if any, sanitary conveniences. During this time there was a vigorous campaign to eliminate the flies and control the disease. The usual method of control was a liberal treatment of the latrines and kitchen sumps with oil and diesel fuel. They tried to seal the old latrines with red clay packed down by running a tank across them. Both Perkins and Col. John H. Collier, commanding officer, 66th Armored Regiment, recalled that even then flies could be seen crawling out of the latrines.

There were many inspections of kitchen sumps and latrines. On one such inspection, Maj. Thaddeus Coykendall and Capt. William Grimes lowered a lantern into a latrine that had been treated generously with diesel fuel and other combustible products. It blew up in their faces, causing injuries that prevented their sailing with the division in October 1942.

Training began to intensify for the 2d Armored. There were long road marches, obstacle courses and a new device—a rope ladder—which was hung about twenty-five feet high between two pine trees. It was easy to climb; but its novelty added to the course. In addition to the physical conditioning, the men resumed weapons training and firing and were expected to qualify with their individual weapons. They also fired their vehicular weapons. This was probably the most intensive and effective training that the division had undergone in such a short time.

Patton was assigned the command of the Western Task Force on August 24, 1942. A few days later, Major General Harmon was called to Washington to meet with Patton and General Marshall. Patton greeted Harmon with the question, "Do you want to go to war?" Harmon replied, "Sure, when do we start?" Thus the 2d Armored Division was committed to the landing in North Africa in a somewhat casual manner. Not to be outdone, Harmon returned to Fort Bragg and called Capt. Urban J. Wurm, the division's Catholic chaplain, into his office and asked him if he were ready for war. Wurm replied that he was there to serve.

In late August or early September, the landing teams were formed and began intensified training. The general plan was to have three landing teams, each with elements of the 2d Armored Division. Usually the team would have two light tank companies, an armored infantry company, an artillery battery, two engineer platoons and a reconnaissance platoon. The landing teams were separated from the remainder of the division, not to be reunited until Christmas Day.

While the division was undergoing its training, it began to receive new equipment, such as gasoline-powered tanks. When the new tanks arrived, the division had to turn in the old diesel-powered ones. These had to be in proper shape and even had to be painted—requirements which took time that the division did not have. The question of half-tracks came up, and for a time it appeared that the infantrymen were on the verge of losing their personnel carriers, because the rear idler spindle was fixed in place and could not bend or give when moving over rough terrain. 1st Lt. Thomas Hauss and M. Sgt. Gerry Noble came up with a scheme to replace the fixed idler with an eyebolt and nut, and a coil spring from a caterpillar tractor. Col. Sidney R. Hinds personally paid for the items and directed that it be tested and that he be informed of the results. It was successful. Hinds took the idea to the division ordnance officer, Lt. Col. Frederick Crabb, who took the suggestion to Major General Harmon. Harmon quickly approved it and had ordnance buy the modification parts and install the device on all the half-tracks slated for North Africa.

Meanwhile, Major General Scott gave Patton advice based on his observations in North Africa: when terrain permitted, tanks should lead their infantry; against antitank fire or direct artillery fire, tanks should lead with artillery fire, infantry, machine guns and aviation. All the tanks should be marked alike so that the enemy could not distinguish the officers' tanks; dummy antenna masts should be installed on all tanks. He urged making night attacks by illuminating the targets and then concentrating all direct fire, which usually resulted in a massacre.

In September, the assault teams were separated from the remainder of the division and began amphibious training at Mott Lake on the Fort Bragg reservation. Harmon kept stressing that the training would save lives. They practiced exactly what was planned for the North African landing, establishing beachheads and making dawn assaults. Harmon was displeased with some performances, especially that of the officers of one artillery battery. The artillerymen brought their guns ashore and then went to sleep without emplacing them or preparing the guns for action. Relieving all the officers, he transferred them to supply units. Harmon thought that officers' education and position demanded a larger responsibility to their men and to themselves. While most officers quickly learned the lesson, he would have to repeat it in the future. The training was good and worth the effort. The troops were not told of the actual plans but knew that something was about to take place.

The combat team from the 1st Battalion, 67th Armored Regiment, went to Camp Pickett, Virginia, was assigned to the 3d Infantry Division and missed the severe diarrhea epidemic that hit the 2d Armored Division. At Camp Pickett, the men found that all preparations, equipment and personnel matters had to be kept up to date. With all the work to be done, extra supply personnel were brought in to supplement the men of the 2d Armored. By working night and day, by begging, borrowing and sometimes by extralegal means, the work was completed and the unit was ready to sail with the convoy. However, life at Camp Pickett was not the most pleasant. The camp site itself had become a bog, after two weeks of rain. The men came under the command of Maj. Gen. Jonathan W. Anderson, commanding general, 3d Infantry Division, and the post facilities were for the post personnel only. The tankers were forced to use the facilities of the 3d Infantry Division for movies and beer, all adding to the crowded conditions. There were few rooms for families to visit, and there was even less time to see the families. The men realized that their departure was nearing.

The landing team and the infantry began to practice amphibious landings, loadings and unloadings in the Chesapeake Bay, Little Creek and Solomon Island in October 1942. Once the training began, deficiencies in organization, training, planning and technique became clear. One ship captain refused to participate because he claimed that his crew was untrained. Rear Adm. Henry K. Hewitt issued orders that landings be limited to one small beach, for fear of damaging the boats' propellers. Because of that edict, the landing teams could unload only their infantry, not vehicles. Originally no night rehearsals were permitted by General Patton. Hewitt changed the order to permit night landings, but then sailing orders were received, and the teams had only one or two exercises.

While the divisional combat teams were training, other members of the division went to Transport Quartermaster School at Norfolk, Virginia, to learn combat loading: the predetermined loading of men, vehicles and supplies so that they could be put ashore in the proper sequence. The original plan was to have the vehicles and their crews on the same ship. Due to a shortage of shipping, however, the vehicles and drivers sailed on the same ship, but the crews went on different ships. At the schools and even while loading, two views had to be reconciled: the army wanted to carry as much as possible; the navy thought that the men should carry the minimum and that heavy supplies and equipment should follow in a later convoy.

In early September, TORCH took final form. The Western Task Force under Rear Admiral Hewitt and Major General Patton was supposed to capture Casablanca and Port Lyautey. The task force was actually composed of three subtask forces, each assigned a separate and distinct mission. The Northern Attack Group was to land and capture Port Lyautey and the airport. The Center Attack Group was to land at Fedala. The Southern Attack Group was to land at Safi, secure that port, block reinforcements from the south and then aid the center group in capturing Casablanca. Harmon instructed that only those persons with a definite need be told the destination and objectives. In the 2d Armored Division, the information went to Col. Maurice Rose, chief of staff, Lt. Col. Lawrence R. Dewey, G-3, Lt. Col. Ralph J. Butchers, G-4, and, of course, Harmon. These men were the only ones to have the full details until the convoy had actually sailed.

In early October 1942, there was a noticeable increase in the tempo of preparations. The War Department directed that only those items necessary for housekeeping and messing be taken. The remainder would be marked for shipment and turned over to local post commanders for later shipment. About 12,000 men and two-thirds of the vehicles would remain behind with Brig. Gen. Allen F. Kingman, commanding general, Combat Command A. While the remaining men were trying to ready themselves, Harmon was worrying about losing trained men to Officer Candidate School. About 3,500 men had passed the test, and based on past experience about 1,000 of those would be selected to attend. It would hurt the mission forces if any of the selected men were taken out of those forces, and it would hurt morale if one out of every fifteen men in the division were taken from it at this time. Harmon told Devers that it would be ''a terrible thing to take leaders away.'' Devers replied that Harmon need not worry about the 2d Armored Division and that the men would deliver when they had to. There was no mention of the Officer Candidate School question that had prompted Harmon to write in the first place.

After all these problems, the assault teams went to Norfolk and dress rehearsal training in the Chesapeake Bay. Harmon was concerned about the men unloading into assault boats, forming into assault waves and landing. During one exercise using a lighthouse beacon, only one boat landed at its assigned place—Harmon's. Even so, while he had landed at the designated place, he was in the first wave, instead of in the third wave, as he was supposed to be. The remainder of the men were scattered, and it required twelve hours to reassemble them. This poor showing was directly attributable to the inexperience of the navy personnel involved. As if that were not bad enough, the training exercises indicated that the chain cargo nets were unsatisfactory and the division had to get rope ones from Fort Bragg.

The 2d Armored Division was ordered to send one element to the New York port of embarkation to load its equipment. The trains were loaded at Fort Bragg so that the loading could be easily done. The first vehicles onto the ships would be the last to come off. While enroute, one flat car belonging to the Missouri Pacific Railroad, wider than allowed on eastern railroads, struck a bridge. The 2d Armored guard riding in the turret of a medium tank thought that the bridge had exploded. He told Colonel I. D. White that he had never seen such a fireworks display. The train in which White was riding pulled onto a siding and stopped. White got out and walked to the front of the train to investigate. The crew was entering a small maintenance shack, having completed their eight-hour stint. They expected replacements to relieve them. The replacements were not there and no amount of urging by White could get the old crew to continue. White spotted a phone nearby and finally reached a vice president of the Pennsylvania Central Railroad, who promised a crew within two hours. This was done and the train continued on to New York, where it arrived twenty-four hours late.

At Fort Bragg, the 2d Armored Division had made efforts to water-proof their vehicles, primarily by covering them with a thick layer of grease. At the port, where there were experts to do the job, the men had to remove the grease which they had used so generously. This only added to the frustrations besetting the command.

The ship, the *Seatrain,* properly the U.S.S. *Lakehurst,* was not very impressive. Having recently been a ferry between Florida and Cuba, it was without bulkheads or compartments. There was no way to block off damaged compartments in the event of being hit by shellfire or torpedoes. White remembered the ship's captain telling him that if the ship were hit it would probably sink in five minutes—that is, if it did not explode because of its large cargo of gasoline and ammunition: 175,000 gallons of gas in five-gallon cans and nearly 4 million rounds of ammunition, mines and grenades. In addition, the *Seatrain* was to carry 13,870 gallons of SAE 30- and 50-weight oil in quart cans.

Before loading the vehicles, the men loaded the bulk items. The gasoline cans needed to be inspected for leakage. They were stacked on top of one another and probably did leak once the ship was under way. Next to the engine room, the men stored the ammunition and the rations for thirty days. Vehicle loading was a problem created by the New York Port authorities and the railroad. White had planned to move the flat cars alongside the ship and then unload them, but the railroad had planned differently. When one car was unloaded, it pulled out, the train respotted, and the next car unloaded—an unnecessarily time-consuming method. When about half of the vehicles were unloaded, it became apparent that the ship could not hold them all. A decision was made to cut the rations by about 50 percent to make room for the vehicles. In order to insure a balanced diet, the men had to call several quartermaster depots to determine the contents of the unlabeled ration boxes. Somehow the division managed to cut its food supply and still maintain a suitable diet.

The rules of the port were strict about ammunition. The port officials originally would not permit the combat loading of ammunition in the tanks and other vehicles: that would have to wait until the ship was at sea. This would have been difficult, if not impossible, for the division to accomplish. After much delay, the division was granted permission to load the ammunition in the vehicles. As the day for sailing neared, plenty of work remained to be done. It was difficult to get civilians to work around the clock and, while the command had a company of military engineers for unloading, union rules prevented using military labor to load ships. White and his men feared that they might not go because the ship was not ready. When the ship was finally loaded, it was angled down four feet at the bow. This was corrected by shifting fuel oil and by loading medium tanks on the stern's upper deck. Some half-tracks that mounted 37mm and twin .50 caliber antiaircraft guns were placed on the top deck for antiaircraft protection.

After the *Seatrain* was loaded and ready to sail to Hampton Roads to join the fleet, the ship's captain announced that they would sail unescorted, except for a blimp that *might* be over them during daylight hours. White called Harmon, who called Patton, and Patton called—someone! But the *Seatrain* received a two-destroyer escort. A few days after the vessel sailed, the harbor of New York was closed because of mines sown by a German submarine.

At Hampton Roads and Norfolk, the loading of men and equipment was progressing smoothly. The headquarters of BLACKSTONE, Harmon's code name, was aboard the U.S.S. *Harris*. On the morning of October 19, 1942, the ships sailed out to Solomon Island, giving the men one last chance to practice landing from combat vessels. On October 22, they had their first abandon-ship drill. The men were confined to ship, and about midnight on the 23d the convoy weighed anchor and headed out to sea. The next morning, when the men went on deck they saw the convoy with its destroyer escorts all around them. As the 2d Armored's Catholic chaplain noted, the destroyers were a very comforting sight.

Earlier, Patton had warned the division that the day would come when they would be using live ammunition. The men were now on their way to war, with the destination known to but a few. They could and did ask themselves if they had trained properly, if they had learned the lessons that the officers and noncommissioned officers and the maneuvers had intended to teach. The 2d Armored Division was one of the best trained units in the army, but until now their opposition had always been their friends and brother units. Now the enemy and the ammunition would be real.

Chapter 7

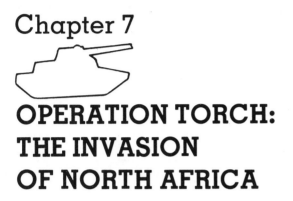

OPERATION TORCH: THE INVASION OF NORTH AFRICA

During the Arcadia Conference in December 1941, President Franklin D. Roosevelt and Prime Minister Winston Churchill agreed that an invasion was necessary to bring the United States actively into the war. The president favored an attack on the European mainland. The prime minister favored attacking either North Africa or Norway, to build a ring around the Nazis, relieve the pressure on the Russians and ease the pressure on the British, primarily in Libya and Egypt. The Americans and British vacillated until July 25, 1942, when the president committed the United States to Operation TORCH.

The outline of the plan was completed about September 6. The Western Task Force assault was to occur simultaneously at three places. One group was to capture Casablanca, another the deep water port at Safi, and a third the airfield at Port Lyautey. Patton estimated that the forces needed would be considerable. In order to capture the airfield, he thought two infantry battalion combat teams and a reinforced armored battalion would be necessary. The main landing at Fedala would require a division

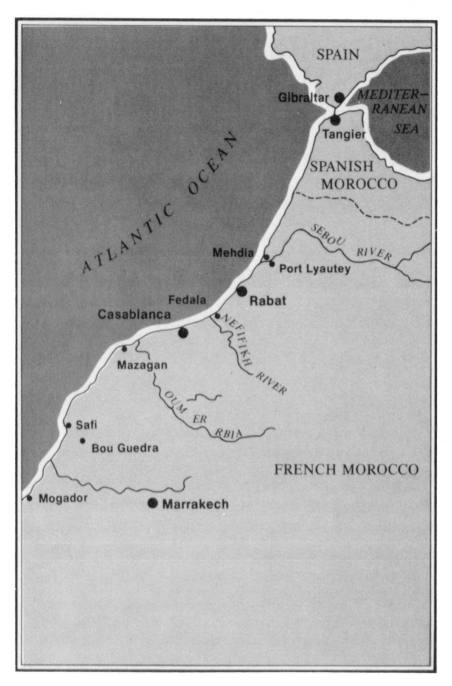

Figure 5. North Africa, 1942.

(minus one regimental combat team), reinforced with an armored regimental combat team. At Safi the forces were to be an infantry battalion combat team, one armored battalion combat team and a floating reserve of one regimental combat team. TORCH was one of the biggest gambles of the war and the largest operation to date. Success depended to a great extent on political rather than military considerations. There was to be no preliminary bombardment or other preparatory barrage. The assault forces would start ashore hoping they did not meet any resistance. The landing on the Atlantic coast of French North Africa was to be strictly an American venture, while those on the Mediterranean Coast, at Oran and Algiers, were to be in partnership with the British.

The Western Task Force, under the command of General Patton, sailed from the United States on October 23, 1942. The convoy numbered over 100 ships, with about 35,000 men and 149,000 tons of supplies (enough for 30 days). The task forces were built around the 3d Infantry Division, most of the 9th Infantry Division and the 2d Armored Division. During the crossing, the troops drilled for hours, climbing down rope ladders and landing nets. The officers and noncommissioned officers studied maps, aerial photographs and terrain models, brought on to the ships just before sailing. The landing teams drilled on their specific assignments, so that each man knew his mission. Because of the problems experienced during the practice landings, Harmon had maps of the Safi area painted on the walls of the ward rooms, and the men memorized the terrain features. Harmon also decided that in future operations every man to the lowest private would be briefed on the plans.

Besides the tactical assignments, the men learned to fire the new bazooka. No one in the task forces had seen this new antitank weapon until they were at sea. The army taught the navy how to use the .30 caliber antiaircraft machine guns. Classes were conducted in the recognition and avoidance of booby traps, the customs of the Moslems, camouflage, naval weapons, first aid, identification of aircraft and armored vehicles, signal training and proper conduct if captured. Each day the men took part in abandon-ship and general quarters drills. Chaplain Urban J. Wurm noted that the men understood the gravity of their undertaking. He was pleased that Patton had been selected to command the task force, noting that the general "knows his men, and [his] men know him; in knowing him love him, in loving him will follow him—anywhere."

The convoy elements did not all sail together; on October 27, Y Force, which had sailed from New York, joined the convoy. Led by the cruiser U.S.S. *Augusta,* it included the carrier U.S.S. *Ranger* with approximately ninety planes. The fighting force was an impressive spectacle. Hopefully the men would not have to hurt anyone, but if the code phrase, "play ball," was passed, then there was going to be "some gore." Two days later, the U.S.S. *Calvert* joined the convoy; on board the *Calvert* was Brig. Gen. Hugh J. Gaffey, commanding general, Combat Command B. The submarine threat was a constant worry. During the voyage, the navy conducted fire, collision and abandon-ship drills, and on October 30, three days after Y force joined them, the convoy experienced its first submarine activity. However, none were actually sighted. Three days later, they were in the midst of a submarine wolf pack, and rumors circulated that a U-boat had been sunk that morning. However, the convoy lost no ships to submarines.

The French Moroccan coast had almost unlimited sites for amphibious landings; generally the beaches had suitable gradients, fair exits from the beaches and few obstacles to landing craft. However, the exits were sandy, which could be a problem for wheeled vehicles. The major hazards were the surf, heavy swells and strong winds. The weathermen predicted only one or two days of acceptable landing conditions, necessitating rapid landings on a wide front. Because there were no navigable rivers and few capes and headlands, obtaining control of the three ports of Safi, Casablanca and Port Lyautey was essential to the allied force. The navy planned to arrive in position by midnight on November 7 and spend four hours unloading the vessels. The attack teams would have to depend on naval air support until they captured the airfields, giving them land-based aircraft support. The Port Lyautey convoy was late in arriving at its destination. It should have been on station at 11:00 P.M., November 7, but did not arrive until 3:00 A.M. on November 8. H-hour was initially changed from 4:00 to 4:30, but that also proved too early.

The battle for North Africa opened in a most unorthodox manner. The president of the United States announced to the people of French Morocco that the American army was coming. His message stressed historic American and French ties. The United States and Great Britain, he said, were striving to restore liberty and democracy to those living under the tri-color. The Allies were attempting to restore the right of self-government, the right of religious freedom, and the right to live as one pleased. The Americans came to destroy the enemy and would leave when the job was done. Concluding, Roosevelt added, "I am appealing to your sense of realism, self-interests and ideals. Do not obstruct this great purpose. Help us and the day of a world of peace will be hastened."

Convoy to North Africa.

The British and American governments issued a joint declaration stating that the landings were the first step in the liberation of France. The immediate objective was the isolation and destruction of the Germans in North Africa. The Allies were there as friends; French sovereignty remained unaffected. They also cautioned the French in France not to do anything yet, for it was not yet time for them to rise up. Lt. Gen. Dwight D. Eisenhower's proclamation said the same: the Allies came as friends to defeat the Italians and the Germans and had no designs on French territory. The Allies would take no offensive action against the French if they did not resist the landings. If the French wanted to comply with the directions and not resist, they were to fly two tricolors or a tricolor and an American flag one above the other during daylight hours. At night, searchlights were to point toward the sky. Orders were issued for the French navy and merchant marine to stay in port and not scuttle their vessels. The coast guard units were to withdraw from their stations and not to man the guns. Aviation units were to keep their planes on the ground. All Frenchmen were to obey the orders of American officers.

The original plan was for the president's message to be broadcast simultaneously with the landings at Oran, Algiers and the western ones. The message was sent at 3:00 A.M. in order not to jeopardize the two Mediterranean landings, but as it happened that time was actually one hour ahead of the Western Task Force landing time. Brig. Gen. Lucian Truscott, commanding general, 9th Infantry Division, observed that due to the premature broadcast, "if the French were not waiting beside their guns, we would indeed be lucky."

Task Force GOALPOST was to seize, stock and maintain the airport at Lyautey and Salé and cover the northern flank of the entire operation. It was the smallest of the three task forces and in some respects had the most difficult time. The ensuing battle was the first tank fight in which elements of the 2d Armored Division participated. To carry out his assignment, Truscott had Col. Frederic J. deRohan's 60th Regimental Combat Team, 9th Infantry Division, and the 1st Battalion Combat Team, 66th Armored Regiment, commanded by Lt. Col. Harry Semmes. Both units were in excellent condition, with the staffs well organized and the units at almost full strength, and both had received some amphibious training.

The planners thought that the French would be defending the Port Lyautey area with a regiment of infantry (3,080 men), twelve antitank guns, artillery and engineers. Reinforcements, which would be available from the Spanish Moroccan border towns, Meknes and Rabat, included two regiments of infantry, a battalion of forty-five tanks and 1,200 mechanized cavalrymen. All could be brought to Lyautey anywhere from D+1 to D+4. Possible enemy reactions to the landings required that the Americans get their tanks and antitank guns ashore as quickly as possible. Unknown to the Americans, there were two opinions among French officers. One group wanted to carry out orders regardless, while the other did not want to fight the Allies. Commanders in the threatened area had authority to open fire on their own initiative.

The Port Lyautey landings originally included two plans. In Plan A the Americans were to land south of the airport, then move onto the field as a unit. Its advantage lay in its simplicity. The disadvantage was that the invading force was about the same strength as the enemy. It was thought that it would require most of the first day for the troops to land and assemble, and bad weather could prevent the landing of other troops. In Plan B, the Americans would land in several locations and advance on the airport from different directions. The advantage was speed and surprise of attack, and the ability to get men and material ashore as quickly as possible. The major disadvantages were that the Americans would not have a superiority of troops at any point and that there would be few reserves. Since the basic factor was the weather, Truscott adopted Plan B.

While the men were loading into their assault craft, five French vessels sailed past the American ships. One flashed a message which read, "Be aware. Alert on shore for 5:00 A.M." It simply confirmed that the task force had failed to surprise the French and that the president's message had not changed the French decision to resist. The armor landing team was to land inside the breakwater at Port Lyautey, on the order of the force commander, beginning about 7:50 A.M. Its mission was to assemble and to protect the south against any enemy approaching from that direction. As the reserve force, it was to be ready to aid in the attacks to secure the airports at Port Lyautey, Rabat-Salé and Sibi-Yahia, and the radio station at Rabat-Salé. To aid the Armored Battalion, one reinforced infantry company from the 3d Battalion Landing Team would be available in a reserve role. The 1st Armored Landing Team personnel were on the *John Penn;* the light tanks were on the *Electra.* The Armored Battalion was to land as quickly as possible after daylight and after the infantry assault battalions.

The surf, rather than French resistance, hampered Truscott's landing. Three of the landing craft bringing the armor ashore were swamped, and a light tank, a half-track and a scout car were lost. The light tank had been amphibiously sealed with compounds containing fish oils. As it drove through the breakers from the landing craft, it went in a big semicircle, rolled back into the breakers, then into deep water and disappeared with the entire crew. Some conjectured that the crew had been asphyxiated by fish oil vapors. By nightfall, six or seven tanks had reached the shore. Semmes was ordered to the south flank and to take command of the infantry and antitank units there. He went into position about a mile south of the lagoon and the next morning had the privilege of fighting the initial 2d Armored action of the war.

On November 9, Semmes had his tanks in position to oppose any threat from the south. About 4:30 A.M., fourteen French tanks, small enough to go under the fig trees, were seen moving north along the Rabat-Port Lyautey road. Pulling back to defilade positions behind a low ridge, the Americans opened fire when the approaching tanks came within range. The French retreated to a eucalyptus grove, which the navy then shelled, driving the French away. The noted naval historian, Samuel Eliot Morison, incorrectly credited the navy with breaking up that attack, when in fact it was the small armored force that initially repulsed the French.

Semmes and his command had their problems. Before leaving the United States, they had been issued new radios but had not had time to calibrate them. While at sea, the command was under radio silence and therefore could not properly care for the equipment. Moreover the tank guns were not bore-sighted (the telescopic sight aligned parallel to the axis of the main gun), and the men were forced to use a trial-and-error method of aiming. After repulsing the first threat to the beachhead, Semmes's small force had about an hour's rest before fighting off an infantry attack at about 6:00 A.M. After routing the infantry, the Americans were attacked a second time by tanks. The old French Renaults were repulsed with four tanks lost. Semmes himself accounted for two of them. The French gunnery had been accurate: two shells were imbedded in the front slope armor of Semmes's tank.

The tempo of the action increased; about 8:15, while observing the naval gunfire rout the French from the grove of trees, the armored group received some reinforcements. At 9:00 about ten tanks from Company C, 70th Tank Battalion, arrived to help the 2d Armored Division take on thirty-two French tanks. The French were attempting to reach the American beachhead. The American tanks counterattacked, driving the enemy three miles inland and forcing them to abandon twenty-four of their tanks. After this fight ended at about 3:00 P.M., Company C of the 70th Tank

Battalion was detached and ordered to help the infantry in its attempt to take the airfield. Semmes, meanwhile, had been reinforced with Cannon Company, 60th Infantry Regiment.

Truscott made repeated appeals for supplies and equipment, but the surf, though rated as only moderate, hampered unloading. The losses in landing craft were high: 70 of the available 162 boats had been damaged or destroyed. During the night, nine additional tanks, a platoon of the 443d Coast Artillery (Antiaircraft Artillery), and the reconnaissance platoon joined their parent units at the south end of the lagoon. To add to the misery, rain began during the night and continued during most of the next day. However, the defenders were in position and ready for whatever the French might try on November 10.

Lt. James M. Burt, maintenance officer in B Company, 66th Armored Regiment, had a marine amphibious vehicle for his landing craft. His section experimented with it in Chesapeake Bay, learning how to use it. The equipment was stored in the hold of the ship. Semmes called Burt to the bridge, asking him if he and his crew wanted to take the vehicle in to the beach. Not trusting his vehicle compass, he measured 135 degrees and hit his beach while the navy missed their beach by two miles. Burt took his vehicle back to the ship to get a cutting torch to repair a tank whose turret had been wedged by a glancing round from a French tank. The navy refused to lend a torch but sent their men to the beach to do the repair work. Then the navy men could not get back to their ship.

On November 10, the French continued their attempt to relieve the Port Lyautey garrison. About 11:00 A.M. the reconnaissance platoon spotted twenty French tanks moving north on the Rabat-Port Lyautey road. Six American tanks and two assault guns from Cannon Company entered the woods east of that road, while the remainder of the American force stayed in their positions. The French sent six tanks into the woods to flush out the Americans while the rest of the French continued northward. In the woods, the French tanks were fired on by the Americans and quickly withdrew. The navy placed heavy gunfire on the French, who pulled back, losing seven more tanks: three to naval gunfire and four to antitank fire.

Semmes and his small force were solidly astride the road the French needed to resupply their garrison. About 4:00 that afternoon, a patrol of four tanks was sent into the valley northeast (toward Port Lyautey) looking for enemy cavalry troops. They found none but did make contact with the 1st Battalion Combat Team from the 60th Infantry Regiment; this

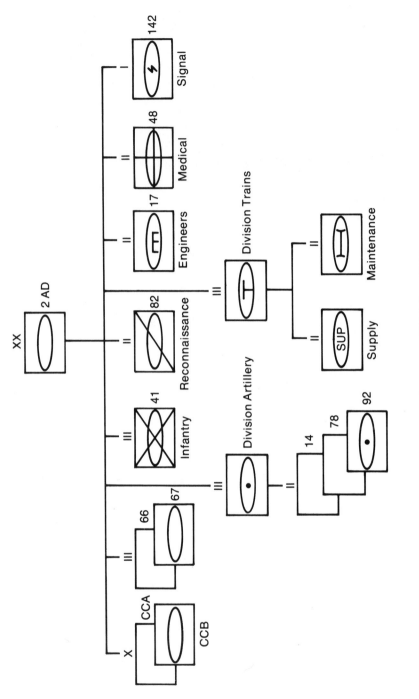

Figure 6. An Armored Division, 1942.

contact encircled the French, making their positions untenable. About 11:00 P.M. on November 10, the Americans received a message that the French wanted to discuss surrender terms. At 2:00 A.M.on November 11, the Americans learned that the French commander, Major General Mathenet, had ordered the French resistance to halt, and a meeting was arranged for 8:00 the same morning. Somehow a message was passed to the French that Maj. Leonard H. "Steamer" Nason was with the Task Force. Nason, who had travelled widely after World War I, was friendly with the French Foreign Legion, having been made an honorary corporal, and had been decorated by the sultan of Morocco with the Star of Islam. Semmes, Nason and a company of light tanks accompanied Truscott to meet the French commander, to "lend something of military display to the event." Major General Mathenet said that he had been ordered to end the fighting, pending decisions of higher headquarters. The local terms were favorable to both the Americans and the ever-sensitive French. The Americans would occupy the port and the airport but would not interfere with the French if the French did not interfere with them. The French had resisted the landing and fought well, inflicting over 200 casualties, but their zeal declined as the battle continued. With their inability to resupply the garrison, caused primarily by the tanks of the 2d Armored Division, the French were, as Burt so bluntly stated, "firing their shot for honor."

The Western Task Force's major objective was Fedala, whence it planned to assault the rear of Casablanca. A direct attack was considered too costly, especially against such well-defended positions. Patton's letter of instruction to Harmon said that the initial mission of the Western Task Force was to assault and capture Casablanca and the nearby airport and then if necessary to build a strike force to secure Spanish Morocco. The second step would be the occupation of French Morocco in conjunction with the Center Task Force that had landed at Oran.

The French garrison at Fedala was estimated at approximately 2,500 men; however, an estimated 6,500 reinforcements were available to aid the defenders. Formidable defenses opposed the landing force. In the Batterie du Port were three 100mm guns which faced northwesterly but could be turned to fire on the center beach. A battery of two fixed 75mm guns could be brought to bear on several of the beaches. The Batterie Pont Blondin, four 138.6mm guns with a range of 18,000 yards, was in sunken emplacement. These major shore defense positions were fortified by machine gun emplacements and by mobile batteries of 75mm artillery in unknown locations.

BRUSHWOOD, code name for the Fedala landing, was assigned to the 3d Infantry Division, commanded by Maj. Gen. Jonathan W. Anderson. Supporting the infantry was the Armored Landing Team built around Maj. Richard E. Nelson's 1st Battalion, 67th Armored Regiment. This group had a combined strength of 19,783 officers and men and seventy-seven light tanks. Their objectives were Fedala and Casablanca, fifteen miles south of the landing sites. Casablanca, considered the key to liberating French North Africa, had a deep water port which could serve as the main supply port for any Allied venture in western Africa. Initially, Anderson planned to land two infantry regimental combat teams, keeping one infantry regiment and the armored landing team in floating reserve. The amor was scheduled to land approximately three hours after the first wave, then join the 7th and 15th Infantry Regiments for the attack on Casablanca.

The infantry landing teams started ashore about 4:30 A.M. on November 8. Several factors, including troop ships and cargo transports being out of their assigned positions, the inexperience of army troops in landing and the lack of skill on the part of the navy, caused a thirty-minute delay. When the operation started, some of the landing craft foundered on the rocks and reefs and were lost.

The officers and men of the 2d Armored Division landing team were awakened by naval gunfire and soon lined the rails of the ships to watch the fight. They had a fright as they saw a transport racing toward the beach. It was fired on but beat a hasty retreat; the ship was the *Biddle*, carrying some of their vehicles. At 4:00 P.M., Nelson went ashore, returning at 6:00 with instructions to start unloading. The loss of landing craft was a hindrance, but by dark a platoon of Company A, 67th Armored Regiment, was ashore and had taken up positions overlooking Fedala; during the night it met no enemy resistance. The remainder of the tanks were to be unloaded the following day.

By 5:00 P.M. on November 8, about 40 percent of the Center Landing Team was ashore. Once again there had been a large loss of landing craft: about half of their 347 boats. In spite of the difficulties, Anderson and his men captured most, if not all, of their initial objectives before sunrise on November 9. Once the port was in American hands, emphasis was placed on landing the tanks. The *Arcturus* was brought to the docks and unloaded, while landing craft unloaded the *Biddle*. By 7:00 P.M., the Armored Landing Team was ashore and in position between the railroad and a highway. It was ordered to move east of the Oued Mellah to guard against possible infiltrators. Defenses were established on the east bank of the river and guards posted on the bridges, but no enemy tested the tankers that night.

At dawn the armored team sent reconnaissance patrols to its front. One platoon of Company A, 67th Armored Regiment, was sent toward Mediouna, where it found the 15th Infantry Regiment and acted as a flank guard for the infantry that day. Southwest of Casablanca, 600 Moroccan Spahis were in position to attack the flank of the 15th Infantry. There was a minor skirmish, but the French forces were driven off without American losses. The remainder of the armored force awaited orders in the BRUSHWOOD reserve. About dark, the Armored Battalion was ordered to move to positions west of Casablanca and to be ready to attack at 8:00 A.M. on November 11. It started to rain, and because of the extreme darkness each tank had to be led on foot. In spite of all precautions, one quarter-ton vehicle went over a cliff. In the morning after the 78th Armored Artillery fired a brief artillery concentration at Casablanca, the tanks started moving forward to launch the assault to capture the major objective of the Western Task Force. At that point, Patton ordered a cease-fire because the French had surrendered.

The French resistance was not as determined as it could have been. One reason was the surprise of the landings; a second was the lack of desire to fight the Americans. Possibly the French fought for honor, but in any event they were willing to join the Allies as soon as they surrendered.

The main 2d Armored Division landing was at Safi, about 120 miles southwest of Casablanca. Patton had issued detailed instructions to Maj. Gen. Ernest N. Harmon. Task Force BLACKSTONE was to land, secure its positions and be ready to assault the land defenses of Casablanca. That mission could only be deterred by actual combat at Safi. Once the troops were ashore, they should move quickly to capture, undamaged if possible, the telephone exchange and radio station, both considered vital to the establishment of civil control.

However difficult and costly the mission, Safi had to be captured and the *Seatrain* unloaded. Harmon was instructed that if for any reason beyond his control he could not unload the *Seatrain,* he was to send it to Fedala. He was admonished to be careful not to expose the ship to unnecessary dangers. As the *Seatrain* carried the only medium tanks in the Western Task Force, the admonitions were heeded. After unloading his command, Harmon was to reach Casablanca as quickly as possible. He had to secure a crossing over the Rbia River, while maintaining his lines of communication to Safi. Any enemy attack against Safi was to be Harmon's only concern. If he felt that it was necessary to abandon Safi, he was to contact Patton for approval; in the event he could not reach him he was authorized to use his own judgement.

Harmon issued orders detailing much the same information that he had received from Patton. In addition, he cautioned the commands that they might have to fight the Marrakech garrison, about 100 miles south of Safi. The landing had three phases: unloading and establishing a 5,000-yard radial beachhead; expanding this beachhead to 10,000 yards; and future enlargement of the beachhead. No plans were made to land any part of the command, except the assault troops, anyplace except on the docks at Safi.

Safi was a dangerous place to try a landing. At that time of year, heavy swells could dash the light landing craft onto the rocks. There were few suitable beaches, and even these were short and butted into high cliffs. The harbor, however, was one of the three deep-water ports on the Atlantic side of French North Africa. It was triangular, with the entrance about 500 yards wide and a narrow opening formed by a long jetty and a pier that came together at right angles. Inside the harbor was a quay which could handle three ships, and in addition there were electric cranes to help with the unloading. Nearby covered storage sheds were connected by a spur railroad track which led to the interior. If the 2d Armored could get to these facilities, the unloading of the tanks would be greatly eased, as no landing craft could handle the medium tanks of the task force.

The invaders expected an opposing force of about 1,000 men. Actually, they found about half that number. At Marrakech there was a considerable number of reinforcements available, including 1,400 cavalry, 2,000 infantry, two battalions of horse-drawn guns, and forty tanks and armored cars. The Safi harbor defenses were covered by artillery and machine guns. The Batterie Roilleuse had four 130mm coast defense guns, three batteries of 75mm guns and four 155mm guns, which could raise havoc with the landing force if the French chose to resist. The convoy arrived at their positions about 10:45 P.M. on November 7. After being fed potato salad, sandwiches and coffee, the men started over the side at 11:30. To their amazement, the harbor lighthouse was blazing, and continued to shine until about 2:00 A.M. Apparently the convoy had arrived undetected. The men loaded into their assault craft as early as possible to minimize losses should the French decide to fight.

From the time of the first alert at Safi (3:20 A.M.) until the Allied landing, the French had about an hour and ten minutes to prepare. A rickety old French vessel, the *Alfonse de Lande,* fired the first shot and was promptly sunk by American gunfire. Shortly after 5:00 Commander Deuve, the French commander at Safi, was notified that ships had been sighted. He refused to open fire until the spotters could identify the ships. Later when he saw a warship enter the harbor, he gave the order to fire. His actions were answered by gun flashes that lit up the horizon.

The first landings were made by the 47th Infantry Regiment of the 9th Infantry Division, commanded by Colonel E. H. Randel; its mission was to establish the initial beachhead. After that, it was to hold the beachhead while the medium tanks were unloaded and the Armored Force prepared to move northeast to Casablanca. Harmon learned that the French had placed a boom across the mouth of the Safi harbor. He suggested that two destroyers ram it and enter the harbor carrying two infantry companies. They needed to take the electric cranes intact if the tanks were to be unloaded. Upon arriving at Safi, however, they found no boom, but Harmon and Rear Adm. Lyle A. Davidson decided to send the destroyers into the harbor anyway. As a result, the port was secured without serious damage to the facilities. The crane was damaged by a watchman, but the next day he returned and repaired it in about three hours. The Reconnaissance Platoon of the 47th Infantry Regiment seized the telegraph and telephone centers intact and successfully cut Safi off from the rest of North Africa. Company L of the same regiment captured the oil storage tanks east of the harbor.

By dawn (about 6:00 A.M.), the harbor, railroad station, post office and highways to the south were held by the Americans, but they did not have the town. The battle to take the town began in earnest and was making such progress that the *Seatrain* sailed into the harbor and began to unload the medium tanks about 2:00 P.M. Just as the ship docked, it was attacked by a French airplane which was shot down by antiaircraft guns on the *Lakehurst.* About the same time, the *Titania,* which carried the light tanks of the armored landing team, tied up to the dock and started unloading. As the tanks were unloaded, they went to an assembly area near Horseshoe Hill, three miles northeast of town.

Harmon moved his headquarters to Safi about 3:30 P.M. on November 8, where he found French sniping and American inactivity. He sent tanks and infantry to clean out the snipers and thus cleared up the unloading problems. The major difficulty was that the task force did not have any army troops to move the supplies inland. The Arabs were slow, indifferent and unreliable. Finally, the men of the 47th Infantry Regiment were used; but they were tired and felt insulted at having to do noninfantry work. They also had to send crews on the destroyers *Cole* and *Bernadau* to Mazagan to resupply the task force as it moved north for the assault on Casablanca.

So far, French resistance had emanated from the garrison at Safi. The French air force at Marrakech did not take off because of "weather conditions"—unlimited visibility. The next morning at 6:30, a French plane strafed and bombed the docks, destroying several vehicles and causing some casualties. It was shot down by the antiaircraft gun crews on the *Lakehurst*. American aircraft attacked the French air force at Marrakech, destroying about forty planes on the ground. Returning to their carrier, the navy pilots spotted and attacked a French column on its way to counterattack the Americans at Safi. The planes slowed the French, enabling Harmon to rush troops to meet their advance.

The French had reached Bou Guedra, approximately fifteen miles from Safi, when they met elements of the 2d Armored Division. About 1:50 P.M. on November 9, Harmon ordered Brigadier General Gaffey to oppose the French. Gaffey moved out at 2:13 with the light tanks of the 2d Battalion, 67th Armored Regiment, while the medium tanks of the 3d Battalion were kept in Combat Command reserve. At 5:00 the light tanks, commanded by Lt. Col. William M. Stokes, encountered the enemy about a mile and half east of Bou Guedra and forced them to pull back to positions in the hills. The Americans went into defensive positions, planning to resume the attack the next morning. After firing about 300 rounds of 105mm howitzer ammunition but not dislodging the French, it was decided to break off the engagement and move northward to Casablanca. A determined attack could have dislodged the French but would have cost lives and tanks that were needed elsewhere. Harmon thought that the 47th Infantry Regiment and Company B, 70th Tank Battalion, could handle the situation while the 2d Armored Division moved north.

Having no word from Patton, Harmon decided to start toward Casablanca on the afternoon of November 10. The move was a risky one, for the enemy still had considerable forces at Marrakech and Mogador. Harmon felt that Colonel Randel (aided by naval gunfire) could hold Safi. If necessary, the infantry could fight its way back to the beach and board the ships.

At noon, as the preparations for the march were being made, the French civil authorities loaned the Americans two buses to transport the headquarters personnel. Combat Command B was ordered to cease operations at 5:15 P.M. and pull back for movement to Casablanca. The march began at 7:00 under blackout conditions, through unknown territory, at excessive speeds and with a time limit. The command had to capture Mazagan, where the navy was sending the *Cole* and the *Bernadau* to refuel and resupply the tanks. The column stopped several times, and each time some of the exhausted drivers went to sleep. On one such stop, Harmon and his G-3, Lt. Col. Lawrence R. Dewey, found an old French soldier standing in uniform beside a rock and holding a light. Harmon listened to the old veteran explain that he had done his duty for the French republic. The division commander invited him to stand aside. The Frenchman did, explaining that he was holding the light because he did not want the Americans to hurt themselves.

The tankers reached the outskirts of Mazagon at 4:30 A.M. Harmon, wanting to avoid a night engagement, decided to wait until dawn (about 6:30) and to attack the town with infantry. Gaffey was sent to capture the bridge at Azemmour, which he did. The Task Force had made alternate arrangements for the bridge. Had the French destroyed it, the 2d Armored was prepared to build a pontoon bridge seventeen kilometers (about 10.2 miles) upstream, where the river was about 215 feet wide, with excellent approaches and exits.

Meanwhile, Harmon met with the French commander and, with the threat of air and naval bombardment, persuaded the French to surrender at 7:45, with full military honors, permitting them to keep their weapons. Chaplain Wurm was of the opinion that the French were truly glad to see the Americans. After the surrender, the column moved to assembly areas just north of town to refuel and prepared to resume the march northward. While refueling, Harmon was informed that the French had ceased operations against the Americans in all of North Africa and that he should stop in place. To show his appreciation, Harmon bought 5,000 eggs for his command, a gesture much appreciated after a steady diet of K-rations.

The Allied landings in North Africa came as a complete surprise to the Germans. They thought that the landing teams which went ashore at Oran and Tunis were destined for the eastern end of the Mediterranean Sea. After the landings, the Germans had the choice of surrendering or continuing the fight, for evacuation was out of the question. The first German broadcasts to the world pictured greedy Americans and British grabbing the territory of their former ally. On the third and fourth day following the landings, German propaganda claimed that the Allies landed in North Africa to make the Mediterranean an Allied lake, because they were short on shipping and could not wait for their ships to go around the Cape of Good Hope. The Nazis dropped the shipping argument on the fifth day and switched to a new line: Fortress Europa had a weak link, which was southern France. Therefore Germany was justified in moving into what had been Vichy France.

The 2d Armored Division had taken part in perhaps the most difficult of all military operations—an amphibious landing on hostile soil. The division proved its training under the most demanding of tests: combat. The tankers had had a variety of missions. At Port Lyautey they defended preventing the French from resupplying the garrison. At Safi, after blocking the reinforcing column, they executed a deep penetration against almost no resistance; Harmon's men were in position to attack when the resistance ended. TORCH showed that an amphibious force could be transported across the ocean, landed against opposition and execute its mission against opposition. It also revealed that better landing methods were needed, if other landings were to be carried out. North Africa was a testing ground for the 2d Armored Division and, in a larger sense, for the army.

Chapter 8

NORTH AFRICAN INTERLUDE

Operation TORCH was the wildest adventure that Major General Harmon and the 2d Armored Division had experienced. The anxiety and suspense were as awesome as they would ever undergo. Everyone, army and navy alike, was inexperienced, but the initial mission of the Western Task Force had been accomplished with only nine 2d Armored Division casualties: four dead and five wounded. French Morocco had been captured. While Port Lyautey and the Fedala-Casablanca venture were primarily an infantry operation, the landing at Safi was mainly a tank action. Following the French surrender, the division settled down to occupation duty. No plans had been made to use the 2d Armored in the Tunisian desert campaign. Patton permitted the French to retain administrative jurisdiction of their colony. As long as the French controlled the native population and did not interfere with the war effort, the United States would not interfere in the internal affairs of French Morocco.

The 2d Armored Division was alerted for movement on November 13, 1942. It was to occupy a bivouac area in the Mamora Cork Forest about eighteen miles northeast of Rabat. Lacking transportation for its headquarters personnel, the division impressed two charcoal-burning buses to take them to Casablanca, where, thanks to the ingenuity of Capt. Maurice T. Fliegelman, the remainder of the trip was made in a deluxe French bus. Chaplain Wurm observed that the area was picturesque and that the division had never had a better bivouac area, even back in the States. However, the sun blazed down during the day and at night there was usually a cold rain.

While bivouacked in the Cork Forest, the division and the Western Task Force faced two serious problems: the French reaction to British participation, especially after the British had attacked Dakar, and the response of the governments of Spain, Vichy France and French North Africa to the invasion. The Americans were especially concerned that the 130,000 Spanish and native Spanish Moroccan troops might cause them problems. Spain had made statements about pushing the frontier south of the Sebou River (Port Lyautey is on the Sebou River), but the Americans were committed to maintaining French possessions as they were.

The 2d Armored Division's mission was to guard the Spanish-French Moroccan border, to prevent attempts by Spain or Germany to attack supply and communications lines and to keep open the single-track railroad between Casablanca and Oran. When the German military archives were captured at the end of the war, a plan for a German invasion of North Africa was discovered. It involved the use of Spanish forces to capture Gibralter and to assist the Germans in severing the American supply lines to the Tunisian front. The Spanish, under Lt. Gen. Luis Orgas Yoldi, continually made threats about their frontier. To discourage any such venture, Patton invited the Spanish general to a review presented by the 2d Armored Division. He came, and as the Spanish did not have any weapon to combat the tanks, there was no more talk about expanding to the Sebou River. Harmon confessed that while he had opposed permitting the Spanish to view the division, the gamble had worked.

The next problem facing the men was how to get along with the native population. The sultan of Morocco was friendly to the Americans, but the situation could become very dangerous if any incident changed his mind. Chaplain Wurm knew that Rabat was the second principal holy city for the Moslems. The young men of the division were warned about "youthful indiscretions." Harmon solved many problems with liberal doses of money. This was especially true if the natives found dud ammunition while scavenging in the target or impact area. He also established

Souk-el-Harmon (Harmon's market), so that the American soldiers could buy products from the Arabs without being robbed. At night the soldiers cooked their purchases over stoves made from number-ten cans filled with sand and soaked with gasoline. Patton initially objected to the consumption of approximately 500 gallons of gasoline a week for this purpose, for gas cost about $8.00 per gallon delivered to North Africa. However, he gave his consent, and morale soared.

All was not work in the division. There was time for socializing and experimentation. Since there was an abundance of wine, but a lack of hard liquor, Capt. Tom Wishard discovered that by heating the wine almost to the boiling point and condensing the steam, a fairly tasty liquid could be distilled. When mixed with grapefruit juice, the "kickapoo joy juice" satisfied most men. However, the still met the same end as most moonshine operations. One day, as a batch was being run off, the "revenooer," Colonel I. D. White, walked into the mess tent and ended the experiment. Sgt. Russel S. Lamison, mail clerk for the 142d Signal Company, was returning from the movies one night when he heard someone calling "Veno, Veno." Many of the men refused to answer, because they thought he had already had enough vino. In fact, the man had fallen into the kitchen garbage pit, breaking his leg, and was calling for his friend Bill Veno. Finally a good samaritan came along and helped him to the aid station.

The men were given some time off from the strenuous training, and taken on tours of the native areas. Lt. Gen. John H. Collier, who became acquainted with some of the French armor officers, recalled his visit to Marrakech. He described the sound of the city as what a person with finely tuned hearing would hear listening to thousands of worms. Other times the officers were treated to horseback rides by French who had managed to escape France and retained their positions or wealth. Some of the native chieftains were, it was thought, required to conduct wild boar hunts for the officers. The enlisted men were treated to some wildfowl shooting. As always, there was the constant danger with men out of a combat zone —social diseases. To combat the situation, the division and I Armored Corps required that anyone returning from pass submit to a prophylactic treatment before being admitted to the division area. Sgt. Frederick Morse was one of the victims of the policy. When he arrived at the main gate to return to the division area, the military police told him that he would have to be treated. He stated that he had not done anything to require treatment. He was bluntly informed that to get the red stamp to enter, he had to be treated. If he didn't submit, he might be declared AWOL. Morse knew there was only one way to get back into the camp. Some who maintained their innocence and refused to submit were forcibly treated.

Gambling was another pastime for the men. Some members of Reconnaissance Platoon, 17th Engineer Battalion, dug a very large foxhole, covered it and used it as their gaming and drinking room. Sgt. Aloysius Villmer remembers one man who, after a long night of wine and cards, appeared for reveille with his leggings on the wrong legs and only a steel helmet without the liner. When the organized games were unavailable, some men improvised. There were repulsive black beetles which lived around the unit latrines, so beetle races were organized. One soldier who had a winner sold his insect for five dollars. The buyer planned to use the tired and almost immobile beetle for stud purposes.

Back in the United States, the remainder of the division was preparing to sail for North Africa. The 702d Tank Destroyer Battalion was relieved from assignment to the division and reassigned to Army Ground Forces. The other units continued training while preparing their equipment for North Africa. After most of the organizational equipment had been packed, Colonels Hinds and Collier both found it difficult to maintain morale in regiments without much equipment. The men spent many hours on the rifle ranges, in calisthenics and on extended road marches. After making the required twenty-five-mile march in full field gear, the division would often continue for an additional fifteen to twenty-five miles. The men were never content with meeting minimal standards.

While the training was demanding, rugged and dangerous, it gave all personnel a preview of combat. Mrs. Sidney R. (Regina) Hinds said that because of the training at Fort Benning, on the maneuvers and at Fort Bragg, there was no doubt in her mind that her husband would come home alive. That is the ultimate compliment to any commanding officer. On November 1, 1942, the division moved to Fort Dix, New Jersey. When the lead elements of the division reached New York, they found a longshoreman's strike in progress. Equally infuriating were the requirements by the quartermaster corps that it take over certain responsibilities when the tanks reached the dock area. The tankers had already stowed some 3,000 pounds of equipment in the tanks, so that jarring motion and salt water would not do any damage. The men had to restow the items in accordance with quartermaster wishes. When the division reached North Africa, H Company, 66th Armored Regiment, found that it had rammer staffs and other equipment belonging to the 78th Field Artillery. Capt. Norris Perkins's maintenance crew had overhauled and tuned the engines of his tanks, but again quartermaster personnel interferred, redoing what had already been done. The one consolation was that Perkins and his tanks were on the sea train *Texas* in the center of the convoy, where they felt safe and snug with their heavy, precious cargo.

The troop ships *American, Ancon, Argentina, Brazil* and *Chiriqui* carried as many as 5,000 men each. On the *Brazil* the men started a newspaper which a contest named the *Convoice*. It was great for morale and kept the troops informed of the war situation, as well as detailing the do's and don't's of ship life. For major offenses—smoking during blackout periods or throwing items overboard—the usual punishment was confinement to the brig, one meal a day and no cigarettes or reading material for the duration of the trip.

While the troop ships were crowded, the sea train *Texas* carried most of the vehicles. The men had full run of the upper deck for calisthenics. They took part in the security of the ship, manning antiaircraft weapons, guard duty, submarine watch and fire guard. Captain Perkins, using his architecture background, constructed dummy traversing and elevating handwheels for the tank cannons from trash and cardboard. He painted a panoramic background on canvas and began training his gunners and tank commanders in the rapid adjustment of tank cannon fire. The instructor would ''sense'' explosive bursts and the men were required to bring the burst onto the target.

The troops landed at Casablanca on Christmas Day. Col. John Collier recalled that he was just sitting down to dinner, when Gen. Hugh Gaffey came striding into the dining room and ordered the men to disembark. He and many others were treated to a memorable dinner—C-rations in the rain. The men of the sea train *Texas,* however, were permitted to dine aboard ship and had their choice of entrees: broiled fish, ham or turkey with all the trimmings. Patton had arranged for the ships to be met with bands playing.

Shortly after landing, the men underwent a German air raid. While the enemy did no damage, some 2d Armored personnel were injured by falling flack. On New Year's Eve, the enemy returned for another raid. Perkins recalled that it was a great fireworks show. The men cheered as the German bombers were illuminated in the searchlights. The antiaircraft fire, tracer bullets and flack added to the strange beauty. The men added to the show with their cheering and impolite but enthusiastic comments to

"Hang it in 'er." The only apparent injuries during that raid were to three men in G Company, 66th Armored Regiment, who jumped into the garbage dump barefooted. Later, both Lord "Haw Haw" and a woman that the men labelled B. S. Bessie claimed that part of the division had been sunk at sea, while the rest had been destroyed at Casablanca. Perkins told his wife not to believe the stories of the German Propaganda Service. In fact, he claimed that the German efforts at propaganda, especially their music, only boosted morale among the men. Chaplain Wurm observed that after the first air raid, there was an undercurrent of petty jealousy among the new arrivals, for when Casablanca was attacked, the men wanted to know how soon they could place a star on their service ribbons.

With the division now reunited, there was a renewed emphasis on compliance with uniform regulations, especially since General Patton commanded the area. Among other things, haircuts were stressed. Col. Herbert Long remembered that 1st Lt. Junius P. Whitehurst, platoon leader of the Reconnaissance Platoon, 2d Battalion, 66th Armored Regiment decided to solve the short hair problem by having his head shaved. The battalion commander, Lt. Col. Charles G. Rau took Whitehurst to task for his excessively short hair. One night at the battalion officers' mess, Colonel Rau told Whitehurst, "Officers do not shave their heads." The platoon leader's answer, respectfully stated, brought the mess tent down: "Yes sir, Colonel Rau, I will grow it back just as fast as I can."

The area around the Cork Forest afforded the division excellent terrain for training. Basics were restressed: crew drills, marches, range firing and tactical problems. Lt. Col. Lawrence R. Dewey was not pleased with the tank sights. Using several destroyed tank hulls as targets, he soon discovered that until the sights were improved, the tankers would have to use the artillery bracketing method to hit the target: firing over and short of the target, then splitting the difference. Col. Thomas H. Roberts, commander of Division Artillery, and Lt. Col. Harry Semmes, commanding officer, 2d Battalion, 66th Armored Regiment, experimented with attacking under overhead artillery fire. The artillery, using time fuses, fired so that the shells burst in the air and the shrapnel fell around the tanks. This permitted tanks to attack with artillery support, forcing defenders to keep their heads down. Collier was in the first tank to run through the exercise. Later, when General Patton was told of the experiment, he came to watch and take part. He rode the bow gunner's seat, firing the machine gun, and burned out the barrel.

Training became more realistic. Major General Harmon remembered that on one exercise, when he stopped a point man and asked him his assignment, the man recited what he was supposed to do. Harmon decided that the men needed to be trained to react, not to recite procedures. The training began to reflect lessons learned in Tunis.

In late November, Companies G and H, 67th Armored Regiment, left French Morocco and joined the British 78th Division at Beja, Tunisia. On Christmas Day they took part in some of the heaviest fighting of the African campaign. The British and the American 1st Armored Division thought that the bigger M-4 Shermans would murder the Germans. In the first battle, the field was littered with the burning tank hulks, including his company commander's. With no more ammunition and almost out of gas, the tank commander, Sgt. John Pelicci, decided to pull back when they were not resupplied and had received no orders. As the tank broke its defilade position, the Germans intensified their fire. Only the excellent driving of Pfc. Bob Burkett saved the tank from destruction. As the tank pulled back, the tank commander was chewed out and ordered back into action. Finally some supplies were brought to it. The tank, named *Gallant*, was the only one to survive that battle. On January 11, 1943, the two companies returned to the 2d Armored Division. That experience was invaluable, because the men had received battle training that the American service schools could not offer.

In January, 1943, the division was alerted that something significant was about to occur in North Africa. While sitting in his tent one night, Lieutenant Colonel Dewey heard a radio bulletin referring to an impending visit by the president of the United States. Realizing the importance of such a message, he ordered the radio operator to answer in code, while he alerted Harmon. Colonel I. D. White's bandleader was ordered to report to division headquarters. White thought it was for some ceremony scheduled by Harmon. When the bandleader returned, he asked White to accompany him to a spot out of hearing of the regimental staff: "My God, colonel, the president is coming here." White, surprised and wondering why the bandleader was given that information instead of himself, asked, "Is that what they told you at division headquarters?" The band leader answered, "Oh no, sir. They wanted to know if my band could play 'Hail to the Chief.'" Company A, 67th Armored Regiment, served as an honor guard for the president and the British prime minister when they met in conference. The meeting was so secret that as President Roosevelt addressed the men of the division and had lunch with them in the field, some doubted that he was in North Africa. Chaplain Wurm, who was meeting with Archbishop Francis Spellman at Rabat, found it difficult to believe that Roosevelt was in Casablanca. He agreed that "anything is possible, though this story to our mind reaches the height of fantasy even though some men swear that they were a few yards from the president."

The Casablanca Conference added another story to the division's legends. Part of the time, the 41st Armored Infantry Regiment detailed soldiers to guard the president's and prime minister's quarters. One night when Churchill was returning to his house, the guard challenged him to identify himself. He did, but the soldier did not recognize the figure or voice. The soldier called for the sergeant of the guard, saying that someone was trying to pass, claiming to be the British prime minister. The guard added that he thought the person was a liar, divinely damned. The sergeant of the guard recognized Churchill and permitted him to enter the house. Later this was one of Churchill's favorite stories, fondly told.

The Casablanca Conference had a direct influence on future operations of the 2d Armored. It was decided to conduct further operations in the Mediterranean to help ease the pressure on the Russians, and since the troops were already there, it would be easier than attempting a cross-channel attack. Any such attack would have to be successful on the first landing, which was not viewed as a definite possibility at the time. The British argued that it would be better to force the Germans to stretch their military forces across the continent of Europe. They felt that the best way to do this would be to eliminate Italy from the war. It was therefore decided to attack Sicily as soon as conditions permitted; meanwhile the Allies would rearm the French. This decision posed a problem, however, since the Americans did not have sufficient shipping to send additional equipment, and the French would require training in the use of the American equipment.

While the 2d Armored Division was beginning to meet the demands placed on it by the Casablanca Conference, in the Tunisian battle the Germans attacked and routed the 1st Armored Division at Kasserine Pass in February 1943. There was an immediate need for replacements. Since the shipping problems prevented resupplying the tanks, self-propelled artillery and personnel from the United States, replacements had to come from the 2d Armored Division. Eisenhower was of the opinion that Hell on Wheels could be relieved of its occupation duty and sent to the Tunisian front, but his supply people told him that additional combat troops could not be supplied and maintained there. For this reason, the 2d Armored and 3d Infantry Divisions were stripped of trucks to send to the front. Eisenhower wanted to send one armored regiment to the east but concluded that there was not enough equipment left in the 2d Armored Division to get a regiment ready for action.

The tank companies were ordered to send the equivalent of one tank platoon, one officer and twenty-four men to the 1st Armored Division. Most units used this opportunity to get rid of their most undesirable soldiers, even some from the kitchens. Perkins thought that this was immoral and decided to send men who were trained and ready for combat. After much soul-searching and personal anguish, he sent his third platoon complete, without any changes in personnel. The remaining part of his H Company, 66th Armored Regiment, were shocked. He immediately reorganized the company, selecting the three best platoon sergeants, fifteen best drivers, gunners, tank commanders and crewmen, and divided them equally into three platoons. He promoted the men to their new ranks and produced a fine organization, to the surprise of everyone. It was a lesson in instant reorganization and what would have to be done in combat due to casualties.

In addition to the 2d Armored's loss of its men and most of its tanks, Harmon was transferred to the front. Originally he was to relieve the 1st Armored Division commander but instead became deputy corps commander and did not have to perform that unpleasant task—yet. After driving the Germans out of Kasserine Pass, Harmon returned to the 2d Armored Division and reported to his men about the fighting on the Tunisian front. Since Patton had replaced Maj. Gen. Lloyd Fredendall, Harmon thought that the division might be called to the front. If the division were not sent there, he indicated to the men that there would still be a bigger job ahead of them. Hinting that something was in the wind, he told them that they would be sent to amphibious school in the second week of March.

Later, when Harmon was reassigned as the new commanding general of the 1st Armored Division, he was replaced by Brig. Gen. Allen F. Kingman. Col. John H. Collier became commanding officer of Combat Command A. Col. I. D. White assumed command of Combat Command B. About this same time, Lt. Gen. Mark W. Clark began looking for a general officer who spoke French and had a technical knowledge of American equipment to become the senior advisor to the French armored units. Since Kingman had studied at the French Armor School between the wars and met the other requirement, he was offered the job and accepted it. When he arrived at his new headquarters, he found that many of the enlisted men assigned to him were the same men he had selected to aid the British a year earlier. Brig. Gen. Hugh J. Gaffey, former commanding general of Combat Command B, and most recently, chief of staff of II Corps (Patton's command), replaced Kingman as division commander. In spite of losing two commanders within thirty days, the men did not display a defeatist attitude; they had confidence in their leaders.

While the division was training for the invasion of Sicily and simultaneously rearming the French and the 1st Armored Division, Gen. George C. Marshall inquired if it were possible to rotate the 3d Infantry and 2d Armored Divisions with those in II Corps reserve. Eisenhower and Maj. Gen. Omar N. Bradley discussed the possibility. They advised against it because a major offensive was to begin in a few days, and the training for the invasion of Sicily was too advanced to justify wholesale transfers. Patton had been asked for his opinion about the transfer and whether the changes could be completed in about a week. His answer, apparently lost from the record, must have been in the negative, for the plan was not adopted.

The division was applying the lessons learned from its observers who had gone to the Tunisian front for extended duty with the 1st Armored Division. When they returned, they passed along their information to the remainder of the division, which was training from dawn until after dark. The division reinstituted chemical training and defenses against chemical agents. Live ammunition was used to make the men more cautious and to accustom them to the sounds of the battlefield. Many times they were supported by fighter-bomber aircraft. The men realized that while they were making progress, they still had much to learn.

Visiting the 2d Armored Division, Major General Harmon compared the battle ability of the Americans and Germans, concluding that while American doctrine was sound, the Germans were superior in their thoroughness and discipline. He was of the opinion that the Americans tried to do many things instead of trying to do a few things well. From experience, he thought that tank battles were won by the combatant which got in the first shot. The Americans needed to be trained to respond automatically, not to think. Addressing the officers and the noncommissioned officers, he advised them to be aware of the battle-weary soldier. When casualties reduced a squad or platoon to two or three men, they should be pulled out of the line and rested; at that point, green but vigorous men would be of more value than tired veterans. He stressed that every man in the unit should be briefed on the mission, since leaders might be killed or wounded and a private might have to assume command. Such a briefing would insure the smooth completion of the mission.

Harmon believed that the Americans should have tank destroyers, with their three-inch guns, up with the tanks, unless the tanks had heavier guns. Tanks should move forward by bounds: one tank firing from a hull defilade position, while the second moved forward. That movement might be rapid or slow, depending on the situation. In addition, the tanks must learn to coordinate their movements with supporting infantry. He was somewhat critical of previous armor theory. Speed was missing from the battlefield; movement was slow and deliberate. The maneuvers had given the soldiers a false picture because of their failure to portray supply situations accurately, their lack of casualty evacuations and their failure to conduct proper reconnaissances. Speaking directly and critically to the division, he said, "In maneuvers we have been guilty of rewarding officers and men for grandstand moves such as would be impossible to make on the battlefield and which gave a false impression of what can be accomplished." He warned the men to be aware that if the Germans lost any ground it was axiomatic that they counterattacked to regain it. When capturing positions from the Germans, the American soldiers must be ready to meet that counterattack.

The plans for Operation HUSKY, the invasion of Sicily, were made in 1943. The assaulting forces, with the exception of Oklahoma's 45th Infantry Division, were battle-tested. The 2d Armored Division was to provide the armor for the assaulting divisions and to be their floating reserve. When the invasion was in the preliminary stage, Colonel Collier told General Kingman that if only one regiment were used in the landing, it should be his—especially since Colonel White and the 67th Armored Regiment had made the North African landing. However, both regiments were used.

In late April and early May 1943, the division moved to Oran to begin their amphibious training. They had been ordered to send one combat command to the Fifth Army training center for attachment to the 3d Infantry Division. Col. John H. Collier's Combat Command A was selected for this duty. The command was composed of the 66th Armored Regiment; 41st Armored Infantry Regiment (minus one battalion); 14th Artillery Battalion; B Company, 82d Reconnaissance Battalion; B Company, 48th Medical Battalion; A Company, 2d Armored Division Supply

Battalion; and C Company, 2d Armored Maintenance Battalion. Combat Command headquarters was augmented with personnel from division headquarters and the 142d Signal Company. Because of a shortage of rail equipment, a flash flood and a heavy concentration of both rail and road traffic it took a month to complete the move. Capt. Curtis M. Clark, F Company, 66th Armored Regiment, was ordered to take his tank company to Arzew. He encountered many delays en route. Finally he told the engineer to make no stops and ran the train at gunpoint. When he arrived at Arzew, he wrote a detailed report, which the remainder of the regiment used as a guide for working with French train crews. Clark received a twenty-three endorsement reprimand for his necessary but impolitic actions.

On his move, Perkins was treated to almost a similar action. At one train stop, the Red Cross appeared and fed the men ice cream with real fruit. He told his wife that at that time if Hannibal had appeared with his elephants loaded with gold and beautiful women, he would have been told to go away. One night, during this move, Perkins was asleep when the train stopped. He awoke and immediately went forward to the locomotive and found the engineer relieving himself with no apparent concern about getting the train moving again. Since the engineer had stopped at the foot of a steep grade, he had to back the train two or three miles before he had enough space to build up the necessary speed to get over the mountain.

After Combat Command A completed its move, Col. Maurice Rose returned to the division and assumed command of Combat Command A. He had gone with Harmon to the 1st Armored Division. On June 3, 1943, Combat Command A moved to Bizerte, became part of the 3d Infantry Division (Reinforced) and began rigorous training for the assault. This training consisted of speed marching, attacks on pillboxes, street fighting and the loading and unloading of various types of landing craft. On June 25, the 3d Infantry Division (Reinforced) made a practice invasion near Bizerte and El Djebel, with apparent success. After this landing the combat command returned to its bivouac area without its vehicles and spent the next several days checking the waterproofing of equipment, completing basic loads and making final arrangements for embarkation. Eisenhower's deputy, Maj. Gen. John P. Lucas, observing the landing, was impressed by the men and the competence of Rose.

At the port of Bizerte, the armor assault landing team was aboard but still waterproofing their vehicles. The metal shrouds, which were to keep water out of the intake and exhaust ports and the air vents in the top of the engine compartment, did not fit properly and required more masking tape and sealing compounds than had been allotted. Perkins tried to get the extra materials, but the quartermaster officer refused, stating that each unit was to receive only the set amount. Perkins argued that if his team failed to get ashore then in all probability the following units would fail also. The quartermaster colonel was not impressed. Perkins gathered his seventeen tank commanders, telling them of the problem and then sent them to find the colonel's supply. They returned with the information, whereupon Perkins took the tankers to the truck and doled out the necessary amounts. The corporal who was guarding the truck rushed away to bring back his captain, who drew his weapon and ordered the raiders away. Perkins showed his own weapon, told the captain to go to hell, and finished the job. The tank commanders rushed their extralegally obtained materials to their LSTs and hid them. They were under orders to admit to no one, not even a general, that they had the material. Perkins leaped into his jeep and headed out of the dock area, only to be stopped by an armed guard. He bluffed the guard, telling him that he was en route to prefer charges against the colonel. He continued on to headquarters, 66th Armored Regiment, where he told Colonel Collier what had happened. Collier had Perkins hide in a tent near regimental headquarters in case MPs were sent to capture him. Later, Collier had Perkins taken across Lake Bizerte, where he hid on the LSTs until the convoy sailed.

The remainder of the division assembled at Monad for the move to Port aux Poules, about twenty miles east of Oran. Moving the tanks and half-tracks of the division took a month, because it was made over a single-track railroad which was subject to frequent washouts, and the number of freight cars available permitted shipping only about one medium tank company at a time. The wheeled vehicles moved overland. While the division was preparing for the invasion of Sicily, it had to resupply itself with tanks and artillery. Since supplies from the United States were slow in reaching North Africa, the division had to get some equipment from the 1st Armored Division. One supply officer, 1st Lt. James M. Burt, recalled signing a hand receipt for "so many acres of armored equipment." 1st Lt. Morton Eustis, who had gone AWOL from the Air Corps to join the 2d Armored, unofficially modified the jeeps of C Company, 82d Reconnaissance Battalion. He mounted British machine guns on them. Feeling that the jeeps did not afford sufficient firepower, he decided to see if he could acquire some machine guns and mounts. Putting on his old Air Corps insignia, Eustis went to an Air Corps base where he got ten British machine guns and 150,000 rounds of ammunition. He designed the mount, taught the men how to use the weapons and finally gained approval for the weapons from his battalion and division commanders.

For the invasion, Colonel I. D. White's Combat Command B had the 3d Battalion, 67th Armored Regiment (minus two platoons); A Company, 41st Armored Infantry; three firing batteries of the 78th Artillery; C Company, 82d Reconnaissance Battalion; B Company, 17th Engineer Battalion, a detachment from Company E of the same battalion; D Battery, 107th Coast Artillery (Antiaircraft Artillery); and a detachment from the 48th Medical Battalion. The remainder of the division, not assigned to Combat Command A, was controlled by the 2d Armored Division commander, to be used at his discretion.

Collier was especially pleased to get to the training area and establish good relations with the navy. They had food, especially fruits and juices. The rear-echelon personnel in Algeria had appropriated the small stoves intended for the use of the tankers so that the support units could have hot water for shaving. The men were living on K-ration supplement, without any of the accessory packs which had breads, seasonings, crackers and jellies. The 66th Armored regimental commander recalled that as they sailed for Sicily his surgeon told him the command was about 15 percent underweight.

Combat Command B trained for the assault in much the same way as Combat Command A. Tactical training consisted of fighting and capturing villages and combined arms team work, all making the maximum use of live ammunition. Sgt. Fred Smith, A Company, 17th Engineers, recalled that one experiment was to build the pontoon bridges on board the LSTs and push them into shore. On a trial run at Arzew, the bridge was being pushed shoreward; the men were riding it and enjoying their "accidental" spills into the Mediterranean Sea. General Patton happened by, and, seeing that only the platoon leader was dry, ordered him into the drink. Patton told the engineer officer that when the men were dripping wet, the officer should be also. The command underwent amphibious training: for the most part, loading and unloading the various types of assault ships; some practice landings to familiarize the troops with landing problems; and experimentation with firing tank guns from the decks of the ships. Major General Gaffey was not entirely satisfied with the naval support. Beach gradients had forced the navy to experiment with various unloading procedures. One method was to unload the tanks from an LST (landing ship tank) to an LCT (landing craft tank) with its sides cut out. This method, slow and laborious during very calm seas, was difficult at night and all but impossible in rough seas. Gaffey later stated that "except for very junior officers" the navy paid little attention to the practice landings and did not mention LST weight limitations. Later, the navy indicated that the LST's were overloaded and that Combat Command B would have to meet weight limitations imposed by the navy. If the division had accepted the weight limitations, only one medium tank company could have been taken to Sicily.

While training was being conducted, Combat Command B started to load the transports. The ships lacked sufficient antiaircraft weapons, so for the second time the 2d Armored Division placed its antiaircraft weapons on the decks to help protect the ships. At this time army personnel were under the control of the navy. When the order came to load, the personnel boarded at night for security reasons. The vacated bivouac areas were taken over by men staying behind. The rear detachment constructed dummy tents and other facilities to convince any spying eyes that all was normal. A signal detachment took over the radio traffic patterns to confuse the Germans and Italians. All orders and plans were kept under guard in a locked room; all orders to subordinates were given without explanation or discussion.

One final inspection occurred before the convoy sailed. On June 23, a review was conducted before King George VI of England. Accompanying the monarch, Eisenhower had an opportunity to inspect the 2d Armored Divison and the 82d Airborne Division, which he pronounced to be in splendid shape with fine discipline. The LST carrying part of C Battery, 14th Artillery, loaded and sailed for Bizerte. Corp. Samuel Tackitt remembered that as it pulled into the harbor, the officers lined the bridge to see the battle damage. The enlisted men tried to come up on deck, but the officers, army and navy, wanted them below. A sniper shot rang out, and the officers came tumbling off the bridge like "turtles off a log," according to Tackitt. The enlisted men then gave a cheer for the sniper.

The convoy sailed from Bizerte on July 6. It stopped at Tunis, rendezvousing with the other elements of the convoy which had sailed later. While awaiting sailing orders, the threat of air attack was on everyone's mind. One night a false alarm caused the LSTs carrying E Company, 66th Armored Regiment, to open fire. The company commander, Capt. John R. Werts, who was from Ninety-Six, South Carolina, had a pronounced southern accent which accounted for his nickname "Ajax

Fo-Fo'' (Four-Four). Sensing that it was a false alarm, he commanded, ''Cease dat fahr! Cease dat fahr! But Lawd, ain't it purty!''

All the elements met off the coast of Malta on D minus one. During the trip, the convoy was hit by a storm, the most severe in recent years, which caused some loss of small craft and equipment. There was also damage to some of the special floating ramps which were to be used to unload the equipment. And the misery of seasickness did little to calm minds or improve morale.

For the second time, Hell on Wheels was about to participate in the most difficult of military operations—an assault landing on a hostile shore. This time, unlike North Africa, the enemy's reactions were predictable. However, large questions were in the minds of the officers and men: would the enemy counterattack before the equipment was ashore or would it wait for the Americans to move inland? The men hoped that their many hours' training had prepared them for the combat to come.

Chapter 9

OPERATION HUSKY:
THE INVASION OF SICILY

The Americans still wanted a cross-channel attack but realized they did not have the men or equipment to stage such an assault in 1943. Sicily was the next logical invasion site if the Allies continued operations in the Mediterranean. The island, located two miles from Italy and ninety miles from North Africa, straddled British supply lines and forced them to keep two fleets in the Mediterranean Sea. The invasion of Sicily was intended to make the Mediterranean supply lines more secure, to ease German pressure on Russia, to intensify pressure on Italy and to keep the United States active in the conflict.

The decision to attack Sicily was aided and abetted by a unique British intelligence plan. MINCEMEAT was carried out in May 1943. The scheme was to plant false documents on a corpse and place it off the coast of Spain, so that Spanish and later German officials could get their hands on the documents. The correspondence indicated that the landing on Sicily was only a cover for landings that were to occur on the Greek coast or on the island of Sardinia. The "man who never was" lured some German reinforcements from Sicily.

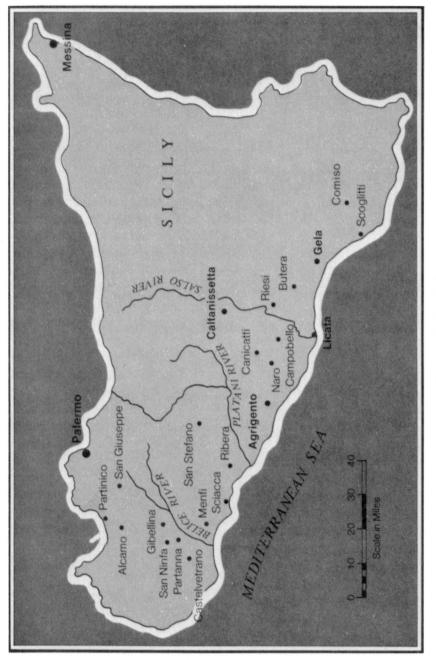

Figure 7. Sicily, 1943.

Intelligence sources estimated that initial resistance would come from six or seven Italian coastal and field divisions and two German divisions, a force of perhaps 208,000 Italians and 30,000 Germans. The German units were the Hermann Goering Panzer Division and the 15th Panzer Grenadier Division. Since the Italian air force was flying obsolete and inferior aircraft, the Germans had taken over the air defense of Italy. Intelligence indicated that the Germans and Italians had about 1,104 planes available, compared to the Allies' 3,680. While at sea, the task forces learned that the German airfields at Gela and Comiso had been bombed and put out of operation; this freed an estimated 3,000 to 4,000 additional Germans to man defenses in the area where Combat Command B was to land. The Americans expected to encounter concrete pillboxes, strong points surrounded by barbed wire, machine gun emplacements, tank traps and tank ditches. It was thought that the beaches were wired and mined.

The Axis navies, while also a concern of the planners, proved to be a negligible factor. The Italians lacked radar and aircraft carriers. Because of their previous heavy losses and the distances involved, the Italian navy was reluctant to use its fleet in Sicilian waters, unless ''an extraordinarily good opportunity presented itself'' and air protection was available. The Germans had a few landing craft at Messina and a few submarines in the Mediterranean, but the German admiralty decided not to reinforce the submarine fleet because of the increased dangers posed by Gibraltar. Due to these factors, the main defensive burden would rest upon the Axis ground forces. Also to the advantage of the Allies was the friction between the Axis partners caused by their own North African experiences.

The enemy seemed to have three options: defend at the beaches and counterattack when the Allied attack slowed; withdraw to favorable defensive positions and battle the invaders there; or surrender—which was not considered a serious possibility. The Americans thought that the Germans would not participate in counterattacks against the beachhead. The Italians planned to fight at the water's edge, with a small force close to the beaches and a reserve force to bolster any seriously threatened sector. The major flaw of the Axis plan was their lack of transportation. The German units would have to form the reserve, because of their mobility. They would be capable of independent action and able to move without orders from the Italian commander; the Germans thought the Italian will to fight had all but disappeared. If a determined counterattack were launched before the Americans could land tanks and artillery, the

Germans felt that it might be possible to push them back into the sea. At Gela this plan almost worked.

The Americans planned to land in the Gulf of Gela over a distance of about seventy miles. About half of that distance was sandy shoreline; the remainder was rocky points and low cliffs, while inland there were plains surrounded by mountains. The three American beaches were considered ideal for landing, but they were also ideal for counterattacks. If the Italians and Germans carried out their plans to defend the island, the Americans could be in for a difficult time. The invasion forces were commanded by British Gen. Sir Harold R. L. G. Alexander. In his opinion, the main effort would fall on the British Eighth Army, commanded by Gen. Bernard L. Montgomery, while the American Seventh Army, commanded by Lt. Gen. George S. Patton, Jr., would shield the British left flank. This plan relegated the Americans to a secondary role, which neither the men nor their fiery, hard-fighting commander thought appropriate.

The Seventh Army was scheduled to land at three different sites. On the east, CENT FORCE, the 45th Infantry Division (the Oklahoma National Guard division), was to land at Scoglitti. In the center, DIME FORCE, the 1st Infantry Division and the 2d Armored Division (minus Combat Command A), was to land at Gela. These two landings were under the American II Corps, commanded by Maj. Gen. Omar N. Bradley. On the west, JOSS FORCE, the 3d Infantry Division reinforced by Combat Command A of the 2d Armored, was to land at Licata. One other division, the 82d Airborne, was supposed to make an air drop in the Gela region to aid the landing force. JOSS was a separate command from II Corps, whose composition had been decided before it left North Africa. The infantrymen and Combat Command A had trained together in landing operations, securing initial objectives and establishing beachheads. Its first-day mission was to capture the port and airfield at Licata and take the high ground soon after. Patton wanted all three forces to take their initial objectives in three days.

Combat Command A sailed with the 3d Infantry Division as its reserve force. It was to be ready to execute one of four missions: to advance north on Campobello di Licata, to move west on Palma di Montechiaro, to move east to reinforce II Corps or to meet and destroy any enemy counterattack from the east, north or west. Col. John H. Collier warned his 66th Armored Regiment that they were to maintain American ideals in human relations. The men were charged with the proper care and treatment of women and children; no misconduct in that area would be tolerated.

The task force arrived at its station at 2:45 A.M. on July 10, 1943, and the 3d Infantry Division and the 3d Ranger Battalion went ashore a few minutes later. Until the convoy had actually sailed, Capt. Norris Perkins was the only man in his company to know the details of the landing. This was in keeping with the decision to tell only regimental, battalion and company commanders of this objective beforehand. While at sea, he faced the task of telling his men. Adding to his problem was the strict radio silence now in force. One day while the five LCTs carrying his company were maintaining their relative positions by circling, Perkins sent his orders and instructions to each vessel by means of 1st Lt. Cameron J. Warren, who stripped naked and swam to each of the LCTs. As the small flotilla neared the coast, the LCT ship captain, a navy ensign, was unable to recognize any terrain features and confessed to Perkins that he was lost and confused. Perkins drew a profile of how the landing area should look from out at sea. When dawn arrived, they located the landing area four or five miles to the west of their position. The initial assault, aided by the 3d Battalion, 66th Armored Regiment, quickly cleared and established the beachhead. By daylight most resistance had been overcome; the landings were accomplished on schedule. The other elements of Combat Command A were to land as quickly as the situation permitted.

Perkins was the first tanker to cross the Salso River and enter Licata. Fearing heavy resistance, he sent Lieutenant Warren's platoon up the east bank of the river to find a point where he could cross and flank the town. Warren had some problems, losing two tanks in the mud or on the slippery banks. The town fell with minimal resistance. They grabbed the abandoned airfield without incident, but began to receive fire from the defended hill mass to their front. Perkins directed his third platoon to attack from the flank while he led the other platoons against the enemy front.

On the trip from North Africa, one platoon leader had not closed the hatch of his tank and lost the use of his radio. Therefore, the platoon sergeant, Hubert Gwinn, was directing the platoon. During the battle, Lt. Col. Amzi R. Quillian, battalion commander of the 3d Battalion, 66th Armored Regiment, was listening in on the company command channel and questioning Perkins. Because of the terrain, Perkins could hear Gwinn, but he could not hear Colonel Quillian. Gwinn, after listening to "Hazel 6 this is John 6, what is your position and situation," took matters into his own hands. Thinking that it might be a German fluent in English,

Gwinn said, "Listen you lousy son of a bitch, if you are a goddamn Nazi, just keep on listening, maybe you'll learn something." After the battle, in which the company destroyed six 75mm guns and several pillboxes, Quillian joined the company and asked to meet the sergeant. Perkins, knowing the situation, introduced the men: "Sergeant Gwinn, this is John 6." The colonel congratulated Gwinn and everyone laughed.

The bulk of Combat Command A spent most of the day on their ships, subjected to continuous bombing. The LCI carrying B Company, 41st Armored Infantry Regiment, was rocked by a near miss. The men were shaken and scared, but uninjured. By noon, infantry and engineers landed at the port of Licata and began unloading. By working all night, the men were able to unload all the personnel and about two-thirds of the equipment. When finished, the men went to assembly areas north of town. On July 11, enemy bombers hit an LST carrying about half the equipment for Combat Command headquarters, a medium tank company and vehicles for an infantry company. Before the LST sank, the men managed to unload fourteen medium tanks but were unable to save the remainder of the gear. Personnel losses were estimated to be about 25 percent of the men on the ship.

During the night of July 10–11, the 62d Armored Field Artillery Battalion and two batteries of the 443d Coast Artillery Battalion (Antiaircraft Artillery) were attached to Combat Command A. For the 62d, this was the first of a long series of attachments to the division. At midnight, Brig. Gen. Maurice Rose was ordered to attack at 6:00 A.M. on July 11, to secure the towns of Naro and Canicatti and the hills to its north, against possible counterattacks from the German 15th Panzer Grenadier Division, which had been spotted returning to the west. Rose gave orders that the remainder of the command close on the main body in company-size units as soon as they landed.

The reconnaissance company moved out at 3:30 A.M., leading the combat command into Naro. The remainder of the command followed at 6:00. Initially the men met resistance from snipers and some machine guns. In addition, enemy planes strafed and bombed the column but inflicted little damage. The worst problems were caused by the poor roads and difficult terrain. Just outside the town, the column was met by two civilians, the mayor and his small son. The mayor told them that the town was unoccupied and the people were not hostile. The father and son rode back into town on the hood of Col. Sidney R. Hinds's half-track, at the head of the column. The exits to the town were quickly secured and two officers and a platoon of infantry were left to police the town, while awaiting AMGOT (Allied Military Government of Occupied Territory) officials. The combat command then moved north, coiling in the woods. The 2d Armored Division had captured its first Sicilian town.

Shortly after Naro was captured, the American Air Corps sent over a flight of eighteen B-26 bombers, which partially destroyed the town. The attack resulted from the Air Corps's refusal to permit direct air-ground communications and its refusal to recognize the fluidity of a battlefield situation. Unfortunately, the Air Corps was using phase lines (prominent terrain features used as control devices in fast-moving situations) and refused to recognize that some advances were more rapid than others. Usually, the Air Corps was about twenty-four hours behind the actual battlefield situations. This was not the first time, nor would it be the last, that American troops suffered because of the uncoordinated efforts of the Air Corps and ground troops.

After taking Naro, Maj. Gen. Lucian Truscott, commanding general of the 3d Infantry Division, ordered the Combat Command to send reconnaissance elements toward Canicatti. B Company, 82d Reconnaissance Battalion, proceeded about a mile before spotting some Italian soldiers. First Lieutenant W. R. Neilson brought up two light tanks and started through the narrow mountain pass. Proceeding along the narrow road, the tanks halted before a curve—that was defended by four large-caliber guns. Two 37mm assault guns were brought forward to help the advance, but Italian machine guns on the high ground took the reconnaissance company under fire. The Americans, however, fought their way out of the trap without a loss. The remainder of the column, moving north behind the reconnaissance company, was attacked by German aircraft. After fighting off the planes, the command proceeded with the infantrymen of G Company, 41st Armored Infantry Regiment, riding the tanks of D Company, 66th Armored Regiment; this was possibly the first time that this happened, at least in actual battle.

Since the enemy was dug in, B Company, 82d Reconnaissance Battalion, called for infantry help. After G Company, 41st Armored Infantry Regiment, arrived with the tanks of D Company, 66th Armored Regiment, they made slow progress against the Italians. Under the cover of darkness, the enemy pulled out and the Americans had the pass, four miles short of their objective, Canicatti. During the night the Americans moved forward to capture the high ground south of the town and made plans to resume the attack the following morning.

The attack to capture Canicatti was preceded by a ten-minute artillery barrage, after which the assaulting forces were to take the town and the hill mass to the north. After the barrage lifted, a white flag was seen from a building in the town. Brigadier General Rose and Colonel Hinds mounted their vehicles and headed into town to receive the surrender. Making their way along the road, they were fired on by artillery. Rose and his party dived into a nearby ditch while their men returned a thirty-minute artillery barrage. Even before the enemy fire, the American assaulting force had been moving into position.

Perkins's H Company, 66th Armored Regiment, and G Company, 41st Armored Infantry Regiment, were selected for the assault. The infantrymen, riding the tanks, were to dismount and assist the tanks when resistance was encountered. When the task force came within three-fourths of a mile of the town, it began to receive accurate and intense artillery fire. The infantry dismounted and took cover. Perkins was ordered to move into the city. He could not make contact with the infantrymen, so he ordered his company to attack through the town with all guns firing at any balcony, window, street intersection or roof parapet which might hide a sniper or bazookaman.

As the tankers reached the north edge of town, Perkins's tank began to draw heavy fire from large-caliber guns some 2,500 yards to his front. After firing one round at the antitank guns, Perkins directed his tank behind a small stone wall. A shell hit the muzzle, forcing it into a violent recoil just as Perkins was reaching into the breech to clear out some spilled powder. The breech broke his arm in two places, and the tank was bathed in flames. The crew jumped out as Perkins cut the bedding loose; the men hastily withdrew to a building some 100 yards to the rear, where they splinted Perkins's arm. Perkins directed the men to accompany him back to the tank. He crawled inside to retrieve a secret code, while the others splinted Sgt. Tim McMahan's leg. Hailing a nearby tank, Perkins rode ahead to finish the battle. Corp. Kenneth F. Grogan, Perkins's driver, told a correspondent for the *Armored News,* that the company commander was finally ordered off the battlefield and forced to have medical treatment. The town fell about 3:00 P.M. and the mystery of the white flag was explained. It was a Red Cross flag flying atop the hospital. For his part, Perkins was awarded the Distinguished Service Cross. 1st Lt. Cameron Warren assumed command of the company.

After the town was secured, the infantrymen mounted the tanks and moved to take the high ground to the northeast. H Company, 41st Armored Infantry Regiment, attacked the ridges north of town. Progress was slow, but the infantrymen secured their objectives against enemy machine gun and antitank fire. During the night the command was reorganized and the following morning (July 13) assaults were launched to clear the high ground northwest of Canicatti. The attack started at 4:00 P.M. and by 10:30 A.M. the enemy had been driven out of positions overlooking the town. After capturing the high ground, Combat Command A sent reconnaissance patrols toward the outskirts of Caltanissetta.

During the night two men, an officer and an enlisted man, moved through enemy lines into Caltanissetta, stole two bicycles and rode them back, reporting to their regimental commander, Colonel Hinds. After seizing Canicatti, Combat Command A was the 3d Infantry Division's reserve force. While in that role, Rose continued to send out reconnaissance patrols which were so aggressive that they captured several towns without the aid of the main body of the command.

Patton, a forceful leader, was not content with conducting secondary attacks and requested permission from Alexander to capture Agrigento. The Army Group commander replied that he would permit that, if Patton could capture the town by a reconnaissance in force. Patton promptly ordered Truscott to take the town by a reconnaissance in force—all the force he had: the 3d Infantry Division, part of the 82d Airborne Division, two Ranger Battalions and a task force from the 2d Armored Division.

On July 17, when it was reported that a strong enemy column was approaching from the northwest toward Aragona and Comotini, the 1st Battalion, 66th Armored Regiment, and the 14th Armored Artillery Battalion were alerted to meet the threat. However, air reconnaissance failed to reveal any such enemy and the armored troops were not used. That night, Combat Command A was ordered to assist the 15th Infantry Regimental Combat Team in its attack on Serradifalco. Again Rose pushed strong reconnaissance elements into the area. Patrols of the 41st Armored Infantry Regiment moved toward San Cataldo and Caltanissetta ahead of the 15th Infantry Regiment. A reserve force of tanks and infantry went into assembly areas north of Canicatti, ready for use. Patrols from the Reconnaissance Company, 66th Armored Regiment, captured and secured Serradifalco by 10:30 P.M. An hour later, Company E of the 41st Armored Infantry Regiment captured San Cataldo. By 7:30 the next morning, patrols from the 66th Armored and the 41st Armored Infantry Regiment had captured and secured Caltanissetta. By July 18, the area of the 3d Infantry Division was secure and Patton ordered Combat Command A to rejoin the 2d Armored Division in army reserve.

The 2d Armored Division (minus Combat Command A) sailed with the assault convoy. KOOL FORCE, as the Seventh Army reserve, was to execute one of two plans. Under Plan A, the tanks would land on an established beachhead, assemble and await the orders of the Seventh Army commander. If the division had to carry out Plan B, it would force a landing at one or more beaches and aid one of the other assaulting forces. Either plan would be carried out on Patton's order. KOOL FORCE, commanded by Maj. Gen. Hugh J. Gaffey (an artilleryman and a pioneer in armor warfare), was composed of two major groups: the 18th Infantry Regimental Combat Team, commanded by Col. George A. Smith, and Combat Command B, commanded by Col. I. D. White. In Smith's force was his infantry regiment from the 1st Infantry Division, the 32d Artillery Battalion, a company of engineers, a medical company and two tank platoons from I Company, 67th Armored Regiment. Combat Command B contained the 3d Battalion, 67th Armored Regiment; the 1st Battalion, 41st Armored Infantry Regiment; the 78th Armored Artillery Battalion; Companies C and D, 82d Reconnaissance Battalion; and B Company, 17th Engineer Battalion.

The convoy arrived off the Gela coast about 2:00 A.M. on July 10. As the reserve, it had to spend most of the day aboard ship, enduring shell fire and bombing attacks. At 1:30 P.M. Gaffey went to the flagship. Patton told him that Plan A was in effect. Gaffey sent a landing party ashore, under Col. Redding F. Perry, division chief of staff, to make provisions for assembly areas, routes and guides. Gaffey had been told that the navy would select the proper beach. However, either Maj. Gen. Terry Allen, commanding general of the 1st Infantry Division, or his assistant division commander, Brig. Gen. Theodore Roosevelt, decided that the tanks should land at a different site, because the beaches might be mined. Other factors in the change were the deep draft of the LSTs, the unsatisfactory gradient of the original landing site and the fact that some of the pontoons to be used in unloading the tanks were damaged, while others had landed at Scoglitti, out of the division zone. These changes, and the task force's arrival in cruising formation rather than landing formation, caused a two-hour delay in the landing. Because of the delay the infantry elements were to be landed first, as it was not feasible to return to sea, regroup and arrive in landing formation.

The first troops to land were the headquarters of Combat Command B, which went ashore about 5:00 P.M. on D day (July 10). Colonel I. D. White decided to use the area near the Gela-Faullo landing zone as the assembly area. The infantry elements started ashore about 6:00 P.M. and

The division practices unloading from LSTs prior to the invasion of Sicily.

by midnight were joined by all Combat Command personnel. The tanks were in the process of being off-loaded from the LSTs to the LCTs, but fatigue and high seas caused the navy to postpone landing more vehicles until daylight on July 11. Two platoons of medium tanks had been landed about 2:00 A.M., but they stuck in the soft sand of the beach. The first day had been a rough one for the Americans. They had withstood several Italian counterattacks but had also lost the pontoons to bring their tanks ashore. If the Germans attacked the beachhead before the 2d Armored Division landed its armored vehicles, the situation could become desperate.

The next morning, when unloading resumed, the third platoon, C Company, 82d Reconnaissance Battalion, received its vehicles and was given the mission of locating enemy tanks operating against the east flank of the 1st Infantry Division near the Acate River. Finding the enemy, they kept him under observation until later in the day, when G Company, 67th Armored Regiment, drove him off. Two German divisions formed in the valley northeast of Gela, attacked toward the beachhead and came very close to defeating the American landing efforts. When the German counterattack began about 8:00 A.M. on July 11, thirty to forty German tanks attacked the 2d Battalion, 16th Infantry Regiment, on the 1st Infantry Division's right flank between Gela and Niscemi. Six officers and forty-five enlisted men repulsed German attacks with one antitank gun, a bazooka and finally a tank destroyer that joined them later in the day. This action saved the right flank.

The headquarters element of Combat Command B had stayed ashore during the night. In the morning Col. I. D. White returned to the beach, attempting to find any LSTs that might be carrying the tanks. The Combat Command executive officer, Lt. Col. Briard P. Johnson, remained at the command post to guide any troops and vehicles to the assembly areas. Johnson and the headquarters personnel were watching the 26th Regimental Combat Team attack along the Gela-Ponto Olivo road toward the Ponto Olivo airfield on the west side of the plain. Thirty or forty German tanks were observed in the middle of the plain and on a small hill about 4,000 meters from Combat Command B's command post. Until then, the enemy tanks had been screened from view by the hill mass to the north, occupied by the 18th Infantry Regiment in reserve. The tanks, heading toward the beach, must have passed through and/or around the west flank of the 16th Infantry Regiment, which was pushing toward Niscemi. This gave the Germans an apparently unopposed approach to the beach.

When the headquarters of Combat Command B landed, it did not have any of its vehicles. They borrowed a quarter-ton truck with a radio and a three-quarter-ton weapons carrier. The light truck and radio were at the beach with Colonel White. Johnson immediately sent Captain Arthur Pottle, Combat Command S-2, to alert Colonel White and to bring 1st Lt. James A. White and his platoon of four tanks to the command post. While Pottle was on his mission, Johnson tried unsuccessfully to locate the 32d Artillery Battalion which he thought was in the area. Surveying the scene through binoculars, he observed shells falling in and around the German tanks. Apparently one was damaged, for the crew dismounted and fled. When Lieutenant White's platoon arrived, he emplaced them while others counted approximately forty enemy tanks on the plain, heading for the beach.

The four American tanks were placed in firing positions astride the Gela-Vittoria road where it entered the high ground on the east side of the plain. Three tanks were on the north side of the road; one (Lieutenant White's) was on the south. The four American tanks began firing, with Johnson standing on the back deck of the platoon leader's tank and pointing out targets. The tanks scored hits against the approaching German panzers at the same time that indirect fire from artillery batteries, 4.2-inch mortars and perhaps naval gunfire was landing in the area. The huge amount of indirect fire concealed the presence of direct fire weapons. About the time that the American tanks started firing, a lone 105mm howitzer from the 32d Artillery Battalion arrived, and the chief of section reported to Johnson for instructions. The howitzer was placed in position about forty to fifty yards from Lieutenant White's tank and started firing at the Germans.

Colonel White rushed Companies D and C (minus one platoon) of the 82d Reconnaissance Battalion, armed only with their individual weapons, to the command post. He feared that the Germans might be supporting their tanks with infantry. The men from the reconnaissance battalion had a grandstand view of the fight, as no enemy fire was yet falling in their location. When the enemy finally discovered that the punishing fire was coming from their flank, they fired at the suspected location, forcing the dismounted men to seek cover. Sgt. Otis Brake, C Company, 82d Reconnaissance Battalion, Johnson's old company, reported to him and offered to help. He acted as a runner between White, Johnson and the three tanks on the north side of the road. The use of reconnaissance personnel in such a manner caused their battalion commander, Lt. Col. Paul A. Disney, to say later that this was a case of "grasping at straws."

Four to six German tanks reached the main road, stopping near a farm building. Johnson, who had visited the howitzer and given the gun crew a lesson in leading targets, returned to the tanks and resumed pointing out targets. The Germans were difficult to see because of the buildings. The tanks on the north side of the road expended their ammunition and pulled back 400–500 yards. The Germans started moving forward and were taken under fire by White's tanks and by the 105mm howitzer. One tank was destroyed and the others pulled back.

Johnson sent Maj. Joe A. Clema to the rear for more ammunition, as White and the howitzer each had about four rounds left. Clema was unable to find any ammunition but did return with an M-7 self-propelled 105mm howitzer belonging to Cannon Company, 16th Infantry Regiment. One German tank that had stayed near the farm buildings had turned its turret toward the Americans. The infantry captain commanding Cannon Company did not think standing guard over a German tank was a proper mission for the self-propelled howitzer, but Clema finally persuaded him. The towed howitzer belonging to the 32d Artillery Battalion departed to find its unit.

The 2d Armored Division was acutely aware that tanks were needed and did not spend time de-waterproofing them, as Samuel Eliot Morison has alleged, but rushed them inland as quickly as they landed. The tank tracks became so entangled in the Summerville matting (chicken wire placed on the ground to give better traction) that it had to be cut from the tracks and drive sprockets. Several tanks tried to avoid the matting by traversing the soft sand, which resulted in their throwing one or both tracks.

When Maj. Clifton B. Batchelder, executive officer of the 3d Battalion, 67th Armored Regiment, came ashore, Colonel White told him to take the American tanks inland to meet the German panzer attack. Batchelder asked what the plans and orders were. White remembered being told later that his rather abrupt answer was "Plans hell! This may be Custer's last stand." The executive officer led the tanks of G Company to the nearby sand dunes at about the time that the Germans started retreating through the smoke and about the time that the self-propelled howitzer from Cannon Company arrived to help the American tankers. Possibly the retreating German tanks became involved with the 26th Infantry Regiment as they disappeared.

The attack of the Hermann Goering Panzer Division was beaten off with a loss of fifteen German tanks, while the Americans had only three men wounded. Sheer bravery won the day for the Americans. During the battle, two tanks had stoppages or malfunctions with their main gun. The sergeant tank commanders calmly got out of their tanks and cleaned the bores of their weapons while under fire. One commander then led his tank to a better firing position.

About 11:00 A.M., the 1st Battalion, 41st Armored Infantry Regiment (minus Company A), was sent to join the Rangers at Gela for a proposed attack on Mount Lapa. The tanks were pulled out about noon to support the regiments of the 1st Infantry Division. By dark, all the tanks of the 3d Battalion, 67th Armored Regiment, were ashore, along with eight light tanks of D Company, 82d Reconnaissance Battalion. The following day, the remainder of the tanks came ashore, giving the force a total of forty-two medium tanks attached to the 1st Infantry Division and twenty-two medium and twenty-one light tanks under Combat Command B.

Late on the night of July 11 Gaffey issued orders for KOOL FORCE to protect the flanks of the 1st Infantry Division and to be prepared to counterattack enemy advances from the northwest or northeast. Combat Command B was to assemble and be prepared to counterattack to the northwest, northeast or southeast. It was to extend reconnaissance efforts to the southeast by sending out the 18th Infantry, tank remnants and the engineers. C Company, 82d Reconnaissance Battalion, took numerous prisoners and established contact with the 45th Infantry Division at Vittoria and Comiso. The engineers (B Company, 17th Engineer Battalion) put in minefields, prepared the bridges for demolition and removed several enemy minefields.

G Company, 67th Armored Regiment, was attached to the 16th Regiment. The following morning this force encountered antitank fire, artillery and bombing and strafing attacks. The tanks were ordered to withdraw. As they began to pull back, 1st Lt. K. E. Beichley's tank was damaged and fell behind. The next four tanks passed him and stumbled into a German ambush. One tank, commanded by Sgt. William Belz, fought the German Tiger tank at a range of 100 yards but lost. However, as three German tanks passed Beichley's position, he destroyed them. The fight raged in the 16th Infantry zone. The German tanks and infantry supported by aircraft attacked several times, apparently seeking to drive a wedge between the American forces or to reach the beachhead. By evening, after losing six tanks and three other vehicles, the Germans withdrew, leaving the Americans in position.

The third platoon of H Company was assigned a separate road-blocking mission. Later in the day, it and A Company of the 41st Armored Infantry Regiment, were put in the gap on Hill 211 northeast of Gela, between the 16th and 26th Infantry Regiments. During the day, the tank platoon destroyed three German tanks and a command car. Being on dominant terrain, these two platoons were subjected to heavy artillery fire. However, they maintained their positions until reassigned to their parent units on July 16.

In the 26th Infantry regimental zone, two platoons of H Company, 67th Armored Regiment, were supporting its advance to capture the Ponto Olivo airdrome. Supported by tanks firing as artillery, the infantry captured Il Costelluccia after the tanks had knocked out several pillboxes and machine gun nests. 1st Lt. Van Valkenberg's tanks overran the airdrome, losing one tank to a land mine. On Hill 211, the third platoon of H Company could see the battle below, and their fire knocked out two tanks, a weapons carrier, a motorcycle and a personnel carrier. As the tankers overran the airfield, they captured a German artillery officer, four enlisted men and uncounted Italians.

The two platoons originally sent to Gela to support the Ranger attack on Mount Lapa received new missions. One platoon stayed to help the Rangers while the other was sent to aid the 26th Infantry. The attack to capture Mount Lapa was scheduled for the night of July 11, and the infantry phase had been accomplished. The attack was supported by Company A, 83d Chemical Battalion, firing 4.2-inch mortars and high-explosive shells. At dawn the tanks were told to expose themselves, hopefully drawing enemy fire—they did! Returning the fire, they destroyed several enemy pillboxes and machine guns. Mount Lapa was captured ahead of schedule. The tanks then reconnoitered the high ground beyond, destroying two artillery and mortar observation posts, and the Rangers took Mount Nicola.

The night of July 13 the Rangers and the 41st Armored Infantry were ordered to capture Butera, which the navy had begun shelling earlier in the day. Company C, 82d Reconnaissance Battalion, was to protect the flanks of the attacking force while the tank company, Company D, 82d Reconnaissance Battalion, was the force reserve. The Rangers, after capturing the city, were to take the high ground around Mount Lungo, which would protect the left flank of the 1st Infantry Division. The attackers had seen a white flag from the town, but they proceeded on schedule. Reaching the outskirts of the town, the Americans encountered heavy resistance. This was overcome; and with the capture of Butera by 3:00 A.M., a large number of Italian prisoners were taken. The reconnaissance platoons continued northward and were in position to aid the 1st Infantry Division capture Mazzarino, Pietraperzia and Caltanissetta.

From July 11 to 14, Combat Command B had attached most of its tanks to the 1st Infantry Division and guarded the flanks and filled in the gaps of the American lines. On the morning of July 14, all the tanks came under the control of the 2d Armored Division. Reports that enemy armor was massing southwest of Caltagirone required that the armor of Combat Command B again protect the right flank of the 1st Infantry Division. The outpost road-blocking units were relieved by the 18th Infantry Regiment and rejoined Combat Command B, which was massed as force reserve from that date.

On the morning of July 16, Allen reported that the 26th Infantry Regiment was being attacked by German tanks and needed help. Gaffey and Maj. Gen. Geoffrey Keyes, who happened to be in the headquarters at the time, departed to examine the situation. The division commander alerted D Company, 82d Reconnaissance, and the 78th Armored Artillery Battalion and led them to meet the enemy. Arriving at Mazzarino, the two generals received word that the attack had been repulsed and that their help was not needed. The armored force returned to its assembly areas near Butera.

That same day, Patton relieved the 2d Armored forces from patrols and outpost duty for maintenance and rehabilitation and ordered the division to assemble near Campobello. This rest period was needed to consolidate the division for a new move. At the time, Patton and others thought that the Americans were being improperly used in the Sicilian campaign. He planned a spectacular move which, if successful, would capture public attention and gain the favorable publicity which he thought the American soldiers needed and deserved.

He created a Provisional Corps under Major General Keyes, the original chief of staff of the 2d Armored Division, who requested the Hell on Wheels division as part of this force. He also had the 3d Infantry, the 82d Airborne and the Ranger Battalions. The missions of this provisional corps were to clean out western Sicily and capture Palermo. The 2d Armored Division was to follow the infantry division, ready to exploit their successes. The city, although a port and the original landing site favored by Patton, had ceased to be of strategic value. It was hoped that by capturing the Sicilian capital, they would seize headlines at home and convince the British that the Americans could fulfill their role in the war. Patton wanted the city taken in five days. The provisional corps assembled 100 miles from their objective, and with little or no transportation for the troops, captured the city in only four.

On July 18, Combat Command A was relieved of its attachment to the 3d Infantry Division. The Combat Command also lost its attachments, the 62d Armored Artillery Battalion and two batteries of the 443d Coast Artillery. By 1:30 P.M., it had joined the division at Campobello. While the division was assembling, the 82d Reconnaissance Battalion sent a patrol to Pietraperzia and captured it by noon; the men were favorably received by the civil population. The 82d Reconnaissance Battalion was then assigned to provide reconnaissance for the Provisional Corps. At the same time the division moved from its assembly areas toward Castelvetrano and went into assembly areas south of Agrigento before morning on July 19.

While the 2d Armored Division was moving and preparing for battle, the intelligence section was making estimates of the situation based on the information being received. The enemy was thought to have about 60,000 Italian soldiers guarding western Sicily. They were believed to be badly equipped, poorly armed and generally second-rate troops. The intelligence section saw three options for the enemy: to defend in place; to defend in successive positions and wage limited objective counterattacks; or to defend in position and counterattack the western flank of the advancing corps. Based on enemy reactions up to that time, it was thought that the Italians would occupy the American troops while the Germans withdrew to final defensive positions near Messina.

For most of July 19 and 20, the 2d Armored Division waited in reserve positions, but late in the evening of July 20 it was alerted to move to Ribera. It had to provide transportation for the 1st and 4th Ranger Battalions and the 82d Airborne Division, to place them in position to attack Castelvetrano. Meanwhile the Italian prisoners were helpfully providing information. They reported that the shoulders of the roads were mined, especially near roadblocks, and that booby traps could be expected. There was a report that the enemy was using gas, but this was considered erroneous. Sicily produced about 95 percent of the world's sulphur supply, and the burning sulphur produced a pungent odor and gas, which was nontoxic.

The Provisional Corps issued the attack order on July 20. The 2d Armored Division, reinforced by the 1st and 4th Ranger Battalions, was to move to assembly areas, refuel and be prepared for offensive action. Combat Command A was to lead the attack, followed by Combat Command B, which was to exploit the success of or support Combat Command A, as well as to protect defiles after Combat Command A had passed through them. The 82d Reconnaissance Battalion was to conduct reconnaissance on the front and flanks of Combat Command A, to block the southern exits from Castelvetrano and to protect the left flank and rear of the division. At the start, all artillery units were to be in direct support of Combat Command A and, except when actually moving, were to be in position to fire. Gaffey authorized and encouraged the use of captured enemy vehicles for clearing enemy minefields and supplementing the division's supply vehicles.

Company C, 82d Reconnaissance Battalion, preceded the 82d Airborne Division, making enemy contact at the Magazzolo River. After a brief fight, the company took fifty-five prisoners and continued to Ribera after removing the mines from the road. In taking the town, they acquired an additional seventy prisoners. On July 21, C Company reached Alcamo, where the Italian garrison surrendered with great pomp and ceremony. The company also captured a gasoline dump outside town and posted guards, while the rest of the unit pulled back to San Ninfa for the night. In the morning of July 22, C Company was to lead the 2d Armored Division into Palermo. Because the company had not been resupplied during the night and their gas tanks were almost empty, they decided to use the captured gas. An armed convoy brought it to the tanks, and apparently none of the vehicles were damaged from the substitute. This situation had arisen because supply vehicles had been pulled off the road by overzealous, ill-advised staff officers attempting to insure that the division's combat elements reached their proper assembly areas.

The 2d Armored's move from Agrigento to assembly areas west of the Belice River was made against great difficulties. The main bridges had been destroyed, causing detours through precipitous gorges and even railroad tunnels. Engineers worked to remove mines, to construct bypasses and to widen trails into roads. In addition, the division had to move across the rear of two infantry divisions, sharing the road with the two Ranger battalions and a separate infantry regiment.

On the move, Corp. Samuel Tackitt, driving a self-propelled howitzer, hit and destroyed a truck carrying troops of the 82d Airborne Divi-

sion. The paratrooper sergeant told Tackitt that the truck should not have
been in the road—a far cry from Fort Benning days when the two units
were "friendly" rivals. Orders were received to attack at 6:00 A.M. on
July 22 to capture Palermo by 8:00 P.M. that same day. The division was
charged with securing the port area and the harbor shipping and preventing their sabotage. It was to patrol the city and docks and maintain order
until relieved by the 3d Infantry Division.

Combat Command A crossed the Belice River line at 6:00 A.M. The
reconnaissance elements had made contact with the enemy, and the advanced guard (3d Battalion, 41st Infantry and E Company, 66th Armored
Regiment) was moving across the river when the command was ordered
to halt to permit the 39th Infantry Regimental Combat Team, 9th Infantry
Division, and the 4th Ranger Battalion to pass through their lines. When
the 2d Armored Division started moving again, it found the defiles defended by antitank guns and machine guns, wisely emplaced and well
defended by infantry. The strongpoints had to be eliminated one by one,
as the Italians defended each position until surrounded by infantry and
shelled by artillery or tanks. These skirmishes were fought by the reconnaissance and leading elements. On one of these squad and platoon type
missions to clear the high ground, Pfc. Philip L. Lamb, H Company, 41st
Armored Infantry Regiment, reached the top of the hill only to find
friendly Sicilians who greeted him as a long-lost relative.

The first determined enemy resistance occurred at the pass north of
San Giuseppe. Company C, 82d Reconnaissance Battalion, having captured San Ninfa at 9:30 A.M., disarmed the defenders and prepared to
continue northward. One of the Italians told them that the road was mined
and there were guns in position at the next pass. The company set out,
using its customary precautions. It was an ideal location for an ambush:
the road climbed up through a series of hairpin curves to a narrow pass at
the top. As they started up the narrow road, they encountered mines.
However, the mines had been stacked by the side of the road, rather than
put into the ground.

Proceeding onward, they met thirty Italians who laid down their
weapons and surrendered. The lead scout car had gone about a hundred
yards farther when the prisoners indicated that something was ahead.
Eustis and 1st Lt. Donald Chace conducted a reconnaissance by fire (i.e.,
firing into an area to see if enemy fire were returned) which was answered
by heavy weapons; the second shot destroyed the scout car. Every weapon
started firing. The two officers were trapped between the German fire and

American artillery fire, which had been called for and was falling in the area. Finally, the American artillery stopped, and the men moved forward, finding the first antitank gun destroyed. All resistance was overcome by 1:15 P.M. and the column moved through the pass. The enemy had been caught off guard and did not have time to prepare for the 2d Armored Division. The original supposition that the enemy would delay in a series of positions had proved correct, but the division was moving so rapidly that, instead of falling back to successive positions, the enemy had to fall back to alternate positions (i.e., instead of falling back from line A to line B, they had to fall back from line A to line C, and so on).

After the battle at San Giuseppe, the next fight was the pass at Monreale. The 2d Armored Division surprised the Germans, who were emplacing mines and demolitions. Colonel Hinds, with the advance guard, had been disappointed with the performance of G Company, 41st Armored Infantry Regiment, and had promised them the regiment's next rough assignment. This was it. The Germans had three or four antitank guns in position and protected with infantry and machine guns. Mortar and artillery fire destroyed several of the enemy guns and the last one was taken out by a platoon of G Company, led by 2d Lt. James K. Maupin. The platoon leader remembered the Fort Benning Platoon Problem A, and in the attack the men killed or captured the entire gun crew. An American assault gun fired a round into the casement, insuring that the German gun would not fire again. The gate to Palermo was open.

About 9:30 A.M. Combat Command B moved from its assembly area, following Combat Command A and bivouacking about Camporeale. Division headquarters ordered Colonel White to advance along the division's west (left) flank, generally along Highway 113. He was to clear enemy resistance to the north and west and to assist Combat Command A's capture of Palermo. White radioed back to Johnson with instructions to assemble the unit commanders in Camporeale. In a house occupied by an old couple, White issued his orders to Lt. Cols. Hugh Exton (78th Armored Artillery Battalion), Harry Hillyard (3d Battalion, 67th Armored Regiment) and Marty Morin (1st Battalion, 41st Armored Infantry Regiment). Within an hour after the meeting the column began to move, with the infantry leading because of the darkness. Another hour later, the leading elements made contact with the Italian delaying force. After destroying four 105mm guns and some mortars and capturing an ammunition dump, the troops continued, encountering resistance all the way into Partinico. When Johnson and the Combat Command command post arrived in the afternoon, the town square was swarming with hundreds of surrendering Italian soldiers.

Light and medium tanks took the lead, and the advance continued against lessening enemy resistance. About four miles south of Terracini, Combat Command B captured 350 mountain troops and continued their march northward. Three miles north of town, leading elements came upon a large crater blown in the road. After the engineers had constructed a bypass and about twenty-five German prisoners had been taken, the reconnaissance elements scouted the defile ahead, removing mines and overcoming several tank traps. The march resumed toward Carini, where the mountain had been blown down over the road, but reconnaissance found a trail over the crest. The command passed over the mountain, descended to the town and captured 600 amazed Italians. White halted his men near Carini for the night in an olive and nut tree grove.

As Combat Command A moved north from Monreale, B Company, 82d Reconnaissance Battalion, sent the first patrols into Palermo about noon. The most advanced elements probably had outposts east of town and on the Palermo-Montelepre road, about seven miles from Palermo. The command post stayed in the grove until moving into the Villa Zucco several days later.

Along with the lead elements of B Company, 82d Reconnaissance Battalion, was Col. Sidney R. Hinds. He had an unusual mission: to capture an enemy battleship which was supposed to be in the harbor. As the reconnaissance elements spread throughout the city, Hinds and his detachment went to the waterfront to survey the situation—how to capture a battleship was not taught at any of the service schools. The advance guard returned to the Combat Command A lines where they were promptly admonished for crossing the corps restraining line, which they did not know existed. The division began moving forward, encountering some resistance from German gun crews. As they advanced, Hinds' was the third vehicle in the column. They were surprised by a Mercedes-Benz carrying Italian staff officers; Hinds radioed back to have the car stopped and returned to him along with its occupants. The vehicle was retained for division use, while the occupants went to prisoner-of-war compounds. One of the occupants, Gen. di Brigata Giuseppe Molenero, commander of the port defenses, voluntarily surrendered to Keyes at 7:00 P.M. at the Royal Palace. The reconnaissance battalion continued to patrol the city until relieved the next day. Patton, guided by the division chief of staff, arrived about 9:00 P.M.

The question of which division first entered the city has been argued ever since. Maj. Gen. John P. Lucas has expressed the hope that someday the debate would be settled once and for all: was it the 2d Armored Division or the 3d Infantry Division that first entered Palermo? It has been alleged that Patton ordered the 3d Infantry to hold back so that he could make a triumphal entry with the 2d Armored. On the other hand, the 3d Infantry Division history maintains that when the tankers entered the city they found the streets patrolled by Lt. Col. John A. Heintges's battalion of the 7th Infantry Regiment.

Meanwhile, Col. Sidney R. Hinds's regiment discovered that the battleship it was supposed to capture had sailed the day previously. Hinds maintained that the only American troops that beat him into the city were the two armored cars in front of his. Combat Command A's after-action report stated that the Reconnaissance Company, 66th Armored Regiment, patrolled the city during the night and was relieved by the 3d Infantry Division the following day. Further evidence that the 3d Infantry Division arrived after the 2d Armored Division was the staff car carrying an Italian general looking for someone to whom to surrender. Had the 3d actually arrived before the tankers, he could surely have surrendered to them.

On July 23, Combat Command A began patrolling and guarding the docks, banks, utilities and other important buildings as a precaution against looting. The same day, Combat Command B was ordered to clean out the western end of the island. Major General Gaffey divided the 2d Armored Division zone of occupation into three parts, assigning the city proper to Col. Thomas H. Roberts, division artillery commander. The combat commands oversaw approximately equal areas on the outskirts and surrounding lands.

By utilizing the speed of tracked vehicles, the 2d Armored suffered losses of only 56 killed, 250 wounded, 32 missing and 5 men captured. During combat, the division captured 16,199 Germans and Italians. However, the division had not been used advantageously. Had it been landed as a whole, then the attacks might well have been quicker and the results more productive. The decision to split the division into combat commands operating separately in different roles illustrated the same vital lesson the maneuvers had demonstrated: senior commanders needed to be familiar with armor tactics. The division learned that something would have to be done toward working more effectively with the Air Corps. During the Sicilian campaign, the Americans suffered more from the errors of the American Air Corps than it did from the Luftwaffe. In one week Combat Command A lost fourteen vehicles and 75 men killed or wounded by friendly aircraft. Brigadier General Rose had ordered the command not to fire on friendly aircraft, but one day the 3d gun section, C Battery, 14th Artillery, shot down a P-38 in self-defense. The pilot bailed out and only his pride was injured. The Air Corps got the message; air attacks against Americans stopped for the duration of the campaign.

The capture of Palermo was a brilliant maneuver which closely resembled exercises in which the 2d Armored Division had participated during the Tennessee and Louisiana maneuvers of 1941. Several men commented that they had executed the wide, sweeping, flanking movement before; some even thought that the maneuvers had been more demanding than actual combat. Any fears that the tankers could not perform as well during wartime as during exercises, proved unfounded. The division clearly demonstrated that its training had been valid; the long hours in the maneuver field saved lives and shortened the battle. Patton, who wanted Palermo taken in five days, started the attack from 100 miles distant. The city was in American hands in four days, and the 2d Armored Division had played an indispensible role.

Chapter 10

THE SICILIAN-ENGLISH INTERMISSION

After twelve days of combat, the 2d Armored Division entered a period of duty as military occupation forces. In contrast to its role in North Africa, the tankers played an active part in the military government of Sicily. The island was the testing ground for the government of occupied territories; the military worked out procedures which were later employed in Germany.

The 2d Armored Division was ordered to be ready to carry out one of several missions. Its primary role was to administer and police the Provisional Corps's zone of occupation. As the Seventh Army reserve, it had to be ready to move east into combat on twelve hours' notice, while division artillery had to be ready to move east on six hours' notice. The men were to be ready to embark and engage in amphibious operations with seventy-two hours' warning.

While planning for their tactical assignments, the men had to get their equipment into battle condition. The first consideration was the thorough maintenance of vehicles, arms and equipment. Afterwards the men resumed training, with calisthenics and other exercises led by officers. The combat vehicles had been in constant use since landing. The light tanks caused the most problems, for their tracks were almost worn through. Combat efficiency was low because of the lack of spare parts, particularly tank engines and tracks. The tank engines needed extensive overhauling or replacing, and the wheeled vehicles had not been serviced during operations. General Gaffey borrowed Patton's C-47, sending Lt. Col. Frederick C. Crabb back to Bizerte for replacement tracks. Patton forwarded a letter requesting that Crabb be given every assistance.

It was after dark when he got the rear echelon 2d Armored Division trucks together and appeared at the army depot near Bizerte. There was only a major on duty; seeing a letter with Patton's signature and dozens of lined trucks, he opened the gate. When Crabb and his men began to loot the place, the harrassed officer called the Eastern Base Section G-4. The 2d Armored Division supply crew found an LST on the beach partially loaded with smoke cans. The disgruntled navy lieutenant in command agreed to sail if he had a full ship; the supply team loaded it before dawn, and the ship sailed about daylight. As Crabb was boarding his airplane, the G-4, a lieutenant colonel, appeared to arrest Crabb. While Crabb was armed, the G-4 had no weapon, no M-Ps, no papers authorizing arrest and not the rank to halt him. After Crabb returned to Sicily, Patton was requested to return Crabb to Africa; the general thought it was a big joke.

Still, Crabb's efforts almost ended in failure. The LST landed and the newly formed Island Base Section unloaded the tracks and engines before Crabb knew about it. It took longer to get the parts out of the Palermo warehouse than it had taken to get them out of Bizerte and across the Mediterranean to Palermo. However, by the time the division left Sicily, the tracks had been replaced and the equipment was ready for use, as the needed parts had finally arrived.

Training resumed in earnest, starting with school for the soldier and progressing to small-unit problems. The men were also given every opportunity to swim. They were cautioned to maintain high standards of military courtesy, discipline and dress; commanders were to stress proper wearing of the uniform. This was in part related to an incident involving the 66th Armored Regiment supply section. Two men had been on the road for several days without sleep. The day that Palermo fell, they pulled into the city; as the assistant driver went to ask directions, the driver fell asleep behind the wheel. The military police arrested him and informed General Gaffey, who in turn directed Col. John H. Collier to prefer charges against the two men for sleeping on duty. After investigation, Collier recommended that the men be awarded Bronze Stars and ordered that this action not be held against them. The men of the division were to shave daily, except when engaged in actual operations, when they would have to shave at least every other day. They were to wear steel helmets and to carry appropriate weapons. The men received instructions in handling civil disorders, one of their primary missions at that time. They took long road marches despite bad weather. One platoon leader, 1st Lt. Morton Eustis, thought it was high time that the men got back into condition.

As much as the vehicles needed maintenance and as much as the men needed to be at the peak of efficiency, the division's main mission was to govern the occupied area of Sicily. The Allies attempted to make maximum usage of the civilian authorities. AMGOT (Allied Military Government of Occupied Territory) was created to keep the military out of government as much as possible. The logic was simple: if the military did not have to worry about the civilian population, it would be free to concentrate on fighting the war. The AMGOT officials worked through local officials, mayors, priests and police. Their goals were to preserve order, feed the people and make few changes, while removing as many of the Fascist trappings as possible. If a local official's record was acceptable, he was retained in office; otherwise, a replacement was found.

Two days after entering Palermo, the 2d Armored Division G-2 warned that while the enemy would probably not interfere with the occupation, sabotage could be expected; therefore guards, sentries and patrols should be on the alert to prevent hostile acts. He cautioned that it would take time to clean out small pockets of resistance, to disarm the civilians and deserters and to institute a system of government. The western end of the island (the 2d Armored's sector) was divided into three sections, with each combat command responsible for the policing of its section. The Palermo military district was the responsibility of Col. Thomas H. Roberts, Jr., the division artillery commander. The three area commanders —Roberts, plus Gen. Maurice Rose of Combat Command A and Col. I. D. White of Combat Command B—were to include route reconnaissances, guard posts and patrols and to draw up plans to repel any attacks, seaborne or airborne.

The division was given military government duty on short notice and without any prior training or instructions. Lt. Col. Briard P. Johnson was called to division headquarters and told that the division was to assume governmental control of the island the following morning, with Combat

Command B on the north, and Combat Command A on the south side of the division's zone. On the way back to the CCB command post, Johnson stopped to inform Colonel Collier, telling him of Gaffey's orders to make the plans and inform Collier who had been attached to CCB. Collier's reply was "Issue the orders and we will carry them out." Johnson worked late into the night writing the orders, issuing them and getting the necessary troops into position. Instructions stressed maintaining order, improving sanitation, safeguarding food supplies and warehouses, protecting banks, enforcing curfews and maintaining proper conduct to troops. The next day, with the troops in position and functioning, Johnson returned to Palermo to find the government affairs officer. He was located having lunch at a restaurant in Monreale. Johnson joined him and made notes of items which had not been covered. Later he issued instructions supplementing the basic directive.

Palermo itself was divided into two equal sections assigned to Companies B and C, 82d Reconnaissance Battalion. The main streets were constantly patrolled, while the less important ones were patrolled at staggered intervals; the outlying districts were screened once daily. Permanent guard posts were established at the railroad yards, water works, fuel pumping stations, public buildings and the radio station. Members of the *Carabinieri Reale,* the civil police, rode in patrol cars with the Americans. Bars and eating establishments were inspected to insure cleanliness; any shortcomings placed them off limits.

When AMGOT officials were not available, the men of the 2d Armored Division were their representatives. Their instructions were carefully detailed and designed to avoid problems. The soldiers were to request permission before using civilian cars and billets or captured enemy supplies and equipment. The town commanders were to call local meetings, establish the local judiciary and reopen minor courts at once. The banks were to be closed except to lend the city money, and if money were not available, then the town commanders were to notify AMGOT, who would supply funds. At Godrano, when tax collectors confiscated private property and alleged that it was for use by the United States government, they were arrested.

Lt. Morton Eustis described the daily life of patrols in his letters home. The reconnaissance personnel conducted raids against black marketeers, stopped riots at breadlines, escorted drunks to the stockades and, on one occasion, while taking a woman to a hospital, almost delivered a baby in their vehicle. As a result of the patrolling, members of the 82d

Reconnaissance Battalion were familiar with all the back alleys and bombed-out rooms. They were attempting to stop the "migrant women" who pursued their trade from room to room. Many took their doors with them to insure some privacy while conducting their transactions.

To help cut down on social diseases, the units established "houses of joy." One unit had its house in a walled villa, "manned" by about twenty-five comely volunteers, handpicked by the battalion surgeon. Each battalion and separate unit in the regiment was given a quota for a specific day; there was always a medical officer to supervise disease control. One day M. Sgt. Edward Ullman, operations sergeant, 2d Battalion, 66th Armored Regiment, came to Maj. Herbert S. Long, battalion S 2-3, saying that Long's orderly was getting skittish and temperamental. Ullman recommended a visit to the house of joy. The official pass was prepared and the orderly summoned. The man was spruced up and given some extra lira. The young man saluted sharply and told Long, "Thank you, sir. Thank you very much, sir. I'll hang one in for the major." Another unit commander, so the story goes, ran his house like a military unit. He dispatched trucks to the loading point, directing that they be loaded and en route back to the unit area by X hour. At X plus so many minutes the ladies were to be doing the deed for which they had been retained.

However, the division chaplains waged their war against the establishments. One man recalled that a Protestant chaplain hand-lettered a sign and attached it to a truck, calling it the "Whore House Special." On September 11, Chaplain Wurm discussed the matter with Gaffey. Three days later there was a staff and unit commanders meeting at which Gaffey ordered that all unit houses be abolished. He also told the officers that they could not require the soldiers to use prophylactics. Wurm commented that this made him a persona non grata with some of the staff and all of the unit commanders. But this stance by Wurm probably was a factor in his being awarded the Legion of Merit on November 5.

In the middle of October, Morton Eustis lamented that they were still patrolling and wondered if the 2d Armored would ever fight again. But all was not work; in September, Gaffey issued a directive that 5 percent of the command could be issued passes in accordance with existing policies. However, enlisted men were forbidden to enter Palermo and Sterrativallo except on official business. In August the troops were treated to a U.S.O. show featuring Bob Hope and Francis Langford. In lighter moments, the officers had parties, which were fun once the generals departed. C Company, 82d Reconnaissance Battalion, had a unique party. The men flooded the town with invitations to a "gentile signorina," with instructions to be at a certain loading point at a certain time. The more than forty girls of questionable virtue may have included some "genteel" ones, but as Eustis confessed, "who cares in that kind of party."

A nonfraternization policy had been instituted after an American soldier was arrested for driving a weapons carrier that contained seven civilians. Black-market activities began to surface, and many civilians possessing government-issue items were arrested. Investigations revealed that the primary offenders were from the 53d Quartermaster Battalion in Palermo.

Much of the credit for stopping looting must be given to the *Carabinieri*, who were under American control. The primary concern of both Sicilian police and Americans was the maintenance of order; the best way to accomplish this was by a rationing system, insuring that the people received a fair amount of food. Many farmers refused to bring their grain to town; instead they held it back to sell at inflated prices or hoarded it. At Pirizzi the citizens rioted when local officials started taking grain from the warehouses, and men from the 2d Armored Division were promptly dispatched. The situation was soon under control. Near San Cipirello a *Carabinieri* was wounded attempting to stop a man for illegally transporting grain. His assailant escaped, and the local police considered the incident part of the Mafia activities. The division G-3 report noted that it was necessary for the division to distribute grain; the local authorities did not give the matter proper supervision.

During combat, Palermo suffered considerable damage. The downtown area was filled with craters and destroyed buildings, while the waterfront was a mass of rubble. When the division took over, the civilians had scattered to the countryside. Those who stayed had been without food and water for about five days. The division began to help make the city liveable again. The engineers removed mines, filled in tank traps, removed roadblocks, constructed bypasses around the damaged areas and restored radio and telecommunications within the division zone. The men extended a helping hand in the restoration of health facilities, food supplies and public finances. The city began to recover, and by the time the division left Sicily signs appeared in hotels requesting officers, under officers (sergeants) and soldiers to pay for their rooms in advance.

While carrying out the military government of the island and while patrolling, the 2d Armored Division arrested those who violated curfew or blackout regulations, possessed weapons or illegally transported grain or flour. The prime candidates for arrest were military-age males who could not account for their absence from the military. Some Italians had deserted their units and obtained civilian jobs while the 2d Armored Division was overrunning the western end of the island. Some Germans were reported on the island, and patrols went out in search of them; apparently several were captured.

The 2d Armored Division had to secure and capture all weapons and ammunition that could possibly fall into enemy hands. All the ammunition was to be collected into a central area. At one dump near Perciani, the ammunition exploded with no apparent cause, sending an American soldier and eight prisoner-of-war laborers to the hospital with second-degree burns. Investigation later revealed that the division ammunition officer, Second Lieutenant L. E. Lawrence had heard a loud pop, probably a booby trap, then seen a flash as the powder exploded. Thirteen people were killed when an ammunition dump exploded near San Giuseppe, and several other dumps mysteriously exploded. Civilians were apprehended for possessing military equipment. One, who threw hand grenades at a guard near the division water point, was arrested and taken to Partinico and his house was locked. A fisherman was arrested and jailed for fishing with dynamite, and a second man was jailed for allegedly giving him the explosives.

About 7:50 P.M. on August 20, 1943, a patrol from the 3d Battalion, 41st Armored Infantry Regiment, found sixty-nine drums of mustard gas. The following day the 2d Armored Division took over sixty barrels of a persistent gas (probably mustard gas) from the 82d Airborne Division. The fifty-gallon barrels totalled 6,450 gallons. This may well have been the division's most frightening experience in Sicily. Earlier the odor of burning sulphur had raised the possibility that the Axis was using gas. The men had received chemical training in North Africa before going to Sicily, and they did have gas masks available.

One of the most serious situations was the apparent sabotage of the 2d Armored Division's communications lines. Patton ordered the lines patrolled according to standard procedure and authorized the shooting of anyone caught trying to sabotage the lines. He indicated that if there were a second attempt at sabotage the nearest dwelling would be torn down. General Rose bluntly ordered the wire guards to shoot on sight anyone cutting communications. Four days after the order was issued, a wire guard shot and wounded a civilian. The same day, Gaffey sent a message to Hinds: "The Commanding General desires to compliment the soldier who shot the wire saboteur today." Apparently, Patton was not entirely pleased; two days later he sent a message to Gaffey: "Target practice for wire guards indicated." Apparently the civilian that had been shot was to be tried for sabotage. On August 11, Keyes said that he wanted to make an example of him. The shooting of the civilian, however, did not stop the wire cutting. Periodic reports and the regimental and battalion logs indicate that sabotage continued and perhaps even increased during the month of August. But as the division spent more time on the island, it decreased and finally stopped.

The Germans, during their stay on the island, had waged a propaganda war against the United States. As the 2d Armored Division's civil government personnel moved through the town of San Giuseppe, they saw a civilian carrying a sign reading, "Long Live the United States. Long Live Liberty. For twenty years we have been forced to keep silent. We welcome you so that we may again have Liberty and Freedom." Many civilians were surprised that the women were not raped and that homes were not pillaged during combat or the occupation, because Americans had been portrayed as vicious, barbaric and bloodthirsty. The Americans did make one startling discovery: the Germans had told their troops the same horror stories they had told to the Sicilians. However, because German prisoners in Canada had been permitted to write about their conditions and treatment, refuting the Nazi propaganda, the troops apparently did not believe the propaganda.

Prisoner-of-war interrogation teams of the 2d Armored Division were busy questioning the many prisoners. The Germans talked about their equipment and munitions. For example, they told of a newly developed mine that could only be removed by exploding it. The Germans also had a new type S mine, which looked exactly like the older model but had an antilifting device built into it. The new model had a hole in its base to install a pull igniter. Also developed was an antitank weapon made of two containers connected by wires; once it had landed on a tank, the weight of the containers pulled the wire that was also the fuze. The Russians had combatted this device by surrounding their tanks with barbed wire. In another type of device, the Germans used the principle of the shaped charge. The hollow magnetic grenade was held on the tank by three magnets, and the detonation was concentrated at one point. Also described was a flamethrower with a range of fifteen to twenty-five meters and a life of seven to eight seconds. The interrogator noted that the informant had said that this piece of equipment never functioned properly.

The questioning also revealed much about American soldiers and their weapons. It was reported that American infantrymen did not take proper concealment measures during advances toward an objective. Their artillery and mortar fire had adverse effects on German and Italian morale. One prisoner, Lieutenant Colonel Altini, said that the main reason many surrendered was to escape the artillery and mortar fire. The American fragmentation grenade was not considered equal to the German one because the American grenade fragmented into large chunks, while the German one burst into smaller pieces.

In the latter part of September 1943, the 2d Armored Division was alerted for movement to another theater of operations. The men were to take their clothing, two wool blankets, two pairs of service shoes and three pairs of light wool socks. They would carry one magazine or clip for their individual weapons. Units were permitted to take housekeeping items that were necessary for administrative work: typewriters, desks, safes and coin counting, duplicating, computing, adding, mimeographing and payroll machines. They could take all signal equipment not mounted in combat vehicles, with the exception of the SCR-299 radios. The division was also permitted to take one steel treadway bridge and the vehicles necessary for it. The division's destination, England, was known to very few. In October, an order assigning code numbers for the movement arrived; the order was sent to several other headquarters, including the CG ETO (commanding general, European theater of operations).

Patton had issued a warning order alerting the 2d Armored Division for movement and directing the division to be organized according to the latest T/O and T/E (table of organization and tables of equipment). The new organization, which would be termed "light" would have the division lose three regiments: the 66th and 67th Armored and the 41st Armored Infantry. In their place, the division gained three tank battalions and three infantry battalions. In effect, the division was to lose over 50 percent of its tank strength and a smaller part of its infantry strength.

The pace quickened; in the last week of October 1943, the division (minus the detachments in North Africa) was ordered to assemble near Capaci by November 3. They were to be relieved of their police responsibility by November 1. Once at Capaci, the men were restricted to the area. On October 27 Gen. Maurice Rose was selected to lead an advance party of seven officers (Johnson from Combat Command B and a major or captain from each regiment or division artillery) and seven noncommissioned officers from each of the separate companies or battalions. This group of fourteen sailed with the 1st and 9th Infantry Divisions. They landed at Liverpool on November 8, exactly one year after the invasion of North Africa. While the advance elements were at sea, someone decided that the group was too small to meet the requirements which it would face. Accordingly, three officers and eighty-one enlisted personnel were also sent to England. This group, primarily from the 17th Engineer Battalion, the Maintenance and Supply Battalions, the 142d Signal Company and from division headquarters, was to make the necessary advance arrangement for the division. Apparently, this augmentation group had been flown from Sicily to England, for Johnson and his party were surprised when they were met by an officer from the division.

The 2d Armored Division was ordered to turn in its property, except for the vehicles necessary to move to the staging area, between October 25 and 29. The equipment was to be ready for use, the vehicles and weapons thoroughly cleaned and oiled. On November 9 General Gaffey issued a memorandum to selected officers stating that the division was going to the United Kingdom. They would draw new equipment and make preparations for the continuation of the war; the troops were to be told of their destination once they were at sea. In North Africa, the rear echelon of the 2d Armored was undergoing the same preparations as its parent unit on Sicily. In the latter part of September, they were ordered to the port of Oran, where they turned in their equipment and prepared to depart. They sailed on November 14.

During the movement from Sicily and North Africa to England, the division took only those items necessary to start again. After the men were at sea, rumors began to circulate about their destination. One story was that the division was returning to Fort Benning; in fact, the ships proceeded so far west that one man swore he saw the Empire State Building. Some of the ships which had been passenger liners before the war were manned by their civilian crews. One night at dinner, the waiter handed Capt. Curtis Clark the menu; he looked at it and handed it back with a one-word order: "Yes."

The officers were quartered in cabins, where they were not as crowded as the enlisted men. Two mischievous officers, Capt. William Marion (Butch) Page and Maj. Herbert S. Long, could not stand the idea of the 2d Battalion surgeon, Capt. Mario de Felice, sporting his new civilian pajamas, a gift from his stateside fiancée. One day while the doctor was out of his cabin, Page and Long entered, armed with a large pair of scissors. They performed surgery on the crotch of the pajama pants, leaving a gaping hole about twelve inches in diameter. That evening, a dozen officers assembled in de Felice's cabin to watch the fun. The doctor, expansive before an audience, was chattering away as he donned his girlfriend's gift: first the jacket, then the pants. He felt a draft where there should not be one. He directed an incredulous gaze downward— then came the pained explosion. The doctor could not believe that anyone, especially a brother officer, would commit such an atrocity. Adding insult to injury, the two culprits, Page and Long, ran a notice in the ship's newspaper offering a reward for the fiend who had hacked the crotch out of Doc de Felice's pajamas.

The doctor was convinced that the culprit was Page. Page loved his cigars, so the doctor borrowed a box and wreaked his revenge. Using capsules from the battalion medical section, he extracted gunpowder from .45 bullets; using his surgical skills, he removed some tobacco from the cigars and replaced it with the capsules of gunpowder. Some were placed about a quarter-inch from the end of the cigar, while others were about a half-inch from the end. Since the doctor operated on only about one-fifth of the cigars and since his skill made the loaded stogies indistinguishable from the unloaded ones, Page could not be certain which were which. Page was shattered—literally. Doc had used about four times as much gunpowder as was used in commercial trick cigars. Long recalled that Page was "too tight to waste a new box of cigars" so he gamely smoked the entire box.

The enlisted men slept in bunks stacked four high and close together; they slept in their clothing. They received two meals a day (as did the officers), and could also buy candy and crackers from the ships' PX (post exchange). Usually there were high-stakes dice or poker games in each of the compartments.

The ships docked at Liverpool, England, on Thanksgiving Day. Sea gulls were everywhere, and the fun-loving American soldier had to make a game out of every situation. Sgt. Russel S. Lamison saw men throw food scraps to the gulls; to experiment, some men began to throw bits of metal. The gulls dived for the metal and the men began to use all the bolts and nuts they could take off the ship. The men were fed Thanksgiving dinner aboard the ship, but as one man recalled, "It was something not to be thankful for."

The advance party did all the supervisory work, the mass of paper

Right (L. to R.): Col. Sidney Hinds, Gen. Dwight Eisenhower, Prime Minister Winston Churchill and Major General Edward H. Brooks.

Below: Members of the 41st Armored Infantry Regiment practice with flame throwers during a field problem in the English training period.

work necessary to transfer equipment, allocate space for the units and plan for the reception of the incoming troops. A battalion of the 33d Armored Regiment, 3d Armored Division, was loaned to the advance group to do the necessary labor. Bunks were made, fires laid ready for lighting and three days' rations placed in every kitchen storeroom; a cadre of cooks handled the first meal until the incoming cooks could assume their duties. All the combat vehicles, with about half the wheeled vehicles, had been drawn from depots and driven to the unit motor parks. Finally, with all that work behind them, the advance party had to arrange to meet forty-three incoming trains at Tidworth and a few at Ludgershall and Grately at the same time. The preparations paid off well. Incoming units went first to their barracks where they left their packs and then to the mess halls for their first meal. Johnson recalled that the men's eyes lit up when they saw that the beds had been made. While the beds were double-deckers with straw-filled ticks instead of mattresses, it was a luxury for men who had been living in the field for a year. Later the division would do the same for the 4th Armored Division.

Tidworth Barracks, the new home of Hell on Wheels, was a former English cavalry post, located on the Salisbury Plain. It was a huge military reservation with all the barracks of red brick and stone. Chaplain Wurm noted in his diary that "it is a severe, pretentious-looking establishment." During the first week, the men settled into their barracks. There was no central heat, but there were coal grates in each room. Although the weather was chilly and damp, the men were not unhappy; they were only sixty-four miles from London. Life in England was enjoyable, at least the soldiers thought so. There were post exchanges, beer, movies, and one theater. They could get daily passes to Salisbury, Andover and Amesburg, forty-eight-hour passes to London and seven-day furloughs to any other part of England or Scotland. The division maintained cordial relations with the British civil and military populations. Weekly dances were held, which were extremely popular with the British women. One especially popular feature of these dances was the food: sandwiches, doughnuts and coffee. On Christmas Day, the division played host to British war orphans. The officers and men had saved their candy rations to share with the children, and later their turkey and Christmas extras. The men also vied with each other over who would wear the homemade Santa Claus suit. Some wondered who had the most fun—the kids or the men.

There were, of course, some complaints about the Americans in

England. Eustis told about the local pub run by an elderly couple that took in the Americans on the strength of their tipping. The pub owners seemed glad to have the Americans. Eustis also noted that the Americans had too much money, that they were too loud and boisterous and that some were stealing British girls from their British boyfriends. This caused friction. As some unknown pundit said, the "Americans were overpaid, over-sexed and over here."

Not all the Hell-on-Wheelers arrived in England with the convoy. Nine or ten men, including Corp. Ralph L. Reints, remained with the signal equipment when the large convoy sailed for England. The small detachment sailed from Palermo on October 30, arriving at Bizerte the following day but missing the larger convoy. A decision was made to keep the men there awaiting the next convoy. The navy decided to use the LST to ferry troops to Italy; as the Hell-on-Wheelers had no place to go, they too made the trip. They were to make several trips with British, French, Polish and South American troops destined for the fighting front.

On the LST the food situation was becoming critical. The supplies for army personnel had long since been depleted. The ship captain permitted the 2d Armored Division troops to eat with his own men. He had begged, borrowed and stolen food but now had to order the army troops to not eat. The sailors initiated a sit-down strike and refused to eat unless the soldiers were fed also. Finally, to solve the situation, an investigating committee of chaplains and colonels arrived. The solution was to attach the Hell-on-Wheelers to the navy, so that the ship captain could then draw rations for the army troops. On December 26, the men were alerted for movement to England and rejoined the division on January 6.

In the later part of its Sicilian occupation and en route to England, the division began to evaluate its performance, seeking improvements. Maj. Clifton Batchelder, executive officer of the 3d Battalion, 67th Armored Regiment, thought that if the division could start training all over again, more time and attention should be given to gunnery, not only with tank weapons, but with all the auxiliary arms, assault guns and mortars. Training and practice should be so thorough that firing and hitting became automatic. To Batchelder's mind, tactics depended on gunnery and straight shooting. Other officers stressed that shooting straight and rapidly was the key to victory. Maj. Herbert Long, while not disputing that much had been done with the cannon, felt that for the most part crews had ignored machine guns. The machine gun gave the tank a weapon against ground troops, forcing them to keep their heads down while the tanks and infantry advanced. These ideas were included in training.

After getting settled in their new barracks, the men drew new equipment and began cleaning and testing the gear. Training resumed in earnest. The division started with the individual and crew drill and went on to driver instruction. The 66th Armored Regiment had a most unusual teaching method for drivers: chasing jackrabbits. The theory was that a rabbit demonstrated all the moves necessary on the battlefield: stops, starts, turns. After crew and squad training, the units progressed to platoon and company training. This was followed by weapons firing and tactical training; then first aid and weapons qualifications, as well as supply discipline. This was basic training all over again, but designed to insure that nothing had been omitted. The division sent its regiments to the Imber and Minehead ranges for maneuvers and firing of tank guns.

The division perfected its team concept at the Imber range. The actions in Sicily had been successful due to American aggressiveness and because the enemy, except for the Germans, fought with little or no resolve. The Sicilian experience pointed out deficiencies which would have to be overcome. At Canicatti, the infantry had dismounted when they first met resistance. This was due in part to the infantry's lacking sufficient and adequate radios for communication with the tankers. At Imber the infantry found that they did not have to dismount at first resistance but could fight better from their half-tracks. They could better stay with the tanks, arrive on the objective, round up the prisoners and move on to the next objective. The artillery demonstrated that it could also serve in the tank-infantry team. It perfected the TOT (all guns of division artillery firing so that the rounds arrived at the target at the same time). After joining the corps, the men were introduced to STONKS (division plus all corps artillery which could reach the target, firing so that the rounds burst on the target simultaneously.)

During the cold, wet winter, training continued for the 2d Armored Division. Many who had been at Fort Benning with Patton remembered that this rugged, demanding training saved lives. Now the division condensed the training into the few months available. Special emphasis was placed on amphibious operations, mine detection and booby traps. Each division in England was required to train at least ten men to use mine detectors in the infantry, artillery and signal battalions. All company grade officers (lieutenants and captains) of infantry and engineers were to be trained in directing artillery fire. The 2d Armored also required this of its tank officers.

In January 1944, the 195th Antiaircraft Artillery Battalion was attached to the 2d Armored Division, and the division was ordered to incorporate it into its training. This attachment was to last throughout the war. On February 8, 1944, the division was assigned to XIX Corps, commanded by Maj. Gen. Charles H. Corlett. Eisenhower told the corps commander to create a family feeling in the organization. He did not want genius or brilliance, but he did want common sense. The 2d Armored Division established extremely good relations with its fellow corps members, a rapport that lasted through the war.

In April 1944, the reconnaissance battalion went to the British antiaircraft range. The men found it better than the garrison life of paperwork, policing and spit and polish. They spent countless hours firing at target sleeves; although not the real thing, it was useful. The other parts of the division were undergoing combined exercises with their corps partners and the British at Broadsands.

While training, the 2d Armored Division was threatened with having to reorganize into a smaller division. Under the proposed plan, it would lose three regiments and gain three tank battalions and three infantry battalions. The new division was to have 10,937 men, compared to 14,620 men in the old structure.

For some unknown reason, perhaps because of influential armor leaders such as Patton, Gaffey and others who were in England, Eisenhower amended the order, permitting the 2d and 3d Armored Divisions to retain the regimental structure and directed them to draw up a list of equipment needed to send them into battle. So, while the division did undergo some reorganization, it was internal. The old regimental structure was altered somewhat, for instead of having two medium and one light battalions per tank regiment, they now had three battalions of two medium companies and one light company. This caused confusion because the light tank companies retained their old unit designation instead of being relettered.

Gen. Ernest N. Harmon, commander of the 2d Armored Division in the landing of North Africa who had assumed command of the 1st Armored Division in April 1943, was in England. Harmon, who probably had more combat experience in an armored division than anyone else in the army at the time, recommended that the infantry and armored elements be balanced to forge a team, with a second infantry regiment attached to the division. He foresaw using the heavy divisions, with one or two infantry divisions on the armored division's flanks, much like the opening exercise in the Louisiana maneuvers of 1941.

The 2d Armored Division commander, General Gaffey, wanted to eliminate the half-tracks from the armored infantry regiment and replace them with trucks. Col. Sidney Hinds opposed the idea. He told Gaffey that if it were done, any infantry could function with the tankers. To Hinds's mind, armored infantrymen were specially trained for their role. In Sicily, the 41st Armored Infantry had used half-tracks with tow hooks attached, permitting the regiment to capture and save enemy equipment found on the battlefield. Gaffey cast some aspersions on the "gypsy caravan," but the half-tracks and their strange assortment of equipment contributed to the health, well-being and, most importantly, the morale of the men. Apparently, Gaffey did not understand that the infantrymen viewed their half-tracks in the same manner that the tankers or artillerymen viewed their vehicles. The half-tracks could closely follow the advancing foot soldier, carrying those items that the infantryman could not carry on his person, such as extra ammunition, mines, barbed wire, weapons and food, and if necessary could be used to evacuate the wounded or dead.

Hinds was of the opinion that the current tables of equipment did not provide for the maximum firepower and recommended that some thought be given to substituting to acquire larger caliber or automatic weapons. Apparently his arguments were successful for Gaffey requested not only what Hinds had recommended but other items which the division needed. The letter slowly wound its way through channels, gaining endorsements but little else. Finally, just before the division sailed for the landing at Normandy, most of the requested supplies were provided.

The preceding year, in late September 1943, General Eisenhower had told Gen. George C. Marshall that he would like to use the newer divisions to make the initial landings and to save the veteran divisions as follow-up units, to pass through and seize the early objectives. The units assigned to the First Army were either battle experienced or supposedly well trained.

In March 1944, the army activated the headquarters of the Third Army, under the command of Lieutenant General Patton. He was supposed to have told Eisenhower that he did not want a brilliant staff, but a loyal one. To get that loyalty, he turned to the 2d Armored Division, taking General Gaffey, the division commander, and Col. Redding F.

Perry, the chief of staff. Replacing these men in the 2d Armored were Gen. Edward H. Brooks (an artilleryman and developer of the M-7 105mm self-propelled howitzer), and Col. Charles Palmer.

In mid-April 1944, all passes and leaves were cancelled. Two weeks later all men were restricted to their regimental or battalion areas. Being restricted to the area did not pose a problem for T5 Harry Stearns, medical detachment, 14th Armored Artillery. Stearns forged a Captain Smuck's name to a pass and was apprehended by the military police for being ten minutes late reporting into the area. Stearns was court-martialed, reduced and sentenced to six months in the battalion area. In later years, he recalled that he marched out of the courtroom straight to the LST which was to take him to France. Laughingly, he added that the ten-minute lateness saved him from facing charges of forgery.

In May, the 2d Armored and the 9th Infantry took part in an exercise of marshalling the build-up units. This problem, done under the protection of fighter aircraft, revealed deficiencies. While preparing for the invasion, the commanders had to attend to many details. On one inspection Col. John H. Collier discovered crimped cartridges in some of his machine gun ammunition. A detailed inspection found that about 90 percent of the machine gun belts had at least one damaged round. The men were immediately ordered to inspect all belts and replace the damaged rounds. Fortunately, these discoveries came early enough to permit corrections; the men did not have to live or die with the problems, as they had in North Africa and Sicily.

As D day approached, the 2d Armored Division engaged in practice landing operations at the actual camps and ports they would be using. Brooks conducted a series of map problems, terrain board exercises and staff conferences. During this time, probably many in the division echoed the thoughts of Morton Eustis, who hoped that the Germans did not collapse until the division had a chance to hit them good from the west; he added, "I hope my platoon is the first to set foot in Berlin."

Gen. Maurice Rose and the advance command post personnel departed from Tidworth Barracks to join the 9th Infantry Regiment of the 2d Infantry Division at the Barry, Wales, marshalling area. They sailed for the rendezvous off the Isle of Wight on June 5, aboard the S.S. *Charles Sumner*. Two days later they were off the coast of France. The advance group landed about 6:30 P.M. and established their command post north of St. Laurent-Sur-Mer. The purpose of the advance group was to gain information on the progress of the operation, receive and organize Combat Command A, and receive, orient and command all units of the division until the division commander landed.

The 2d Armored Division moved from Tidworth Barracks on June 6-7 to the marshalling areas of Portsmouth and Southampton. The major part of the division loaded and started for France that night, landing on June 9. While the division was not entitled to its third bronze arrowhead for being part of the initial landing group, it was in its third combat landing, as part of the initial follow-up force. The division was about to take part in battles that would test it as it had not been tested before.

From July 1943 to June 6, 1944, the 2d Armored Division circled from war to peace and back to war. In Sicily, after landing as separate units, the division united and for the first time in its history fought as a division. It did not take part in the final two-thirds of the Sicilian campaign but served in a military government role. This proved beneficial, for it would have to assume that role again. While acting as "policeman," its secondary mission was to be ready for deployment if the Seventh Army commander thought it necessary. He never did. When in England preparing for the landings in France, the 2d Armored often trained even harder than it had in the past, drawing on the operations in North Africa and Sicily for battle experience. While the previous battles had been against second- and third-rate troops fighting without conviction, this time the enemy would be top-notch: the battle-tested, battle-hardened German army.

Chapter 11

THE COTENTIN PENINSULA

The Allied operations in France were planned and executed in three phases. Gen. Dwight D. Eisenhower wanted to establish a beachhead on the continent, build up the forces and then break through into the Brittany-Normandy area. The final step was to be a pursuit on a broad front. The major emphasis was placed on the left flank, while the right joined Allied forces moving northward from southern France. The 2d Armored Division, the first armored division to land on the continent, was to have a major role in executing all parts of this plan.

The combat commands were structured so that maximum firepower could be brought quickly ashore. Gen. Maurice Rose's Combat Command A had the 66th Armored Regiment as the basis of its command. In addition Rose had the 82d Reconnaissance Battalion, two battalions of the 41st Armored Infantry, the 14th and 92d Armored Artillery Battalions, battalion headquarters and Company A of the 17th Armored Engineer Battalion, Company A of the Maintenance Battalion, Company A, 48th Medical Battalion, and a detachment of the Supply Battalion. Combat Command B, led by Colonel I.D. White, was a smaller force destined to

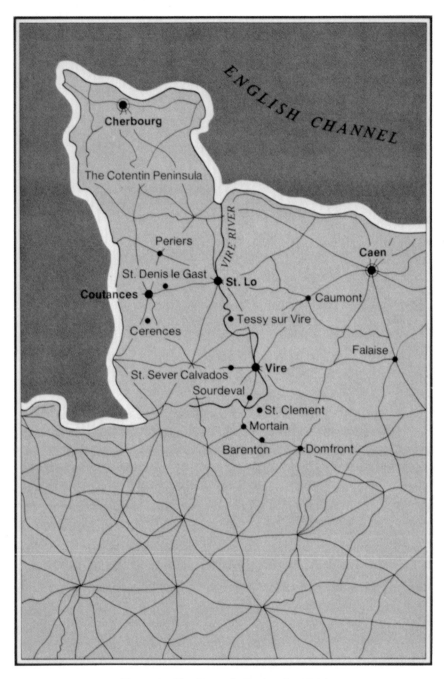

Figure 8. The Cotentin Peninsula, 1944.

land after Combat Command A. It consisted of the 67th Armored Regiment, the 78th Armored Artillery Battalion, one battalion of the 41st Armored Infantry, Companies B and E of the 17th Engineer Battalion, Company B of the 48th Medical Battalion, Company B of the Maintenance Battalion and a detachment of the Supply Battalion. Division headquarters controlled the remainder of the division and two important attachments: the 195th Antiaircraft Artillery Battalion and the 702d Tank Destroyer Battalion.

The bulk of the division loaded onto their LSTs on D day and started across the channel. They arrived off Omaha beach in the afternoon, spending the night on the ships. In the darkness, the Germans fired an occasional artillery round at the ships. One LST hit an enemy mine and sank, taking to the bottom seventeen medium and fourteen light tanks, six quarter-ton trucks, six half-tracks and three assault guns. The sixty-six casualties included seven killed, but most of the wounded or missing returned to duty within two days. The explosion was so strong that it jarred the ship carrying General Brooks and the division staff.

This landing was easier than those in North Africa and Sicily. The men drove the vehicles off the ships and onto the beach with only a few having to move through a small amount of water. On June 11, the division commander, with the advanced command post, landed and assumed command of the division. The 2d Armored Division, in its follow-up role, was to be ready to help expand the beachhead and exploit the successes of the initial landing. The first two echelons, the combat commands, were ashore on June 14. The third echelon, primarily division trains, was ashore by June 28, and all division troops had landed by July 2.

Pfc. Albert J. Isacks joined D Company, 17th Engineers, in England shortly after the main body had departed for France. He spent endless hours smearing waterproof grease on vital engine parts. Apparently, even after the landings, many thought that the vehicles would have to move through deep water. The LSTs sailed in the evening, arriving off the coast early the next morning. On the first approach, one ship hit a sandbar with the water just off the ramp so deep that no vehicle could be unloaded. A second attempt placed the LST on dry beach, with the vehicles getting only their tires damp. All the work, Isacks thought, had been in vain. After the men and equipment came ashore, the vehicles went to dewaterproofing points and then to assembly areas near Mosles, France.

Once ashore, the division reorganized into two almost equal strength combat commands and a division reserve of one tank battalion and one infantry battalion under Col. Sidney R. Hinds. The division retained control of the 82d Reconnaissance Battalion, the 195th Antiaircraft Artillery Battalion and the 702d Tank Destroyer Battalion. While in the beachhead area, the 67th Armored Regiment reorganized so that each battalion had two medium tank companies and one light tank company, instead of the regiment having two medium tank battalions and one light tank battalion.

With the landing of the 2d Armored Division, the first phase of the invasion was completed. The Allies began to build up supplies and troops for the breakout and for carrying the fight to the Nazis. The division's tank and infantry regiments and reconnaissance battalions sent patrols to make contact with the enemy and if possible to capture some prisoners. While in its reserve role, the division also had the tactical mission to repulse any counterattacks.

While the convoys were at sea, the air corps conducted reconnaissance of the peninsula for the land forces. Early in the afternoon of June 5, approximately fifty German tanks were reported in the landing area or in nearby positions. On June 6 and 7, reports indicated that the Germans were massing a counterattack which included armored elements. On June 12, after being ashore for five days, V Corps reported that even though they had encountered no tanks, the reconnaissance battalion of the German 17th SS Panzer Division was fighting on their front. The corps's G-2 guessed that air corps raids had prevented the Germans from moving their armor to oppose the landings.

Almost simultaneously with the initial landings, the 2d Armored was called on to assist some of the landing forces. V Corps called for two armored infantry companies to be sent to the 29th Infantry Division to secure the bridgehead near Auxilie sur Mer. The Reconnaissance Company of the 66th Armored Regiment and the 82d Reconnaissance Battalion sent patrols to make contact with friendly forces in the front and on the flanks. On June 11, the Intelligence and Reconnaissance Platoon of the 41st Armored Infantry and elements of the 101st Airborne Division were patrolling south of the railroad tracks toward Montmartin-en-Caignes where they encountered heavy machine gun fire. A platoon of G Company, 41st Armored Infantry, rushed to their aid. In the brief but determined encounter the Hell-on-Wheelers lost two men and captured five, after killing an estimated fifteen members of the 4th Company, 915th Panzer Grenadier Regiment.

The American V Corps scheduled a June 12 attack by three infantry divisions, supported in reserve by the 2d Armored Division. The objectives were the high ground south of the Foret de Cerisy and the town of Caumont. Before the American attack could get started the Germans launched their own counterattack into the boundary between Utah and Omaha beaches. It was designed to split the American beachheads and if possible push them back into the sea.

The Germans attacked the 101st Airborne, which had few, if any, heavy weapons to stop a tank attack. General Bradley ordered the 2d Armored Division to send a task force of one tank battalion and one infantry battalion to secure the bridgehead at Isigny. Protected by fire from three American battleships, the USS *Texas, Arkansas* and *Nevada,* patrols began scouting the route. Before the troops could be committed to action, their mission was changed and they were sent to support the 101st Airborne. Brooks also secured permission to enlarge this force, sending Rose's Combat Command A. En route to Carentan, they passed through Isigny, where two military policemen were standing. After spotting the unit designations, one reportedly turned to the other and said, "That's Patton's old outfit. Toughest bunch in the army. Hitler never saw nothing like them." In the ensuing battle, Hell on Wheels was about to acquire a new nickname.

The attack of the 2d Armored Division was in the bocage, or hedgerow, country. It was the only type of action for which the division had not trained at Fort Benning, during the maneuvers or in North Africa and Sicily. The countryside was dotted with small fields surrounded by thick hedgerows, sunken roads and many intersections. It was premium defensive country, placing an added burden on the attacker.

Rose sent his reconnaissance forces to scout the route to Carentan. They encountered elements of the German 12th SS Panzer Division and a few Tiger tanks. About 4:00 A.M. the Reconnaissance Company, 66th Armor, was attacked by twenty Tiger tanks plus infantry, but they repulsed the enemy with little effort—perhaps an indication that the Germans were not that determined to stand. Collier and the lead elements of Combat Command A raced into Carentan, joined with the 101st Airborne Division and assaulted the German 17th SS Panzer Division.

The tankers and the paratroopers launched their attack at 2:00 P.M. with deadly seriousness. As events—so strange in warfare—happened, the 2d Armored and the 101st Airborne attacked just as the Germans launched their own attack. Thus, many of the enemy were already out of their foxholes and in the open when first contact was made. At 5:30 P.M.

Left: Typical bocage country with sunken roads and hedgerows.
Below: Battle damage near the Carentan, France, railroad station.

the remainder of Combat Command A arrived and joined the fight. The first day's action drove back the enemy, who suffered an estimated 500 losses compared to 8 killed, 45 wounded and the loss of 4 tanks for the 2d Armored Division.

The tankers took several prisoners who identified themselves as Polish deserters from the 2d Battalion, 914th Infantry Regiment, 353d Infantry Division. They had been ordered to cover the front while the German paratroopers withdrew. They identified the enemy forces south of Carentan as the 6th Parachute Regiment and the 37th SS Regiment. The prisoners reported that they had had no food or ammunition for seven or eight days, that losses had been heavy in their unit but that morale was still high among the Germans. The division learned from its prisoners that the enemy would not surrender, they were determined to fight to the death. The division also learned that the 2d Panzer Division was near Caumont but had not been committed to action.

During the night, Combat Command A coiled but encountered severe shelling, mortar and artillery fire. The same night, the 66th Armored Regiment received its first replacements. The young men were nervous. Collier recalled that they fired at anything that moved: leaves, shadows, insects. Finally, the experienced men were able to stop the trigger-happy newcomers.

The next morning, when the attack resumed, the enemy was driven back with increasingly high losses, along the road to Periers. Combat Command A pushed the Germans back across the small canal or stream. Just as they were clearing the approaches to the bridge, Maj. Gen. Maxwell D. Taylor came forward asking Collier if the bridge had been cleared. Collier replied that the area had been cleared to the bridge, but he had not yet been across. Taylor did not hesitate; he went across, effectively linking the two threatened beachheads. Having gotten the 101st Airborne Division beyond Carentan and having stalled the German counterattack, Combat Command A was pulled out of the line. However, the 1st Battalion, 66th Armor, remained attached to the 101st Airborne and later the 83d Infantry Division, until July 6.

The division's first continental combat was successful because of two factors. The Germans apparently did not know that the Americans had landed armor. The tanks caught them by surprise and systematically pushed ahead. Second was the adaptability of the American soldier, his skill in finding solutions to new problems. Although the men had no hedgerow experience, they soon found how to penetrate them, especially by using the bulldozer tanks of the 17th Engineer Battalion. However, the Germans hid in back of the hedges, let the tanks pass and then fired on the following infantry. To counter this, the Americans started through the hedges with their main guns loaded with canister and pointed to the rear and to the flanks. As the tanks crashed through, they fired parallel to the hedges, literally wiping out the enemy. For their part the 2d Armored Division, particularly Combat Command A, earned the grudging respect of German army and political leaders, who nicknamed the division, "Roosevelt's Butchers," a name which the division gladly accepted.

Bradley ordered the tankers, Combat Command A, to push a vigorous reconnaissance toward Periers. The mission was given to the Reconnaissance Company, 66th Armor, one tank company and one infantry company, supported by the 14th Armored Artillery Battalion. Crossing the line of departure at 6:50 A.M., the force quickly ran into heavy machine gun, small arms and antitank fire. The remainder of the 3d Battalion, 41st Armored Infantry, and the 1st Battalion, 66th Armor, advanced to aid the reconnaissance force. In the later afternoon the 14th Armored Artillery reported their radio frequencies were being jammed, primarily with music and messages to the effect, "14th Field Artillery we know who you are." Later that evening, the tankers were pulled out of the line and were replaced by the 101st Airborne. The 2d Armored Division had determined that the enemy was holding the area in force.

While Combat Command A was engaged, Combat Command B was in the assembly area, clearing mines from the roads and fields. Brooks had devised three plans to repulse possible enemy counterattacks. The first would use Combat Command B to repel close-in attacks by the German 2d Panzer Division from the direction of St. Germain de Elle. According to the second plan, Combat Command B would attack to St. Germain or even deeper. Plan three envisioned using all of the division: one combat command would be used on the west flank as in plan one, while the second combat command would execute plan two.

Within a week after landing, the armor section of the future 12th Army Group demonstrated the new M-4 tank, which carried a 76mm gun. Most of the armor commanders were at the test firing: General Patton and Maj. Gens. Hugh J. Gaffey (Patton's chief of staff), Robert W. Grow (6th Armored Division), Lunsford E. Oliver (5th Armored Division) and Walton H. Walker (XX Corps). The spectators were impressed with the new tank but were unwilling to replace the battle-tested M-4 which carried only a 75mm gun. Finally, Patton accepted the weapon but placed it in a separate battalion. Later, the demand for the new tanks became so great that instead of putting them all in Third Army, the decision was made to feed them into all the armored divisions. Originally, only about a third of the tanks were to have the new 76mm gun; however, as more became available, they represented almost 50 percent.

Combat Command A was pulled out of the line and returned to division control. The division had primarily a reserve role for the period of June 19 to July 26. During this time they camouflage painted their vehicles and combat clothing and performed needed maintenance on their vehicles and weapons. The division continued to train, emphasizing tank-infantry-artillery cooperation in hedgerow fighting. It stressed knowing the use and characteristics of enemy weapons (especially enemy tanks and bazookas), using flamethrowers, practicing demolitions and using mine detectors.

From the military point of view, the hedgerows offered small fields of fire. A concealed enemy could, as at Carentan, wait until the attacker was within approximately 100 yards or less before firing, usually with deadly accuracy. Attempting to find a better means of getting through the thick hedgerows, besides crashing through, the division tried using satchel charges to blow holes through the dense shrubbery. Some members of the division proposed mounting bulldozer blades on the tanks. This would be more satisfactory, as the tank could move through the hedges without climbing over and exposing their thin underbelly. Hedgerow fighting was especially dangerous in the first encounters, for the German machine gun and rifle fire caused the men to drop to the ground. Then, with telling accuracy, the enemy fired mortars onto the prone attackers. The best defense against this tactic was to keep moving. Based on the Carentan experience, First Army authorized canister as 30 percent of the basic load of ammunition for the light tank. Typically, they wanted reports on its effectiveness and further recommendations for its usage.

The division assembly area was often subjected to bombings and strafings. Most attacks were repulsed by the 195th Antiaircraft Artillery and the antiaircraft weapons mounted on the division vehicles. On June 20, two German planes bombed the assembly area of the 2d Battalion, 67th Armor, causing a crater eighty to ninety feet in diameter and twenty-five to thirty feet deep. Most of the casualties, seven killed and fifty-one wounded, were caused by flying chunks of clay, some of which were as large as a quarter-ton truck. After this, slit trenches were deepened by several feet.

On the last day of June, the 2d Armored Division was ordered to relieve the British 7th Armored Division in an area east of Caumont. Once in position, the 17th Armored Engineer Battalion prepared routes to meet possible counterattacks from any direction. The infantry dug in and outposted their positions, while the mortars and artillery were registered along possible routes of approach. The two tank regiments manned reserve positions, ready to come to the aid of the infantry if needed. To ease the pressure on the frontline soldiers, two infantry battalions were kept in the line while the third was in reserve, and rotated to relieve one front line unit at a time.

After assuming their defensive positions and getting them ready to repel counterattacks, the 41st Armored Infantry and the 82d Reconnaissance Battalion constantly sent out patrols to gather information about enemy strengths and locations. At 11:10 A.M. on July 2, the first patrol from the 2d Battalion, 41st Armored Infantry, started for the small village of Briquessard. The British reported it to be well defended. They got almost to the village before drawing fire and withdrew without loss. The next morning a patrol from the 3d Battalion, 41st Armored Infantry, consisting of one officer and twenty men, reached the edge of Buquet before coming under heavy machine gun, small arms and mortar fire. The patrol returned the fire and attempted to maneuver, but the open terrain and the intensity of enemy fire prevented such movement. Forced to withdraw, they lost the patrol leader and had one enlisted man wounded. A second patrol later returned to the town, attempting to retrieve the officer's body, but failed. Finding that the area was heavily booby-trapped, it determined that the Germans were going to resist the advance of any patrols. This pattern continued while the division manned the front lines.

Division officers and observers made frequent visits to the front to view the situation and to observe tactics. General Rose made daily visits to the frontline battalions, exposing himself to enemy view and fire. As if by magic, moments after Rose had departed, the Germans would fire artillery, mortars and Nebelwerfers, or "screaming Mimis," where he had been. The division commander may have said something to Rose, for while he continued to visit the front, he did so with much less exposure. The general saw as much as before, but the infantrymen received much less shelling.

The division artillery, working on improving their firing, perfected the technique of firing the "stonk" and time on target. The first division concentration (all guns fired) occurred at 1:00 A.M. on July 2. The target was an enemy build-up in Anctoville. Two days later, First Army planned a salute to the independence of the United States. First army artillery, V Corps artillery, the 74th Artillery Battalion, the 96th Artillery Regiment and division artillery planned to fire a single round at high noon in honor of the Fourth of July. The British, apparently forgetting the day's historical significance, also requested permission to join. It was granted and the British Royal Horse Artillery took part in the salute. At noon on July 4, approximately 280 guns fired an Independence Day salute at the Germans in the town of Anctoville.

During three days, July 5 to 8, the 92d Armored Artillery Battalion fired in support of the Royal Horse Artillery and the 50th British Brigade. The Americans helped to break up a counterattack west of Hottot, destroying four Mark IV tanks and killing eight infantry. Later the 14th Artillery found that the Germans were firing in the same sequence as the Americans, hoping to trick the American infantrymen into thinking that they were being shelled by their own guns. It did not work. Another favorite German tactic was to place guns so that they could fire down the American lines. To counter this, the division artillery air observers flew missions about dawn and dusk. When the muzzle flashes of the German guns were located, effective counterbattery fire could be brought onto the targets.

The armored infantrymen holding the line wanted to have all the .30-caliber machine guns on their half-tracks replaced with the longer-range .50-caliber guns. Some replacements had been made in England, but not all the guns had been changed. While holding the line, the men saw many American planes crash near their positions. The soldiers rushed to the crash, salvaged the .50-caliber machineguns and helped the pilots if they could. The regimental and division maintenance sections made mounts so that the aircraft machine guns could be used in the infantry half-tracks. Procurement of supplies in this manner required a liberal interpretation of regulations about items found either on post or on the battlefield.

The division also conducted its own psychological warfare against the Germans. Psychological warfare personnel moved sound trucks close the the front and played Strauss waltzes, followed with statements encouraging surrender. The finale, if the appeals did not work, was a forty-eight gun artillery barrage on the German positions. This played havoc with their morale. Another type of psychological warfare was waged. On July 9, starting at 3:00 P.M. and lasting for 1½ hours, the 2d Armored

Division called a halt to the war so that it could return several German nurses to their lines.

In turn, the 2d Armored Division received a fright in the latter part of July. A liaison officer reported that a sound truck had passed through announcing that the Cherbourg area had been gassed. The division commander asked the V Corps to investigate the situation. It was even more frightening a few days later when two Hell-On-Wheelers found twelve bottles of gas which they could not identify. Several days later, the 702d Tank Destroyer Battalion found a container of gas and some powder, thought to be a decontamination agent, as well as the morning report of the 14th Company of the Panzer Grenadier Regiment ''Goetz Von Berlichingen.'' This gas proved to be nonlethal tear gas.

The landings on the Cotentin peninsula were largely successful because of the blunderings of Adolf Hitler. He refused to permit the movement of troops to the beachheads. In his ''military wisdom'' the landings were feints to cover the real assault that would occur in the Pas de Calais area under George S. Patton, Jr. Initially, then, the Germans committed their armor to the defense of the Seine basin, primarily near Caen, to prevent the linking of the British and Americans after their landing at Calais. By mid-July the Germans had two armor divisions on Bradley's front, the 2d SS Panzer and the Panzer Lehr Division, but still kept most of their armor near Calais to meet the nonexistent threat.

Against the background of these German preparations, Gen. Omar N. Bradley planned one of the most spectacular actions of the war—Operation COBRA, the breakout from the Cotentin peninsula to the plains of France, where the armored elements would teach the Germans a lesson in *blitzkreig*.

In the week prior to COBRA, the 2d Armored Division was alerted to be ready to turn its part of the line over to the 8th Armored Brigade, British 50th Armored Division, and retire to the area west of La Mine. During this week, the division and its attached units practiced tank-infantry teamwork and attended demonstrations of the same. Each battalion practiced limited objective attacks in hedgerow country. The infantrymen, especially the attached regimental combat team, were taught how and at what tanks fire, how to ride the tanks and how to help them. A new device, the external telephone, mounted on the tanks, was a great benefit.

Besides the tactical training, the men performed maintenance on vehicles and individual equipment. Some medium tanks carrying the 75mm gun were replaced with the 76mm gun. Wire cutters were placed on all the open-topped vehicles to prevent decapitation by wire strung over the road. Sgt. Curtis G. Culin of the 102d Cavalry Reconnaissance Squadron designed and tested a hedgerow cutter (heavy steel prongs welded to the front of the tank); about 75 percent of the tanks were equipped with them. This new tool was kept secret until COBRA was actually underway. The "Rhinoceros" disrupted German defenses, buried many defenders alive and caused many to surrender when attacked from several directions at once.

The 2d Armored Division was a heavy division; it had two tank regiments and one infantry regiment. With the attachment of an additional infantry regiment and its artillery battalion, two other artillery battalions and a reconnaissance squadron, each combat commander had more battle strength than did that of a light armored division. In effect, the division commander wielded a small corps. When planning for the Normandy invasion, each division was permitted 15 percent overage to cover casualties; replacements were based on the larger figure. The older Table of Organization and Equipment designated a tank crew to be six men, not five. Each armored regimental maintenance section had twelve additional tanks for replacements. With the excess tanks and trained personnel, each armored regiment had almost a company of extra tanks. In COBRA, the division suffered moderate to heavy casualties which in no way affected its tactical efficiency, because of the extra strength.

Supply columns were organized for the attack. The division quartermaster organized an eighty-four-truck column to resupply each combat command. Combat Command A, which had a semiindependent mission, was to get twenty-four trucks (twelve to carry gasoline, one to carry diesel, one for grease and oil, ten to carry a balanced load of ammunition, mostly artillery shells). The remainder of the eighty-four vehicles were to support Combat Command B and the rest of the division. Each tank was to carry three days' rations for the crew and its supporting infantry, as well as extra ammunition and gasoline for 200 miles of operation. Capt. James M. Burt, B Company, 66th Armor, recalled that the tanks often carried more food and water than the orders required. To aid the attached infantry, the tankers also had extra pioneer tools: shovels, picks and axes. This important addition helped infantrymen to dig their foxholes or slit trenches faster. It created a feeling that the tankers wanted and needed them.

Field Marshall Erwin Rommel noted that after four or five days the Allied forces had given clear indications of their plans. They wanted to establish a bridgehead, then break out into the interior of France, probably toward Paris, or cut off the Cotentin peninsula and secure the port of Cherbourg. While Rommel was pleading with Hitler for the use of the idle panzer divisions and being rebuked for his efforts, the German situation was deteriorating. Personnel replacements were few and insufficient to change the course of battle. Tank losses exceeded gains. There was lack of fuel, repair parts and ammunition because of the effective disruption of German supply lines by United States' air operations. As if that were not enough, the officer corps was reeling from the purges following the plot to assassinate Hitler. The German enlisted personnel were becoming disillusioned because of the lack of air support and the superiority of the Allied troops. The much-promised "miracle weapons" were not forthcoming. All of these factors, combined at the right time with a determined Allied effort to break out of the peninsula, would make the American effort succeed.

For approximately six to seven weeks, the Americans bolstered their forces for an attempted breakout of the Cotentin peninsula. The Allies had two choices: they could attempt to roll back the Germans along a broad front; or they could attack along a narrow front, pierce the German lines and attempt an enveloping movement. COBRA was built around the second choice. It was an attack against prepared German defenses, which if successful would propel the Allies into the heart of France.

The plan had three phases, opening with a carpet bombing intended to clear a corridor 2,500 yards deep and 6,000 yards wide. The air bombardment was to be quickly followed by two infantry divisions, attacking to secure the shoulders of the corridor. In phase two, the exploiting forces were to pin the enemy against the sea; and during the final phase, the V, VIII and XIX Corps, which would be applying pressure during the two earlier phases, were to increase that pressure, hopefully taking advantage of enemy disorganization to block an escape into the interior of France. Simultaneously, the Americans had to prevent enemy reinforcements from entering the battle area.

The VII Corps was to be the exploiting force; the 1st Infantry and 3d Armored Divisions were to attack through the gap created by the bombing attack. The 2d Armored Division was to have an important but secondary role. After the attack began, however, the exploiting forces became heavily engaged. The 2d Armored Division then formed the spearhead and the success of COBRA depended on the success of Hell on Wheels.

Brooks was ordered by VII Corps to move the division (minus one combat command) through the gap created by the bombing attack, to seize the le Mesnil Herman–St. Sampson de Bon Fosse–Hill 183 area. This mission, given to Combat Comand A, would cover the assault of the 1st Infantry and the 3d Armored Division. The order further directed Brooks to push one combat command to the southwest along the Pont Hebert–St. Gilles–Canisy road. It was to be prepared to execute one of the three possible missions: to seize and secure objectives in its zone between Cerences and St. Denis le Gast, blocking enemy reinforcements; to move on Coutances to reinforce the 3d Armored Division; or to move to the southwest to support the remainder of the 2d Armored Division.

The official histories of the United States Army in World War II state that on the east flank, where the 2d Armored was to operate, the division had essentially a protective or defensive mission. However, when the division started moving, Brooks gave no indication of a defensive posture. The original plans did not call for the 2d Armored to bear the brunt of the attack, but when Gen. J. Lawton Collins, VII Corps commanding general, used the words ''seize the area'' and directed the other combat command to ''seize and secure objectives within its zone,'' he was speaking of offensive, not defensive, action.

At the conclusion of its attack, the 2d Armored Division was to take up blocking positions at Brehal, Cerences, Lengronne, St. Denis le Gast, Hambye, Villeboudon and Tessy sur Vire. These positions would stretch the Allies across the Cotentin peninsula, effectively preventing any escape for the trapped German troops or the arrival of German reinforcements. COBRA entailed a two-pronged envelopment, with the 2d Armored Division used in the easternmost thrust.

The 30th Infantry Division was to protect the left flank of VII Corps by securing crossings over the Vire River and blocking the arrival of reinforcements from the east. After that division had moved its vehicles from the road, the 2d Armored Division was to attack in a column of combat commands, then splitting to make independent attacks. This was necessary because of the nature of Brooks's mission.

Brooks organized the combat commands so that, while appearing to be of equal strength, Combat Command A was the larger and more powerful of the two. His reasons were the nature of its mission and the possibility that Rose might be cut off once underway. Rose commanded the 66th Armored Regiment, the 22d Regimental Combat Team and its normal attachments, the 14th Armored Artillery Battalion, Companies A and C of the 17th Armored Engineers Battalion, the 702d Tank Destroyer

Battalion (minus Company B), Company A and half of Company C from the 48th Medical Battalion, D Battery of the 195th Antiaircraft Artillery Battalion, and a detachment of the division's Maintenance Battalion.

Combat Command B had the 67th Armored Regiment (minus the 3d Battalion), the 1st and 3rd Battalions, 41st Armored Infantry Regiment, the 78th Armored Artillery Battalion, Company B from the 17th Armored Engineer Battalion, Company B of the 702d Tank Destroyer Battalion, the 48th Medical Battalion's B Company, A Battery of the 195th Antiaircraft Artillery Battalion, and a detachment of the division Maintenance Battalion.

Division reserve, commanded by Col. Sidney R. Hinds, contained the 3d Battalion, 67th Armor, and the 2d Battalion (minus one company) of his own 41st Armored Infantry Regiment. Division artillery made its plans along with the remainder of the division. Once committed to battle, the 62d Armored Artillery Battalion was to be used in direct support of Combat Command B. The 92d Armored Artillery Battalion was to be in direct support of the 41st Armored Infantry Regiment (division reserve). Batteries C and D, 129th Antiaircraft Artillery Battalion, (90mm guns) were to be used initially in antiaircraft roles, but on division order they would revert to a tank destroyer role.

Rose issued his operations order on July 20. Combat Command A was to move by two routes, seizing the high ground near le Mesnil Herman, St. Sampson de Bon Fosse and Hill 183, which would protect the attack of the 1st Infantry and 3d Armored Divisions. After capturing the initial objectives, the men were to be ready to attack any enemy forces moving from the east or south between Conde sur Vire and Hambye. The reconnaissance units (the 82d Reconnaissance Battalion and the 24th Cavalry Squadron) were ordered to overrun light resistance and to outpost the objectives until relieved by the advance guard. On July 22, the combat command was placed on a two-hour alert; at 6:00 P.M. on July 25, it was alerted for movement to an assembly area south of Pont Hebert, from which it was to lead the 2d Armored Division attack.

COBRA began with a saturation bombing attack along the Periers-St. Lo road, after which the 9th and 30th Infantry Divisions attacked to force open the shoulders of the gap. The bombing had mixed results. The American fliers either misread their maps or, as one man recalled, the Germans threw the smoke pots marking the forward bombline back into the American lines. In either case, the American bombers dropped their loads short, causing many casualties in the 30th Infantry Division. This short bombing also killed Lt. Gen. Lesley J. McNair, who was visiting the front lines.

From the German positions, Gen. Fritz Bayerlein, commanding general of the 130th Panzer Lehr Division, said later that the units holding the front were almost totally wiped out, with tanks overturned and buried, artillery positions destroyed, infantry positions flattened, all signal communications cut and no command possible. He added that the shock to the men was indescribable; several German soldiers went mad. Bayerlein, may have been correct, but the 30th Infantry Division history noted that when the division attacked "they found the enemy doing business at the same old stand with the same old merchandise—dug-in tanks and infantry." Enemy artillery was splattering on the main routes of attack. The air attack probably did not produce many German casualties, but it certainly created confusion, disrupted communications and hindered the flow of supplies.

In the early afternoon of July 25, the 2nd Armored Division received a message that the Germans were felling trees across the road and covering them with antitank guns all the way to St. Gilles. After the infantry attacks began, with the troops meeting only moderately light resistance, Collins decided to commit the exploiting force the next day, July 26. In spite of the limited success of the air attack, he guessed that there was more to be gained in committing the troops to battle than in permitting the Germans to regroup and prepare for a delayed attack.

Rose, alerted to move south of the assembly area on July 25, began moving at 10:30 P.M. that day. At 2:00 A.M. he assembled his unit commanders and gave them verbal orders for the attack. The original plan was changed because of recent information. They were to attack in one column, two battalions abreast, instead of in two columns as originally planned. Combat Command A would attack with the 2d Battalion, 66th Armor, on the right and the 3d Battalion, 66th Armor, on the left of the road between St. Gilles and Canisy. Two infantry companies accompanied the lead tank battalions, while the remainder of the infantry (in trucks) followed the 1st Battalion of the 6th Armor.

The Panzer Lehr Division, whose assignment was to defend the route chosen by the 2d Armored Division, had been almost totally destroyed. Because of this, it was replaced by the 352d Infantry Regiment. The American attack hit in the boundary areas of the LXXXIV and II

Above: Troops await the carpet bombing attack before the breakout at St. Lo, France.
Below: German tank in a bomb crater caused by carpet bombing at St. Lo.

Parachute Corps. As a result, Combat Command A received a heavy volume of flanking fire, but at the same time it constantly outflanked enemy positions.

General Brooks told Rose to get started; he did. Crossing the line of departure at 9:45 A.M., Combat Command A passed through the 120th Infantry Regiment, 30th Infantry Division, and deployed because of the difficult terrain. By 10:35, the tankers had broken through the thin crust of German defenses, about 1½ miles north of St. Gilles. The tanks had, to that point, encountered artillery fire, some antitank fire, at least one tank and an occasional defended hedgerow. Bomb craters caused greater delays than the enemy; the division engineers practically had to rebuild the roads. Combat Command A took their first prisoners about 10:35, sending them to the rear for questioning. The POWs were thought to be from the Panzer Lehr Division, the 5th Parachute Division and the 275th Infantry Division. They reported that the 275th Engineer Battalion had suffered heavy losses from the bombing attack. The attack continued against "not heavy" resistance.

While north of St. Gilles, Rose learned that air reconnaissance had reported seven Mark VI tanks south of that town. Later, Combat Command A confirmed that the German tanks had indeed entered the town. At 3:00 P.M., the advance guard of the 2d Battalion, 66th Armor, on the right side of the route of advance, reported that it had encountered a roadblock 800 yards north of St. Gilles. This destroyed overpass was defended by antitank guns and infantry. The leading units called for air support, which eliminated the obstacle. About ten minutes later, the 2d Battalion, 66th Armor, circumvented a minefield and entered the town from the northwest. In a short, brisk fight, the tankers destroyed two tanks and a self-propelled gun, while the air corps accounted for two additional tanks.

After passing through the town, the command split into two columns. The 2d Battalion, 66th Armor, stayed on the road toward le Mesnil Herman, while the 3d Battalion, 66th Armor, moved southwest toward St. Sampson de Bon Fosse. The objectives were the extensive road networks leading into the main battle area from the east and south. The Germans tried with artillery and antitank fire but failed to interrupt the columns. When these efforts proved fruitless, the Germans quickly manned a defensive position behind a stream as a tank ditch, but this too was unsuccessful. The 2d Battalion, 66th Armor, flanked this position from the east, driving the defenders out. Artillery fire increased as the Americans took the high ground 1,400 yards north of Canisy. During the advance, the combat command had burned several fuel dumps, destroyed several armored vehicles and captured almost a hundred prisoners.

Rose's command met its first determined opposition at Canisy. The Germans were using a bombed-out overpass as a roadblock. About 5:00 P.M., D Company, 66th Armor, moved into firing positions atop a hill overlooking the town. Meanwhile, A Company flanked the town and entered it from the east. As the infantrymen helped clean out the town and the tanks regrouped to continue southward, they were bombed by a flight of American P-47s which apparently mistook them for Germans. The Americans were using their identification panels and yellow smoke to signal the airplanes; the Germans were using orange for the same purpose. The colors must have looked much the same from the air.

During the battle, Sgt. Frederick Morse of the maintenance section, A Company, 82d Reconnaissance Battalion, was driving a truck hauling prisoners back to the hastily constructed prisoner cages. The driver and guard had somehow commandeered a German Volkswagen pickup truck to make their trips. At the time, the front was a swirling mass of pockets of resistance. The Germans had a machine gun covering the looping curve of the road they had to travel. They drew fire on the trip back to the cages, but for some reason—perhaps the German machine gun crew thought their countrymen were trying to escape the trap—they received no fire as they went forward. After three trips, Morse and his guard believed that they had used all the good luck in their charms and were relieved when the tanks arrived to assist them.

Rose, an aggressive, single-minded person, continued to push southward. The tankers advanced until they met opposition. At that point, the infantry, who were riding the hulls, dismounted, scouted ahead to find the obstacle and reported back to the tankers. The Germans greatly aided the American efforts by leaving the engines of their tanks running, which betrayed the enemy's position. When the infantry reported on the opposition, the tankers would then attack or outflank the German positions. At 11:00 P.M., the 3d Battalion, 66th Armor, entered St. Sampson de Bon Fosse; by 2:00 A.M., the 2d Battalion, 66th Armor, was very close to le Mesnil Herman. Rose then permitted his men to rest for the night, while the Reconnaissance Company, 66th Armored Regiment, established outposts around the area.

At dawn on July 27, the 2d Battalion, 66th Armor, was at the crossroads northeast of le Mesnil Herman, where it came under heavy artillery and mortar fire and suffered a few small-scale infantry attacks.

For approximately three hours (9:00 A.M. to noon) it engaged in tank-versus-tank fights and fired at antitank guns. During the fight, the Americans lost three tanks. Corp. William L. Giblin was badly burned when his tank was destroyed. His company commander, whose tank was also knocked out of action, had been taken prisoner. Giblin, however, managed to rescue the captain and capture the three Germans—more candidates for Morse to haul to the rear. During the height of the battle, Capt. Mario de Felice, medical officer of the 2d Battalion, 66th Armor, moved deep into enemy territory to aid the wounded. Though he was surrounded and the aid man beside him was killed in action, the doctor refused to leave until the wounded had received care and been evacuated. For his actions, de Felice was awarded the Distinguished Service Cross.

Reports that Hill 183 was in friendly hands proved to be erroneous. The area around the slopes had been taken, but the enemy still held the crest. The 2d Battalion, 66th Armor, was ordered to take the hill, and it did by 3:00 P.M. Meanwhile, the 22d Infantry Regiment was ordered to comb the brush to eliminate snipers, then relieve the 2d Battalion on Hill 183.

During the battle, Maj. Lindsey Harkness, commanding officer of the 2d Battalion, 66th Armor, was supervising the removal of a roadblock created by several burning German tanks. As the officer pursued this task, a German soldier leaped from the hedgerow and wounded Harkness in the chest. Harkness refused to be evacuated and continued with the operation. Later in the day, he arrived at Rose's command post to discuss continuing the operation and to make plans for the night advance. Hal Boyle, a newspaper correspondent, was at Rose's command post and was impressed at the bleeding commander's determination to carry on the fight. When Boyle mentioned the incident to Harkness's hometown newspaper, the major's family was understandably concerned and contacted the War Department, asking why a wounded man was still in action. Wires crisscrossed the Atlantic demanding answers. Days later and many miles north, Harkness was called out of action to assure the Red Cross that he was in good health and still fighting.

Rose ordered the 1st Battalion, 66th Armor, to make a reconnaissance in force toward Tessy sur Vire. This force (the eastern task force), which had been Combat Command A's reserve, met intense antitank opposition and had to overcome strong infantry delaying actions. Enemy infantry infiltrated the tank column, fired and escaped before the Americans could swing their weapons on them. The tankers took the high ground near le Mesnil Opac, about two miles southeast of le Mesnil Herman, and captured about twenty-three prisoners, including three officers of the Ground Luftwaffe Army, German air corps personnel used in a ground combat role. Part of the 24th Cavalry Reconnaissance Squadron relieved the tankers, who then pulled back to an assembly area near le Mesnil Herman.

The western task force (3d Battalion, 66th Armor) moved south toward Villebaudon, where it was to turn east toward Tessy sur Vire. The tankers ran into heavy delaying action; the enemy used tanks and infantry to maximum advantage, and it was 11:00 P.M. before the task force reached the crossroads at la Denisiere. Soon thereafter the Americans pulled back about three miles to spend the night and resupply their vehicles. While supervising the attack, Col. John H. Collier was almost killed. An armor-piercing round from a tank or antitank gun passed between his legs, nicking his trousers. An engineer private next to him had his leg shot off below the knee. A medic nearby immediately came to the scene and with Collier's assistance rescued the wounded engineer. Reflecting on that event years later, Collier realized that the enemy was Wehrmacht troops, not SS, because though he was armed and a legitimate target they did not fire on the rescue party.

Later in the evening, Rose assembled the unit commanders and ordered them to resume the attack at 6:30 A.M. and to seize, organize and hold the ground, denying the enemy an opportunity to use the approach routes that would disrupt the main attack of COBRA. At 2:00 A.M. Rose was notified that the 113th Cavalry Group was to be attached to the combat command and that Combat Command A was detached from the 2d Armored Division to operate under the supervision of XIX Corps.

In late afternoon, the 2d Armored Division began warning Rose that reports indicated the Germans were moving toward his position. The nearest ford on the Vire River was at Tessy sur Vire. At 8:30 P.M., the division air officer reported the road between le Mesnil Herman and Villebaudon was crowded with enemy infantry and armor. Aircraft strafed the enemy column, and bomber attacks were requested.

While Combat Command A was holding off the German reinforcements attempting to relieve their trapped comrades, Combat Command B, led by Brigadier General I. D. White, prepared to enter the fight. Combat Command B had been assigned to seize four areas: the high ground west of Pont Brocard; Notre Dame le Cenilly; the area around Lengronne; and Cambernon. Their ultimate objective was the

Cerences–St. Denis le Gast line, blocking the escape bridge at Gavray. Rose had notified the division that the roads were mined and in bad shape as a result of the bombing which had preceded the ground attack. During the night of July 26–27, the engineers worked to remove mines and to make the roads passable. Brooks had decided to commit Combat Command B in its planned role to take Lengronne; the attack was to be launched on the morning of July 27. Division artillery, two armored artillery battalions and five antiaircraft batteries would be in support. Troops under division control would bring up the rear. Altogether the force numbered about 11,000 men.

Brooks sent the 82d Reconnaissance Battalion ahead of the division, ordering them to keep moving to the limit of their responsibility. He observed that the zone appeared clear, but the battalion was to keep him informed. Lt. Col. Wheeler Merriam, commanding officer of the 82d Reconnaissance Battalion remembered that optimism was a Brooks trademark—nothing was ever in front of the division. Except this time, it was the German Seventh Army.

Combat Command A had attacked on July 26. Combat Command B attacked at 10:00 A.M. the following morning. Following the route of Combat Command A as far as Canisy, White moved from Pont Hebert to Canisy, where he turned southwest and divided his force into two columns. The right column moved on the Dangy–Pont Brocard–Notre Dame le Cenilly road, while the left column proceeded along a road about a mile east and south of the right column. When passing through Canisy, Brooks told White: "Your mission has been changed. Move at once on Cerences and Brehal. Cut off withdrawal of [the] enemy from the north." With new orders came a change in tactics. Speed became the prime consideration; White and Combat Command B were racing an enemy who had a head start. To execute the new mission, it would be necessary to seize key traffic control points and to destroy those bridges over the Sienne River not already destroyed from the air. Enemy forces encountered were to be contained and bypassed until the objectives were secured. Thus Combat Command B became the spearhead of VII Corps.

First enemy contact was made at Quibou, about a mile southwest of Canisy. A German force of four Mark V tanks, antitank guns, artillery and infantry had already knocked out an American assault gun and captured, among others, a sergeant with a map indicating phase lines and routes of attack. The right column's advance guard arrived, deployed and, with the aid of P-47s flying cover, outflanked the position. The

Germans retreated, the sergeant escaped to be evacuated for battle fatigue, and the column continued toward Dangy.

Unknown to the Americans, Maj. Gen. Fritz Bayerlein, commander of the 130th Panzer Lehr Division, was conducting a staff meeting in Dangy as the American tanks roared through the village. The German general and his staff were trapped; the tanks fired high-explosive shells and machine guns at the front of the house, and the back windows were barred. However, Bayerlein and his staff slipped away after dark and called the corps commander, telling him that nothing remained of the 130th Panzer Lehr Division. The Americans rolled on.

Pont Brocard was taken after a sharp clash between the advance guard and German armored cars. The American advance guard went into Notre Dame le Cenilly, destroying several vehicles and taking about twenty-five prisoners. The American commander motioned the prisoners to the rear, only to find that the main body was not in sight. Lt. Col. Richard E. Nelson, commanding officer of the 1st Battalion, 67th Armored Regiment, looking for his advance guard, rounded a corner in Notre Dame le Cenilly and saw a large group of Germans leaving a church. Reacting quickly, he killed more than forty as they rushed out.

Later, the right column went into defensive positions for the night. The next morning, several destroyed vehicles were found in front of the roadblocks. The left column was slowed more by difficult terrain than by enemy resistance. The 188th Field Artillery Group, supporting the division, attempted to occupy positions near Pont Brocard but were blocked by German infantry. Col. Thomas A. Roberts, division artillery commander, called for fifty men from each artillery battalion to act as infantry and help the 183d Artillery Battalion, which was having the most difficulty. At 3:00 P.M., tanks arrived to aid the "infantrymen" and in the struggle captured 175 prisoners, a large ammunition and supply dump, and a four-gun pack howitzer battery. The 2d Platoon, 67th Armored Regiment's Reconnaissance Company, fought its way into its bivouac area, capturing 300 prisoners and a German payroll, which later caused considerable paperwork for the company. During the night D Company, 17th Armored Engineer Battalion, took thirty-two prisoners and weapons while the Germans were trying to pass through their area.

The next morning, the right column, under orders to capture Cambernon, encountered a stiff enemy attack from Cerisy la Salle directed toward Pont Brocard and Notre Dame le Cenilly. The Germans were repulsed with the aid of the division reserve; destroyed vehicles and dead or dying Germans were scattered over a forty-acre field. By midnight Hinds had taken Cerisy la Salle and secured it.

A small task force, composed of a tank company, an armored infantry company, a platoon of engineers, a medical detachment and an air control party, captured Cambernon, established a roadblock and then fought off annihilation. They were under constant pressure and could not be reinforced. By utilizing protective air and artillery cover, they improved their position and rendered valuable assistance in the next thirty-six hours.

The main body of the combat command continued the attack. The right column was assigned to seize key road junctions in the St. Martin de Cenilly area while the left column captured road junctions near Hambey and the town of Lengronne. The armored fence which the 2d Armored was building could trap the German army, if the division beat the main body of Germans to the river crossings. About 6:35 P.M., the division's prisoner-of-war interrogation center notified G-2 that they had questioned a member of the 353d Infantry Division, who stated that the Germans were in full retreat but still facing north. His division was unaware that the 2d Armored was behind them.

The 82d Reconnaissance Battalion had won the race and was manning outposts along the Sienne River. Merriam had inspected them and found them all peaceful. When he returned to his command post, north of Notre Dame le Cenilly, he found it under attack by German infantry. Battalion Sgt. Maj. Victor S. Prawdzik walked behind his line of non-combatant defenders, urging and encouraging them with his then famous words, "God damnit, trooper, get a move on; get a move on, trooper!" Many seemed to fear Prawdzik more than the Germans. The attack was beaten off with few casualties to the headquarters personnel.

Combat Command B had won the race but now faced its most severe test. It had to meet any German attempt to break out and prevent reinforcements coming into the area. In its vulnerable position it might suffer tremendous casualties in men and materials. If it were unable to repulse the German attacks, the German army would escape to fight again. The success of COBRA depended on the ability of Brooks, White and Hinds to hold the St. Denis le Gast–Sienne River line.

Brooks and White guessed correctly that the Germans would attempt to break out of the trap. Late in the afternoon of July 28, they pulled in their men and established a defensive line about seven miles long, from Pont Brocard to St. Denis le Gast. This accordian-type move left a gap of ten miles from St. Denis le Gast to the sea. However, the Germans were handicapped by geography. The Sienne River flows southwest to northeast. It is wide, with steep banks, and forms an effective barrier. The defensive positions of the 2d Armored and the Sienne River formed a funnel-shaped figure with the small end at Gavray, which the Germans held. The 2d Armored Division's positions, however, blocked access to the town and its all-important bridge.

The first German attack occurred about 4:00 A.M. at the crossroads southwest of St. Martin de Cenilly. Led by a self-propelled 88mm gun and wildly yelling "Heil Hitler," German infantry almost overran the American position. The German crew worked the gun into a position to rake the American defenders with deadly fire. Seeing the immediate danger, Sgt. Robert Lotz, I Company, 41st Armored Infantry Regiment, destroyed the periscope and then shot the gun commander. Later, when the battle was over, the motor on the gun was still running and a shell was found in the breech. Had the German attack been successful, it would have created a path large enough for a considerable number of the encircled troops to escape the trap. At dawn the attackers withdrew, leaving seventeen German dead and 150 wounded.

The second attack occurred at approximately 9:00 A.M. near the crossroads at la Penetiere. A company of the 4th Infantry Division manned outposts protecting the 78th Armored Artillery Battalion. The cannoneers were also supported by four tank destroyers and an antiaircraft artillery section. The infantry was driven in by a German force of fifteen tanks and several hundred paratroopers. One battery fired indirect fire, two batteries and the antiaircraft section lowered their guns for direct fire, as did the tank destroyers. For about thirty confused minutes this was the only force preventing a breakout. The attack was turned back, and elements of the 41st Armored Infantry Regiment reestablished the outpost. The Germans had 126 men killed and nine tanks destroyed. More importantly, however, the line remained intact.

The outposts were pulled in again for the night of July 29-30. The division reserve moved to positions near Lengronne and captured 169 Germans while moving into its bivouac area. The 78th Armored Artillery Battalion occupied positions near la Chappelle. Unbeknown to the units, the moves were of critical importance.

The 92d Artillery, moving to a new position, had to fight its way into its area near Bois de Soulles. When Combat Command B called for fire support, the battalion complied even though under attack at the time. The Germans came so close that one self-propelled howitzer was sent to engage a German self-propelled gun with direct fire, while C Battery fired in another direction to destroy a second gun. When the Germans finally broke contact, the artillerymen found 150 dead, along with many damaged or abandoned vehicles.

About midnight, an estimated 600 infantry, the vehicles of a panzer battalion from the 2d SS Panzer Division "Das Reich" and the 17th SS Panzer Grenadier Regiment overran the command post of the 2d Battalion, 41st Armored Infantry Regiment. Lt. Col. Wilson D. Coleman was establishing outposts when the enemy attacked. He sighted the lead German tank and destroyed it with a bazooka shell, then hastily mounted his jeep and returned to alert his command. While preparing his men to meet the assault, Coleman was killed. Gradually, because of the size of the enemy forces, the battalion roadblocks and outposts were driven back into their areas. The determined defense, however, bought time for the remainder of the division reserve.

Next in the line of attack was the 3d Battalion, 67th Armored Regiment. Lt. Col. Harry Hillyard, battalion commander, was inspecting his roadblocks and outposts when the Germans hit his headquarters. His men fought gallantly, not knowing whom they were fighting in the dark night. Sometimes the fighting became brutal hand-to-hand combat. As three Germans came through a hole in the hedgerow, Staff Sergeant Joseph Barnes cut each of their throats. The battle ended when a German tank forced its gun over the hedgerow and systematically destroyed the vehicles. The area, illuminated by burning vehicles and barraged by fire from tanks, panzerfausts and small arms, was abandoned.

After overrunning two command posts, the Germans next came upon the headquarters of division reserve, or the 41st Armored Infantry Regiment Reinforced. The headquarters came into their area, even though it was being swept by heavy enemy small arms and machine gun fire. The men began to organize a perimeter defense, and as survivors from the 2d Battalion, 41st, and 3d Battalion, 67th, entered the area, they were immediately pressed into service. The noncombatant specialists fought their first battle, demonstrating a discipline and training unmatched by many line units: they did not fire at each other or into the stragglers approaching their lines. That night, they served as a rallying point for many isolated groups which fought to survive the confused battle. Throughout the night, the specialists rescued many wounded and brought back bodies. Several times noncommissioned officers, on their own initiative, ventured out of the perimeter to man abandoned American tanks, to stalk German tanks and to establish better defense positions.

During the battle, 1st Lt. William H. Hough had led his platoon of tanks from the 3d Battalion, 67th Armored Regiment, to the town of St. Denis le Gast. Some enemy soldiers had gone around Hind's position and attacked the town, driving out Hough and his tanks; at the same time Hinds had lost radio contact with the infantry accompanying the tank officer. Hinds, Lt. Col. Robert B. Galloway (regimental executive officer) and several enlisted men decided to take a half-track to the town some few hundred yards to their rear to determine who held it and to reestablish communications. Backing the half-track into town, they came upon an enemy armored car. The American officers, armed only with their pistols, killed the driver and wounded a sentry, then escaped in a hail of machine gun fire. The headquarters men called for artillery fire from the 92d Artillery Battalion, who placed the fire only 200 yards in their front. When dawn came, the damage was assessed: 139 enemy soldiers had been shot through the head or shoulders. Remarkably, the American force which served as a rallying point for isolated groups had not killed any of their own men.

However, a group of Germans broke through the line, headed for St. Denis le Gast and then turned west on the main road to the bivouac area of the 78th Armored Artillery Battalion. At about 2:15 A.M., an officer from the Reconnaissance Company, 67th Armored, stopped in the 78th Armored Artillery area to report the fight at St. Denis le Gast. About the same time, an American tank destroyer limped in to repair its damages. At approximately 3:00, German infantry attacked the battalion outposts and were repulsed, leaving forty dead and five prisoners.

After beating off the attack and learning that St. Denis le Gast had been overrun, Lt. Col. Hugh Exton, commanding officer, 78th Artillery, moved three howitzers close to the road, where they would be in position for direct fire against enemy vehicles. One gun was the third section of A Battery, of which Pfc. James S. Crawford was the loader. He loaded an armor-piercing round in the gun and sat down with another on his lap, ready for instant reloading. He went to sleep and missed the ensuing battle. All across France, Belgium, Holland and Germany, he was to hear about sleeping through the fight. While the battalion intelligence officer, Capt. Naubert O. Simard, Jr., was questioning the prisoners, he heard an armored column approach and challenged it in German. The reply, "Vas ist?," caused one battery commander to yell, "That ain't American." All weapons opened fire: the .50-caliber machine guns, the 105mm howitzers and the 3-inch gun on the tank destroyer. About ninety Germans were killed and eleven vehicles destroyed. The artillerymen took about 205 prisoners, while suffering only four dead and seven wounded.

While the attacks on division reserve and the 78th Armored Artillery were bloody and savage, the most brutal was near Grimesnil. A company of infantry, a tank company, the headquarters company, 2d Battalion, 67th Armored (minus the assault gun platoon), and an engineer platoon were establishing a defensive position near Grimesnil, about 600 to 800 yards southeast of the American force at Cambernon. Tanks were being put into roadblock positions when the company commander, Capt. James R. McCartney, executive officer, 2d Battalion, 67th Armor, heard the distinctive sound of approaching German infantry and challenged them. The enemy force, estimated at 2,000 to 2,500 men and ninety vehicles, was a mixed force from many units.

The Germans attacked, driving in the tank outpost, but were stopped by the actions of Sgt. Hulon B. Whittington, whose Medal of Honor citation reads:

For conspicuous gallantry and intrepidity at the risk of life above and beyond the call of duty. On the night of 29 July 1944, near Grimesnil, France, during an enemy armored attack, Sergeant Whittington, a squad leader, assumed command of his platoon when the platoon leader and the platoon sergeant became missing in action. He reorganized the defense and, under fire, courageously crawled between gun positions to check the actions of his men. When the advancing enemy attempted to penetrate a roadblock, Sergeant Whittington, completely disregarding intense enemy action, mounted a tank and by shouting through the turret, directed it into position to fire pointblank at the leading Mark V German Tank. The destruction of this vehicle blocked all movement of the enemy column, consisting of over 100 vehicles of a Panzer unit. The blocked vehicles were then destroyed by hand grenades, bazookas, tank, and artillery fire and large numbers of enemy personnel were wiped out by a bold and resolute bayonet charge inspired by Sergeant Whittington. When the medical aid man had become a casualty, Sergeant Whittington personally administered first aid to his wounded men. The dynamic leadership, the inspiring example, and the dauntless courage of Sergeant Whittington above and beyond the call of duty, are in keeping with the highest traditions of the military service.

The Germans tried to envelop the American positions, but they were repulsed in savage hand-to-hand, grenade and bayonet fighting. About 3:30, fearing that they would be overrun, Capt. W. C. Johnson (I Company, 41st Armored Infantry) radioed the 78th Artillery for fire support but heard an order, "B Battery fire direct," meaning that the artillerymen were fighting in their own positions. About an hour later, the 78th and 62d Armored Artillery fired, using map data and adjusting by sound and flash; both procedures are highly dangerous when used in close proximity to friendly forces. For three hours, twenty-seven guns fired 700 rounds most effectively.

The Germans made one final effort to overrun the Americans. Their infantry tried to sneak through a swamp and attack from the flanks and rear. However, tanks were sent to intercept them, and in the morning almost 300 German bodies were found in the swamp. The Germans were stopped by the bravery of the Americans. When dawn came, the scene rivaled Dante's *Inferno:* almost 600 dead, including three women and a major general, over 1,000 German prisoners and all ninety vehicles destroyed. Maj. Jerome Smith called the scene "the most godless sight I have ever witnessed on any battlefield." Capt. James R. McCartney, a veteran of French Morocco, Tunisia and Sicily, said that he had not seen such horrible carnage in all his battle experience. Bulldozers had to be used to clear the roads.

On July 30, the 82d Reconnaissance Battalion combed the area for survivors and stragglers. During the day, they killed 100 more Germans and took about 250 prisoners. At 11:15 A.M., they reported to division headquarters that "100 men from the 2d SS Panzer Division had just walked in and gave up." That same day the division (minus Combat Command A) was ordered out of battle to regroup, refresh, perform maintenance and prepare for another attack. During Operation COBRA, Combat Command B killed 1,500, captured about 5,200 and destroyed about 331 vehicles, while suffering 42 killed, 284 wounded and 69 missing in action.

The door had been opened for Third Army and General Patton to race through into the interior of France. He led the attack with the 4th Armored Division. Since it was new to combat, the division was perhaps a bit nervous. The first shots it fired were at Hell on Wheels. After determining that the 4th Armored Division was in fact firing at his troops, Hinds radioed it, saying that it was firing at "Powerhouse," the division's radio call sign. Apparently the 4th Armored suspected that Hinds was a German

Above: Troops of the 82d Reconnaissance Battalion enter a French village during the breakout at St. Lo.
Below: Brig. Gen. I. D. White inspecting battle damage during Operation COBRA.

fluent in English and continued firing. He finally told them that if the fire did not stop he would call their P (Maj. Gen. John S. "P" or "Professor" Wood, the division commander). The firing ceased.

Operation COBRA was the first time that an armored division had been used to pass through a gap and then exploit a breakthrough. The air-ground teamwork that had evolved in the peninsula—putting an air corps officer into a tank and using him to spot targets and call for air support—was one of the reasons that the operation was successful. The primary success came because the men had been ordered to keep moving regardless of losses. Many times when the lead tank drew fire, the following one flanked the opposition. This simple maneuver, nose-and-seat-of-the-pants theory, saved lives and material. The alternative, deliberate maneuver, would have given the Germans time to bring their reserves to the battle area. Another factor in the success of COBRA was the disrupted communications of the Germans and their inability to see the main direction of attack. COBRA opened the door for the battle of northern France. It had been successful and Third Army was to be loosed upon an unsuspecting German army. The singlemindedness of the 2d Armored Division commanders, to concentrate on the objective and to bypass opposition until the objective had been attained, was the keystone for the 2d Armored's success.

Chapter 12

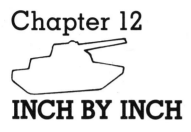

INCH BY INCH

By July 28, 1944, both combat commands were confronting strong enemy opposition. Large numbers of Germans were attempting to break out of the iron ring that White's Combat Command B was building. Simultaneously, strong enemy forces were attacking to assist their comrades. These German troops ran directly into Rose's Combat Command A, which had been ordered to seal off the Vire River as an approach route. Rose had accomplished this initial mission by the afternoon of July 27. After cutting the roads into the COBRA area, he sent strong patrols toward Tessy sur Vire and Villebaudon and planned to resume the attack in the morning of July 28. However, Combat Command A was transferred to XIX Corps the night of the 27th. Maj. Gen. Charles Corlett's XIX Corps had been given the mission of supporting the left flank of the American breakout and was responsible for action on the far bank of the Vire River. Meanwhile, the Germans moved the 2d Panzer Division to the river, hoping to break the Americans' grip. When the enemy crossed the Vire, they collided with Combat Command A and the 30th Infantry Division.

Rose had assembled his unit commanders and had scheduled an attack for 6:30 A.M. on July 28, in order to capture Tessy sur Vire and Villebaudon. When Combat Command A was transferred to XIX Corps, its objective was changed to the corps objective, which was around the town of Percy and the high ground around le Chefresne, across the Vire River southeast of Percy. The reasoning was that this would eliminate the German bridgehead at Tessy sur Vire. This caused the attack to be postponed until 3:00 that day, a delay that proved to be extremely costly. To carry out his new mission, Rose divided his combat command into three columns, each with a company of the 22d Infantry Regiment, a company of medium tanks and a platoon of light tanks from the 66th Armored Regiment, plus supporting units.

Before the original attack was postponed, Rose had sent a reconnaissance in force toward Tessy sur Vire. The Americans, avoiding the main roads, which were littered with the burning wreckage of German vehicles, were still strafed by enemy planes. American fighter bombers drove off the Luftwaffe, shooting down one German plane and not losing any American ground or air forces. About noon, U.S. forces secured Villebaudon after a sharp fight in which they destroyed six enemy reconnaissance vehicles and a Mark IV tank and killed about fifty enemy soldiers. The Americans had one man killed and lost three tanks, which were later recovered and returned to use.

Three German tanks had taken up positions at the la Denisiere crossroads behind the American force, threatening to cut the road between le Mesnil Herman and Villebaudon, which would isolate the combat command spearhead. The 14th Armored Artillery Battalion moved to positions south of the crossroads, firing in support of the advancing American tanks. Once in position, the battalion had to fire in two directions: south to support the American attack on Villebaudon, and north to dislodge the German tanks. The battery concentrating on the tanks was firing Charge 1: the Germans were not more than 500 yards away.

The prolonged duel caused additional hazards. In order to resupply the artillerymen, the supply convoy had to pass the crossroads. To get by this danger point, some of the supply personnel dismounted from their trucks and engaged the German tanks, while the drivers raced across the critical area. The drivers were not always successful and several vehicles were damaged, although none were destroyed. The Germans held out another day before being dislodged from their positions. During the fight, the 14th Artillery fired 2,275 rounds, an enormous expenditure reflecting the almost incessant artillery bombardment.

After taking Villebaudon, Rose strengthened the American hold on this town with the 113th Cavalry Group and later with the 14th Armored Artillery. He then sent the task force toward Tessy sur Vire. Lt. Col. Amzi R. Quillan, who was forward directing the fight, was mortally wounded by fire from elements of the 24th Cavalry Squadron. The Americans encountered a strong enemy armored column and retired to positions near le Mesnil Herman for the night. Taking Tessy became a struggle to hold Villebaudon.

At 7:30 A.M. on July 29, the column attacked again, this time to capture Percy. This attack met strong enemy antitank gun and artillery fire. The Americans paid a heavy price, losing one platoon from G Company, 66th Armored Regiment. At times German infantry could be seen crossing the road from east to west—entering the battle area, not leaving it. German tanks began firing onto the flank of the column and were quickly engaged by part of the 702d Tank Destroyer Battalion. After an intense firefight, the Americans pulled back for the night. Still, despite being cut off from the rear, the advance continued the morning after a powerful German counterattack which inflicted heavy casualties on the infantry was beaten off. Percy was captured at 3:30 P.M. When the infantry rejoined the fight, they were able to consolidate the hold on Percy. After securing the town, the tankers continued southward, gaining about a mile before the attack was halted at 6:30 and they were relieved by the 175th Infantry Regiment, 29th Infantry Division.

The assault resumed the next morning, and during a day of bitter fighting the Americans took part of the high ground. The 14th Armored Artillery Battalion, which had escaped from the embroilment at la Denisiere crossroads, was preparing to move from Villebaudon. The cannoneers were already in column, ready to pull onto the road, when the Germans attacked. The battalion immediately assumed firing positions and answered the enemy, while all the time receiving artillery, mortar and small arms fire. Again they had to fire simultaneously in two directions and at ranges of less than 2,000 yards. Friendly infantry was overrun and fell back through the artillerymen's position, hotly followed by German infantry. All hands, including cooks and clerks, manned the hedgerow defenses. Finally the battalion pulled out of its position to move south but first transferred its fire control function to the 44th Artillery Battalion, 4th Infantry Division. In the late afternoon, the column was relieved by infantry and turned its area over to them.

The second column that Rose sent out (the middle column) was to advance as far south as Villebaudon and then turn eastward, advancing down the ridge to Tessy sur Vire. This force included two infantry battalions from the 22d Regimental Combat Team and the 2d Battalion, 66th Armored Regiment. Initially, the force was to seize Beaucoudray, severing the main road between Villebaudon and Tessy sur Vire. They met light ground resistance but were dive-bombed by five German ME-109s. The advance guard entered Moyen against fierce resistance, but the main body of the column got only to the high ground north of the town before their advance halted. The enemy garrison consisted of eight companies of panzer grenadiers and tanks from the 116th Panzer Division. Late in the evening of July 28, the two battalions from the 22d Regimental Combat Team disengaged from their positions, moved west to join their regiment and then moved south on the Percy highway. Casualties had been high on both sides, but the 2d Battalion, 66th Armored, had been ordered to hold the high ground until relieved by the 29th Infantry Division the next day.

Rose withdrew his forces from the area around Moyen. The men were to attack through la Denisiere and Villebaudon, then turn east toward Tessy sur Vire. If this move were successful, the Americans would flank the German positions at Moyen and on the Marcron River. Recognizing the danger, the enemy launched a strong tank-infantry counterattack, supported by heavy artillery fire. In the ensuing thirteen-hour fight, part of the 702d Tank Destroyer Battalion destroyed eleven enemy tanks, while its supporting infantry captured 120 Germans and killed 180. The tankers finally repulsed the Germans and secured Villebaudon for the second time in three days. The success often rested on individual action. During the fight, Technical Sergeant Arnold O. Pederson was unable to move forward against the intense tank and antitank fire. He dismounted, organized a bazooka team and led it against the enemy. He was able to dislodge the Germans, and his own tank moved forward.

The third column that had attacked on July 28 was ordered to move east from le Mesnil Herman toward le Mesnil Opac, turn south towards Tessy sur Vire and then advance southward to capture Pontfaroy. The task force encountered small arms fire near le Mesnil Opac but overcame it with little difficulty. But when they turned southward they found the strong enemy force that was holding up the center column at Moyen. After searching for a crossing over the small stream and fighting all day, the column was ordered to disengage and assemble for the night. While moving to their assembly area, the Americans were infiltrated by German infantry and tanks. The attack resumed the next day, with the tankers getting to about a kilometer north of Moyen before being ordered out of the line to be relieved by the 29th Infantry Division.

After the west column had been cut off at Villebaudon, Rose believed that further efforts at that time to take the corps objective would endanger the combat command and possibly cut off the entire command. He convinced the corps commander, who had authorized the efforts to take Tessy sur Vire. Now Corlett told Rose to concentrate on Percy and the Vire River. Once across the Vire, it would be easy to encircle Tessy from the west and cut it off from the south. Late on July 30, Corlett attached Combat Command A to the 29th Infantry Division, whose mission was to attack east and capture the elusive Tessy and the high ground about 1½ miles south of the town.

Combat Command A's mission was to aid the infantry in securing the left flank of XIX Corps, by capturing Tessy sur Vire and the high ground near la Poemeliere, about a mile west of Tessy and overlooking the town. The attack began about 9:45 A.M. on July 31. The 1st Battalion, 66th Armored Regiment, reached a point south of Beaucoudray, where it encountered enemy forces in a strong defensive position. The Germans held a wooded area on the far side of an eighty-foot-deep ravine. Even though four enemy tanks were destroyed, the battalion and its support troops spent nearly seven hours under heavy artillery fire, trying to find a way around this obstacle. At about 9:00 P.M. they were ordered to hold their positions.

Reports that the Germans would begin to withdraw prompted Corlett to resume the attack the following day. It was also reported that the Germans would resist any advance with strong delaying actions. At 3:00 P.M. on August 1, Combat Command A led the 29th Infantry Division into Tessy sur Vire. The command formed a box of five tanks to lead the attack. Two medium tanks were in front on both sides of the road; their mission was to flush out German tanks. About a hundred yards behind these tanks, a light tank moved down the center of the road—bait. Following and completing the box were two tank destroyers on either side of the road; their mission was to aid the medium tanks and to protect the light tank. No infantry rode these vehicles. The 3d Battalion was further north, paralleling the route of the 1st Battalion. Both battalions, though meeting heavy artillery, tank and antitank fire, made steady progress.

The 3d Battalion, 66th Armor, attacked toward Tessy, but along a secondary road through Chevry. After a week of steady fighting, the battalion had been reduced to twenty-four tanks, less than half strength. The early morning ground mist helped their movement. One company commander remembered that as the haze lifted his unit passed several German tanks with their crews standing beside them. The Germans made no effort to oppose the Americans and Capt. James M. Burt ordered his men not to fire unless fired upon. After the mist cleared, however, hard fighting continued all day. A German detachment of reconnaissance and personnel vehicles was overrun and destroyed. Later, five Panther tanks hit the column from the north. The Americans turned back the German efforts but at heavy cost.

H Company, 66th Armor, encountered three German Panther tanks which delayed their advance for about three hours. The Americans tried sneaking some tanks forward through a smoke screen. Finally Sgt. Joe Young maneuvered his tank to a protected position only about 200 yards from the Germans. Even at that close range, the first three armor-piercing rounds bounced off the sides of the Panther. The first round from the German tank penetrated their turret, killing one tanker and wounding Sergeant Young. A platoon leader, Lieutenant E. V. Helms, had orders to take the position at any cost. In a final desperation move, he and a skeleton crew charged the enemy, alternately firing smoke and armor-piercing shot at the Germans. Other tanks followed the lieutenant, with orders to continue the attack if he were knocked out. The Germans apparently lost their nerve and withdrew without firing. The 3d Battalion, already reduced in number, lost an additional fourteen tanks, reducing their strength to ten. By midafternoon, they had taken the high ground near la Poemeliere and sent a patrol of two tanks into town, only to have them destroyed.

Meanwhile the other two battalions of the 66th Armored were attacking astride the main road from Villebaudon toward Tessy sur Vire. They encountered strong opposition from antitank guns and artillery, as well as tank fire from the German units attempting to hold the Vire crossings for their retreating troops. B Company, 120th Infantry Regiment, 30th Infantry Division, entered Tessy thinking that Combat Command A had already preceded it. The infantrymen began setting up roadblocks, but finding the enemy still very much there, they were driven out. The tankers thought that too much artillery fire was falling in the town to risk the tanks, but four M-4s were sent to aid the infantrymen. The infantry company commander supposedly asserted that the tanks could have had wooden weapons for all he cared, for their mere appearance boosted American morale and deflated that of the enemy. After fighting all day, the Americans had secured the town and, with its capture, sealed the fate of the Germans caught west and north of the Vire River.

Following the capture of Tessy sur Vire, Combat Command A re-

Tanks of the 66th Armored Regiment enter Tessy sur Vire.

turned to the administrative control of the 2d Armored Division, even though it remained attached to the 29th Infantry Division and subject to their tactical orders. Rose pulled his men back to assembly areas near Villebaudon for reorganization and maintenance. The dense vegetation, rough terrain, sunken roads, thick hedgerows and severe opposition had induced heavy losses. After the fight the combat command had eighty medium tanks, fifty-six light tanks and fourteen armored cars in operation. The 3d Battalion, 66th Armor, suffered 105% losses in medium tanks, and 73% of its tank officers, as well as 43% of its enlisted personnel, had been killed or wounded. During the night of August 3-4, the 2d Battalion, 119th Infantry Regiment, 30th Infantry Division, was attached to Combat Command A. Since attachments usually indicated the tankers were about to reenter the battle, they were alerted to be ready to attack at 6:00 A.M. on August 4.

Gen. Charles Corlett, commanding general of XIX Corps, ordered the attack continued, hoping to defeat a fleeing enemy. The 28th and 29th Infantry Divisions each had a combat command of the 2d Armored attached to support the corp's advance southward toward Vire. The 2d Armored, which came under XIX Corps control at noon on August 2, was ordered to be ready to resume operations any time after 6:00 P.M. Seventy minutes later, at 1:10, the division was placed on a two-hour alert. Brooks was ordered to begin movement at 4:00 to secure the corps objective—generally the high ground between St. Sever Calvados and Vire and that south of that line.

Combat Command B, on the southwest flank of the corps zone, was assigned to capture St. Sever Calvados. After moving through Villebaudon and Percy, it crossed the Vire River, heading south into enemy territory. The Reconnaissance Company, 67th Armor, leading the tank elements, made good progress until it reached a roadblock west of Margueray, which was defended by several 88mm antitank guns. In the fight, the Americans lost three armored cars before pulling back to await reinforcements.

The main body of Combat Command B had moved from bivouac areas near Notre Dame le Cenilly and had covered about thirteen miles before coming under extremely heavy artillery, antitank, mortar and tank fire from le Chefrense, about 1½ miles northwest of Margueray. At the same time that the 1st Battalion, 67th Armor, was receiving enemy fire, elements of the 28th Infantry Division began falling back toward the tankers. The ensuing congestion delayed their efforts to send aid to the reconnaissance company which already had pulled back. The 2d Platoon, H Company, deployed and, supported by a platoon of C Company, 41st Armored Infantry Regiment, laid down a base of fire. The 3d Platoon, H Company, moved forward, breached three hedgerows and was preparing to move through a fourth when they drew fire. The platoon leader, seeing his machine gun bullets ricochetting, fired an armor-piercing round and scored a flaming hit on a German Mark IV tank. Nonetheless, after having one tank destroyed and another damaged, the platoon pulled back.

The 1st Platoon of H Company was called forward to replace the 3d, which had moved to try to secure the flanks against a possible counterattack. The tankers tried to reach the crossroads that were holding up the reconnaissance platoon but could not force the Germans out of their positions with air and artillery. The battallion consolidated for the night, west of Margueray.

During the night, the Germans pulled out of their positions and infantry patrols moved on to the high ground without opposition. The Reconnaissance Company, 67th Armored, went into Montbray, finding that the enemy had just departed. The following morning, Combat Command B resumed its attack to capture St. Sever Calvados. Heavy resistance from enemy rear guard units, mines and log roadblocks continued. To compound their problems, it started to rain, hampering movement off the paved roads. The 1st Battalion, finding that the Germans had destroyed the bridge north of St. Sever, had to detour east through Sept Freres, only to discover that the road junction west of town was mined. After removing the charges, which slowed their attack, the command turned southwest and had proceeded about three hundred yards when it met strong antitank fire that destroyed the platoon leader's tank. By late afternoon, the command had still not reached the initial objective, but it prepared to resume the attack the following morning.

The 2d Battalion, 67th Armored, which had followed its sister battalion, reached la Cavee the first day without encountering any opposition. It camped, preparing to pass through elements of the 28th Infantry the following day. The next morning its move was delayed by a blown bridge. Finally, after moving south along mined and muddy roads to Montbray, it began following the route of the 1st Battalion. It bivouacked north of Courson, because the enemy, attempting to defend a destroyed bridge south of town, had the town under heavy mortar and artillery fire.

White resumed the attack at 6:00 A.M., and Brooks told him to push

hard under the cover of the morning fog. Yet things did not go according
to plan. The route was heavily mined, and while turning around a tank
detonated at least four mines that had been wired together and turned
over. The bottom armor was split open as if with a can opener. The
tankers finally reached the town, secured it and started moving through,
with the advance guard encountering dug-in infantry, artillery, mortar
and bazooka fire about a mile to the southeast. Suddenly, the Germans
shifted their fire to St. Sever Calvados because the 28th Infantry Division
was passing through it to the south and southwest. The 2d Battalion held
its positions while the 1st went to the aid of the infantry.

On August 4, the 82d Reconnaissance Battalion had sent patrols into
the Foret de St. Sever and toward Vire, scouting to secure routes of
advance for both combat commands. The first resistance was a roadblock
of fallen trees which seemed unmanned. First Lieutenants Morton Eustis
and Frank W. Jordan led with the tanks they had borrowed from the 67th
Armored Regiment. Moving forward, C Company encountered a very
cleverly prepared defensive position. The tanks and dismounted men of
the scout sections received heavy fire. The American volleys were ineffective, for the Germans had well hidden their guns. The company finally
had to pull back, after suffering four killed and eleven wounded. Officers
and enlisted men made repeated trips through the fire-swept area to bring
out the wounded. Aid man Pvt. Melvin Andrade continued to treat the
casualties, even though he himself was painfully wounded.

On August 5, White attacked with two columns through the Foret de
St. Sever. The right column was to capture Champ du Boult, while the left
sought St. Manvieu Bocage. The right advance made fairly good progress
until about two miles southeast of St. Sever, where it met a small delaying
force that fled when fired upon. In this brief fight, the Americans destroyed one Mark V Panther tank and lost one of their own to a land mine.
After regrouping, the force continued toward the objective, meeting
strong opposition after about a mile, at a destroyed bridge. The enemy
was entrenched on the high ground, looking down onto the approaching
American column.

The Germans had already destroyed four tanks when Col. Thomas
H. Roberts decided to move ahead to adjust artillery fire, alleging that the
forward observers were not adequately doing their job. White urged
Roberts not to go, but the intrepid artilleryman insisted. His tank was
destroyed and the crew's bodies so badly burnt that Robert's body was
identified only through the serial number on his pistol. After losing five

A tank of the 67th Armored Regiment enters the village of St. Sever Calvados.

tanks in a short period, White decided to break contact and to resume the attack the next morning.

The left column met lesser opposition because they were attacking through hedgerow country, not a forest. Initially, the 1st Battalion, 67th Armor, was held in combat command reserve, but at 6:00 P.M. it was given the mission to take St. Manvieu Bocage. It met some strong resistance and one local counterattack but captured the town and outposted it for the night.

On August 6 the attack resumed with the two columns again making progress against determined resistance. The right column (2d Battalion, 67th Armor), attacking at dawn, could not advance against the entrenched enemy on the high ground. The terrain was not suited for armored vehicles and the column had insufficient infantry until the 1st Battalion, 41st Armored Infantry Regiment, arrived about noon. The enemy still resisted and at dusk, after making some gains, the command pulled back to regroup. During the day, the tankers suffered no losses, but the infantry suffered heavily because of the artillery and mortar fire that continued to rain down on them. The left column made good progress against lessening resistance, reaching le Gast (on the southwest side of the Foret de St. Sever) that afternoon. After taking the town, they turned it over to the 115th Infantry Regiment, 29th Infantry Division.

Combat Command A had been pulled out of the line and permitted to rest its men and conduct maintenance on its equipment. On August 3 they were ordered to proceed south, protecting the left flank of XIX Corps, and seize the key road junction at Martilly, about 2,000 yards west of Vire.

At 6:00 A.M. the command started its attack. Leading with the 3d Battalion, 66th Armored Regiment, it made contact four hours, or about 5,000 yards, later. The advance was held up by roadblocks, dug-in tanks, antitank guns and infantry. By 5:30 P.M., after fighting all day, the command was held up at a stream crossing two miles north of their initial objective. Rose requested additional infantry, as the artillery fire and mortars had taken a heavy toll during the day, but his request was denied. Later in the night he repeated the request, saying that without more infantry he could stay in operation for only one more day.

The attack resumed at 8:00 the next morning, with the combat command coordinating with the 29th Infantry Division. The left column, led by the 1st Battalion, 66th Armor, moved west of Vire and captured Hill 219, overlooking the city and the Vire River. The 1st Battalion was then ordered to take the high ground immediately south of the town. It found all the bridges and roads mined and defended by dug-in infantry and tanks. Additionally, the Germans had infiltrated the American positions; it was all they could do to hold the critical hill. The 2d Battalion, leading the other column, fought its way to Martilly (the crossroads northwest of Vire) against the same type of opposition faced by its sister battalion. During the attempts to advance, Corp. William D. Yockey spotted an enemy force trying to flank his platoon. He turned his tank to meet the threat and in routing the enemy was killed. When his tank was hit and set afire, T4 Floyd Allan helped to evacuate three wounded crew members. He then returned to the tank, extinguished the fire and drove it to safety. The battalion, after being unable to move, disengaged for the night and prepared to resume the attack on the following morning.

During the day, unable to dislodge the opposition facing it, Combat Command A had taken some prisoners who revealed that two infantry regiments and an artillery regiment had moved into the area to relieve the 2d SS Panzer Division, which had begun moving out of the area the previous evening. Corps assigned the division a new mission: Combat Command A was to continue the attack, completing its original task, and then continue southeast to capture Domfront. The renewed attack on the following morning was to be aided by a heavy shelling of the town all night and by the attachment of the 2d Battalion, 41st Armored Infantry.

Corps and division artillery shelled Vire heavily during the night of August 5. Brooks ordered Rose to take the town the following day. If he could not, then he was to go around it and continue with the new corps order. He was also given the additional battalion of infantry he had requested. The attack started at 8:00 A.M. and met heavy artillery, mortar, antitank gun, tank and small arms fire. After an entire day of trying to advance, the command made only 500 yards. Taking the city was crucial, for Gen. Dwight D. Eisenhower had decided that it was to be the pivot at which he would turn the Allies north and east. So far the Germans had denied the city to Combat Command A for two days. At 9:22 P.M., Rose was ordered to report to division headquarters. He was relieved of the command of Combat Command A to become commanding general of the 3d Armored Division. Col. John H. Collier now assumed command of Combat Command A.

The struggle to take Vire had been savage. The Germans resisted the advance with artillery, mortars, tanks, antitank guns and infantry. While the Americans did make some progress, the Germans denied them Vire. This city, the intersection of five major roads, was a vital communications center. Control of it would enable the Americans to pursue the Germans at a faster pace. The attack had been conducted to keep pressure on the Germans and to deny them time to dig in and prepare elaborate defensive positions, but the fight to hold Vire was as fierce as any that the division had encountered during the war. One tank company lined up behind a hedgerow, planning to rush the Vire River. German fire knocked out ten of the tanks; when the other nine moved out to cross the river, four of them were promptly destroyed. Reconnaissance units scouted to find alternate crossing sites, but the ground proved too soft.

The American force on Hill 219 posed a threat to the Germans in Vire which could not be ignored. They conducted a strong counterattack to drive the Americans off the hill, but the 116th Infantry Regiment, 29th Infantry Division, arrived to help the tankers retain their hold. During a momentary lull, Corp. Arden Gatzke received a letter from his mother, giving him the address and outfit of a high school buddy. After reading the letter, he went to a company meeting where orders and plans for the upcoming fight were given. As the meeting came to an end, the company commander told the tankers not to run over any infantry and named the unit of Gatzke's friend. He went to the nearby infantry and asked where his buddy was—only about ten yards away. They visited for several hours before the tanks continued the attack.

On August 7, the combat command was ordered into corps reserve, but the 29th Infantry Division would not grant permission for the 1st and 3d Battalions, 66th Armored, to leave their positions on Hill 219. The men conducted as much maintenance as they could while in this reserve status.

In its next action, the 2d Armored Division received unexpected help. The British had cracked the German high command's code and read their messages during the war. One such code was received on August 2. Hitler directed Gen. Gunter von Kluge to prepare an attack to recapture the city of Avranches. If successful, the Fuehrer hoped to divide the American forces and roll those on the north side back into the sea. For this attack, Hitler released four armored divisions from the Caen front with sufficient infantry support to make a decisive thrust. It was a repetition of the successful 1940 strategy of the Battle of France. The ULTRA decoding teams intercepted the message, and Churchill immediately informed General Eisenhower. Surprise was the one factor which could make the scheme successful. In this campaign, surprise would be an Allied weapon, not a German one.

General Eisenhower and Lieutenant General Bradley, aware of the concentration of German armor through battlefield intelligence and ULTRA, thought that the Germans would launch a strong counterattack. The American generals began shifting forces to meet the threat and, in doing so, created a gap between Mortain and Mayenne. This danger caused Maj. Gen. J. Lawton Collins, commanding general of VII Corps, to request that the 2d Armored Division (minus one combat command) be assigned to him. The Germans gathered their forces for an attack on Avranches. If successful, they would split the First and Third Armies and ease the pressure on the rapidly developing movement to trap the German army at Falaise.

Almost certainly neither Corlett nor Brooks had the information to place the 2d Armored Division in the position that it would have during the German counterattack. On August 6, Corlett ordered the division to aid the advance of VII Corps to their objective of the Domfront-Ambrieres line. The Germans did not launch their attack until August 7. What resulted was the ultimate in warfare: a double envelopment of an attacking force. For years historians and military officers have argued whether the double envelopment was planned or whether it was one of those successful accidents. We now know that it was deliberately planned and executed in such a manner to lead the Germans to conclude that it was an accidental placement of Allied troops. To aid the VII Corps, the 2d Armored was ordered to attack south from Vire toward Gathemo, then turned eastward to capture Hill 367, approximately five miles south of Vire. The Germans launched their counterattack the day that the division was shifting forces; the division, minus Combat Command A, was ordered south to Barenton.

Combat Command A stayed on the north flank of XIX Corps, aiding the 28th Infantry Division in its advance southward. To carry out its mission, the command organized a task force designated Task Force A, composed of the 2d Battalion, 66th Armor; 14th Armored Artillery Battalion; one platoon from A Company, 17th Engineer Battalion; 2d Battalion, 41st Armored Infantry Regiment; and a company of the 702d Tank Destroyer Battalion. They were to first capture Gathemo, then turn down the ridge and attack Hill 367. Their advance was slow and difficult because of the terrain and enemy action. During the attack, they destroyed several antitank guns and artillery pieces and killed or captured numerous enemy infantrymen.

Combat Command A, in reserve near Vire during August 7-9 (except for the task force which had taken Hill 367), was aware that the

Germans were building their forces for an attack. Air observers reported considerable enemy activity along the base of the hill mass near the Foret de Mortain, about ten miles south of Combat Command A positions. The division had turned the town of Gathemo over to the 28th Infantry Division, who lost it to attacking German forces. A prisoner stated that the Germans had massed a large tank force that was moving north toward the city.

On August 10, XIX Corps attacked to recapture Gathemo and moved toward the town of Tinchebray, about seven miles east of Gathemo. Collier organized two task forces. One was attached to the 28th Infantry Division, with the mission of recapturing Gathemo—which it did, driving out the remnants of the German 84th Infantry Division. The second task force was commanded by Lt. Col. William M. Stokes, who replaced Collier as commander of the 66th Armored Regiment. They attacked at 6:00 A.M. to capture Vengeons and St. Sauveur de Chaulieu, both between Gathemo and Tinchebray. The attack progressed smoothly across broken terrain and in the face of intense enemy fire. By nightfall the command had advanced about two miles toward its final objective.

By August 11, the Germans saw that their attack had stalled. The German commander sought to get out as many men and as much material as possible, to form a new defensive line near Le Mans. Conducting a savage defense, they forced both combat commands to fight for every foot of ground. At 8:00 A.M. Collier resumed the attack for Tinchebray, the mission being to capture Hill 338 (east of Vengeons) and to recapture Hill 367. They met resistance more determined than any in their battle. experience. The Germans had antitank battalions equipped with 88mm guns, which took a heavy toll on the Americans. Orders now changed the mission of the combat command. Instead of taking Tinchebray, Collier was to attack southward toward Sourdeval, five to seven miles south of Vengeons and about the same distance north of Mortain.

In German headquarters the situation maps showed that Combat Command A was attacking south, while Combat Command B was attacking north from Barenton. Their objectives were to cut off the LXXXIV Corps and the XLVII Panzer Corps while the Germans were attempting to rescue their trapped forces. Combat Command A continued to attack on August 12, while Task Force A captured the crossroads on Hill 338. Following its success, the task force rejoined the main body of the combat command that afternoon, being relieved by elements of the 28th Infantry Division at 1:30 P.M.

Task Force 1/66 (1st Battalion, 66th Armor) was leading the attack south down the Vengeons-Sourdeval road in the face of intense artillery, mortar and antitank fire. It bypassed the town and seized the crossroads about two miles south of Sourdeval. Task Force 2/41 (2d Battalion, 41st Armored Infantry Regiment) which was following the tankers, quickly moved forward to assume responsibility for security of the crucial crossroads.

Meanwhile the 3d Battalion, 66th Armor, which had been in combat command reserve, passed through the lines of Task Force 1/66 and made excellent progress, moving through Roche Fichet and St. Clement and cutting the main road between Mortain and Ger, near Les Haies Martinet. After a stop for reservicing, it resumed the attack at 7:00 A.M., reaching Butte Ducics, where Task Force 1/66 joined it and both forces spent the night. During the day, a prisoner from the German 941st Infantry Regiment said that his regiment was retreating because of the American attack. He did not know of an ordered withdrawal and had seen no tanks and very little artillery.

On August 13, the combat command consolidated its gains and regrouped forces, while the division (minus Combat Command A) was released from attachment to VII Corps and returned to the operational control of XIX Corps.

Late in the evening of August 6, Brooks was ordered to lead the division south toward Barenton to aid the advance of the 1st Infantry Division. The 82d Reconnaissance Battalion led the march, the advance guard departing at 12:10 A.M., while the division followed at 5:30. The battalion left the St. Sever area and crept along dark roads toward Mortain. South of St. Poisthe the 82d Reconnaissance Battalion encountered machine gun fire. A few miles further south it drew heavy mortar fire. Merriam began to suspect that the division would have to detour to reach Mortain. The next morning, after contacting elements of the 9th Infantry Division, it was apparent that the 82d Reconnaissance Battalion was hitting the spearhead of the German counterattack. Probing around the German units, the battalion moved west to Brecey, turned south to St. Hilaire and then to Barenton. Along the route, the French were pleased to see the Americans and gave them cognac, wine and cider. During the night, the headquarters and Headquarters Company, 67th Armor, traded chocolate and cigarettes for butter and eggs. For the first time since leaving England, the men were treated to fried eggs.

After a fifty-mile road march, the division (minus Combat Com-

mand A) reached Barenton about 4:00 P.M. and contacted the friendly
forces. Battle Group 2, Task Force X of the 3d Armored Division and the
3d Battalion, 120th Infantry Regiment, 30th Infantry Division, had been
sent to aid the American forces. But the Germans arrived first and in the
ensuing battle reduced the 3d Armored and 30th Infantry elements to
about eighty men and ten tanks. These units were attached to Combat
Command B by Gen. J. Lawton Collins, VII Corps commanding general.

The terrain around Barenton was unfavorable for armored attacks. In
the hilly area, the tanks would be roadbound; control of the defiles and the
high ground was absolutely necessary for the attack planned for the next
morning. The 3d Battalion, 41st Armored Infantry, was given the mission
to capture Ger, northeast of Barenton. To protect the infantry attack, Task
Force X of the 3d Armored was supposed to capture the high ground north
of Barenton to guard the defiles. Both attacks, however, failed to reach
their objectives; the attack scheduled for the next morning would have to
be carried out with that handicap.

The attack to take the high ground west of the Barenton-Ger road
could cut the major German attack-escape route: the Ger-Mortain road. It
started at 8:00 A.M., with two infantry battalions abreast: the 1st Battalion, 41st Armored Infantry, on the right; the 3d Battalion, 41st Armored
Infantry, on the left. They advanced more than three miles through
minefields and antitank guns. During the attack the infantry was covered
by the 2d and 3d Battalions of the 67th Armored Regiment. That night the
columns consolidated their gains and maintained contact with the enemy
through patrols.

By August 8, the Americans, having blunted the German offensive,
geared for counterattacks. Instead of finding a soft spot in the Allies'
lines, the Germans had found the strength of the American First Army. A
major German attack was planned for the morning of August 9, but the 2d
Armored Division was on their flanks, like a spear in their sides. This
threat would have to be removed before the Germans could advance to
Avranches. They committed the 19th SS Panzer Division to break the 2d
Armored Division's hold on Hill 250 northwest of Barenton.

Before the enemy could launch its attack, the Americans resumed
their attack on the morning of August 9; the objective was the high
ground about four miles north of Barenton near the tiny village of le Gue
Rochoux. Its capture would place the 2d Armored about three miles south
of the Ger-Mortain road and make it a more serious threat to the German
supply and escape route. Infantry carried out the attack, as the terrain was

too rugged for tanks. However, the tanks supported the advance from firing positions a mile away. The attack was led by a patrol of H Company, 41st Armored Infantry Regiment, commanded by 1st Lt. Roy Green. As the patrol approached the stock shed near the crest, they ran head-on into a German patrol with apparently the same mission. The shooting started and the enemy was driven off. The balance of the 1st and 3d Battallions, 41st Armored Infantry, followed immediately to consolidate the objective and to prepare for the certain counterattacks which followed. Green set up a left flank outpost which proved to be the most valuable position on the hill. His post overlooked the area where the enemy was forming for their counterattacks. Using his radio, he was able to direct artillery fire so that all shells burst simultaneously on the enemy before they could get underway.

After taking the positions, the Americans beat back a two-pronged German counterattack. A platoon of the 702d Tank Destroyer Battalion, sent northward to cover the Ger-Barenton road, was in position to rake German tanks and armored personnel carriers moving down the road. The tank destroyers destroyed five vehicles and left an unknown number of enemy dead. The second attack came against the west flank of the American positions, hitting in the area between the objectives taken on August 8 and their present positions. The 3d Battalion, 67th Armored, and 102d Infantry launched their own counterattack with such speed and vigor that the Germans withdrew. The positions were secure for the night, although they were subjected to constant artillery, mortar and small arms fire. The Luftwaffe also conducted several raids on the 2d Armored's positions, killing and wounding several men and destroying many vehicles.

Nighttime brought little rest for the infanrymen holding the hill. As the men were pulled out for their evening K-rations, they were issued engineer sandbags full of hand grenades, one per man, two if they could carry them. One evening Pvt. "Tiny" Hurtado complained to the medics that he was barely able to move his arms. An examination revealed no damage. A doctor asked what Tiny had in the sacks. "Grenades," he answered, then adding that he had thrown six sacks full during the previous night attack. The doctor gave him a bottle of liniment, telling the private to apply liberally for "charley horse." During the night the Germans attacked again. Four enemy grenades bracketed Hurtado's foxhole; the fifth bounced off his helmet. Hurtado threw almost half a sack of grenades back into the darkness, along with various uncomplimentary comments about the enemy and his ancestors. Despite the ferocity of the fight, there was no firing on the German medics who came to aid their wounded.

During the night of August 9, there were indications that the Germans intended to launch a large-scale counterattack against the 2d Armored positions. The French resistance reported that the Germans were moving many tanks to the vicinity of Domfront for a possible assault. At 7:30 A.M. a French civilian reported that the Germans were planning a counterattack from the area of Domfront, but his credibility was considered doubtful. However, as a precautionary measure the 82d Reconnaissance Battalion and some attached engineers blew up the bridges between Barenton and Domfront.

During these intense counterattacks, Hinds was visiting the frontline commanders, Lt. Cols. Marty Morin (1st Battalion) and Marshall Crawley (3d Battalion, 41st Infantry). On one such visit, Crawley admitted that he did not know if they could hold out much longer and that they might not be there in the morning. Everything was committed, there was nothing anyone could do but hang on. Hinds answered as bravely as he could, "If you are not here, I don't know where in the devil you will be." Again that night the enemy attacked with a vengeance to dislodge the defenders. Capt. Thomas H. Carothers led the grenade and bayonet attack to repel the Germans. For his actions, he was recommended for the Distinguished Service Cross. Fate however intervened to deny him the nation's second highest award.

The infantry believed that anything found or captured on the battlefield belonged to the captor—in this instance, a German paymaster unit. The funds were divided among the captors and some were used to buy a cow for a company barbecue. One of the men was wounded and evacuated to a hospital in England where the hospital inspector general asked the soldier how he had obtained such a large amount of money. The man told the story, and the IG immediately started an investigation. The report came to Maj. Gen. Ernest N. Harmon, who had returned to command the division. Harmon called Hinds into his office and asked about the incident. Hinds argued that to court-martial Carothers would be detrimental to the individual, his company, battalion, regiment and division since he was one of the best company commanders in the infantry regiment. Harmon's solution was to withdraw the recommendation for the DSC and its accompanying citation and issue instead a Silver Star and a reprimand.

One night, faced with the possibility of losing one battlion from the

35th Infantry Division, Hinds went to see the chief of staff to protest the loss of a needed unit. Just as he arrived at the blackout tent, the enemy planes struck. Both Hinds and the chief of staff dived into a nearby foxhole, as Hinds tried to convince the chief of staff that the outcome of the war might hinge on that one battalion. After a loud and close near-miss, the chief of staff told Hinds to "get the Hell out of here and not to mention that battalion again." Hinds took the answer to mean that the 2d Armored Division could use the battalion for a few more days. Hinds groped his way in the dark to where he had left his Jeep and driver, Sgt. Lyle Doak, hoping that after the attack he would find them both intact. Both had escaped any damage; Doak was in a nearby ditch calmly eating a midnight snack.

Other members of the division were not so fortunate. Maj. Everett Hackenberry, 41st Armored Infantry regimental surgeon, was wounded in that same air raid. Returning from one frontline battalion aid station, he was caught in the attack and immediately dived into a nearby ditch. Unfortunately a piece of metal lacerated the doctor's derriere, causing a good deal of local bleeding. When he arrived at the regimental aid station, the medics cut his trousers from him and applied a voluminous bandage to the injury. When the damage was assessed the next day, the bandage was replaced with a band-aid, but Hackenberry rode on a pneumatic donut and ate standing up for some time.

During the day of August 10, Combat Command B acted as a covering force, while the 3d Battalion, 120th Infantry Regiment, attacked to open supply and communications lines to the 2d Battalion of the same regiment, isolated on a hill near Mortain. The Intelligence and Reconnaissance Platoon of the 67th Armored Regiment conducted an extended patrol along the Mortain-Barenton road to determine if it were clear of enemy. About two miles north the patrol encountered a defended roadblock and beat a hasty retreat. In doing so, one driver backed his jeep over the edge of the road, injuring both occupants. One had to be evacuated, while the other was able to stay on duty with the regiment.

Patrols which had been sent toward Ger encountered the enemy in strength. One detachment pulled back and the Germans followed it toward the American positions, but they were repulsed by division artillery. Another patrol made enemy contact about 200 yards from their front lines. When the Germans tried to surround the Americans, their move was detected. Though not actually encircled, they were cut off by extremely heavy small arms and artillery fire. Maj. Clifton B. Batchelder

American artillery observation post near Barenton.

was notified of the action, and he directed tank and artillery fire on the German positions. During the artillery duel, a concentration of nebel-werfer fire landed at the observation post of the 3d Battalion, 67th Armored, killing one man, wounding another and destroying the jeep of the battalion commander. The Germans were driven off, however, and the Americans were able to return to their lines.

During August 11, the 2d Armored Division continued to defend its positions north of Barenton. It had moved its reserves forward and as a result of the previous day's action had them on thirty-minute alert. Patrols continued and they penetrated the Foret de Lande Pourrie, northwest of their lines. The Germans tried their earlier tactic of following the Americans back to their lines, but it was stifled by artillery and tank fire.

The division was ordered to attack northward on August 12, cutting the Ger-Mortain road, while division reserve was to take over and defend The Combat Command B zone. It was also to be ready to counterattack to restore any lost roadblocks and any area lost to the Germans. The American attack started at 11:00 A.M. with the 1st Battalion, 41st Armored Infantry Regiment, on the right and the 3d Battalion on the left. Again the terrain was so rugged that tanks could support the infantrymen only from a distance. The right column advanced about 800 yards against light opposition, while the left one was caught in intense artillery and small arms fire. During the fight the Germans attempted to skirt around the left flank of the 3d Battalion. With the devastating fire to its front and the enemy to its rear, the 3d Battalion was unable to move. A counterattack against the Germans relieved the threat and the attack continued until about 10:00 P.M., when the VII Corps commander ordered the tankers to assume defensive positions for the night.

Seeking something to divert the enemy's attention, General Brooks conceived a plan to destroy enemy escape routes deep into their own territory. To carry it out, he designated a platoon from A Company, 82d Reconnaissance Battalion, supported by Capt. George L. Youngblood, 17th Armored Engineer Battalion. To protect this small group, a platoon of tanks from D Company, 82d Reconnaissance Battalion, was strung out along the route. The patrol reached the bridge at Lonlaye l'Abbaye and silently prepared to destroy it. To the Americans' dismay, the local townsfolk discovered the tankers and immediately began to celebrate their liberation. Nonetheless, the bridge was destroyed along with several nearby houses. The explosion brought instantaneous reaction from nearby German tanks and infantry. The Hell-on-Wheelers hid in the woods along with the entire male population, who claimed to be members of the FFI (French Forces of the Interior). During their hiding, the Americans captured some sixty-five Germans who entered their area. The small task force managed to return to their lines the next day. Some of the FFI members were clothed and armed and served as scouts for the Americans. One such FFI member did yeoman service until someone discovered that he was in fact a deserter from the German forces. Another did an excellent job with A Company's assault gun crew until General Brooks ordered *her* out of the company.

XIX Corps was meeting less resistance than other corps and Combat Command A was making good progress, while Combat Command B was defending as ordered. The division received information that Domfront was defended by an engineer battalion, which was reportedly armed only with rifles and machine guns. Lt. Col. Wheeler Merriam, commanding officer of the 82d Reconnaissance Battalion, and a task force were ordered to capture Domfront. Since the town is on a high hill overlooking the approach route, surprise would be impossible. On August 14, Merriam and the task force departed, under German observation all the way.

Leading the attack, Lt. Morton Eustis was killed when a German panzerfaust hit his tank. The columns stopped for the night, planning to attack the apparently strongly held position the next morning after an air attack and rolling artillery barrage softened the resistance. The next day, Dame Fortune smiled on the Americans. The bridge at the foot of the hill was prepared for destruction, but artillery fire cut the demolition wires. The commander of I Company, 41st Armored Infantry, sent a patrol around the flank, surprising the guards protecting the bridge. As the Americans began to move forward, they were surprised to see a white flag and an entire company marching out to surrender. The enemy company commander, who had been captured by the Americans during World War I, had told his men of the Allied treatment and of his plans to surrender. He informed the remainder of the company that they could do as they chose. With this opening, the task force dashed into the town. The local commander had his adjutant form the battalion for surrendering. He was apparently more concerned with military protocol, his car and his two girl friends than with fighting.

While the 82d Reconnaissance Battalion was capturing Domfront, Combat Command A was ordered to seize the high ground west of Ger and Hill 329, then move on to Fliers. If it were necessary to take Fliers, the command was authorized to bypass Ger. Colonel Collier began the attack at 7:00 A.M. and made steady progress until encountering a minefield which was covered by mortar and small arms fire. The infantry and engineers succeeded in clearing the obstacle, and the advance resumed. A destroyed bridge across the Egrenne River, which was defended by artillery and self-propelled antitank guns, delayed further advance until late into the night. Collier had received orders earlier in the day that he was to continue to attack only until August 15. By 10:00 A.M. of that day, the 3d Battalion, 66th Armored, reached its objective, linking up with the 82d Reconnaissance Battalion which had captured the city of Domfront. Combat Command A was relieved the same afternoon by the 112th Infantry Regiment, 28th Infantry Division, and Collier led the tankers to the division assembly area near Barenton for a few days' rest. The next mission was one designed for armor: a rapid deep pursuit of a routed enemy force.

Chapter 13

MILE AFTER MILE

The 2d Armored Division was pulled out of offensive action on August 14–15, 1944, and went into bivouacs near Barenton for rest and maintenance. Pfc. Albert J. Isacks, who had gone with a patrol to destroy the bridge at Lonlaye l'Abbaye, returned to the division bivouac area after several days of maneuvering. His company, D Company, 17th Engineers, had their old area and Isacks slept in the same slit trench that he had used before. While there, the division test-fired tanks equipped with rocket launchers, apparently without success or enthusiasm, and trained the 99th Infantry Battalion (Separate) in tank-infantry tactics. To break the monotony of battle and military food, the men enjoyed a visiting USO show and a doughnut wagon.

Some American soldiers did not let the language barrier prevent their getting food. One man in the Reconnaissance Platoon, 17th Engineers, wanted some fresh eggs. He tried in vain to talk with a French farmer. Finally, in desperation, the soldier squatted and began cackling like a hen. "O oui," replied the farmer, who left and returned shortly with a helmet full of fresh eggs.

255

The division's rest was about to end. XIX Corps was ordered to rush to the Seine River to trap the enemy attempting to escape from the Falaise pocket. The corps commander, General Corlett, thought that the move was to be "à la Patton." Brooks alerted the division for possible movement eastward, perhaps to the Eure River, with combat commands abreast. Division reserve was to follow Combat Command B, while division artillery was to follow Combat Command A. Movement orders could be expected anytime after 7:00 A.M. on August 19. Emphasizing the seriousness of the mission, the division commander stressed that each man was to stay alert when moving, to prevent a surprise by the enemy. Each vehicle was to have guards watching the rear. All personnel were to wear steel helmets at all times. The men were not to sleep in their vehicles but to be ready with all weapons at all times.

On August 18, the division moved along two routes, with Combat Command A on the south and Combat Command B on the north. After spending the first night at Sees, they then proceeded to assembly areas about five miles from Mortagne-au-Perche, covering ninety-nine miles in two days. While passing through Sees, the division halted to permit the 2d Armored Protoge (French armored division) to pass on its way to attack and later capture Paris. In their new assembly area, the Hell-on-Wheelers sent out patrols to make contact with the enemy, but none was located. The division prepared to launch attacks northward to seize crossings over the Seine and to prevent the Germans using them to escape back to their lines.

XIX Corps on the left of the Eure River, with XV Corps on the right, planned to attack northward, capturing the Seine crossings at Elbeuf. The attack, to be led by the 113th Cavalry Group and the 30th Infantry Division, was to be followed rapidly by the 2d Armored and 28th Infantry Divisions. The leading divisions were ordered to bypass towns for the following infantry to clear. The attack was launched on August 20, at 8:00 A.M., with combat commands abreast: Combat Command A on the right and Combat Command B on the left. Initially division reserve followed Combat Command B. Instead of leading with an infantry division supporting the 113th Cavalry Group, the formation was the same as in the first exercise in the Louisiana maneuvers. The 2d Armored was in the center, with the 28th Infantry on the left flank and the 30th Infantry on the right flank. The attack began in rain and mud.

On the right Combat Command A met little opposition on its move from Longny au Perche to the Avre River, northwest of Brezolles. There they found the destroyed bridge well defended by artillery and antitank guns. After pushing a bridgehead force across, Company A, 17th Engineer Battalion, built a thirty-foot treadway bridge. Collier ordered the 2d Battalion, 66th Armored, and the 2d Battalion, 41st Armored Infantry, along with Company A of the 702d Tank Destroyer Battalion, across before nightfall. The remainder of the combat command crossed after dark.

On the division's left flank, White's Combat Command B advanced in two columns, wanting to cross the Avre River at Verneuil. However, the Germans chose to defend that town and the river crossings. In the fight, the Americans were at a disadvantage. The routes to the town were exposed; the attacks had to be frontal, directly into the strength of the German defenses. Air support was summoned, and it inflicted considerable losses on the defenders. But they had taken a heavy toll on Combat Command B personnel and equipment. Capt. John Erbes, Medical Corps, and his medics, attempted to aid the wounded but could not reach them because of the intensity of the artillery and small arms fire. Finally he waved his Red Cross flag; the Germans stopped firing while the doctor and his assistants saved the wounded. After finding a river crossing four miles east of town, the tankers received orders to break contact and go around the opposition.

The following day, both combat commands continued the attack in the face of artillery, nebelwerfer, antitank, tank and small arms fire. On the right flank, Combat Command A progressed about ten miles, capturing the town of Damville, after the 2d Battalion, 41st Armored Infantry, and a tank company forced the defenders to the high ground to the north. In the fight for the town, the attackers killed some thirty defenders, while capturing ten times that number.

On the left, Combat Command B, after crossing the Avre River east of Verneuil, headed for its objective of Breteuil, encountering enemy opposition about four miles south of the town. This pocket was reduced and the men continued. While the attack progressed, several wounded needed medical aid. Pvt. Bennie F. Boatright, A Company, 41st Armored Infantry, medical aid man, went forward, meeting heavy machine gun fire. The Germans were so close that they could see his Red Cross brassard, but continued to fire, driving him to cover. He held the brassard up where the enemy could see it and started forward a second time, only to be driven to cover again. Trying a third time, he was mortally wounded at almost point-blank range. He was awarded the Distinguished Service Cross posthumously.

A platoon of C Company, 67th Armored, while consolidating a

stream crossing, destroyed two German command cars and killed thirty-five infantrymen mounted on bicycles. The American platoon leader, 2d Lt. John Zablocki simply said, "We mowed 'em down!" Both combat commands consolidated their positions and planned to renew the attack the following morning.

Leading the attack, the 82d Reconnaissance Battalion met an enemy column of trucks and armored cars near La Bochelle destroying fourteen vehicles and capturing 274 surprised Germans. Patrols later reached about five miles south of the Seine River. The combat commands resumed their advance, hampered more by the lack of stream crossings than by enemy action. The 2d Battalion, 67th Armor, found the Germans defending Le Neubourg and, with a battalion of the 28th Infantry, blocked the roads south of town. During the night the German air force bombed the town, hitting their own troops but not causing a single American casualty.

Once across the Iton River, the primary factor in the limited gains of the previous day, the division made excellent progress. Collier had Combat Command A in two columns. The left one cut the road between Le Neubourg and Elbeuf, preventing the Germans' using it to get their retreating forces to the crossings on the Seine. The other column moved to about a mile south of Elbeuf, where it encountered dug-in tanks and antitank gun fire. Pvt. Jose R. Trojo, 66th Armored Regiment, attacked a German tank with his carbine. Later he used a bazooka to kill a German soldier trying to attack an American Tank. 2d Lt. Bernard Deehan hunted down a Mark V Tiger, setting it afire with a thermite grenade. Both men manned an abandoned tank to carry on the fight. The command stopped, consolidated their positions and planned to assault the town the next day.

Combat Command B, attacking in the left portion of the division zone, cut the Conches-Le Neubourg road and the Le Neubourg-Iniville road. The 3d Battalion, 67th Armor, while moving to cut the road from Iniville, encountered heavy tank fire and quickly lost three tanks to a cleverly hidden German tank. The battalion pulled back, deployed for action and called for tank destroyers and a heavy artillery barrage to help clean out the enemy. The coordinated attack that followed the barrage cleared the town about the time that two Mark V tanks made an attempt to escape. One was destroyed immediately; the other almost ran into the quarter-ton truck of the battalion commander, Lt. Col. Harry L. Hillyard, before it too was destroyed. During the day, Combat Command B had isolated the town of Elbeuf, while Combat Command A moved forward to attack Elbeuf the following day.

During the night a light rain began falling, and the Luftwaffe, apparently trying to aid their trapped forces, sent bombers to attack Elbeuf. From the 2d Armored's point of view, the attack was a success because the bombers again missed the Americans and hit the German positions. The amount of damage and casualties was unknown, but thought to be extensive.

At 8:00 A.M., Collier began the attack to capture the crossings over the Seine River at Elbeuf. One column moving along the Le Neubourg-Elbeuf highway met minimal resistance, while the column that had reached a point about a mile south of town the previous evening encountered almost impossible terrain, made even worse by the rain, strongly dug-in tanks and antitank guns supported by artillery. The attackers reached the outskirts of the town but suspended further action, pending the arrival of reinforcements. Combat Command B had been ordered to attack from the southwest to support the advance of Combat Command A. The 3d Battalion, 67th Armor, encountered enemy fire about a mile south of their objective of Tourville la Campagne. The commander sent scouts ahead to find the location of the enemy guns and to determine if the town were defended. The attack order was given, and about 3:30 P.M. Americans entered the town against slight resistance.

Enemy opposition was beginning to fade in spite of the defense offered at Elbeuf. The Germans were more interested in retreating than defending the crossing sites. At 11:00 A.M., Combat Command A renewed its attack with the intent of clearing the town and securing the river crossings. With three columns advancing, Collier had his forces in the city by nightfall and was prepared to continue the attack the following morning. All day the men had endured artillery, mortar, antitank and nebelwerfer fire which, while slowing them down, did not stop their assault. During the fight, the 82d Reconnaissance Battalion had captured several Germans who stated that their mission was to hold the Americans south of town while the bulk of the retreating Germans crossed the river.

During the night, the 41st Armored Infantry captured a messenger with instructions for the 116th Panzer Division. The German corps commander was displeased that the division had not complied with his orders to hold for forty-eight hours. Resorting to Hitler antics, he ordered the division to hold. Later, the messenger admitted that the plan was for the division to hold until midnight of the 26th and then fall back. With this knowledge, Collier planned to renew the attack on the following morning. All three columns of Combat Command A, 41st Armored Infantry

Regiment, with the 99th Infantry Battalion, reached the center of town about noon; mopping up continued until late in the afternoon. The capture of Elbeuf cut all German escape routes out of the Falaise and the Pas de Calais area.

Remembering the British claims that they, and not the Americans, had captured Vire, Brooks ordered Collier to get a receipt for Elbeuf before turning the city over to the Allies. A Canadian officer rather reluctantly gave it. The receipt read:

> *From: 7 Canadian Inf Brigade 261954 (26 August 1945 [7:45 P.M.])*
> *To: 2 US Armd Div*
> *7 Canadian Brigade will assume operational command of Elbeuf west from line of road 113973-118991 and south from line of R[iver] Seine. All boundries inclusive to Canadian Forces. Command to pass 262000 hrs.*
> *Signed by Major J. Stevens*

Hinds accompanied Collier when the receipt was given. Returning to their respective command posts, they encountered several severe nebel-werfer concentrations. This fire hit the command post of the 3d Battalion, 41st Armored Infantry, and the 2d Battalion, 41st Armored Infantry, aid station, where Hinds and his driver, Sgt. Lyle Doak, were visiting casual-ties. They dived for some deep tank tracks nearby, but Hinds was not quite quick enough. Holding his helmet on with his left hand, he received several wounds in the left arm and shoulder. Others were knocked over like "tenpins." One man, next to the driver, was cut in half at the waist. It was, as Hinds remembered, "like a midsummer thunder and lightning storm striking all over."

The colonel returned to the regimental command post. His executive officer, Lt. Col. Robert B. Galloway, sent for the regimental surgeon, Maj. Everett Hackenberry, saying that Hinds wanted to see him right away. The day before, Hinds had asked the doctor for a laxative. When the doctor got this summons from Galloway, he said, "Oh, damn, I forgot all about that laxative." To which Galloway answered, "Never mind the laxative—he won't need it now." The medics wanted to evacuate Hinds, but he refused. Hackenberry dug out the larger pieces of metal, bandaged the wounds, gave him a bottle of aspirin, and everyone continued about their business.

In seven days the 2d Armored Division had advanced about ninety-five miles, routing elements of four enemy divisions—the 2d SS Panzer, 116th Panzer, 17th Luftwaffe Division and the 344th Infantry Division—and closing the last escape route of the retreating German army. After turning Elbeuf over to the Canadians, the division was pulled out of the line and moved about forty-five miles eastward to assembly areas near Mantes Gassicourt. From there it was ordered to continue the rapid pursuit on a wide front, covering the corps advance if the infantry divisions could not keep pace with the tankers. Also, the tankers were to maintain contact with the British XXX Corps on their left flank.

At their assembly area, the division underwent a two-day period of maintenance and rest. A small detachment of Combat Command B had been ordered across the Seine and had proceeded to positions north of St. Martin le Garenne. On August 28, White crossed the Seine to resume the pursuit of the rapidly retreating German army. At this time the enemy was not capable of holding a defensive line; instead he was trying to evacuate as many troops as possible with meager transportation. Germans were surrendering or were captured en masse. Even the rear guard delaying actions were not determined efforts. When strongpoints were encountered, they were either overrun or bypassed for the following infantry to clear.

Gen. Edward H. Brooks ordered the division to cross the bridge at Rosny, advance and protect the XIX Corps's left flank. To do this, it would be necessary to seize the high ground northwest of Villers and Arthies. Combat Command B received that assignment, while the remainder of the division was to maintain their positions. Estimating possible enemy action, Brooks stated that the Germans might oppose the advance with two fresh, but second-rate, infantry divisions and might make determined stands at natural obstacles. There was also the possibility that the Germans had reinforcements farther to the northeast.

Led by the 82d Reconnaissance Battalion, Combat Command B crossed the Seine on August 29, 1944, and attacked through the lines of the 79th Infantry Division. Moving against almost no resistance, they reached their objectives in the afternoon. After consolidating their position, they were detached from XV Corps and reassigned to XIX Corps. The temporary attachment had enabled the XV Corps to come abreast of XIX Corps.

Brooks ordered Combat Command A to cross the Seine, come abreast of Combat Command B and resume the attack. For once, all three divisions in the XIX Corps—the 2d Armored, the 30th Infantry, the 79th Infantry—were to be on line abreast of each other. At 6:30 A.M., Combat Command A crossed the river, came up on the right flank of Combat Command B and continued northward. By the end of the day, against light resistance, it had reached a point about eight miles south of Beauvais. At 7:00, White attacked, after being delayed by a fire fight that developed in the Combat Command B area. At Fleury, the 3d Battalion of the 67th Armored Regiment came upon the tail of a German column, which they shelled. About a mile north of the town, however, the Germans retaliated with devastating antitank fire. The American assault guns deployed; a white phosphorous round set a haystack afire, with the smoke blinding the Germans, who quickly withdrew. During the day, many prisoners and much equipment were captured.

Both combat commands moved out, bypassing resistance and continuing to pressure the retreating foe. The next major hurdle was the Somme River, where the Germans had seemingly destroyed all the bridges. Brooks wanted Combat Command A to use the bridge at Peronne and Aubencheul au Bac. Lieutenant Colonel Merriam briefed the 82d Reconnaissance Battalion and they conducted reconnaissance at thirty miles per hour. After capturing several officers and enlisted personnel at Herbecourt, Brooks ordered more speed from the reconnaissance battalion. The 2d Platoon of C Company found that the Germans had not destroyed the bridge at Peronne; the platoon's approach had been so rapid that the Germans did not have time to detonate the explosives. The first scout car attacked the bridge with both its guns firing; the second stopped short of the bridge to prevent the arrival of reinforcements, while the third protected the first. The platoon leader promptly cut the demolition wires, saving the bridge. He then deployed his platoon to protect the span until a larger force could relieve them. The Germans brought a 20mm antiaircraft gun to the scene, attempting to detonate the explosives by firing at the bridge. The platoon's mortars took the gun under fire and destroyed it. About this time, the 1st Platoon of C Company arrived to support the 2d. The major obstacle to continuing the advance had been surmounted through a German oversight.

Company D, 82d Reconnaissance Battalion, was to capture the bridge at Aubencheul au Bac. As the tanks raced northward, the night was clear and cool. During the march the maintenance half-track radioed ahead to the company commander that a column of German vehicles was

Right: As a patrol of the 2d Armored Divisions moves in to mop up resistance in Daneilie, France, a loyal Frenchman shows them a fleeing German party.
Below: A Sherman Tank, D Company, 66th Armored Regiment, rolls past a burning German vehicle in Aubencheul au Bac, France.

overtaking them and trying to pass. The company commander ordered the tanks to the far right side of the road; when the German column drew even, it was decimated. Luckily, the bridge was also found intact. The tankers, with the aid of the grateful French, set an ambush. All night long, small groups of enemy vehicles approached and were promptly destroyed. The prisoners were turned over to the French, while D Company dragged the destroyed vehicles into the town square so that any approaching enemy would not be forewarned. By daylight the square was filled with disabled hulks.

Combat Command A continued its advance against almost no opposition, and by evening it went into position about four miles south of Montdidier—about thirty-six miles in one day. Combat Command B had about the same success. South of Bresles it was held up by antitank and small arms fire. This was overcome and the town was taken about 3:00 P.M. As the advance continued, the tankers surprised several German columns which had no idea that enemy troops were in their vicinity. The advance of both American columns was aided greatly by air support. Not much friendly column cover was needed and this freed more planes to attack the Germans fleeing the rapidly advancing tankers.

To stop the German retreat and eliminate the forces already at Tournai, General Eisenhower planned to stage an airborne drop, cutting the major Lille-Brussels highway. General Bradley had little faith in airborne operations; he argued that land forces could capture the city before the paratroopers could arrive. Several factors apparently motivated him. Tournai was in the British zone and the slowness of Montgomery's northward advance posed a threat to Maj. Gen. Courtney Hodge's First Army. Second, Eisenhower planned the airborne attack against Bradley's advice. Third, Bradley thought that the planes could be better used to resupply gasoline to the hard-charging tankers. Bradley told Corlett that he had forty-eight hours to be in Tournai.

During the night of August 31, two liaison officers from Corlett's headquarters arrived at the command post of the 2d Armored Division. They reported to Brooks, saying they had an impossible order for the 2d Armored. Subduing his anger, the general asked for the impossible order. They told him that the division was to capture Ghent (Tournai) in forty-eight hours. Brooks returned his compliments to Corlett, supposedly telling him to get a good night's sleep and that the objective was in the bag. After dismissing the two officers, Brooks turned to his chief of staff,

Col. Charles Palmer and asked, "Charlie, where the hell is Ghent?" They were unable to find the city on their map; it was beyond the intended operating range of the division at that time.

Assembling the major unit commanders, Brooks told them of the mission. During the advance, they were not to give the Germans an opportunity to delay them. The attack began at 6:00 A.M. on September 1, with the 2d Armored as spearhead, while the 30th and 79th Infantry Divisions, mounted in trucks, were to follow as quickly as possible. XIX Corps was also to be ready to make night marches if necessary.

The division headed northward in six columns, Combat Command A on the right, Combat Command B on the left, with division reserve, commanded by Col. Sidney R. Hinds, in the middle. By the end of the day, hampered more by a shortage of fuel than by enemy action, Collier had Combat Command A near Hamel and Aeleux, with the reconnaissance elements at Cambrai. White's Combat Command B was delayed briefly by five enemy 88mm guns at Montdidier, but they were scattered by fire from the tank destroyers and the 78th Armored Artillery Battalion. Division headquarters notified corps that the town was not secure and requested that the following infantry be used to clear it. By nighttime, Combat Command B was about twelve miles north of Moidain.

The XIX Corps, which had originally been relegated to a minor role in Belgium (because the British were supposed to get the glory), stole the show. 1st Lt. James Hartford, executive officer of A Company, 82d Reconnaissance Battalion, received the order to attack toward Belgium. After studying the map, he found that the shortest route would be straight north into the British zone and then back to the southeast. The company moved northward. All the while, Hartford was radioing back that they were encountering no opposition. The next day when CCA followed, they found the route to be less peaceful than Hartford had described.

At 7:30 A.M. the attack resumed, and at 9:30 the 82d Reconnaissance Battalion became the first Allied soldiers to enter Belgium. Brooks was hard on the heels of the reconnaissance battalion. He came upon Companies A and B, which had stopped to refuel their vehicles. Brooks asked Lt. Col. Wheeler Merriam why he had stopped short of Belgium. Merriam answered that they were already ten miles inside Belgium. During the day they captured about 800 prisoners, destroyed three 75mm self-propelled guns, eight vehicles and many horse-drawn carts. Immediately behind the reconnaissance battalion, Collier had Combat Command A moving at a rapid rate. It crossed the Belgian border only eleven minutes after Merriam's battalion and was the first large Allied force to enter that country.

The Belgians were ecstatic—even more so than the French, if possible. While moving in column, the soldiers were given fruit, wine and cognac. Through the built-up areas, the citizens threw flowers, fruit and other items. One officer of the 41st Armored Infantry Regiment was accidently hit in the face with a beer bottle, splitting his nose and knocking him unconscious. The Belgian reception caused one mild surprise for Pfc. Albert J. Isacks. After a couple of months on the continent, he had perfected his high school French so that he was able to converse. When an elderly lady presented him with large bottle of Cognac, he began to thank her in his most fluent style. In a broad Cockney accent she replied, "You're quite welcome, Yank." The English lady had married a Belgian and lived there many years without losing her accent.

On the left flank, Combat Command B met small pockets of resistance. North of Hayrincourt, civilians reported that Germans were dug into a beet field, which offered them excellent cover. The tankers tried to cross the field, but the Germans defended fanatically. Someone decided the tank commanders could lean out of their hatches and drop hand grenades into the foxholes. This caused several tank commanders to be killed or wounded. Finally, Lt. Col. Hugh Exton decided to saturate the area with low artillery airburst. After 700 rounds, sweeping back and forth over the field, the survivors surrendered; the dead were too numerous to count. Combat Command B began to suffer the gasoline shortages that occurred in rapid advances. Several units ran out of gas and had to wait for fuel to be delivered later that afternoon. Both commands sent elements into the objective that evening, with Collier reporting that his command arrived with two hours to spare. They were to take the town by midnight, but had it by 10:00 P.M. At 2:30 A.M. on September 3, division headquarters received a message from the commanding general of the Guards Armored Division "expressing hope that 2 AD understands Tournai to be totally within the British Zone." Brooks kept the division in the Tournai area for three days, mopping up pockets of resistance, resting the men and performing needed maintenance. However, the major reason for staying was the shortage of fuel.

Division Reserve, or the 41st Armored Infantry Regiment Reinforced, had been following the advance of the two leading combat commands. Hinds had stopped his force about a half-mile short of the cross-

Above: The 82d Reconnaissance Battalion as the first Allied troops to enter Belgium.
Right: Troops of the 2d Armored Division relaxing between battles.

roads. He and General Brooks were standing and talking, as they waited for Combat Command A to pass and gain some distance. The rear elements had just gone by when a German column came "barrelling down the street through Marchiennes." Hinds fired his machine gun to be sure it was working; General Brooks fired one round from his armored car's .50 caliber before it jammed. Both commanders were on the wrong side of the road; the Germans were between them and their 2d Armored troops. Brooks turned both his armored car and jeep around, escaping over plowed fields and farm paths to catch Combat Command A. All this happened so quickly that his aide, Capt. William Hershey, was left behind. He took cover in a drainage ditch.

To gain some time, Hinds manned the machine gun on his jeep while Doak radioed Colonel Galloway that Germans were approaching and told them to be ready to "take them in." Hinds expended one box of 250 rounds and reached for the second, only to find that it contained Doak's shoe brush and cleaning materials. About all Hinds and Doak could do was keep Galloway informed of what was coming. Aid came immediately. Galloway sent several half-tracks across country into the center of the German column. Tanks bottled up the enemy front and rear; a steep railroad embankment on the west prevented any escape. Trapped, the Germans had to fight but their entire column was destroyed: 123 vehicles demolished, 300 enemy killed, and 30 prisoners taken. Captain Hershey escaped unscathed but, covered with drainage ditch mud from head to foot, he was thought to be an enemy soldier. Both Doak and Hinds had the aide in their sights several times, but neither fired. Later, they delivered the aide back to Brooks, who had joined CCA. His jammed machine gun was immediately repaired. For the general's part in the shooting, Hinds recommended Brooks for the Silver Star. It is not often that a division commander takes part in the actual fighting.

To save fuel for an emergency, Hinds halted his command about ten miles short of the objective. Had the supply troops been able to keep pace with the combat elements and had higher headquarters foreseen the German army's collapse, the Americans might well have been on the Rhine before the end of September. The division spent three days in the Tournai area awaiting gasoline. This delay permitted the Germans to regroup and establish defensive positions. On September 4, the XIX Corps notified the division that no Class III (gasoline) was available anywhere and not to send vehicles to try to find any; when fuel became available, it would be on a strict priority basis. Further complicating the situation was human error. Gasoline intended for XIX Corps was mistakenly sent to VII Corps. When XIX Corps did get fuel, it went to the 79th Infantry Division so that it could then join Third Army.

The men of the 2d Armored Division did not have long to rest; they were ordered to advance east quickly in five columns, clearing out resistance and establishing a bridgehead over the Meuse River. They were to advance as far as their gasoline supply permitted. Probably because of the fight outside Marchiennes, Collier ordered that the last major element of his columns be a platoon of medium tanks, which because of the nature of the operations became standard operating procedure. From prisoner-of-war interrogation reports, the division learned that the Germans no longer had any organized units in France or Belgium. The units there were, for the most part, without officers; the men had been told to make their way back to Germany as best they could. They had been moving by horse-drawn vehicles and bicycles taken from the French.

On September 5, the XIX Corps began their attack eastward, moving behind the screen of the 113th Cavalry Group. The 82d Reconnaissance Battalion, aided by the Cub airplanes of division artillery, led the division's advance. Near Tirlemont, the pilot and air observer noticed German infantry in a field. Armed only with pistols, carbines, tommy guns and a few grenades, the air crew swooped close to the enemy, dropping grenades and firing their weapons. The observer and pilot radioed for an armored car to take the Germans in while the plane held them in place. In his excitement, the observer fired forward, hitting the propeller and forcing the plane to land among the potential prisoners. Fortunately, armored cars arrived, freeing the Americans and ending a dispute as to who was whose prisoner. The reconnaissance personnel found several German tanks near Jodoigne and in the fight destroyed them and took forty-three prisoners. Merriam's battalion was aided by the Belgian resistance, who revealed German troop dispositions. The remainder of the division, moving along five routes, met only scattered resistance and made about seventy miles during the march.

One means which the Americans used to resupply the front was to divert bombers from their strategic missions. 1st Lt. Earl E. Wassom, a B-24 pilot in the 466th Bomb Group, was to fly gas into an abandoned Luftwaffe base at St. Dizier. The group had been told that Brussels was clear and that it was safe to fly over the city. After delivering some gasoline, he and another pilot decided to do some sight-seeing, flying low circular routes around the Belgian capital. The diversion turned to tragedy as his friend's plane was shot down, with the loss of the entire crew. Wassom returned to his home base, telling the debriefing personnel that the town might be cleared but the surrounding area still contained enemy soldiers.

On another mission he encountered enemy fire which damaged his landing gear. The plane was low on fuel, but the bomb bays and cargo compartment were filled with five-gallon gasoline cans. The tower at a small field refused him permission to land; but he was at such a low altitude that he had to land and do so with one approach. Wassom told the tower to get the planes out of the way, he was coming in. The aircraft was so low that the crew could not use their parachutes. He came in low, permitting the crew to jump or to gamble on riding the plane in with the pilot. The crew jumped, rolling and tumbling away from the strip, while Wassom kept the plane level down the runway. He was able to land without accident. The pilots and crews were especially irritated at these fueling missions, because they did not receive combat credit for resupplying gasoline. Those in positions of authority considered these missions milk runs. Those in the aircraft knew they were as dangerous as daylight bombing raids into Germany.

On September 6, while heading for the Albert Canal, the 2d Platoon of C Company, 82d Reconnaissance Battalion, ran into a retreating German column which wanted to fight. The platoon formed a line and fired .30 and .50 caliber machine guns and 37 mm canister and high-explosive shells at the 120 to 150 enemy, who quickly surrendered. The Americans captured seventy-nine Germans, several of whom were seriously wounded. Patrols of the 82d Reconnaissance Battalion reached the outskirts of Hasselt, capturing 283 prisoners that day. The remainder of the division moved to assembly areas south of Brussels, meeting only minor resistance. That afternoon, when the British Guards Armored Division asked what the division planned to do, they answered that on XIX Corps orders they planned to seize a bridgehead over the Meuse River at Maastricht.

After a sharp clash on September 8, A Company, 82d Reconnaissance Battalion, seized Hasselt and rushed patrols to the Albert Canal. They found that the Germans had destroyed the bridges and were defending them with small arms, artillery, antitank guns and pillboxes. Brooks brought the remainder of the division forward to assembly areas outside the town. Division artillery and the reconnaissance personnel manned forward positions to prevent the Germans from slipping combat troops across the canal and surprising the tankers.

While the 2d Armored Division was on the Albert Canal, Capt. James M. Burt accused one of his men of cowardice. One night the accused swam the canal, captured several prisoners and had them swim back across with him. He turned the prisoners over to another company and got a receipt for them. The next morning, the soldier walked up to Burt, saluted, handed him the receipt and asked if he still thought that he was a coward.

The Albert Canal, a narrow and deep body of water, posed problems for the division. Furthermore, intelligence summaries suggested that the enemy would defend the canal vigorously. The German forces were thought to be a mixed group from at least twenty different units, including stragglers, deserters and isolated groups. They had battle groups from at least three Panzer divisions, the 1st SS, the 2d SS and the 2d Panzer. Because of the terrain, the enemy could defend the Albert Canal, then fall back to successive defensive lines along the Vaart Canal, the Maas River and the Juliana Canal. Also, the identification of the 347th and 719th Infantry Divisions, which had formerly been around Utrecht and Rotterdam, suggested that infantry replacements might be sent into the critical area. To determine enemy strength and intentions, the 82d Reconnaissance Battalion was ordered to push patrols across the canal. Later that same day, Merriam reported that the Germans were withdrawing men and vehicles, covering the withdrawal with automatic weapons, mortars and some short-barrelled cannons.

Meanwhile back in the United States, events were taking place that would have a decisive influence on the future of the division. Maj. Gen. Ernest N. Harmon had been assigned to command XXIII Corps, stationed at Camp Bowie, Texas. At San Antonio, en route to his corps, Harmon received orders from General Marshall to return immediately to Washington. Reporting to Marshall, Harmon found that the 2d Armored Division would soon need a new commanding general and he was asked if he wanted the job back. He accepted and rushed to Holland to take command from Brooks, who had been given V Corps. Harmon, as he visited the various units, found that he was still remembered. He overheard one soldier ask another if he knew who the short two-star general was. When the other replied that he did not, the first soldier said that was the general who had bought eggs for his men in North Africa. Harmon stopped his vehicle and asked if the man had been in North Africa. Getting an affirmative reply, Harmon was also told that it was good to have him back with the division. In his own style, which earned him the nickname "Profane Ernie," he replied that it was good to be back with Hell on Wheels.

When the division had liberated Hasselt, the foreman of a local mine came to the command post and told them that the Germans had taken all there was to take, but that the hot water showers at the mine could be used if they desired. Harmon said that the gesture was appreciated and the men headed for the showers with delight. Sgt. Waldo B. Timley, wiping the soap from his eyes, claimed that it was his first real bath since leaving England. Most of the time, the division had been moving so fast that the men had not had time to wash their faces.

Harmon's first task was to get the division across the Albert Canal. While a student at the Command and General Staff College, he had faced a similar problem. One added element had been a ford, some distance from where the crossing was to occur. Harmon had used that ford to cross the river and attack the enemy in the flank and rear. The instructor had ruled that was not the proper solution, the students were to have brought artillery forward, mass the fire of the cannons and send infantry across the river to seize the bridgehead. Then the engineers were to have built a pontoon bridge. The more Harmon reflected on the problem of getting his men across the Albert Canal, the more certain he became that the solution of his student days was correct.

Informed that the British had seized a crossing at the town of Beeringen, Harmon ordered the 82d Reconnaissance Battalion to cross the canal at first light on September 11 and attack southward, clearing the zone for the division. C Company crossed first, followed by Companies B and D. Initially the men received small arms, artillery and mortar fire, encountering more delaying type resistance than heavy opposition intended to deny ground to an attacker. During the day they captured two Germans from the 39th Fusilier Battalion, 453d Infantry Division, wearing G.I. clothing. They also captured five members of the reconnaissance battalion of the 176th Infantry Division, who claimed that their division was supposed to follow them to the area. The prisoners reported that they expected a parachute regiment to join in defense of the crossings.

At dawn, the Germans counterattacked, driving the 82d Reconnaissance Battalion out of Zonhoven, but the Americans regrouped and recaptured the village at 8:10. Merriam and the reconnaissance battalion continued clearing the zone for the division. At the crossroads south of Zonhoven, D Company found the roads to be heavily mined. A destroyed British armored car and felled trees blocked the road. Attempting to work around the road block, D Company lost five tanks in as many minutes. Colonel Merriam arrived on the scene in his armored car to rally the troops and push them forward. An armor-piercing shell hit his ear, severed the driver's legs and shattered those of the radio operator. After removing the wounded, the battalion commander was content to wait for heavier tanks and artillery to overcome the determined resistance.

That afternoon Colonel Collier began moving Combat Command A to Beeringen, awaiting orders to cross the canal. Late that night the division received some encouraging news: they found a document signed by a Colonel Schmidt, which revealed that the mission of the 275th Infantry Division was to hold the enemy while others worked on the West Wall. Meanwhile the combat commands were patrolling their areas, clearing out pockets of German infiltrators. The 3d Battalion, 41st Armored Infantry, which had been assigned to Combat Command B, found a large group of Germans hidden in the woods near Stevoort. Reinforced by a light tank company and another company of infantry, they killed or captured the entire force. The commands did not want to have to worry about their rear areas while fighting on their front.

At 6:30 A.M. on September 13, Collier's Combat Command A crossed the canal and began their attack south to clear the east bank of the river. Using two columns, one moving east and the other south, the men of Combat Command A encountered roadblocks of felled trees. The trees were usually booby-trapped and covered by automatic weapons and infantry. Soft ground restricted the tanks to the road; which meant the Germans did not have to spread their defenses to meet the American threat. Two slag piles to the front and east of the east column overlooked their route of attack, offering the Germans excellent observation posts. Both columns made good progress throughout the day; at night the infantry formed defenses for the tankers.

The 82d Reconnaissance Battalion, filling the gap between the two columns, encountered the same type of opposition and resistance. The 2d Platoon from A Company patrolled through Neerblabeek to Waterloo, where it turned south to the nearby woods. They found a group of Germans washing their clothes. The Germans were not dug in nor had they posted sentries. The platoon, with the aid of a British reconnaissance officer, deployed, placed every weapon in firing position and laid out their ammunition. On signal everyone opened fire with devastating effect: 186 dead or dying Germans.

Prisoners taken during the day reported that their orders were to retire to Genck and that the 1st and 2d SS Divisions were moving into the area east of Genck. Later in the afternoon, a motorcyclist from the Dutch army met an officer of the 82d Reconnaissance Battalion and gave him a note which read: "Dutch Army wishes to know how many Dutch SS Pw's you have and if you are willing to turn them over to the Dutch." The division had encountered members of the Dutch-manned SS Nederland Division, who had fought gamely to prevent being pushed back into Holland. Apparently this message remained unanswered, for no reply was found.

Harmon ordered Collier to continue clearing the division zone; at every opportunity he was to use multiple columns, to cover more ground. Collier started his attack at 6:45 a.m., with one column heading from Genck toward Asch. Making steady progress they reached the area of Bret and Gelteren by noon. The 82d Reconnaissance Battalion, still protecting the combat command flanks, maintained contact with the British while sending patrols eastward to maintain contact with the Germans. By the end of the day, the men had cleared the zone, except for the area between the Vaart Canal and the Meuse River, and had moved onto Maastricht Island as the last defender was pulling out.

To clear the area between the Vaart Canal and the Meuse River, Harmon created a special task force commanded by Lt. Col. William M. Stokes, commanding officer, 66th Armored Regiment, and consisting of the 3d Battalion, 66th Armor, 99th Separate Infantry Battalion, 65th Armored Artillery Battalion, the 82d Reconnaissance Battalion, and D Company, 17th Engineer Battalion. Reconnaissance showed that there were two bridges over the Vaart Canal. A wooden one at Smeermaas, north of Maastricht, could support tanks; the other, partially destroyed, at Neerharen, could not hold such weight but could support infantry in a single file. Both had disadvantages but could be used until the engineers bridged the canal. Stokes had three options in his attack. He could cross the canal at Reckheim and work north, cross at Lanklear and work south or bridge the canal in the center and move in both directions at once. Stokes chose to cross at Reckheim where friendly troops protected the rear, existent bridges facilitated the crossing, and where he could estab- lish a bridgehead for the engineers' bridge at Reckheim. To cross in the center would split the force and permit the Germans to have tanks and antitank weapons near the bridge site. The enemy defenses reportedly numbered 550 men near Boorsheim and about 500 SS troops in Meeswyck; however, there was no information about antitank guns or the extent of the enemy defenses.

Lacking detailed knowledge, Stokes planned to have the infantry cross the canal and establish the bridgehead, then the tanks would cross to attack Lanklear. The Americans needed to use maximum speed in order to prevent the enemy's reinforcing the local garrison. About 7:00 P.M. on September 14, the infantry crossed the canal and attacked northward. They moved rapidly, needing to move out of the narrowest part of the corridor before dark. The attackers met resistance from dug-in infantry without antitank weapons. As the Germans fired, their positions were raked by tanks and artillery, after which the infantrymen moved in quickly to clear away the defenders. Using this method, they took large numbers of prisoners and by nightfall had reached the wide portion of the corridor. The command consolidated for the night and prepared to resume the attack the following day.

The next morning, the force encountered strong hostile fire from the woods near Neerharen. The tanks deployed and, protected by infantry, moved into the trees and eliminated the automatic weapons. Near the bridge that was their objective they found an enemy pillbox. Tank fire prevented the Germans' manning their weapons; the infantry quickly followed, eliminating the strongpoint. The east side of the canal was secure. The 99th Infantry Battalion (Separate) crossed to continue the attack.

Once Stokes had his force across the canal, it advanced northward against increasingly heavy fire and difficult terrain; by nightfall it had reached a point about 300 yards south of Reckheim, where it consolidated. On September 16, the attack resumed and the zone was cleared from the city of Maastricht to the border with the British army. This three-day effort secured the rear of the 2d Armored Division, a difficult task because of the nature of the terrain.

After Collier and Combat Command A had cleared the east bank of the Albert Canal, Harmon ordered White's Combat Command B to bridge the canal to the island of Maastricht, clear the island, move up the east bank of the Juliana Canal and then attack toward Sittard. This move would put the 2d Armored on the flank of the 30th Infantry. White's engineers began building the bridge, but just as the last few feet were to be finished, the bridge fell into the canal, delaying the attack by one day.

When issuing his field order for the renewed attack, Harmon was able to give more information about the enemy. The heaviest opposition came from the 176th Infantry Division and from the 1st Battalion of the 1st SS Grenadier Regiment "Lanstrum Nederland," which had shown great determination in defending the Hasselt bridgehead. Other second- and third-rate units were hastily organized but had withdrawn to the east of the Meuse, apparently to establish a defensive line, entrenchments and field fortifications. The active defenders were thought to be supported by six battalions of artillery, mortars and possibly tanks. Harmon concluded that the 2d Armored could expect a determined defense. To add to this grim but realistic appraisal of the enemy, a message from XIX Corps said that only 225 rounds of 105mm howitzer ammunition were available per gun for the next ten days (an average of twenty-three rounds per gun per day). Artillery, which had thus far opened the way for the tankers, was about to be restricted. That could have serious implications if the Germans decided on a stubborn resistance against the division's attack.

While Combat Command A continued to mop up small pockets of enemy resistance and occupied the entire division zone north of the Albert Canal by 11:00 A.M., Combat Command B was waiting for the engineers to complete the bridge, which they did by 4:45 P.M. Leading Combat Command B, the first troops across were the 3d Battalion, 67th Armored Regiment, serving as the advance guard. After crossing at 6:45, Combat Command B entered Holland at 7:00, attacking along the Maastricht-Sittard highway. The advance progressed well until the tankers came to a destroyed bridge over the Geul River. The battalion went into bivouac while the engineers began building a bridge. However, a satisfactory bridge was soon found upstream, and with other elements of Combat Command B following they went into assembly areas south of the Geul River for the night.

On September 16, both combat commands launched full-scale attacks, using four columns across a seven-mile front. Combat Command A attacked Valkenburg. Collier and his men came under intense fire and needed the entire day to cross the Meuse River and reach the railroad north of town. White and Combat Command B encountered the same stiff resistance. The enemy had organized the terrain into excellent defensive positions. While Harmon and Hinds were watching B Company, 41st Armored Infantry Regiment, advance, they were showered with leaves as enemy machine gun fire cut through the branches above them. B Company, which was advancing perpendicular to the fire, was hit. They immediately turned their .50 caliber machine guns onto the trenches from which the fire was coming. Nearby tanks, from the 67th Armor, turned their guns to aid the infantry and within fifteen minutes some 200 enemy soldiers were dead or taken prisoner. Patrols sent out during the night returned, indicating that the enemy was dug in just north of the Guel River. A force of tanks and infantry tried to cross but were held up by heavy artillery, mortar and small arms fire. Engineers tried to put in a treadway bridge. Incoming enemy fire delayed them until the air corps could be contacted later in the day for the air support that the tankers needed. Finally, about 8:00 P.M., the tanks were able to cross to aid the infantry which had crossed six or seven hours earlier.

Task Force 2 of Combat Command B, finding a bridge intact, attacked at first light to take Hoogveld in Holland and the high ground near Beek. After an all-day struggle, the task force captured the crossroads and the high ground near Kruisberg. By the end of the day, both task forces of Combat Command B had filled out their bridgeheads and were ready to continue pushing the Germans back the following day.

The Germans, fearing an envelopment, started to retire toward Sittard. They had been led to this belief by the probing of the 82d Reconnaissance Battalion, which was working across the Maastricht Canal, north of Maastricht. The Germans thought Combat Command A would turn north after clearing the east bank and Combat Command B would attack southward, linking up with the VII Corps. When Combat Command A continued to attack eastward, and Combat Command B, northward, the Germans, having shifted their forces to meet what they had anticipated as the goal of the 2d Armored, found that they had actually cleared the route for the tankers.

Both combat commands resumed their attack against stiff resistance from dug-in infantry, artillery and antitank guns. A minefield blocked the advance of Combat Command A, until the engineers were brought up to clear it. After getting through the minefield, the columns of Combat Command A had to cross a stream strongly defended by German infantry. It required most of the day for the two lead infantry battalions (2d Battalion, 41st Armored Infantry, and 2d Battalion, 117th Infantry Regiment, 30th Infantry Division, attached to the 2d Armored for this operation) to get across the stream. Late in the day, tanks were sent across to aid the infantrymen. By nightfall, they had reached the vicinity of Schimmert and Terstraten.

When Combat Command B's attack had been slowed by bridging

A tank of Combat Command A moves through an arched gate into the town of Valkenburg, Holland.

operations, this delay gave White an opportunity to regroup the force for the attack northward. The 2d Battalion, 67th Armored Regiment, sent patrols forward to find the enemy. Before proceeding far, they ran into heavy small arms and artillery fire. At 9:00 A.M., two medium tank platoons attacked and by noon had taken Gerlach. The remainder of the battalion followed and an hour later had progressed about 1,000 yards north of Gerlach and captured Censel without meeting any opposition. Patrols continued northward, without making contact with the enemy. After 11:00, the attacks met little or no opposition, because the air corps gave continuous air support.

Attacking in two columns from Schimmert and Drieschen, Combat Command A continued to move eastward, reaching the area around Nuth by 12:00. The bridge at Geleenbeek had been destroyed and the approaches were mined. After removing the explosives, the engineers were able to build two bridges. The advance continued to the vicinity of Amstenrade, where Collier stopped his men for the night.

White and Combat Command B made excellent progress on the north flank of the division zone. The attack moved through six successive objectives against light to moderate resistance. By late afternoon Combat Command B had captured Sittard, which Corlett, XIX Corps commander, wanted to be his anchor for the attack on the Siegfried line. In Sittard, 1st Lt. Robert E. Lee, D Company, 67th Armor, was helping to gather prisoners when he spotted a German officer about to draw a palm pistol from a shoulder holster. Lee grabbed the officer and slammed him against a stone wall with so much force that it broke the prisoner's neck and back. Later 2d Lt. George Adler's 1st Platoon, F Company, 67th Armor, moved into Wehr, becoming the first members of the 2d Armored Division to "enter, conquer, and occupy German soil." Both combat commands had made about six miles that day against resistance best described as indifferent.

Collier was ordered to capture the ground between Gangelt and Geilenkirchen; the latter a strongpoint in the Siegfried line. That attack, launched at 7:00 A.M., progressed nicely until reaching the area around Schinveld, where it encountered severe artillery, small arms and antitank fire. About 9:30 P.M., the objective was finally captured, the ground near Gangelt was organized for defense and roadblocks were established east of the town, toward Geilenkirchen.

While preparing the defensive positions, the 1st Battalion, 66th Armor, was hit with a counterattack by eight tanks and a company of infantry. Unbeknownst to the Germans, the air observer of the 14th Artillery spotted the attack forming. He immediately radioed a warning to the 1st Battalion. At the same time, he guided the 2d Battalion, 66th Armor, around the enemy's left flank and onto their rear, where they launched a surprise attack. The Germans, caught between two forces, fought gallantly but lost all their tanks and self-propelled guns and almost all their infantry.

On September 19, White and Combat Command B attacked to strengthen the division's north flank. The Germans were attempting to destroy a bridge near Wehr. Because of the heavy ground fog, their attempts were disrupted by artillery and automatic weapons fire. About 9:00 A.M., the tankers drove off the Germans and kept the bridge from being destroyed.

Meanwhile, the 3d Battalion, 67th Armored, was attempting to take Millen. After finding the railroad underpass destroyed, they located a bridge over a canal and stream which could support tanks. About this time they started receiving heavy artillery and mortar fire, but it did not slow the tankers. A relief column, after finding a crossing at Overhausen, encountered dug-in infantry. The Americans called for artillery, which drove the Germans out of their positions. Then the Americans captured the town and prepared it for defense. Suspecting that enemy forces were in Hongen, E Company, 67th Armored, sent a patrol into the town to investigate. They destroyed part of an enemy artillery regiment which was attempting to withdraw with a huge quantity of ammunition.

The 2d Armored Division progressed two to five miles against increasing resistance. They had taken their objectives east of Gangelt and were poised to threaten the West Wall, the Siegfried line. Corlett ordered the division to continue attacking, seize the area east of the Sittard-Geilenkirchen road and maintain contact with the 30th Infantry Division. He also told the division to prepare to attack on September 20, to break through the West Wall, cross the Roer River (only nine miles away) and then turn south to help encircle Aachen.

Corlett planned to attack the Siegfried line with a saturation bombing attack, followed by the 30th Infantry Division attacking the line near Rimberg, about nine miles north of Aachen. Harmon was ordered to protect the corps left flank along the Sittard-Geilenkirchen line but to be ready to send a combat command into the breach which the attack was to create and to exploit the gains to the east. However, the planned attack did not occur because of a shortage of artillery ammunition and a heavy fog which lasted until about noon. Fearing the shortage of artillery would encourage the Germans to rush the defenders into the area, and because the Americans on XIX Corps's south flank were not keeping pace with the corps, Corlett ordered the 2d Armored Division into defensive positions until the south flank situation had improved.

While in defensive positions, the men of the 2d Armored conducted maintenance of their vehicles and rested, then began training, emphasizing the lessons learned from the previous action. On September 22, the Germans launched a strong counterattack of two infantry battalions, supported by horse-drawn artillery and antitank guns. Division artillery repulsed the attack, and the attackers never got closer than 150 yards. "The Road March War," or the pursuit phase, ended after the crossing of the Albert Canal. The division knew that now gains would be made in yards, not miles, because the Germans would be defending their homeland.

Chapter 14

BREACHING
THE SIEGFRIED LINE

The pursuit phase ended with the crossing of the Albert Canal. German resistance stiffened and was aided by the American fuel and ammunition shortages. In early and late September, the delays enabled the Germans to pull back the remnants of their Seventh Army and, with other forces, to man the Siegfried line. The Germans had demonstrated a strong ability to recuperate and were still a dangerous enemy. When the 2d Armored Division entered Germany at Wehr, many tankers correctly believed the enemy intended to make their main defensive stand at the Siegfried line or at least in that sector. It was a tenacious struggle, as bitter and as fiercely contested as any which Hell on Wheels faced. The Germans were fighting for their homeland.

The 2d Armored Division was allowed a brief respite before September 19 when Harmon issued Field Order Number 30, stating that the XIX Corps was preparing to breach the Siegfried line. The 2d Armored Division was to defend the corps's left flank and be prepared to exploit any breakthrough. That same day, the division learned from a prisoner-of-war who had worked on the Siegfried line only three weeks earlier, that the line started at Geilenkirchen and moved northward. According to the prisoner, there were two types of pillboxes, one for machine guns and one for antitank weapons. The machine guns were placed four to a pillbox and could fire in four directions. In the antitank positions, two weapons were placed so as to cover possible routes of approach. The fortifications were protected by mines and tank traps. The Germans had also prepared their defenses in depth to the Rhine River. A French informer even told the corps intelligence officer that the Germans had prepared the Maginot and Siegfried lines for the release of toxic Arsene gas after their capture.

The Siegfried line was Germany's border defense, a defense of the holy soil. It spanned the front of the American XIX Corps, from the Dutch border to near Basel on the Swiss border. It was primarily concrete pillboxes with few open earthworks or prepared artillery positions. However, there were some hastily dug trenches for infantry. The pillboxes themselves were generally 20-30 feet by 40-50 feet and 20-25 feet high. At least half, if not most, of this height was underground. The walls and roofs were 4-8 feet thick and often steel plated. The firing slits were angled 50 degrees, permitting mutually supporting fire. Years of neglect had made the natural camouflage excellent and the defenses difficult to spot.

The first row of defense, hastily dug antitank ditches, was followed by five rows of tank obstacles, or ''dragon's teeth,'' consisting of steel rails driven into the ground with concrete molded around them. They were about four feet high. The first line of pillboxes was about 200 to 500 yards behind these teeth. About 300 yards to the rear was another line of pillboxes, and further back was a third but sparser line. On all three lines, between the pillboxes were machine gun positions which afforded interlocking and grazing fire (fire that does not rise above the height of a man). This defensive position presented a formidable barrier to an attacking force. 1st Lt. Irving M. Edelberg said, ''If the recon outfits can't find an underpass or the engineers can't build a bridge over it, I guess we'll just have to take it apart and go through it.''

The terrain was generally flat, with a multitude of slag piles and mine entrances affording good observation posts. The Wurm River, which flowed through the area, was about 30 feet wide and 3 feet deep, with 4–6 foot steep banks—a definite hindrance to mechanized vehicles.

The German troops manning the line were second- and third-rate, inferior to the positions they manned. The units were formed into small combat teams without any thought to overall unit identity or integrity. Before and during the attack, the division intelligence officer identified the 12th, 49th, 183d and 246th Infantry Divisions. The 183d was the only one that had any semblance of being complete with all its elements present. The other ones were missing either infantry regiments, antitank gun battalions, machine gun battalions, artillery or engineers. In addition, there were the 771st Guard Battalion, 992d and 460th Artillery Battalions, the Field Replacement Battalion 49 and the combat teams "Grohe" and "Dietrichsdorf."

The Siegfried line protected the Ruhr-Rhine River valleys and was not viewed as a static defense. Rather, the Germans intended it to weaken the Allies and make them vulnerable to counterattacks. The greatest power of the Siegfried line, for attackers and defenders alike, was its psychological effect.

The mission of Corlett's XIX Corps was to penetrate this West Wall and form a pincher to encircle the city of Aachen. It was to cross two water barriers (one of which was the Wurm River), cover thirty miles of front with only two divisions, establish a bridgehead and force a gap in the line. When the British moved to Arnhem, an additional fifty miles of the left flank was exposed to possible enemy attack. Hoping that the Allied airborne offensive to take Arnhem would be successful, Col. Sidney R. Hinds ordered the reconnaissance elements of the 41st Armored Infantry Regiment to make an unofficial reconnaissance to Arnhem to determine if the Siegfried line could be flanked. Unfortunately, the scheme failed. The 2d Armored Division then faced breaching the line. To accomplish their first task, Corlett decided to attack with the 30th Infantry Division, breaching the line and pouring the 2d Armored through the gap, then turn north and eastward to protect the north flank of the corps while the 30th Infantry wheeled southward to aid the VII Corps in capturing Aachen. Basically the 2d Armored was to have a defensive mission. This plan irritated Harmon, who argued that armor was not designed for defense.

On September 29, Harmon issued his attack orders, stating that their purpose was to advance eastward to seize a line along the Roer River. By doing that, the division would be protecting the flank of the 21st Army Group on the north and the American First Army on the south. Combat Command B was to follow the 30th Infantry Division through the Siegfried line, clearing the area between the Wurm and Roer Rivers and securing a crossing at Linnich. Combat Command A was to follow, doing the same task, with its crossing to be at Julich. These two bridgeheads would open the door to the Rhine River. Some optimists began to think that the war might be concluded by Christmas. However, the frontline soldier knew that it would be a bitter struggle. Division Reserve was to follow Combat Command A, ready to support either force. Initially, the division was to have six artillery battalions in support and to obtain the 228th Field Artillery Group (three battalions) after it had passed through the gap.

The intelligence annex detailed its assessment of the enemy's capability. The tankers could expect mostly self-propelled guns and artillery, although twenty-four tanks were thought to be in Geilenkirchen, a strongly fortified road and rail center. As a thorn in the side of the Ninth Army, it would have to be removed if the Americans were to pull up on the Roer. Individual tanks, supported by infantry, were also thought to be operating in the area. Since the penetration of the line would pose a serious threat to the Cologne-Dusseldorf population centers and the Ruhr-Rhine River industrial areas, Harmon told the division to expect strong enemy resistance, including artillery, air and counterattacks.

On September 26, in preparation for the attack, twenty-six battalions of artillery began shelling the attack zone. On September 29, the 29th Infantry Division Artillery relieved the 2d Armored's Artillery. The following day, the 115th Infantry Regiment, 29th Infantry Division, relieved the 2d Armored Division between Gangelt and Teveren, making additional armor available for the attack.

At that point, the weather changed to snow and rain. To determine if this would seriously impede the attack, Gen. William H. Simpson, Ninth Army commander, went into the field and asked the soldiers. They replied that it would not. The attack by the 30th Infantry Division was scheduled for October 1, following a carpet bombing attack. However, the air attack was postponed because of bad weather, and on the next day the air corps was able to bomb the target area for only two hours and even then the overcast skies made its effect doubtful. The 30th Infantry's attack encountered heavy resistance and progressed slowly.

Corps engineers bridged the Wurm River at Palenberg, finishing about 10:00 P.M. on October 2. The next day, because the 30th Infantry was meeting determined resistance and making little progress, Harmon requested and received permission to start the tanks across. Combat Command B was ordered across to help the infantry clear the town of Ubach. This would give the 2d Armored room to maneuver. General I. D. White organized his combat command for the fight, directing tankdozers, flamethrowers and engineers to be well forward in the columns.

On October 2, the lead task force of the 2d Armored Division began crossing the Wurm, behind the 30th Infantry Division. The remainder of Combat Command B was to follow as quickly as the infantry cleared

Ubach. The crossing, scheduled for 11:00 A.M., progressed slowly—too slowly for Harmon. He called White at 12:55, asking what was the problem. White replied that the bridge was busy and that the infantry was not deep enough for the tankers to get into town. At 2:00, Harmon called the commanding general, 30th Infantry Division, Maj. Gen. Leland S. Hobbs, saying that the 2d Armored needed the south bridge to push Combat Command B across piecemeal and to shove Combat Command A the same way. Besides the tenacious German defense which was delaying the infantry, the ground was soggy, restricting the tracked vehicles to the roads. Division artillery was also handicapped as by midnight it had only two forward observers across the river.

The forces that were across the Wurm reached Ubach after meeting intense artillery, mortar and small arms fire from German infantry who were resisting stubbornly from their pillboxes and trenches. After passing through the lines of the 30th Infantry Division, the tankers aided the 117th Infantry Regiment's move to the north edge of Ubach before the tankers stopped for the night. The taking of Ubach was merely a sample of the bloody yard-by-yard fighting which the division was to endure for the next ten days.

By evening, neither the tankers nor the infantry had progressed beyond the outskirts of the city, nor were all the buildings in friendly hands. The next morning, however, before the Americans could move, they were hit with a stiff counterattack from three directions. One Combat Command B column was to attack directly into the strength of one prong of the German attack. Harmon told Corlett that the tankers were meeting very heavy artillery fire from three directions. The enemy guns were out of range of division artillery, and bad weather prevented American aircraft from locating them. In addition, the intense enemy fire had destroyed some vehicles on the bridge, preventing the rest of Combat Command B from crossing.

After beating off one of the German counterattacks, Task Force 2 of Combat Command B, commanded by Hinds, started attacking northward, parallel to the pillboxes. Its mission was to clear the zone of the enemy and to take the high ground overlooking Hoverhof, which would anchor the bridgehead. In addition, they were to reduce all pillboxes they encountered. The advance was slow because of intense artillery, mortar, antitank gun and dug-in tank fire.

The Americans fired time artillery fire (airbursts) to drive the defenders into their pillboxes, then smoke to blind the fortification's occupants, so that the pillboxes could be flanked. Originally, the men thought that they would have to use the battalion of 155mm self-propelled guns to drive the defenders out of the bunkers. However, they found that the rear steel doors of the pillboxes could be penetrated by the antitank round of the 75mm tank gun. The solid shot did more than just penetrate the doors; it bounced around inside, inflicting casualties, exploding ammunition and lessening determination to resist. This was a slow, time-consuming process. Once the final attack was launched about 4:00 P.M., the task force was able to reach its objective without losses.

At 8:00 A.M., Task Force 1, commanded by Col. Paul Disney, regimental commander, 67th Armored Regiment, was ordered into the fight. He met stubborn resistance crossing the Palenberg Bridge, but passed through the 30th Infantry Division and headed east. The 3d Battalion, 67th Armor, was under deadly, incessant fire from artillery and direct, heavy-caliber weapons. The supporting infantry could not advance because of the enemy fire. Two platoons from G Company, 67th Armor, were ordered to take the high ground east of Ubach. The mission was considered suicidal, for the murderous fire was the heaviest the battalion had yet encountered. During the attack they met seven enemy self-propelled antitank guns and destroyed three of them, losing two tanks in the process. The task force was trying to outflank the Germans, but the enemy had well entrenched their weapons and were fighting with determination. By the end of the day, Disney's task force had gained about 1,800 yards, stopping 600 yards short of Beggendorf.

That evening two companies of German infantry (about 240 men) launched a counterattack trying to circle to the rear of Ubach and to cut the road into the city. The Americans had either intercepted or captured the attack order, for they knew about the Germans' preparations and were ready for them. The entire force was killed or captured. The prisoners told their interrogators that if the division "gave them hell tomorrow then they could reach Cologne." The Americans obtained an overlay showing the defensive lines between the rivers; the prisoners told them that there was not much to the last line.

In the afternoon Corlett attached the 3d Battalion, 116th Infantry Regiment, from the 29th Infantry Division, to Combat Command A. Harmon ordered Collier to be ready for battle by noon the following day, October 5. Corlett had warned Harmon that until the combat command was actually committed, it was the corps reserve; with the infantry's attachment to Hell on Wheels, the corps had no reserve.

The 2d Armored Division was attacking against mutually supporting, fixed defensive positions which dominated the open terrain. The pillboxes were linked by fire trenches, affording cover for machine guns and riflemen. Antitank guns were also in the open areas between the boxes and tanks were dug into defilade positions covering the approaches to the fortifications. Adding to these man-made hazards, a chilling mist covered the already muddy plain, preventing air support when the attack resumed at 7:00 A.M. on October 5.

Task Force 1, of Combat Command B made slow progress through the thick fog, artillery and antitank gun fire. The 3d Battalion, 67th Armor, made about 1,000 yards, reaching the outskirts of Beggendorf before being stopped by a hail of fire. The tanks battled with German tanks and antitank guns until they had expended their ammunition and had to pull back to resupply. At 1:00 P.M. they attacked again, reaching Beggendorf for the second time. Again they were stopped. The infantry were pinned down by the heavy volume of artillery and mortar fire and could not help. The tanks were finally able to advance and progressed to about 600 yards south of Waurichen before enemy fire drove them back.

On October 4, H Company, 67th Armor, had been assigned the mission of cutting the north-south road 1,000 yards east of Ubach. The next day, I Company, 67th Armor, was ordered to move forward to assist H Company. The force inched its way forward against a virtual wall of steel. In the afternoon, the two companies finally broke through to the road and moved 1,000 yards east before dusk. The attack stopped about 1,200 yards short of its objective, Baesweiler, and the men dug in for the night. German infantry tried to entrench only a hundred yards in front of the Americans, but they were repelled by assault gun and mortar fire.

Because of the intensity of the German defense, the 1st Battalion, 67th Armor, and G Company, 41st Armored Infantry Regiment, were ordered out of Combat Command reserve to fill the gap appearing between Task Forces 1 and 2. They were to attack north from Ubach toward Waurichen. Like the other American troops, this force met stiff opposition but by the end of the day managed to reach a point about 500 yards southwest of town. In that attack the battalion lost nine medium tanks and one light tank.

Task Force 2, which was advancing northward on the left flank of the Combat Command B zone, resumed its attack, using much the same tactics that had been successful the previous day. Sgt. Ezra Cook discovered that the communication lines were intact in one bunker. He called the Germans in the next pillbox, telling them that their comrades had been captured and that they were next; they chose to surrender. Colonel Hinds used airbursts to drive the defenders into the pillboxes. He observed that the explosions were of a uniform height and bursting with a consistency that he had not witnessed in previous actions. An artillery liaison officer commented that he had heard of a new type fuze but had not seen it fired. Hinds thought then, and still does today, that the artillery was firing the new POZIT (veritable time) fuze. Moving northward, the tankers and infantry encountered stiff resistance along the roads. The task force progressed about a mile and a half, the best that Combat Command B had for that day. On reaching Frelenberg, it stopped on the edge of town for the night.

Combat Command B had been able to get most of its vehicles across the bridge, including the "thin skin" ones (those other than tanks). At that point, Harmon decided to commit Combat Command A to the fight. He called the chief of staff, Col. Clayton J. Mansfield, and told him to have Collier start moving at 12:30 P.M. Collier had organized two columns for the attack. At 11:45, the left column moved to cross the Palenberg Bridge, which was still being heavily shelled. This detachment advanced about 1,000 yards east of Ubach by dark but had lost two tanks to the enemy shelling. The right column stayed on the west bank, waiting for the other pincer to clear the bridge. After crossing, Combat Command A was to assist the 30th Infantry Division's attack to capture Aachen.

The Germans had taken a heavy toll of 2d Armored tanks: approximately 50 percent of Combat Command B's tanks were damaged or destroyed. This was the heaviest fighting that the division had yet endured. In the late afternoon, Harmon directed the chief of staff to order the Maintenance Battalion forward to work on the tanks that had been damaged. He did not want them to have to go too far back for repairs.

Harmon issued his attack order, stressing that the main effort was to be south and southeast to assist the 30th Infantry in the capture of Alsdorf. Combat Command A would have the heaviest burden, while Combat Command B defended the front line. He warned the division to be ready for a possible counterattack on October 7. Two battalions of the 246th Infantry Division had already been identified. The bulk of this division was expected to arrive in the area during the night of October 6. To thwart their aiding the enemy, all pillboxes were to be destroyed.

The attack opened with heavy artillery barrages by corps and divisional artillery and by fighter bombers. Combat Command A began its attack about 7:00 A.M. but ran into the same intense fire that had previously handicapped the division. About 10:00 A.M., the left column split in two. The first element received the mission of capturing Beggendorf, while the remainder of the force went to positions west of Baesweiler. The first group (Company D, 66th Armored Regiment; Company K, 116th Infantry Regiment; and a platoon from Company A, 702d Tank Destroyer Battalion) had captured its objective by 4:30 P.M. The remainder of the day was spent in mopping up the remnants of the enemy force that had defended the town.

The second part of the left column was ordered to capture Oidtweiler. After splitting, the second force attacked toward Baesweiler and continued southward to take its objective. The advance was slowed by heavy enemy fire falling along the route of attack. By evening, Company E, 66th Armored, Company I, 116th Infantry Regiment, and a platoon of the 17th Engineer Battalion had progressed to positions about 800 yards west of Baesweiler and prepared their positions for the night.

The right column of Combat Command A, which was still on the west bank of the Wurm, began crossing at 1:00 P.M. on October 6, moving toward Oidtweiler and reaching Ubach. A small force (Company I, 66th Armor, and two platoons of I Company, 116th Infantry) was ordered to move toward Alsdorf to aid the 117th Infantry Regiment, 30th Infantry Division. The area was heavily mined. Herds of cattle crossed and recrossed these obstacles with little concern. One cow stepped on a mine. A mess crew of the 14th Armored Artillery Battalion saw the accident, drove through the mine field and began to butcher the animal, while both Americans and Germans watched. Brig. Gen. John H. Collier, who witnessed the action, was so incensed that he could be pacified only by a generous portion of the loin.

At 7:30 A.M., Task Force 1 of Combat Command B started its attack attempting to reach the main highway between Geilenkirchen and Duren, at the town of Waurichen. Its attack followed a rolling barrage, with the medium tanks leading. Enemy automatic weapons, artillery and mortar fire kept the infantry pinned down, so they could not aid the tankers. German antitank guns quickly began to exact a heavy toll of the medium tanks slowed by the soft ground. The Americans faced the German Mark V and VI tanks and in the unequal fight lost 21 of their 34 tanks, or a 63% loss. It appeared that the command was going to make little or no progress that day until someone suggested that instead of trying to capture the objective with medium tanks, why not use light tanks and execute an old style cavalry charge?

Up to this point, the nature of the European battlefield had dictated that few, if any, cavalry type charges would occur. For the most part armor had been used for feeling out opposition, maneuvering and capturing positions in sequence. Since Combat Command B had already lost 63% of its tanks, another attack would be useless. It would be suicidal to try an infantry attack. The M-5 light tank carried a 37mm cannon and several machine guns but could be destroyed by small arms fire. It was hoped that the speed of the light tanks would so surprise the Germans that they would not be able to traverse their antitank guns quickly enough to bring fire to bear. If the Germans could track the tanks, the results would be as disastrous.

The light tanks of C Company, 67th Armored Regiment, were pulled out of the line and formed behind what was left of the mediums. With throttles wide open, they passed through at thirty-five miles per hour. Not bothered by the mud or soft ground, with few minefields and no antitank ditches, they sped toward the Germans. The Germans, perhaps terrified when they realized that they could not track the light tanks, began to flee and were cut down by the tank-mounted machine guns. The light tanks hit a depression and were out of sight for a moment. In the meantime the medium tanks and infantry started forward.

Once on the objective, the light tanks overran enemy artillery, antitank guns and entrenched infantry. They crushed the guns and machine-gunned the crews. When the tanks turned to attack Immendorf and Floverich, they began to receive fire. West of Waurichen, three tanks stalled in a tank ditch and were destroyed by antitank fire, but the crews escaped. The remainder of the tanks cut the road between Immendorf and Floverich, overran an artillery battery, destroyed the guns and killed the crews. About this time the tanks ran into an enemy platoon of five Mark VIs. The 37mm gun of the American light tanks was useless against the German tanks, but by running circles around the bigger and heavier German tanks they caused so much confusion that the enemy fled. The light tanks had pried open the Siegfried line; the Americans were now on its eastern fringe. The light tank attack also enabled the remainder of Task Force 1 to move forward and take up defensive positions in and around Waurichen.

At 4:00 P.M., while Combat Command B was consolidating its gains around Waurichen, the Germans launched a savage counterattack to drive the 3d Battalion out of its newly won positions. The attack, preceded by an artillery concentration of "unbelievable volume" was finally repulsed by the battle-weary troopers. For their part, C Company was awarded a Presidential Unit Citation.

Task Force 2, which was still on the left flank of the Combat Command zone, continued its attack toward the Geilenkirchen-Duren road. After an all-day assault against increasingly heavy fire, the Americans were finally stopped about 1,000 yards short of the strongly defended German positions. However, the attack by Hinds and Disney, of Task Force 1, placed the Americans in a strong position to defend against possible counterattacks.

About noon, Corlett visited the command post of the 2d Armored Division and recommended that the push to the east be limited until VII Corps on the south flank made contact with XIX Corps. He ordered that a good defensive line be established and that the division be prepared to move northeast, east, southeast or south. Harmon may or may not have agreed with his corps commander's assessment of the situation, but he requested additional infantry. He knew that the division lacked sufficient support for a defensive mission. Harmon said that he had lost a lot of tanks, the division having taken "quite a beating. Enemy artillery is worse than anything division has seen." Four hours later, Harmon told Corlett that though fifty tanks had been lost, the division and its infantry were not badly hit. Combat Command A was not able to clear bypassed resistance because of a shortage of infantry, and the lack of reserves.

About 7:00 A.M., Collier began his attack to aid the advance of the 30th Infantry Division. Company I, 66th Armor, and two platoons of infantry from the 116th Infantry Regiment moved along the Ubach-Alsdorf road to a position about one-half mile north of Alsdorf, where it formed abreast and to the left of the tank elements of the 30th Infantry Division.

The right column of Combat Command A attacked to take Oidtweiler and the high ground northeast of Alsdorf. The Germans resisted with an ever-increasing heavy volume of indirect fire. Antitank guns covered the intervening ditches. Reaching a point about 400 yards west of town, the command consolidated its positions for the night. The left column was still attempting to enter Baesweiler. Using two different approaches, from the northwest and the north, the combat command seized the town at 8:30 A.M., overrunning dug-in infantry. The tankers and their supporting infantry spent the remainder of the day clearing the Germans from the village.

That afternoon, Harmon told Collier to dig in his tanks, because it appeared that the division would be in the same positions for a few days and he did not want to surrender any ground. Collier reported that they had information from a reliable civilian that a German regimental size

Sgt. Alton McDaniel moves his dozer tank through the mud near Baesweiler, Germany.

artillery unit was stationed at Aldenhoven. Combat Command A had been shelled from that direction all day; apparently the German weapons were larger than the American.

Combat Command B began to prepare its defensive position from the Wurm, arching around to Beggendorf to tie in with Combat Command A on the south flank. These positions would permit the 2d Armored to protect the north, northeast, east and southeast from attacks, while the 30th Infantry Division attempted to join VII Corps around Aachen. Task Force 1 made a limited attack to clear the town of Waurichen. The 3d Battalion, 41st Armored Infantry Regiment, led the advance while the tanks protected the infantrymen. Later in the day the 1st Battalion, 67th Armor, became responsible for the defense of the town. As a result, White was also ordered to dig in his tanks to prevent losing ground during a possible counterattack.

Task Force 2 did not attack on October 7, but strengthened its positions in preparation for manning defensive positions. In the early afternoon, the Germans launched a counterattack southwest of Waurichen. Hinds sent the 2d Battalion, 67th Armor, to blunt the threat. The tankers and their supporting infantry captured about 100 prisoners after a forty-five minute fight.

Combat Command B improved its positions, emplaced its assault guns and mortars, and prepared to hold on to the salient in Hitler's West Wall. The men cleared pockets of bypassed resistance, including six pillboxes. Patrols were sent out to gain information and, if possible, prisoners. The fighting had taken a heavy toll on Combat Command B. The 2d Battalion, 67th Armored Regiment, was understrength in both tanks and men; A Company of that regiment had one tank, which was inoperable because it had no crew.

The 82d Reconnaissance Battalion, which had been given the mission of protecting the division's right flank, was clearing the zone between the Wurm River and the right column of Combat Command A. About 11:30 A.M. on October 8, A Company told the battalion commander, Col. Wheeler Merriam, that it would be delayed and requested a tankdozer to be sent to its position at the end of a tunnel. American soldiers fluent in German tried to persuade the defenders to surrender, but the enemy refused. The tankdozer was finally used to close the end of the tunnel, burying the enemy troops alive.

The right column of Combat Command A attacked at 7:30 A.M. to capture Oidtweiler. Two columns converged from the west and the north, while the south exits were blocked by a third force. The enemy resisted with its by now traditional heavy artillery and small arms fire. A forward observer, noting a number of vehicles and a large amount of enemy activity in the town, requested that corps artillery fire its big guns at the target. When the fire lifted, two platoons of German infantry surrendered immediately. The attackers reached the edge of town by 10:00, secured it and started preparing it for defense at 3:00 P.M.

While Combat Command A was taking Oidtweiler, General Harmon told Collier that the 30th Infantry Division was receiving a counterattack from the northeast. If the German column entered Schaufenberg, about 2,000 yards south of Oidtweiler, Collier was to attack its flank and destroy it. To aid Combat Command A, Harmon said that he could give Collier a reconnaissance company and one tank company from the division reserve. After a series of exchanges between Collier and Harmon, Collier started a platoon of medium tanks to the aid of the 117th Infantry Regiment, 30th Infantry Division. When XIX Corps questioned Harmon about the situation, the reply, in typical Harmon fashion, said the armor was moving into position, while the remainder of the battalion was under cover. He added, "Let them come."

There was a later series of exchanges concerning Schaufenberg: whose zone of responsibility it was, and who was to capture it. Finally, XIX Corps told Harmon that its map showed that Schaufenberg was in the 2d Armored Division area. Harmon alerted Collier that Combat Command A would have to move into the town. Collier replied that since he would have to use his reserve (an infantry battalion and one tank company) for the assignment, he wanted to wait until morning because he had not yet looked over the terrain.

The next morning Harmon called Collier to ask if anything were happening. Collier replied that the 117th Infantry Regiment said they would take Schaufenberg, and Collier had volunteered a tank company to help the regiment. The infantry wanted to attack at 7:00 A.M., but the fog was so thick that it was questionable whether the tanks could see. Apparently the fog lifted somewhat, for Company I, 66th Armored Regiment, attacked at 7:30, against only sniper fire, cutting the Bettendorf-Schaufenberg road. The infantry occupied the town by 10:00, while the remainder of the division installed minefields and booby traps around their positions, indicating that they planned to stay a while.

One reason for the 2d Armored Division's assuming defensive positions was the failure of the 30th Infantry Division to capture Aachen. This was caused by several factors, including the inability of the American VII Corps to break through the Hürtgen Forest, south of Aachen, and swing north to link with the 30th Infantry Division. Another factor was that the infantrymen were attacking what was thought to be a German staging area for counterattacks against the Americans.

To capture Aachen, the 30th Infantry Division had two choices: attack and capture Wurselen, then move south to take Aachen; or stage a river crossing over the Wurm River, attacking the Siegfried line frontally for the second time. General Hobbs, the division commander, chose the former plan and requested aid from XIX Corps. Corlett, knowing that replacements could not be supplied except from within the corps, loaned him two battalions of infantry from the 29th Infantry Division, and the 3d Battalion, 66th Armored Regiment.

Companies B and G of the 66th Armored supported the attacks of the 1st and 2d Battalions of the 116th Infantry Regiment, 29th Infantry Division. Their mission was to seize three objectives near Wurselen, cut communication routes north and northeast from Aachen and close the Aachen gap by linking up with VII Corps, which was coming from the south. The tankers and their infantry support encountered antitank, artillery and small arms fire in the built-up area around Wurselen. Savage street fighting developed in the town and the nearby villages. Some Mark V and VI tanks were being used as roadblocks; others were roving the battlefield. The American tanks were forced to use the town streets, as the other routes were strongly defended by antitank guns.

The fighting raged for four days with the ferocity revealed in the citation which accompanied the Medal of Honor awarded to Capt. James M. Burt:

> *Captain James M. Burt was in command of Company B, 66th Armored Regiment on the outskirts of Wurselen, Germany, on 13 October 1944 when his organization participated in a coordinated infantry-tank attack designed to isolate the large German garrison which was tenaciously defending the city of Aachen. In the first day's action, when infantrymen ran into murderous small-arms and mortar fire, Captain Burt dismounted from his tank about 200 yards to the rear and moved forward on foot beyond the infantry positions, where, as the enemy concentrated a tremendous volume of fire upon him, he calmly motioned his tanks into good firing positions. As our ground attack gained momentum, he climbed aboard his tank and directed the action from the rear deck, exposed to hostile volleys which finally*

Medal of Honor winner Capt. James M. Burt, H Company, 66th Armored Regiment, 2d Armored Division.

wounded him painfully in the face and neck. He maintained his dangerous post despite point-blank gunfire until friendly artillery knocked out those enemy weapons, and then proceeded to the advanced infantry scout's position to deploy his tanks for the defense of the gains which had been made. The next day, when the enemy counterattacked, he left cover and went 75 yards through heavy fire to assist the infantry battalion commander who was seriously wounded. For the next eight days, through rainy, miserable weather, and under constant, heavy shelling, Captain Burt held the combined forces together dominating and controlling the critical situation through the sheer force of his heroic example. To direct artillery fire, on 15 October, he took his tank 300 yards into the enemy lines where he dismounted and remained for 1 hour giving accurate data to friendly gunners. Twice more that day he went into enemy territory under deadly fire on reconnaissance. In succeeding days he never faltered in his determination to defeat the strong German forces opposing him. Twice the tank in which he was riding was knocked out by enemy action and each time he climbed aboard another vehicle and continued to fight. He took great risks to rescue wounded comrades and inflicted prodigious destruction on enemy personnel and material even though suffering from the wounds he received in the battle's opening phase. Captain Burt's intrepidity and disregard of personal safety was so complete that his own men and the infantry who attached themselves to him were inspired to overcome the wretched and extremely hazardous conditions which accompanied one of the most bitter local actions of the war. The victory achieved closed the Aachen gap.

The Aachen gap was closed on October 16; the 3d Battalion, 66th Armor, assumed defensive positions for the following three days. Action continued, however, as they had to fend off counterattacks and prevent German reinforcements from arriving. On October 20-21 the battalion was pulled out of the line to return to the 2d Armored Division and, except for Company H, joined division reserve.

For the second time since landing in Europe, the tankers were manning a static defense with the tanks dug in and outposted by infantry. The positions were improved with barbed wire and trip wires. Many times the enemy was only 300 yards away and any daytime movement usually resulted in heavy barrages of artillery or mortar fire. The Americans had taken heavy losses in the battle to breach the Siegfried line. The 2d Armored Division suffered 126 killed, 737 wounded and 36 missing. The

48th Medical Battalion treated 1,933 patients, including 90 civilians and German military personnel. The Combat Exhaustion Center, headed by the division psychiatrist, treated 211 men for battle fatigue and returned them to duty. During the battle, the division lost 28 tanks that could not be restored to duty by the Maintenance Battalion.

Hell on Wheels was making limited objective attacks against well-prepared static defenses. The Germans had surveyed the terrain and knew the ranges from their guns to any point on the ground. With that knowledge, they could bring devastating fire onto any attacker and inflict heavy losses. The theorists of the 1920-1930 era had predicted that when armor was used in such a mission the attacker would suffer even if he managed to accomplish his mission.

Chapter 15

OPERATION QUEEN

The Ninth Army's name for the attack to the Roer River was Operation QUEEN. For the 2d Armored Division, the move was a slow and savage struggle through mud, rain and snow. For the Germans, it was a defense of their homeland, protecting the vital Ruhr and Rhine valleys. To both sides it was the largest tank battle on the western front. For thirteen gruelling days, the Germans sought to deny the Americans an advance of nine or ten miles. It was the most determined resistance faced by the 2d Armored Division in the European theater of operations.

After breaching the Siegfried line, First Army, which still controlled the 2d Armored Division, notified the division that its authorized tank strength had been cut to 200 medium and 150 light tanks. Originally the division had been able to keep the extras and draw replacements when the total dropped. However, because of a shortage of replacement tanks, First Army decreed that the division would have to give up any tanks in excess of 200—forcing the surrender of eleven medium tanks. Harmon told his officers that there would be no command tanks except for battalion commanders and down. Six medium tanks would be equipped with a 522 radio: one for each of the combat commands and two for each regiment. The regiments could have five dozer tanks, the remainder to be returned to their units. The shortage of light tanks necessitated that the four tanks in each of the regimental maintenance sections be issued for immediate battle use.

At noon on October 22, Ninth Army, commanded by Lt. Gen. William H. Simpson, assumed control of XIX Corps and the 2d Armored Division. Ninth Army had been employed to capture Brest; now the Army was available to participate in the main drive against the enemy. The transfer, however, did not change the division's responsibility or mission. For the planned attack, Simpson would employ two corps abreast. The XIII Corps on the north was to seize Ruhr crossings at Linnich; while the XIX captured crossings at Julich. Once across the Ruhr River, both corps were to drive for Dusseldorf.

Weather was a prime concern for the tankers; Harmon mounted a tank and found that it could make only two or three miles per hour. Still doubting the ability of the tanks to cross wet, soggy ground, he asked the driver. They could, the driver replied; and Harmon, never doubting the American soldier's ability or confidence, notified Ninth Army that the tanks could take part in the attack.

The weather conditions further deteriorated when snow began to fall. The ground was not frozen and this handicapped the tankers. Ordnance personnel inspected the tanks to make sure that they had "duckbills," or track extenders, to increase their flotation (traction). These locally produced extenders were not totally satisfactory for the medium tanks, but they were all that was available. On the light tanks, the extenders were simply unusable. By the time that the attack took place, about three-fourths of the medium tanks had the extenders mounted. In spite of having the duckbills the vehicles could still become mired in the boggy ground. All light and medium tanks carried logs, approximately nine feet long and four to six inches in diameter, intended to help increase flotation. It turned out that they were not used because the tanks could traverse the ground in first or second gear; most tank crews cut loose their unneeded burden.

Having partially solved its problems with the environment, the division planned several ways to overcome man-made obstacles. The antitank ditches had to be bridged; it was a problem magnified by the intense antitank fire which was thought to be covering the ditches. One scheme called for certain tanks to be driven into a ditch and then quickly dozed over, forming a bridge. Another possibility was to use a bridge built by the 17th Armored Engineer Battalion. It was carried on a T-2 tank retriever, yet was capable of supporting the medium tanks. This early version of the portable bridge was to accompany the leading tanks, ready to span any ditch encountered.

The terrain over which the division would attack was considered tank country. A plain about 300 feet above sea level, it was dotted by many villages, usually 1,000 to 2,000 meters apart. On the plain itself were cultivated fields, crisscrossed by shallow ditches and sparse hedges. It sloped gently to the Roer River, with two main roads crossing it: the Aachen-Linnich highway, in the 2d Armored's area; and the Aldenhoven-Julich road, in the 29th Infantry Division's zone.

All across the plain the Germans assumed positions already favorable to defenders and steadily improved them with minefields and antitank ditches, then covered the obstacles with antitank, artillery, mortar and small arms fire. The level ground gave the built-up areas even more importance. The towns and villages usually commanded the crossroads and bridges. The Roer River, normally about 200 feet wide, was flooded to over 300 feet. The Germans controlled three dams upstream which could be destroyed and the river flooded if the Americans threatened a crossing.

Unknown to the Americans, the German commanding general of the XLVII Corps had been ordered to hold at all costs; no ground was to be given up. The 2d Armored Division acted as a magnet drawing the German 9th Panzer, the 15th Panzer Grenadier and the 10th SS Panzer Divisions against it. General der Panzer Truppen, Hasso von Manteuffel, commanding general, Fifth Panzer Army, persuaded General der Panzer Truppen, Heinrich Freiherr von Luttwitz, commanding general of the German XLVII Corps, to move the 9th Panzer Division across the Roer, even though it would be within American artillery range. This would place them in position readily available to counterattack if the Americans attacked. Later, during the assault, the 2d Armored met units from the 9th Panzer, the 15th Panzer Grenadier, the 183d, 246th and 340th Volks Grenadier Divisions, and the 207th and 506th General Headquarters tank battalions, which were equipped with the Mark VI Tiger Royal Tank. This was the first time that the division had confronted this vehicle. The division encountered extremely heavy indirect fire which emanated partly from the 766th Artillery Brigade and the 902d Assault Gun Brigade.

Maj. Gen. Raymond S. McLain, the new commanding general of

Above: Lt. Gen. William H. Simpson, commanding general, Ninth Army, and Maj. Gen. Raymond McLain, commanding general, XIX Corps, inspect the crown of Charlemagne following the capture of Aachen.

Below: Inspecting U.S. troops, Eisenhower, Churchill and Bradley fire the army's new carbine at 200 yards, scoring 29 hits out of 45 shots.

XIX Corps, who had replaced Corlett, sent the initial orders to the division with enough time for Harmon and his subordinate commanders to make their plans and to communicate those plans to the men. The division staff prepared a sand table which displayed all available information about the terrain features and enemy installations. The importance of the upcoming operation was emphasized by the appearance of Eisenhower, Bradley and Simpson for a briefing on November 10. The use of the sand table so impressed Simpson that he directed all units of the Ninth Army to adopt it.

On November 6, Harmon issued his field order, stating that XIX Corps's objective was to secure a bridgehead over the Roer River. The 29th Infantry Division was to lead the corps's attack. The 2d Armored Division, leading with Combat Command B, was to seize initial objectives and to secure the corps's left flank. The bulk of the division was to be ready to attack eastward and seize assembly areas to cross the Roer River at the bridgehead controlled by the 29th Infantry. Combat Command B was ready to exploit any weakness found toward Linnich. It was to use the 2d Battalion of the 406th Infantry Regiment to capture Immendorf and the high ground north of that town, after which the infantry battalion was to defend the area until the danger of counterattacks had passed.

The intelligence annex to the field order stated that since the fall of Aachen there had been no large-scale counterattacks against American positions. There had been considerable movement of troops and vehicles behind the front lines and "strategic moves far to the rear." The enemy's main concern seemed to be defense: regrouping forces and improving positions. They would probably delay the division's attack in successive positions to a strong defensive line along the Roer River and also they were attempting to "build a substantial striking force." Evidence indicated that the Germans had about 2,110 men in the line, with about fifty tanks in reserve. However, it was known there were three German divisions within two days' travel of the battle area.

Despite optimism in the American press, the commanders on the scene were not overly confident. Harmon had tried to get the 102d Infantry Division to attack and secure his north flank (left), but they refused. He told General White that he was not sure that the plans were going to work out very well. Since the delay had permitted the Germans to regroup and prepare defenses, Simpson said bluntly that he expected "one hell of a fight."

The men in the division were understandably jittery. There had been little action for several days, just patrols and intermittent shellings. Sgt.

Louis Clark, communications sergeant in F Company, 41st Armored Infantry Regiment, heard a team of horses pulling a wagon toward the American lines. Because of the fear that it might be filled with explosives, the men were ordered to let it pass through the lines and then take it in hand to be destroyed. When found the next day, the wagon was empty. Someone suspected that it might be a means for enemy patrols to infiltrate the American lines. The same thing happened the next night; again the wagon passed unmolested. Again, the third night and a third wagon. Now the officers knew it was used to infiltrate patrols; any further wagons were to be destroyed before they reached friendly lines. On the fourth and fifth nights wagons were destroyed by hand grenades; both times they were empty. It was a psychological game the Germans used to play on the nerves and emotions of the Americans.

The attack was to be preceded by an air attack similar to the one during the St. Lo breakout and the one that opened the attack on the Siegfried line. The weather was the deciding factor, however, and XIX Corps set D day for the first clear day after November 10. This caused the division to be alerted and to move to their attack and firing positions several times. The first few times that Combat Command B moved, it received heavy artillery and mortar fire. After a few days this nighttime movement failed to excite the Germans, who fired only the usual amounts of harassing and interdiction fire. This was to be to the division's advantage. Harmon realized that secrecy and suprise would be almost impossible to attain. These movements would mislead the Germans; they would not know which move was the real one. After several delays the attack was scheduled for November 16.

During the final planning sessions, Harmon was able to get the 102d Infantry Division to agree to a boundary change, permitting the 2d Armored Division to envelop Immendorf from the west. The commanding general of the 29th Infantry Division agreed to shift his boundary southward, permitting the 2d Armored to envelop Loverich from the south. The attack was intended to create a gap between the right flank of Combat Command B and the 29th Infantry Division, through which Harmon planned to send Collier's Combat Command A wheeling behind the defending Germans.

Harmon conveyed to the new commanders his philosophy of armor and leadership. The attack was to be bold and aggressive; commanders were to impress upon the men that fast, daring thrusts would cost less lives than nibbling at an objective. In a memorandum he called a checklist for the attack; he wanted all commanders briefed. The platoon leaders would brief their own men. All information—sand tables, maps, aerial photos—was to be studied, because "we feel the enemy had not enough troops to adequately man positions shown." Finally, all commanders were to check communications, ammunition and fuel in their units.

The 2d Armored Division was alerted that the air attack was scheduled for 11:15, and the lead units were to attack at 12:45. The air strike was larger than at St. Lo, with 1,204 American and 1,188 British bombers taking part. Immediately following the air strike, White's Combat Command B attacked without an artillery preparation, catching the Germans by surprise since it was axiomatic that the artillery shelled objectives before a tank or infantry assault.

Combat Command B was organized into three task forces. Task Force 1 (on the south flank) commanded by Col. Paul A. Disney was to take Loverich and Puffendorf. Task Force 2 (in the center) commanded by Lt. Col. Harry Hillyard was to capture Floverich and then aid in the capture of Apweiler. Task Force X (on the north flank) commanded by Lt. Col. James C. Reeves was responsible for capturing Immendorf and preventing German reinforcements from arriving from Geilenkirchen.

McLain directed that Harmon attack initially with one combat command because of the narrow front allotted the 2d Armored. XIX Corps (three divisions) was attacking along a ten-mile front, of which the 2d Armored had approximately two miles. After White had taken his initial objectives and the 29th Infantry Division had captured Setterich, the other combat command could be committed to battle.

Disney divided his command into three sub-task forces. The tanks were to attack Loverich from the south, while the infantry was to approach the town from the west. Following the tanks, the third group was to be sent to Puffendorf to seize and defend the town against possible counterattacks. Prior to the attack, 2d Armored's infantry moved into foxholes behind the frontline troops (3d Battalion, 406th Infantry Regiment, 102d Infantry Division).

At 12:45 the lead tanks crossed the line of departure, heading for the first objective. When the attack began, the artillery fired a rolling barrage ahead of the lead tanks. This kept German infantry and bazooka men pinned in their holes until they were overrun by tanks or infantry. Barbed wire and fire trenches were of little concern. About four minutes after the assault started, the Germans opened fire. D Company, 67th Armored, which was on the south flank, concentrated on the German guns in Setterich, stopping the enemy fire for the time being. Eight minutes and 1,200 yards after the attack started, the American tanks reached the orchard east of Loverich. The enemy began surrendering en masse, and twenty minutes after the attack began the town was secured.

After taking Loverich, Disney turned his task force toward Puffendorf to aid the third section of the attack. Lt. Col. Lemuel Pope, commanding officer, 2d Battalion, 67th Armor, followed the lead battalion to Loverich and then bypassed the town for his objective of Puffendorf. The advance went well, considering the soft ground and the intensity of enemy fire. Four tanks spun deeper into the mud and had to be retrieved, while six others had their tracks blown off by mines. The force bypassed Floverich, which was later cleared by infantry, and by 4:30 P.M. had Puffendorf surrounded and secured. Harmon, who was monitoring the progress of the attacking force, constantly urged the column onward, so the men would have a dry place to sleep.

After securing the two towns, the next mission was to capture the high ground, Hill 102.6, north of Puffendorf. The terrain and weather worked against the tankers, for they were getting mired in the wet ground. As one tank was being pulled out, the platoon leader found a gap in the antitank ditch. He had a dozer tank build a crossing and the attack resumed. Heavy enemy fire kept the Americans off the ridge, but the tankers could command the crest by fire from the south and southwest. They dug in for the night, prepared to attack again the following morning.

Leading with his M-4 Sherman medium tanks, Colonel Hillyard planned a frontal attack against Floverich. The infantry, supported by light tanks, was to follow 200 yards behind, thereby missing the German artillery fire which would be directed against the medium tanks. The attackers encountered a heavy volume of friendly artillery fire which was keeping the Germans pinned in the foxholes. The town was taken within two hours and after consolidating their gains Task Force 2 moved toward Apweiler. G Company, 67th Armored, which had been screening the attack on Floverich, ran into retreating Germans on a hill 500 yards east of the town. Several tanks charged the slope, captured enemy soldiers and motioned them to the rear.

After consolidating their gains, the Americans continued toward Apweiler with the medium tanks leading the attack. The German antitank emplacements in the woods south of the town spotted the approaching Americans and let the tanks come to within about 300 yards before opening fire with deadly accuracy. Two minutes later three tanks were burning; four others were immobilized. Unable to move forward, the Americans pulled back and established defensive positions along the highway about 800 yards east of Floverich. The savage defense of this town was thought to be of major significance. During the night, the men reported hearing armored vehicles moving behind the German lines.

The third task force of the combat command attacked with the others. Task Force X (2d Battalion, 406th Infantry Regiment, and Company H, 67th Armored Regiment) attacked at 12:45 from Waurichen and had only about 2,000 yards to move to their objective of Immendorf. Advancing through heavy artillery and mortar fire and losing four tanks to minefields, they took the town by 1:50 and prepared for defense by 3:50. Reeves's task force had planned to keep one company in reserve. When Task Force 2 had to pull back, it left a gap in the line, forcing him to put his reserve company into the line.

While the day's attacks had been successful and Combat Command B had all their initial objectives, the men were in dangerous positions. They occupied a salient into the German lines and were drawing heavy enemy fire from three directions. Any further advance was dangerous until the flank units came alongside the spearhead. In addition, their winding supply routes were hindered by many detours. Ammunition and fuel did not arrive at the forward positions in sufficient quantities to resist a determined counterattack. Had the enemy made a determined effort to push back the 1st Battalion, 67th Armored, on Hill 102.6, then perhaps all the gains of the day would have been negated.

The 67th Armored Regiment established its headquarters in the house of the mayor of Ubach. He was an anti-Nazi and probably was in a concentration camp. The house, a three-story building with a basement, had slate roofing. The German gunners had surveyed the area with extreme accuracy and knew the ranges to all points—road crossings, intersections, buildings, possible concentration areas, bridges and other major terrain features. An occasional round bursting nearby would shake loose a tile on the roof. At that time the officers were getting a one-quart liquor ration per month. The rations had just been distributed when the Germans decided to shell Ubach heavily. One staff officer in headquarters, 67th Armor, was nervous; as a slate rattled to the ground he would pop the cork and enjoy hearty swallows. One round hit the roof directly; someone urged the nervous officer to take a mouthful, which he did. Ubach continued to receive fire until the latter part of November.

Harmon was getting angry about the situation at Setterich: the 29th

Infantry Division, which was supposed to take the town, was apparently not making serious efforts to do so. XIX Corps told the division chief of staff, Col. Clayton J. Mansfield, that the infantry doubted they could take the town before November 17. He asked if a boundary change would be acceptable, permitting the 2d Armored to take it. Permission was denied.

The first day's attacks of the 2d Armored had been successful, resulting in almost complete destruction of the 350th Infantry Regiment, 183d Infantry Division. The attack order for the next day said that the resistance had been light but could be expected to stiffen. Localized counterattacks of perhaps battalion strength, supported by armor, could be anticipated. Combat Command B was to resume the attack at 8:00 A.M., while Combat Command A was to be ready to move an hour later to seize Ederen.

November 18 was perhaps the most disastrous day in 2d Armored Division history. Task Force 1, which had taken Puffendorf, was to take the high ground south of Geronsweiler, while Task Forces 2 and X were to capture Apweiler. All three were then to combine their efforts to take Geronsweiler. By capturing that town, the 2d Armored Division would be looking down on Linnich, about 3,000 - 4,000 yards away. The Germans had shelled Puffendorf all night on November 16, and outposts reported that they could hear tracked vehicles moving behind the front lines. In the morning the German artillery shifted their fire to the exits from Puffendorf. This prevented escape or the arrival of reinforcements to aid the tankers. About 7:00 A.M., D Company of the 67th Armored reported that it was receiving small arms fire, which the tankers returned. They could not see its effect because of the darkness and the heavy morning mist.

Shortly after dawn, between 7:30 and 8:30, the 1st and 2d Battalions, 67th Armor, began to move out into the open to form for the attack on Geronsweiler. They were in line and in an exposed position when at least twenty German tanks, supported by infantry and artillery, attacked. The German tanks were more maneuverable and more heavily armored and also out-gunned the 75mm and 76mm weapons on the American medium tanks. The 2d Armored fought back bravely, but soon the Germans found the range and began inflicting heavy losses on the tankers. The infantry of both sides was pinned down by the heavy artillery fire, thus it was a tank-versus-tank fight—which the Americans lost. Realizing that they could not maintain their exposed positions, the Americans decided to pull back to Puffendorf and use the thick rock-walled buildings in defending against the German attack.

First Lieutenant Robert E. Lee, commanding officer, D Company,

67th Armored, went to each infantryman's foxhole, telling him that the tanks were withdrawing to Puffendorf and directing him to fall back. Lee's actions probably prevented panic among the foot soldiers. He kept his own tank in an exposed position, covering the retreat. The situation changed when the Americans reached the buildings. Now the Germans would have to expose themselves to enter the town. They chose not to do so, probably because of the arrival of Task Force A, Combat Command A. This force, which had planned to use the town as a route for a different attack, accidentally arrived at a crucial moment.

The fight lasted about six hours; Disney's men took a severe beating, perhaps the worst that had been inflicted on an element of the 2d Armored. At noon, responding to Harmon's inquiry, White said that he had lost two medium companies and a light company. XIX Corps was alerted to the possibility that the 2d Armored Division had lost the equivalent of a tank battalion. Later in the day, the actual figures were not quite so grim. A German prisoner reported that he was a member of the 9th Panzer Division and that the attack was to retake Immendorf. In addition, he told them that the Germans had two regiments of infantry, along with supporting artillery, reconnaissance and armor units near Beeck, about four miles to the northwest.

While Task Force 1 was attempting to repel the savage German counterattack, Task Force 2 and Task Force X were launching coordinated attacks to capture Apweiler. The attack started at 8:00 A.M. and came under heavy artillery, mortar, machine gun and tank fire. A platoon of I Company, 67th Armor, which was leading the assault, made about 500 yards before it had to turn back. Hillyard told White that it was impossible to progress over open ground; they would have to work their way up through the draws in the area. At that time White ordered the task force commander to hold his position until further orders. The fire was so intense that when Capt. John Erbes went forward to aid the wounded, his Red Cross flag was riddled by small arms fire. The intrepid doctor and his medics continued their rescue mission, for which Erbes received his second Distinguished Service Cross and the men received Silver Stars. Shortly before noon, the division command post received a message that Task Force 2 was "having a hell of a time and was no closer than they were yesterday."

Task Force X was making its final plans for the attack on Apweiler when the Germans attacked with three companies of infantry from the 10th Panzer Grenadier Regiment and ten tanks from the 9th Panzer Division. Artillery and mortar fire broke up the enemy formations and fire from the 771st Tank Destroyer Battalion knocked out three of the German vehicles. After an all-morning fight, the Germans pulled back. Following the fight, White placed Col. Bernard F. Hurless, commanding officer, 406th Infantry Regiment, in command of Task Force X, which was reinforced with the other two battalions of that regiment. At 6:00 P.M., the Germans began a second counterattack against Immendorf intended to drive the 406th Infantry and H Company of the 67th Armored out of town. Three German tanks broke through the defenses but were destroyed: two by mines placed by the infantry, the third by H Company at a range of less than twenty yards.

The XIX Corps commander, General McLain, granted permission to use Combat Command A. Harmon ordered General Collier to seize Ederen on Combat Command B's right flank. Planning for the attack on Ederen, Capt. John R. Werts, commanding officer, E Company, 66th Armor, a Southerner with a quick wit, summarized the problems which the task force would encounter. A flat plain stretched for a thousand yards in front of the objective. After studying the map, Werts said, "Man, can't you see them cannon balls comin' across there!"

At 9:00 A.M. on November 17, Task Force A, Combat Command A, moved from its assembly area toward Puffendorf and then was to attack northeast to take Ederen. The task force arrived about the same time that the Germans were pushing Task Force 1 of Combat Command B back to Puffendorf. The tanks of Combat Command A pulled back and waited for the situation to develop. At 11:00, Lt. Col. Ira P. Swift, task force commander, ordered the tanks to positions southwest of town. The infantry dismounted and took cover in an orchard, while the tanks moved to positions north and northeast of town, trying to continue their mission.

The tanks headed east from Puffendorf and encountered a tank ditch twelve to fifteen feet wide and ten to twelve feet deep, whose sides formed a V. On the opposite side of the ditch the Germans had about fifteen tanks. The only solution Harmon saw now was to flank the obstacle, moving through the town of Setterich, which was in the 29th Infantry Division zone. He had offered to send an armored column to help the infantry division, but General Gerhardt declined the aid, saying that his men could capture it. To cause more problems, a report was received that sixteen German tanks were moving into town and would be in position to fire on the flank of any force trying to cross the tank ditch.

The day had been disastrous for the 2d Armored. Except for Combat

Command A's Task Force A, the division had not gained a foot of ground. The situation in Setterich was not to Harmon's liking. At 7:54 P.M. White reported that during the day eighteen medium and seven light tanks had been destroyed, while sixteen medium and twelve light tanks were out of action. Combat Command A had lost four mediums; both groups had a total of 56 men killed, 281 wounded and 29 missing. The Germans were known to have lost seventeen tanks and approximately half of their attacking infantry.

During the night, the German patrols infiltrated into Puffendorf. One group was captured and told interrogators that they were part of a 400-man force that was to attack the next morning. The prisoners were surprised at the size of the American force; they had been told the town was only lightly outposted. Later in the night, German infantry was heard in the streets. Some thought it was the prisoners being brought in by 2d Armored patrols. The error was soon discovered; in the fight twenty Germans were killed and ten were captured, none escaped.

Other prisoners reported that they were to attack Immendorf at 6:00 A.M. When the Americans discovered this, they shelled the German assembly areas, breaking up the attack. An assault was launched at 5:00 P.M. but was repulsed by artillery and the 1st Battalion, 406th Infantry Regiment. The German effort was supported by eight Panther tanks, three of which were destroyed by tank destroyers, while the other five retreated.

On November 18, Harmon issued a new attack order. In summarizing the German defensive ability, he concluded that the main defensive line was the Roer River. The division commander thought that east of the Roer they might run into the mobile reserves of the 6th Panzer Army (1st SS, 2d SS, 9th SS, 12th SS and Panzer Lehr Divisions). Combat Command B was to take Apweiler, while Task Force A, Combat Command A, was to defend Puffendorf. Task Force B, Combat Command A, was to move near Setterich, ready to attack and seize the high ground northeast of that town. Combat Command Reserve was to send a tank destroyer platoon and a company of medium tanks to Loverich, where they were to repel counterattacks from the east or northeast. The remainder of the reserve was to move to Baesweiler and make plans to move to either Immendorf or Puffendorf on Harmon's order.

November 18 was to have been a day of rest for the division, but the German counterattack of the previous day changed that. The standard tactic of tank-infantry teams would not work because of the open terrain and the long range of the German weapons. White decided to try an old method to capture Apweiler. He sent a battalion of infantry without armor along the approach route from Immendorf, while a tank company worked its way up through the draws trying to reach a small knoll southeast of the town. The attack, starting at 2:00 P.M., proceeded rapidly, with the infantry reaching the edge of town by 2:25 P.M. and capturing it by 3:15. Within forty-five minutes, the town was prepared for defense with the arrival of H Company, 67th Armored, a platoon of tank destroyers and the 1st Battalion, 406th Infantry Regiment.

At 4:00 P.M. a platoon of I Company, 67th Armor, and two companies of infantry attacked the high ground east of Floverich. They met little opposition; the ground was safely in American hands by dark. With the exception of these two assaults to strengthen Combat Command B's positions, the combat command maintained its defensive positions, ready to repel the counterattack that did not occur. The most action, other than the two attacks, was artillery duels with the enemy.

So far, Combat Command B had carried most of the fight. Harmon was anxious to commit Collier's combat command to the battle. Combat Command A's Task Force A was in assault positions on the outskirts of Puffendorf, waiting for the 29th Infantry Division to capture Setterich. Once that was done, Force A was to assemble in the town, attack through a bridgehead across the tank ditch and capture Freialdenhoven. After three days, Harmon had lost patience. Setterich was the key to the success of the 2d Armored, while it was merely of nuisiance value to the 29th Infantry. He finally convinced McLain that the tankers should be allowed to take the town, which they did late in the afternoon of November 18. Now Harmon could commit the full battle strength of Hell on Wheels to the fight.

On November 19, Combat Command B improved its defensive positions while preparing for an advance the following day. At 5:20 A.M., Force X, which had captured Apweiler the previous day, was attacked by two reconnaissance companies from the 9th Panzer Division supported by nine tanks. By 9:00 all the German tanks had been destroyed and the infantry repulsed. Late in the day three more enemy tanks came near Task Force X's positions and were destroyed by tank destroyers. During the night, patrols from the 406th Infantry Regiment reached the outskirts of Geronsweiler; this was a good indication, for that town was Combat Command B's objective for the following day.

Combat Command A was to move east from Puffendorf and cross

the tank ditch that had blocked its advance. At 3:00 P.M. Task Force A attacked to force a crossing and capture Ederen. After Collier's men moved about a half-mile, the Germans attacked the seemingly exposed left flank with about 100 infantry and four tanks. The Germans apparently forgot that the Americans were in Puffendorf; Task Force 1, Combat Command B, protecting the flank, caught the Germans unaware. The American artillery and mortars routed the infantry, while tanks and tank destroyers knocked out three of the German vehicles. In spite of this aid from Combat Command B, Combat Command A made little progress toward Ederen against the heavy, accurate fire it was drawing from the Germans. At the end of the day, Task Force A dug in on the banks of that tank ditch and prepared to breach it the following day.

Company F, 116th Infantry Regiment, 29th Infantry Division, established a bridgehead across the antitank ditch at Setterich. With that accomplished, Harmon decided to commit all of Combat Command A to the battle. Task Force B, Combat Command A, which had not yet seen action, was now ordered to cross the antitank ditch and attack Freialdenhoven. At 10:30 A.M., the 2d Battalion, 119th Infantry Regiment, 30th Infantry Division, which had been attached to the 2d Armored, relieved the 29th Infantry elements which had captured the town and bridgehead. The remainder of Task Force B moved from Baesweiler, crossed the ditch without going through the town and moved through a gap in a minefield. By nighttime Hinds had his force about 1,000 yards from Freialdenhoven, where he then manned defensive positions.

In spite of a driving rain, Harmon decided to resume the attack to capture Freialdenhoven, Ederen and Geronsweiler on November 20. The commanders decided to use the flamethrower tanks of B Squadron, Fife and Forfar Yeomanry, which had been loaned from the British army since November 19. During the battle, the Germans launched an attack with sixty to eighty Tiger and Panther tanks, which they called "the greatest tank battle of the western front." The 2d Armored Division repulsed the attacks, using all its weapons: tank destroyers, infantry, artillery, fighter bombers and tanks.

The 702d Tank Destroyer Battalion, commanded by Lt. Col. John A. Beall, had recently received the new M-36 tank destroyers which mounted the 90mm gun. The men were anxious to try them against the Germans. To assist the division tanks, Beall revised a German trick of luring the enemy to the guns. Some of the American tanks, clearly no match for the German tanks, ventured forward, drawing fire, and then fell back as though retreating. The Germans gave chase, only to find that they had been lured within the range of the deadly 90mm antitank gun. For six days the Germans tried to rout the 2d Armored Division, only to be turned back. The Americans pushed slowly onward.

On the division's south flank, Hinds's Task Force B, Combat Command A, attacked through a driving rain and into a minefield of both metallic and nonmetallic mines that halted its progress until the mines were removed. When the attack resumed, the infantry dismounted from the tanks and moved forward supported by the flame-throwing Crocodiles. The German infantry manning the trenches quickly surrendered when confronted with the flamethrowers. Three of the British tanks were lost to mines; one stuck in a ditch. By then, however, the American infantry was in the town and had begun clearing it for the night's defense.

In the center of the division's zone, Task Force A, Combat Command A, had the same objective it had faced for several days: Ederen. Capturing this town would help Combat Command B move onto Geronsweiler, which was about 2,500 yards to the northwest and linked by the same road. Collier moved his group out at 10:00 A.M. and described the scene: "Visibility poor, mud knee-deep and receiving direct fire."

With a tank and infantry company on each side of the road, the attack made slow but steady progress through minefields and against enemy Mark VI tanks and infantry. While D Company, 66th Armored, was moving through the tank ditch, it lost a tank destroyer and five medium tanks (three were later recovered and restored to action). The company was ordered to disengage and follow E Company, 66th Armored. By accident, a shell set four haystacks on fire; the smoke blew perpendicular to the route of advance, forming a perfect smoke screen for the Americans. I Company, 66th Armored, was detached from Task Force B and attacked north from Freialdenhoven, approaching Ederen from the southwest. The infantry, advancing behind the tanks of E Company, 66th Armor, rounded up the surprised German infantry, who had not seen the Americans because of the accidental smoke screen. At 3:30 the tanks of both Companies E and I were in position to attack Ederen. Collier ordered them to oversee the capture by the infantry and the securing of the objective. By 5:30 the Americans had the town and prepared it for defense.

White's attack to capture Geronsweiler, scheduled for 9:00 A.M., was delayed because of the heavy rain and the sea of mud. Task Force 1 was to proceed north and northeast, capture Hill 106.2 and the

Geronsweiler-Ederen road, then maintain contact with Collier on Task Force 1's right flank. Task Force 2 was supposed to advance and capture the southern half of the town, while Task Force X seized the northern half.

Task Force 1 attacked and forty-five minutes later had secured its objective without losses in tanks or men. In its advance, Task Force 2 encountered heavy machine gun fire which trapped the infantry in the mud. I Company, which was supporting the advance, started firing at two Mark V tanks. In the duel, the American tanks could not score a killing hit; instead the shells bounced off the German vehicle, hitting an oil dump and setting it afire. As the smoke drifted across the town, it made a perfect smoke screen for the infantrymen. C Company, 41st Armored Infantry Regiment, reached the edge of town but was pinned down by automatic weapons fire. No amount of urging by the officers could move the men forward. The company commander told the forward observer from the 83d Armored Artillery Battalion that the two officers should start walking into town and see if the men would follow. The officers walked, and the men followed.

When the smoke screen was formed, I Company, 67th Armor, moved forward to help the infantry's advance. It destroyed a machine gun nest which protected about thirty riflemen in foxholes. As the tankdozer started filling in the foxholes, the Germans raised a white flag, climbed out of their holes and then fled toward their lines. The Americans, however, had experienced that trick and raked the fleeing figures with machine gun fire.

Task Force X attacked at the same time as the other task forces. It encountered heavy antitank and machine gun fire from the direction of Prummern and Beeck. Company C, 771st Tank Destroyer Battalion, went to the task force's aid and in the fight lost all but three of its vehicles. However, the infantry continued to advance against small arms and machine gun fire. Coming onto the flank of the town, Task Force X was in position to intercept retreating Germans, and did so. By 2:00 P.M., the town was occupied and the task forces began consolidating the buildings and the outlying areas for defense.

When the action around Geronsweiler had somewhat stabilized, the 82d Reconnaissance Battalion was ordered to help guard the left flank of the division. In the grayness of a false dawn following a night of intermittent showers, the men were cold and miserable. Company A maintenance section's armored car driver, Bobbie Ellis, was seen bailing out his water-filled foxhole. Sgt. Charles F. Morse, who had the hole next to

Ellis, heard him mutter with each dip of the steel helmet, ''They even give you running water in this man's GD army.'' Morse correctly thought that the men were living the part of Bill Mauldin's ''Willie and Joe.''

On November 21, the 2d Armored resumed the attack with all five task forces. Task Force B, Combat Command A, was to take positions for an attack on Merzenhausen. Task Force A had an easy job, for they had only to advance a few hundred yards to seize Hill 97.6, east of Ederen. Combat Command B was to attack and capture the high ground east and north of Geronsweiler; with a single exception, it too had an easy time. Hinds had split his command in two for the advance. The southern group, scheduled to attack at 9:00 A.M., was delayed for two hours to refuel their vehicles. Their objective was Hill 105.6, about 600 yards south of Merzenhausen.

The advance across potato and beet fields met little resistance until the tanks were on the hill. There, six German Mark VI tanks fired on F Company, 66th Armored. The Americans destroyed two and the other four pulled back. The infantry had been slowed by artillery and mortar fire but they were on the hill shortly after the German tanks retreated. The left column was assigned the high ground about 300 to 400 yards west of Merzenhausen. The ground sloped toward the town and the attacking force was under observation all the way. However, it received only sporadic artillery and mortar fire. Patrols worked their way into town and reported that tanks and infantry were there.

Hinds and Collier met to discuss the patrol's report at the spot where an 88mm gun had been destroyed. The crew's foxholes dotted the area and were available if needed. When the two commanders arrived at the scene, they immediately selected foxholes for themselves and their drivers. They knew the antennas on their vehicles might well be targets for enemy gunners. As if cued, the Germans opened fire on the vehicles and the small command meeting. The men dived for foxholes; Collier, known affectionately to his men as Pee Wee because of his diminutive size, almost drowned in the water and muck in his hole. Since tanks and infantry were in the town, the commanders decided to delay the assault.

Task Force 1, Combat Command B, was ordered to advance about 300 yards east to capture Hills 96.3 and 95. The 1st Battalion, 41st Armored Infantry, was detached from Force 2, assigned to Force 1 and given the assignment. One officer in the battalion believed it was ''a damned fool mission as we already had the commanding ground.'' At 10:00 A.M. the attackers moved out and immediately came under heavy artillery and mortar fire but reached their objective and made contact with flank units by 2:30. They suffered no tank losses and few infantry casualties. The weary soldiers stayed in these positions for three days before being relieved by the 771st Tank Destroyer Battalion on November 24.

Task Force 2, Combat Command B, attacked to seize the high ground north of Geronsweiler and met only heavy artillery fire. After twenty-five minutes they were on the objective. The Germans launched two counterattacks from the direction of Lindern but were beaten off by artillery and tank destroyer fire. The second attack came later in the day, and for a moment some of the infantry panicked. The tankers restored the line, and the enemy fell back. The defenders maintained their new positions until relieved on November 23.

Task Force X was assigned the high ground about one mile north and northeast of Geronsweiler. If the three task forces of Combat Command B seized their objectives, they would be overlooking the Roer River crossing at Linnich. At 11:00 A.M. Task Force X moved out with the other two task forces, following a rolling artillery barrage which cost the enemy dearly. About thirty-five minutes later, the infantrymen were on Hill 98.1 and began to consolidate the objective. At 5:45 P.M. three companies of the 11th Panzer Grenadier Regiment raised a white flag as if surrendering. When they raised their hands, some had hand grenades cleverly concealed. Two platoons of A Company of the 406th Infantry Regiment were almost destroyed; the enemy penetrated the combat command line. Tanks from the 3d Battalion, 67th Armor, and tank destroyers of B Company, 702d Tank Destroyer Battalion, arrived and restored the line about 6:30 P.M. Company A had suffered heavily and was down to only fifty-four men, but the other companies of the 1st Battalion, 406th Infantry, suffered as well; they stayed in the line. General Harmon's comment, after being informed, was "the infantry must have gotten a little excited."

After a full day's fighting, the 2d Armored Division was in a strong position to resist counterattacks. Harmon issued instructions that the division was to assume a defensive posture until noon on November 23, Thanksgiving Day. By that time, all parts of the division were to be relieved in the line. The artillery and tanks were to stay either in their positions or in adjusted locations to support the infantry manning the front lines. There was some evidence that the enemy was beginning to pull back to positions behind the Roer River. Artillery forward observers reported heavy traffic on the Lindern-Linnich road in both directions, but more going east than west. However, there was no real evidence that it was a full-scale withdrawal.

The saddest day· in the war for Corp. James S. Crawford was

Thanksgiving Day, 1944. Crawford, the loader on gun number three in A Battery, 78th Armored Artillery Battalion, had slept through the German attack at St. Denis le Gast. Thanksgiving morning, he and his gun chief, Sgt. Walter Horner went to breakfast and had real eggs. Horner complained that he received only one egg. The remainder were being saved for dinner. Crawford told him that matters could be worse, they were still alive. Crawford went to bed, for he had been on duty with the gun most of the night. Horner went back to the gun. A few hours later, Crawford was awakened with the news that Horner had been killed by enemy artillery fire.

The following day, the attack resumed. Merzenhausen was the most strongly defended town the division had faced in operations west of the Roer River and was the key to the enemy's defensive positions west of the river. With its capture, the town of Barmen would fall and the division would be on the Roer River. Merzenhausen's importance lay in the fact that it secured the north-south communications lines. It was heavily defended by fire trenches on the north, west and south, with infantry, supported by tanks and assault guns, making the task of capturing the town most difficult.

Hinds organized two groups for the attack. The 1st Battalion, 66th Armored Regiment, was to advance from the south; the 2d Battalion, 119th Infantry Regiment, 30th Infantry Division, from the west. Both battalions had flame-throwing tanks spearheading the attacks. On the south, the flamethrowers caused the Germans to raise white flags. When the tanks moved to exposed positions, however, they were destroyed and the bitter fighting resumed. The tanks slowly worked their way into the orchard on the western edge of town, which permitted the infantry to enter the narrow roads. By 5:30 P.M. the infantry had cleared about one-third of the village. Then the Germans counterattacked. Led by Mark VI tanks, the German infantry pushed the Americans back to the edge of town. A battalion of the 41st Armored Infantry was sent to aid the 119th Infantry, but nightfall prevented their attacking until the next morning. American patrols reported that a battalion of German infantry was massed east of town and that two tanks were in the draws to the north. That night the Americans organized tank stalker crews and the main street was mined to prevent an enemy surprise attack. The defenders then rested and prepared to resume the attack the following morning.

Shortly after midnight the enemy tried to clear the mines from the streets but was stopped by the infantry in the village. The attack to secure

Merzenhausen resumed at 8:00 A.M. It immediately encountered heavy machine gun fire, but that was stopped by dug-in tanks. One American tank was destroyed by a German tank hidden in a barn and firing through a sliding door. A bazooka and molotov cocktail team was organized and the barn was set ablaze, but heavy fire kept the Americans away so they did not know if the tank was destroyed. It was house-to-house fighting, with the Germans throwing hand grenades from second-floor windows. Nevertheless, by 3:00 P.M. the Americans controlled about half the village and began to consolidate their gains. During the day, Collier, who was watching the fighting, told Harmon that a prisoner reported a German infantry division was digging in around Barmen. The general stiffened at the bad news; Barmen was the next target.

On November 26, Ninth Army redrew the boundaries between XIX and XIII Corps. This pulled Combat Command B out of the fight. Harmon assigned them responsibility for Ederen, making Combat Command A responsible for the fighting in the division zone. On the morning of November 27, Collier launched a three-pronged attack to secure Merzenhausen and the high ground northeast and east of the town. The 1st Battalion, 119th Infantry Regiment, was to capture Hill 100.3 northeast of town, while the 3d Battalion, 41st Armored Infantry captured Hill 98.1 to the east. The 2d Battalion, 119th Infantry Regiment, supported by Company I, 66th Armored, and Company A, 17th Armored Engineer Battalion, was to capture Merzenhausen itself. The attack was supposed to take Merzenhausen and Barmen and cut enemy communication lines west of the Roer.

At 7:15 A.M., infantry in the right column, the 3d Battalion, 41st Armored Infantry, advanced over muddy ground, without tank support against dug-in infantry, artillery and mortar fire. They reached the line of German trenches before being counterattacked by eight tanks and a strong infantry force. Using the German trenches, the Americans held off the enemy. Before the end of the day, the 2d Battalion, 41st Armored Infantry, was sent to their aid and to fill the gap that was appearing between the right and center forces. With the commitment of the reserve force, German resistance quickly faded.

Collier thought that the tanks would be most needed to help the 1st Battalion, 119th Infantry, capture Hill 100.3, but the terrain and enemy positions hindered their use. Collier told Lt. Col. Robert H. Herlong that if he could find a covered route for the tanks, then he could use them; if not, then the infantry alone would have to take the hill. In the morning mist, the infantrymen advanced to within 400 yards of the objective before being stopped by small arms fire. The artillery forward observer called for and received heavy fire on the German positions. When the 1st Battalion attacked again, they encountered the same intense fire that had stopped them before. Reconnaissance found railroad tracks, which the tankers could follow up a draw to the crest of the hill. The tanks arrived and after a heavy artillery barrage started moving forward with the infantry following at a distance of 100 to 200 yards. The German fire slackened, then stopped, as the tanks appeared near the crest. The infantry quickly cleared the objective and prepared it for defense.

One noncommissioned officer had a rather effective method for teaching his men to stay alert. Sgt. Lemuel P. Viala was a quiet, soft-spoken, completely unflappable individual. Remembered as "utterly unlike the typical sergeant," he was a long-timer, having served in the old horse cavalry before World War II. To keep his men alert and to teach them to keep their heads down, he would peep over the edge of his foxhole, and if he saw a helmet raise a little too high he bounced a small rock off it. The wearer was usually scared enough to be more careful the next time.

The center force was assigned the roughest mission: clearing Merzenhausen. The 2d Battalion, 119th Infantry Regiment, used two companies for the bitter house-to-house fighting. Tanks and tank destroyers were held out of the town because of mines and the threat of bazooka fire. The method adopted by F Company on the north side of the street and E Company on the south side was relatively simple. One squad would fire at the windows and doors while a second squad rushed the house to flush out, kill or capture the occupants. Repeated charges against snipers, dug-in tanks, bazookas, artillery, mortar and long-range tank fire slowed the advance. At one point a German tank inside a two-floor building was holding up the attack. Hinds directed a forward observer to call for an eight-inch howitzer (the most accurate artillery piece in the world) to fire on the position. The first round, using a delay fuze, took off the roof and the second floor; the second round destroyed the first floor and, more importantly, the German tank. This was perhaps one of the few times that an eight-inch howitzer was used as an antitank gun. By midafternoon the enemy had been driven back only a few hundred yards. The reserve platoon was called to the front. It executed an old style bayonet charge which demoralized the Germans, causing them to pull out of the town.

By 6:00 P.M. the Germans had retreated and the infantry started preparing their defenses for the night. About 9:30, the Germans launched a counterattack with two tanks supported by infantry. Artillery fire drove off most of the attackers, but a stubborn few made it to the defensive minefield that had been installed by the 2d Battalion, 119th Infantry. While flares illuminated the sky, bazooka teams and the infantry defenders fired on German infantry, killing about eight and driving the others away. This day had been a good one for the Americans; they had captured 337 prisoners, including the battalion commander and staff of the 1st Battalion, 695th Infantry Regiment, 340th Infantry Division.

By midnight, the 2d Armored Division had secured its positions and now posed a threat to the final communication route through Barmen. They needed to clear the last few pockets of bypassed resistance and take the town. Barmen, their ultimate objective, was relatively easy, for the two hills taken the previous day overlooked the town. The plan was simple. Three forces were to be used: the right column was to cut the Barmen-Kosler road, preventing the arrival of reinforcements; the left column was to protect the north flank and seize the high ground to the northwest; the center column would conduct the final attack. The assault started at noon and the Americans were in the town thirty minutes later, having met only sporadic rearguard action. On the north flank, the Americans reported that ten to fifteen enemy tanks were in Flossdorf and that they were getting heavy artillery fire from the east bank of the Roer. A platoon of C Company, 702d Tank Destroyer Battalion, went to aid the north column and destroyed one enemy tank. Attacking fighter bombers destroyed six more. Later, several explosions in the town indicated that the aircraft had hit ammunition or fuel or that the Germans were destroying those supplies preparatory to moving to the east bank of the river.

During the battle for the Roer River, Headquarters, 67th Armored Regiment, stayed in Ubach. It was charged primarily with the administrative functions for the regiment; Combat Command B had tactical control. Maj. Francis H. Barnes received notification that he had just been promoted to lieutenant colonel and was to be the regimental executive officer.

Meanwhile, a motorcycle messenger approaching Ubach was taken under fire by an 88mm gun. The motorcycle overturned and the rider suffered numerous cuts, bruises and a compound fracture of one leg. He was brought into the headquarters building where Capt. John Erbes, a battalion surgeon, was present. He asked the newly promoted Barnes to

A machine gun crew of Headquarters, 1st Battalion, 41st Armored Infantry Regiment, 2d Armored Division, follows an American tank during an assault in Germany.

help set the leg before the man was evacuated to the rear area hospital. After the injured man was given a shot of morphine, Barnes held him by the arms while Erbes began to set the leg. Without thinking, Barnes lit a cigarette; the pulling and tugging caused the ashes to drop into the man's eyes. He immediately called Barnes all the most vile types of sons of bitches. He demoted the lieutenant colonel to the level of a moron. All the while, Erbes was splinting the leg. Later, the surgeon told Barnes that the ashes had been the most helpful thing possible, because they took the patient's mind off his leg.

By the end of the attack to the Roer River, the division had received sufficient track extensions to equip each medium tank and to have an adequate reserve. Combat Command A went into defensive positions, while Combat Command B conducted extensive maintenance and rested its personnel. On November 29, Division Trains opened a replacement pool and reception center, processing thirteen officers and sixty-six enlisted men in 2½ days. One of the new officers joining the division was 2d Lt. Frank L. Culver. Assigned to D Company, 66th Armored Regiment, he went to the company, only to find that it was out on an assignment, with only the headquarters personnel present. They greeted him politely, but with the coolness reserved for "virgin second lieutenants." The same day he experienced an attack by German aircraft. Culver recalled that the planes appeared to be coming directly at him. He dashed to the basement air raid shelter. Not realizing that the corridor made three turns, he stopped, thinking he was trapped. Some of the headquarters men came to his aid, escorting the new officer safely into the cellar.

The enemy had reached a new peak in mine warfare. Explosives were emplaced in streets and on the shoulders of roads. In the attack, the 2d Armored Division encountered no fewer than twenty-two minefields. However, the charges did not unduly hamper the tanks, and most got through without extensive damage. Nonetheless, the division suffered more in this twelve-day period than at any previous time. It had 1,505 casualties: 203 killed, 1,104 wounded and 198 missing. They killed an estimated 830 enemy, while capturing 2,385 and destroying 86 tanks, 12 self-propelled guns and 113 miscellaneous vehicles. The division lost about 80 tanks, 41 of which could not be restored to duty.

The battle for the Roer River touched off a newspaper battle in the United States about the merits or demerits of American equipment. Correspondent Jack Bell of the *Chicago Daily News* sent back reports which contained several derogatory quotations from soldiers. An unidentified tank officer told the correspondent that "we won because of sheer numbers. The men had too much will to win for Jerry to stomach. We knew we were licked tank for tank, but the boys went in in a free-for-all, ganging on the Tiger until they knocked him out." The *Armored News* quoted directly from the news release: "American tanks cannot beat Germans in open combat. The Panther and Tiger armor will repel our tank gun shells while their 75 and 88mm guns will shoot straight through our best armor." The answer, at least according to Sgt. Louis Weir, was a tank mounting a 90mm gun. One officer and at least thirty tankers nearby agreed with him; at the same time, they hoped the war would be over before America could build them. Weir also told Bell that given sufficient Shermans and dry footing, the American tanks could out-slug the enemy, because the Shermans were more maneuverable and faster than the enemy tanks.

After thirteen days, the American 2d Armored Division had advanced about nine or ten miles. Bradley wrote Montgomery that the First and Ninth Armies had not made the progress that had been anticipated because of the determined German resistance. They did improve their positions and inflict heavy casualties on the enemy. The 2d Armored had several clues as to why the Germans were waging such a savage defense, and the general conclusion was that the Germans were preparing for defense once the Americans were across the Roer, rather than getting ready to launch a massive counterattack to halt the American drive. The possibility of the Germans' launching a counterattack on the scale of the Battle of the Bulge did not occur to most Americans. In actuality, that was the purpose of the brutal battles west of the Roer River.

Chapter 16

THE BATTLES OF THE BULGE:
Blunting the German Spearhead

Traditionally the Battle of the Bulge is told in terms of the gallant American defenders at St. Vith: "Nuts," the one-word rejection of the surrender offer at Bastogne; and the Third Army's turn from their attack eastward to attack northward against the south flank of the German salient. All that is true; those units deserve the credit and glory earned. However, little is said about the actions on the northern flank, perhaps because it was under the supervision of British Field Marshall Bernard Montgomery. It was on that northern flank where the attack of the 2d Armored Division, temporarily in the American First Army, and VII Corps stopped the German advance three miles short of the Meuse River and blunted the German spearhead. Had the 2d Armored Division failed, the Germans would most probably have realized their goal of splitting the Allies and may have been able to achieve a stalemate on the western front.

During the last few days of November and until December 19, the 2d Armored manned defensive lines on the Roer River. Plans were prepared and sand table exercises were conducted for an attack across the Roer toward the Rhine. Patrols searched for crossing sites and brought back

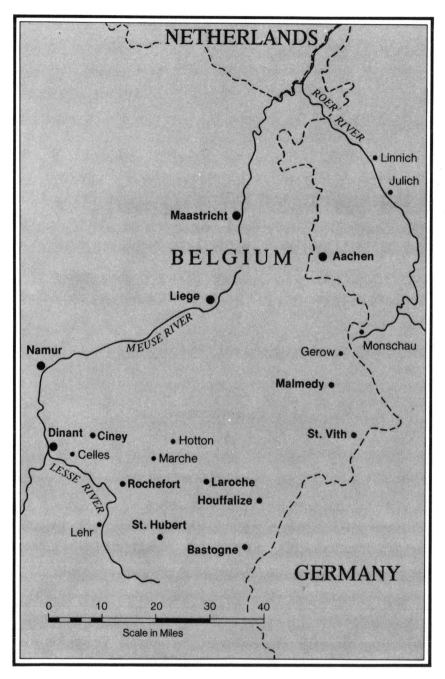

Figure 9. The Battle of the Bulge, 1944.

the information that the enemy was improving their defenses in the Julich and Broichmersh areas. They also discovered that the German 12th Panzer Division was in the Hambach Forest directly opposite the 2d Armored Division and ready to meet any attack, especially an armored assault, across the river.

In addition, the intelligence annex to Field Order 40, issued on December 2, stated that the Sixth Panzer Army, 1st SS, 2d SS, 9th SS and 12th SS Panzer Divisions, in addition to remnants of the 9th Panzer, 10th SS and 15th Panzer Grenadier Divisions, were available for counterattacking any thrust across the Roer. They reportedly had 350 to 450 tanks and assault guns; a dangerous threat if they were not committed piecemeal. The blunt statement that the "Germans [were] unable to launch large-scale counterattacks" proved to be incorrect.

The division spent the period resting and conducting needed maintenance after its grueling struggle to reach the Roer. It also began training, starting with the individual soldier and working up to the platoon and company. During this time it received replacements and worked to integrate them into the division and their units. The men test-drove the LVT (Landing Vehicle, Track). The 41st Armored Infantry Regiment test-fired their new assault guns, 105mm howitzers mounted on tracks. The 702d Tank Destroyer Battalion fired the new M-36 tank destroyer, mounting a 90mm gun (it had been used in the Roer offensive). The units also had demonstrations on the proper use of the British flamethrower tanks and the POZIT fuze. In addition, the 66th Armored Regiment reorganized. While still retaining three battalions, the first was a reconnaissance and security battalion, and the second and third had three medium companies and a light company each. The 67th Armored Regiment retained its three-alike battalion structure.

Part of the mission of the 702d Tank Destroyer Battalion was to fire night harrassing missions from positions covering the Julich-Cologne road. One day Colonel Beale came to Division Artillery headquarters confessing that he had forgotten to remove the drift factor from the firing data and thus the rounds must have been landing to the right of the road. Later, after questioning some prisoners, Beale was relieved to learn that the errant rounds had landed in a fuel and ammunition dump.

The division permitted some leaves and passes for the tankers. Col. Wheeler Merriam and Maj. Herbert Long took a three-day pass to the 2d Armored rest center at Hasselt, Belgium. After having dinner, the two officers returned to their room at the Three Pistols Hotel. In the early morning hours, Long was awakened by flashing lights on the ceiling. Trying to find the source of the lights, he discovered that the floor was covered by broken glass. Then looking out the window, he saw hundreds of people milling around the town square. A German buzz-bomb, probably aimed at Antwerp or London, had fallen short and hit Hasselt. Somewhat like Pavlov's dogs, the two combat officers, who had grown accustomed to the sounds of the battlefield, had been awakened not by the thousand-pound bomb but by the flashing lights of emergency vehicles.

Hitler planned the Battle of the Bulge, or the Ardennes offensive, in order to regain some of the initiative lost since the Allies had landed in Normandy and to drive a wedge between the British and the Americans. After splitting the two army groups (British 21st and American 12th) the Germans hoped to destroy the British forces. According to Hitler, this would force Canada out of the war and compel the United States to negotiate on terms favorable to the Germans. That was a possibility; but, all the same, if Germany lost the battle, then the war was over. The Fifth and Sixth Panzer Armies received all the equipment, the Germans having stripped other units to make these two armies battle-ready. They collected about twenty-seven divisions and supplies under the code name, "Watch on the Rhine," which succeeded in misleading the Allies into thinking that the Germans were preparing a defensive move. For some unknown reason, Hitler and the German general staff did not use the Enigma coding machines. Because of that precaution, Allied intelligence did not detect the significance of the build-up through ULTRA. These precautions also fooled one German supply officer, who stored the reserve gasoline on the *east* bank of the Rhine. This fuel did not reach the soldiers who needed it, and the mistake had crucial consequences.

The German plans were simple. The attacking force would strike through the Ardennes at a point known to be lightly defended and under adverse weather conditions, so that reconnaissance aircraft could not spot them and fighter bombers could not attack them. Expecting little opposition, German armored units planned to secure bridgeheads across the Meuse River and then attack to capture Brussels and Antwerp.

On the morning of December 16, the German attack broke through the American V Corps. Before the spearhead was blunted, a bulge some sixty miles deep and forty-five miles wide at the base was created. The Americans were caught completely off guard. While manning the front lines, Hell on Wheels notified corps headquarters that they could hear German units moving south. While the defenders fought gallantly, the enemy made steady progress toward the Meuse. The first reports received by Ninth Army and the 2d Armored Division indicated that it was a local attack with the Germans only trying to secure better defensive positions. The 2d Armored continued to study sand table terrain for their proposed attack across the Roer River. Lack of aerial reconnaissance prevented the Americans from discovering the real nature of the assault. At 11:00 P.M. on December 16, Harmon issued a letter of instructions which attached Combat Command A to XIII Corps and placed it on a three-hour alert beginning at daylight the next morning. The present pass and training policies of the division were not to be affected by the attachment, an indication that the seriousness of the German attack was not realized.

The division continued to receive news about increased German air activity, the capture of German paratroopers and the killing of civilians and prisoners-of-war by the Germans. The mounting reports forced the division to realize the gravity of the situation. The division instituted alerts and patrols against paratroopers and glider troops. For the first time in the division's history, officers and sergeants drew phase lines on their maps, but to the rear of the 2d Armored's positions. The seriousness of the threat sank home when A Company, 67th Armored, was sent to guard XIX Corps headquarters.

On December 19, the division began to make plans for any eventuality. Collier's Combat Command A was placed on a six-hour alert to meet any threat in any part of the XIX Corps zone; White's Combat Command B was assigned the task of defending the division's area. White created a task force of a light tank company and one infantry company, plus a troop of the 1st Fife and Forfar Yeomanry, to be used in the event of an airborne attack. That afternoon, XIX Corps notified Harmon that the 29th Infantry Division was to relieve the 2d Armored Division. However, the tankers would stay in their present area. At 4:54 P.M. McLain told the division, "You will not be moving." Later, at 7:35, an exchange between the corps and the division commanders altered the previous message:

Corps 6 (McLain): Could you move a big force if called on?
Powerhouse 6 (Harmon): Yes. In about six hours. I can roll the whole outfit when the change is made! Would it be south?
Corps 6: No, the other way.

The only direction that the division could move was west; east would be across the Roer River, south had been refused, north would mean moving against friendly troops.

The 702d Tank Destroyer Battalion in position to fire across the Roer River.

On December 20, the 29th Infantry Division relieved the 2d Armored Division in its defensive zone. The 2d Armored moved to positions immediately east of the Wurm River, where it became Ninth Army reserve. Later that night the division was relieved of its attachment to Ninth Army, assigned to First Army and ordered to plan for movement to assembly areas about a hundred miles west.

Eisenhower had no reserves; to meet the German threat, he had to shift forces. Patton was placed in command of the southern front, while the First and Ninth Armies were placed under Montgomery's command. The British field marshall wanted Gen. Joseph Lawton Collins to command VII Corps in a counterattack. However, Montgomery and the First Army commander, Lt. Gen. Courtney Hodges, thought that it would be after the German attack had lost momentum. Collins ordered VII Corps to assemble in the Marche-Hotton-Modave area, ready to counterattack. Collins's command was to be the two heavy armored divisions (the 2d and the 3d) and two infantry divisions (the 84th, which had some battle experience, and the 75th, which was new to the theater).

On December 21, the 2d Armored began to prepare for one of the most spectacular moves of the war. At 3:00 P.M. it was placed on a one-hour alert. Harmon was called to Simpson's headquarters and at 4:00 P.M. received orders to move the division. Harmon called his chief of staff, telling him to leave as soon as possible on two routes. Col. Clayton J. Mansfield replied that he would get the reconnaissance started at 5:00 A.M. the next morning. Harmon abruptly told him to get started right away. At that point, General White interrupted to say that the command did not have any maps and they would need some time to find the way. Harmon relented but added that the division could not delay beyond midnight. At 8:00 P.M., Harmon again called Mansfield, asking if they had the maps. Mansfield replied that they did and that the division would be moving ''at 2300.'' Harmon approved, saying that he was returning to the division.

Arriving at the division command post about 10:00 P.M. Harmon briefed the senior commanders. The division was ordered to move from Baesweiler, Germany, to new positions near Modave, Belgium, starting at 11:00 P.M. on December 21. The move would be conducted under blackout conditions and with radio silence, which would be lifted on order of the division commander or on enemy contact. The rate of march at night was to be six miles per hour, with sight distance between the vehicles. During the day, they travelled at twelve miles per hour and the interval increased to seventy-five yards between vehicles. The route was to be posted by road guides from the military police platoon of division headquarters and by the 82d Reconnaissance Battalion, which were to drop off sentries at every crossroads.

The movement of the 2d Armored Division, especially in a congested combat zone, created enormous traffic problems. At regulation fifty-yard intervals, the division's more than 3,000 vehicles would have formed a convoy over 100 miles long. Using two routes, the 2d Armored began one of the most spectacular road marches of the war. Once again, it was racing an enemy that had a head start; if the enemy won the race for the Meuse River bridges, the Allied position would be perilous.

The weather created the worst possible conditions; roads were crusted with ice, snow and mud; visibility was hampered by fog. At 10:15 P.M. Companies A and C of the 82d Reconnaissance Battalion departed to mark the routes to the new assembly area, whose exact locations were not known to the division. Three hours after the order to move, leading elements were on the road; and after a twenty-two hour blackout march of 100 miles, they began arriving near Huy, Belgium. Thirty vehicles—six medium tanks, two light tanks, three armored cars, nine 2½-ton trucks, seven jeeps and three motorcycles—had breakdowns or collisions but were restored to duty. One indication of the morale of the division occurred as part of the 2d Armored passed a column of the 3rd Armored; someone yelled at the 3d Armored personnel, "Come to attention, you Joes, the 2d Armored is passing by." It may have been a bit crude but reflected the Hell-on-Wheelers' attitude.

While the 2d Armored was moving to its new area, the Germans had varying degrees of success. Leaving a force to reduce Bastogne, their armored elements slipped around that town and headed for the Meuse River and Liege. The Germans were attacking the 3d Armored Division but pulled back, broke contact and turned west, where they encountered the 84th Infantry Division. They pulled the same maneuver again by breaking contact and turning west. By midnight of December 22, about the same time that the last elements of the 2d Armored reached their assembly areas, the German 2d Panzer and 116th Panzer Divisions had their leading elements at Grandmenil, Marche, Humain, Buissonville, Leignon and Ciney. German patrols reached Celles only three miles from the Meuse. They thought that they had won the race for the bridges.

The 2d Armored Division's march was a glowing tribute to the grueling hours spent in peacetime maneuvers, to lessons learned on the

European battlefields and especially to the men of the division. Harmon, after arriving at the division command post at Havelange, forbade any civilian traffic on the roads. He promised the Belgians that the Germans would fail in their mission. Harmon had never lost an armored battle and had won the grudging respect of the German army. They dreaded him more than any other armor commander. At the same time, Harmon inspired the respect and admiration of his men. Lieutenant Culver remembers how in Baesweiler he saw the general's jeep coming down the street and immediately saluted Harmon. The enlisted men looking out a nearby window shouted and waved at their commander, who returned the greeting with the same genuine affection.

Immediately patrols were sent to locate the enemy and guard the bridges over the Meuse. Harmon sent reconnaissance parties to the southeast, south and southwest to locate the enemy and primarily to establish contact with friendly forces. Because of the bad weather, no one really knew where the Germans were. Otherwise, air observation certainly would have revealed that on December 23 the leading elements of the 2d Panzer Division were only a few miles from the Hell on Wheels command post.

At 11:30 A.M., near Haid, a patrol led by 1st Lt. Everett C. Jones was moving toward Rochefort, when it was fired upon by several German tanks laden with infantry. The unequal fight, occurring on the facing slopes of a hill while a train passed between the combatants, resulted in Jones being wounded and his armored car destroyed. Since Harmon had notified all the major commands at 11:00 that "under no circumstances will radio silence be broken, no one will be captured," Jones and his crew started back to division headquarters to report their activities. On the way they were picked up by a friendly patrol and hurried to tell the division commander what had occurred.

Lt. Col. Wheeler Merriam took Jones to the chief of staff who, after listening to the report, said that he would tell Harmon. Merriam, not satisfied, took the patrol leader to tell Harmon his story himself. Harmon listened and then checked the map. Haid was ten miles south of the command post, twelve miles from Dinant and twenty miles from Namur. The Germans had turned north for a third time and were heading for the Meuse. Any further movement north would threaten the rear of the 84th Infantry Division and put the Germans between the Meuse and the 2d Armored Division.

The period December 16–23 was a time of confusion for senior

American commanders, resulting in a series of orders and changes to those orders. This confusion was primarily caused by the Americans' lack of solid information. Harmon now had a problem. Collins wanted to keep the Belgian location of the 2d Armored Division secret until he could commit it to battle later in January, giving the Germans a real shock. Up to this time, the enemy had not known that the 2d Armored had moved from positions north of Aachen. However, now that the Germans were only ten miles away, there was scarcely time to get approval from the VII Corps commander for committing the division to battle. The division's location would no longer be a secret once the Germans read the unit designations on the destroyed vehicle. They had to be stopped from moving north; the gap between the 2d Armored and the Meuse had to be closed.

Gen. John H. Collier had gone to division headquarters to ask how much time the units would get for maintenance. While there, Harmon asked him if he would like to stay for lunch and a drink. Collier gladly accepted the invitation. After hearing the report, Harmon raced out of the division command post to a nearby tank company, asking how long would it take to get the company on the road. The company commander, Capt. Charles B. Kelley, D Company, 66th Armor, said that if radio silence were lifted, it would take about five minutes. Harmon told him that the ban was lifted then and there. Thus what was to have been twenty-four hours of maintenance proved to be about an hour and a half. Captain Kelley was to get to Ciney and block the roads immediately. The company started moving with throttles wide open. They reached Ciney and found no enemy present. Immediately Captain Kelley established a perimeter defense and then reported to his battalion commander that they were in position.

Lieutenant Culver had placed his tank near a house, waiting like the rest of the company. A woman appeared from the house with a large bowl of soup. While Culver debated whether to accept or refuse, Kelley came by and told him to go to Maj. Herbert Long's jeep for further orders.

Harmon found Lt. Col. Hugh O'Farrell and told him to get his battalion to Ciney and hold the town until the division arrived. With those verbal orders, the 2d Armored Division leaped into the Battle of the Bulge. After making his decision, Harmon called the corps commander and told him that the division was committed to battle. Combat Command A was ordered to secure Ciney, four miles north of Haid, in the gap between the 84th Infantry Division and the Meuse. With the commitment of Collier and Combat Command A, Harmon threw the 2d Armored squarely across the route of the attacking German tanks. As so often in the past—at Port Lyautey, Safi, Gela, Palermo, Carentan, St. Lo, Barenton, Mortain, Elbeuf, Tournai, the Siegfried line—success or failure of the Allies in stemming the German tide rested squarely on the turrets of the 2d Armored Division.

The advance to Ciney was a miracle; the town was ten miles from the division command post and only four miles from the spot where the patrol had received fire. Apparently the Germans were creeping along, cautious of what lay ahead. Task Force A, Combat Command A, began its movement southward at 2:20 P.M. Composed of the 2d Battalion, 66th Armor, 2d Battalion, 41st Armored Infantry, and a platoon each from A Company, 17th Engineers, and A Company, 702d Tank Destroyer Battalion, the column arrived in the town at 3:15 P.M., without opposition. After securing Ciney, Collier was ordered to hold the bulk of his forces there and send reconnaissance elements toward Namur and Dinant. Later Harmon ordered him to head toward Buissonville where the tankers would pose a dual threat to the Germans. If the Germans continued northwestward, they would meet the 2d Armored Division head on; if they continued west, then Collier would be on their flank, still a serious threat.

Task Force B, Combat Command A, composed of the 3d Battalion, 66th Armored Regiment, and E Company, 41st Armored Infantry Regiment, arrived at Ciney about 7:00 P.M. Fifteen minutes earlier, Collier had received orders to attack and secure Buissonville and ordered Task Force B to secure Ciney, while Task Force A moved to the new objective. Maj. Herbert Long led the task force toward Buissonville, passing through Lengonne. As he rounded a sharp curve, Long drew antitank gun fire which "almost parted his hair." The lead tank fired, dispersed the gun crew and crushed the gun. Collier learned from civilian reports that the Germans had about 600 troops and a few tanks in Buissonville. He was advised that the move south should be a strong one. He divided his task force into two columns, one on the main road, the other on a secondary road about 1,000 yards to the east. After progressing about three miles, the advance guards of both columns were fired on by two self-propelled antitank guns and automatic weapons manned by the reconnaissance battalion of the 2d Panzer Division. Immediately, support units were called forward, and after destroying two half-tracks and one self-propelled antitank gun the Americans resumed their advance.

Lieutenant Culver said that he was beginning to feel scared. He could feel many eyes watching him in the dark night. As they approached one small town, the lead tank fired at an antitank gun which was illuminated by the light from the open doors of two nearby houses. The gun, and the crews which were leaving the houses to man it, were flattened. The medium tank leading the advance called for the others to join him in the town. The second Sherman tank started forward, down a steep grade and around an S-shaped curve. Suddenly an exploding shell illuminated the area. Kelley called, asking Culver if the tank in front of his was hit. He could see the tank commander standing in the turret and could feel the heat of the fire. But the tank had somehow escaped any damage. Then he saw a German half-track come barrelling down a side alley, crashing into a nearby house. The tanker, fearing that the destroyed enemy vehicle would trap him, backed out over the half-track, crushing it. The tankers pulled back to occupy a position in an open field and called for infantry to clear the town. A platoon from the 41st Armored Infantry appeared, marching silently down the road with only a occasional clink of their equipment. Within a few minutes, they secured the village and the tankers moved into it for the evening.

While Major Long's column was advancing over a secondary road toward Buissonville, Task Force A was moving down the main road to the same Belgian town. The night was bright, a thin blanket of snow covered the ground, and the temperature was below freezing. The infantry of F Company, 41st Armored Infantry, commanded by Capt. George E. Bonney, led the march, followed by their half-tracks, two other infantry companies and a tank company. Bonney was patrolling the column. At its head he heard the sound of approaching armored vehicles. Bonney quickly deployed his men off the sides of the road and waited. Elements of the 2d Panzer Division were unwittingly advancing north on the same road by which the Americans were moving south. The results, one of the most successful ambushes of World War II, caught the Germans by total surprise. The burning German vehicles lit the area for the infantry, tankers and tank destroyers. About twelve vehicles were destroyed and thirty to forty Germans were killed, while a similar number were captured. The Americans suffered few casualties, though Captain Bonney's leg was almost severed by American tank fire. Following the ambush, Collier ordered the task force to coil for the night and resume the attack the following morning. The leading elements were now only about eight miles from Rochefort.

While Combat Command A was attacking, information was being received at the division command post which helped clarify a confusing enemy picture. At 2:30 P.M. the police at Haversin notified the police at Havelange that five tanks had passed through the town at 11:00 and that paratroopers had landed there at noon. This information gave Lieutenant Colonel Merriam the idea of conducting a reconnaissance by telephone. He called the neighboring towns, to determine if and when the Germans had been there and to request that he be informed if the enemy appeared. The request was productive; enemy locations were easy to follow once the Belgian telephone operators and police began to cooperate.

Since the 2d Panzer Division had flank guards and blocking parties to protect its flanks and communications, the attack of Combat Command A was not unopposed. Collier's attack was oblique to the axis of the German advance, intended to intercept the Germans at Buissonville. At 6:30 A.M. on Christmas Eve, the advance continued, with Task Force A on the main road to Rochefort and Task Force B attacking cross-country in two columns. Task Force A had some difficulty in moving. As the column crossed the Haversin-Forzee road, antitank guns fired on the lead units. They had to maneuver around the roadblock, which consisted of an enemy half-track and a Panther tank. Culver, fresh from Officer Candidate School, was thinking that the terrain would lend itself to an ambush. As the lead tank topped the hill, it fired and hastily pulled back when confronted by a German tank with a "long barrel." An American tank destroyer tried to get a clear shot but could not, because the road formed a T. The German tank was firing with telling accuracy which prevented the tank destroyer's getting an accurate shot. Finally the tank destroyer crawled up the face of a defile, coming broadside to the German Panther and destroying it with three well-placed shots through the turret. With the roadblock reduced, the task force continued the advance at 1:00 P.M. North of Buissonville, it flushed several tanks out of position and destroyed them. Going into position to assault Buissonville, the task force spotted a German column moving north from Havrenne, but the town was taken without opposition.

Task Force B joined the advance on Buissonville, passing through Haid at 9:30 A.M., encountering only sporadic artillery fire. Near Forzee, three German tanks fired on the Americans, who responded by destroying one of the enemy vehicles. The west column of Task Force B encountered a skillfully concealed, dug-in antitank gun near St. Philippe. As the tankers maneuvered around it, the German gunners fled. The Americans destroyed the gun, which could have done considerable damage had the enemy decided to stay and fight. After arriving at the hill mass overlooking Buissonville, Task Force B protected Task Force A's entry into the town.

From its hillside position, Task Force B saw a German force approaching from the south. The men could see for ten miles, and their vantage point permitted them to look right down the Germans' throats. The 14th Armored Artillery Battalion fired its allotted ammunition at ranges of 4,000 to 10,000 yards. When the Germans started retreating, the artillerymen followed them with accurate fire, destroying thirty-eight wheeled vehicles, four antitank guns and six pieces of artillery. An unknown number of Germans were killed and 108 surrendered. After the battle Task Force B was given the mission of defending the town, which it did by posting roadblocks about 800 yards to the south and covering them with tanks and mines.

Collier planned to continue the attack southward and to aid the 4th Cavalry Group which had been attached to the 2d Armored Division at noon the previous day. Commanded by Col. John C. MacDonald, the group was composed of the 4th and 24th Cavalry Squadrons, the 759th Light Tank Battalion, the 635th Antitank Battalion (equipped with towed weapons) and the 297th Engineer Battalion. Harmon had ordered MacDonald to fill the gap between the 84th Infantry Division and the left flank of the 2d Armored Division. Troop A of the 24th Cavalry Squadron was given that mission and by midnight had entered Humain without meeting opposition.

While Combat Command A and the 4th Cavalry Group were attacking, Combat Command B was ordered to secure Ciney against counterattacks and to prepare for a possible offensive. While that movement was being carried out, the division received reports of a large enemy concentration of men and tanks at Celles, only a few miles to the southwest. The French and Belgian underground reported that the Germans at Celles had little or no fuel. This German force was identified as the 2d Panzer Division, the precise counterpart of the 2d Armored Division. In the two previous meetings of these units, the 2d Panzer had pulled back, and it was thought that it might do so again. Both divisions were attacking, both were a little removed from their supporting troops, both were apparently in fine battle condition, and both wanted to destroy the other and continue the attack. Harmon, never one to avoid a battle, began to make plans for attacking the German force at Celles on Christmas Day. However, he could not commit either Combat Command B or Division Reserve without the approval of the corps, army or army group commander. Attempting to get that approval caused one of the war's most bizarre episodes and one of the war's greatest decisions.

On Christmas Eve, Field Marshal Montgomery and General Hodges met at First Army headquarters. During the talks Montgomery decided that the 21st Army Group had to hold the Andenne-Hotton line. The British field marshal wanted to tidy up the battlefield by shortening, strengthening and stabilizing his line, and to secure his flanks before attacking. Montgomery also authorized the corps commander to fall back to that line if necessary.

Harmon began to make his plans for the Christmas attack. He called VII Corps to ask for permission. The call was taken by Brig. Gen. Williston B. Palmer, commanding general, VII Corps Artillery, who was aware of the decisions made by Hodges and Montgomery. He told Harmon to wait, that General Collins was en route to Harmon's command post. A few minutes later Harmon called again, requesting permission to attack. Palmer told him to make the necessary plans but to wait for Collins's arrival. Harmon was furious: he had an opportunity to defeat the enemy, but he did not have authority to attack.

Palmer called First Army and talked with Maj. Gen. William B. Kean, First Army chief of staff. During their conversation, Kean asked Palmer if he could see a town beginning with A and a second one beginning with H on his map. Palmer located Aachen and Le Houissee, both of which were *in front* of the 2d Armored positions and along the attack route that Harmon wanted. To further excite Palmer, Kean told him that Collins now had unrestricted use of all troops in VII Corps. Palmer immediately sent his aide to the 2d Armored command post to inform Collins of the new situation.

Kean called Palmer back, perhaps worried about a possible misunderstanding and uneasy about the tone of voice of the artillery commander. Kean told Palmer to listen closely, to roll with the punch; he asked him a second time if he could spot the two towns A and H. He did: Andenne and Huy, thirty miles to the *rear* of the 2d Armored positions. Palmer immediately sent a second message to the 2d Armored Division command post, telling the corps commander of the error. Collins told Harmon to plan and execute the attack, unless specifically ordered not to do so.

With those instructions, Collins returned to his headquarters, where he found Colonel R.F. Akers, assistant First Army G-3. Akers delivered oral instructions that differed from the telephone conversations that Palmer had had with Kean. Remembering his history—the Major

Hentsch episode from World War I—Collins ordered Akers to type out his instructions. Hotton was the H of the A-H line; Collins was authorized to fall back, but he was not ordered to do so. The corps commander had more control of his troops than had been indicated. Collins and his staff discussed the Akers report, realizing that to pull back would open the Meuse River and the roads to the Germans. After the discussion, Collins called Harmon and ordered the attack. Harmon approved, saying that "the bastards are in the bag." With that order Collins exercised *his* best judgement, which was perhaps in opposition to the wishes of his army and army group commanders. However, his actions demonstrated that the officer closest to the scene should make the decisions. If the 2d Armored Division were successful, Collins would be the hero of the Battle of the Bulge. If Hell on Wheels failed, Collins would be responsible for a disaster.

On the evening of December 24, Harmon issued his attack orders. Combat Command A was to help the 4th Cavalry Group seize and hold Humain and the road junction south of the town. Combat Command B was to seize and hold Celles. Combat command reserve was to be ready to attack south of Marche, aid the 4th Cavalry Group's effort to take Humain or be prepared to protect the division's right flank. The 4th Cavalry Group was ordered to capture Humain, maintain their present roadblocks and patrol the ten- to fifteen-mile gap between Combat Commands B and A.

As the Americans were planning to attack on Christmas Day, the Germans were also active. Gen. Fritz Bayerlein received information that the 2d Panzer Division was stalled at Celles, facing possible destruction. He ordered the Panzer Lehr Division to attack north from Rochefort to take Humain and Buissonville, loosening the American grip at Celles. The Germans managed to capture and hold Humain but failed to ease the pressure on the 2d Panzer Division.

Before moving from Germany, White had organized Combat Command B into two task forces. After moving to Ciney, it still retained that structure. The plan of attack was simple. Celles sits in a valley with long ridges on each side. White decided to send one task force down each ridgeline. After reaching a position south of the town, they would come together, trapping the Germans in a pocket. Greatly aiding this plan was the fact that the Germans were almost out of fuel.

Task Force A (3d Battalion, 67th Armored Regiment) on the right of the combat command zone, began the assault at 9:30 A.M. It moved south without meeting much resistance. While trying to skirt the Bois de

Geauvelant, the lead tank company was fired on by three Panther tanks from Ferme de Mahenne. This fire stopped any further movement south as the task force pulled back and called for air support. Finally, twelve P-38s strafed and bombed the German positions, destroying the tanks. Then the attack continued, with the task force capturing the village of Soinne and the high ground southeast of Celles. The men were now in position to attack.

Task Force B (1st Battalion, 67th Armored Regiment) converged down the eastern ridge, starting the assault with its sister task force. North of the village of Conneux, the force met stiff resistance from artillery, antitank and small arms fire. An added problem for the Americans was getting their tanks through the thick woods. The solution was to block the Germans in the woods and to go around with the major portion of the command. Once around the German positions, the command made rapid progress and after a brief battle at Conjoux, both task forces captured Celles without opposition. During the attack, the Germans had attempted to relieve their comrades who were eventually trapped in the Celles pocket. Division artillery, which fired 2,080 rounds, broke up the German efforts, knocking out seven Mark IV tanks, two antitank guns and forty-eight other vehicles. The casualties were unknown but thought to be considerable.

North of Celles in the thick woods events were not progressing satisfactorily. Company B, 41st Armored Infantry Regiment, was attempting to clear the woods but needed armored support. But the tanks could not penetrate the terrain: thick woods, underbrush, draws and gullies. As 1st Lt. Victor S. Corpron's tanks tried to work their way along a draw, two were promptly destroyed. While the other section of tanks kept the enemy heads down, Corpron went forward to determine the extent of casualties. Some distance from the first burning M-4, he found two wounded tankers, both of whom had been hit by solid shot after they had dismounted. He gave one man morphine, but he died shortly afterwards. The other had had his right leg and left foot shot away. As Corpron was applying tourniquets, ammunition in the second tank exploded; the turret blew off and fell not more than thirty feet from the men. Medical personnel trying to reach the scene were repeatedly driven off by intense enemy machine gun fire. Desperate, Corpron went into the nearby woods armed only with his pistol, found a stretcher, captured a prisoner and forced the enemy to help carry the unconscious man to the aid station. He returned to his tank, waited for darkness and then pulled back. He called for artillery fire but was told that none was available because friendly troops were supposed to be in that sector. Corpron was awarded the Silver Star for his bravery.

After Celles had been secured, a platoon of light tanks was supposed to secure the western approaches, while the main attack proceeded southward. 2d Lt. Cecil L. Sterling's tank and one to his left were hit and burned. As the lieutenant dismounted, he was severely wounded by machine gun fire. The medical officer, Capt. Albert I. Rosenblatt, and his three aid men, Technicians 5th Grade Dominic Rago and Paul F. Goodwin and Pvt. Everett Jones, worked under that heavy fire, giving aid to four wounded men. Four other tankers had died immediately when the tanks had been hit. The doctor knew that the wounded needed to be evacuated, but the half-track ambulance could not carry all the men. Lieutenant Sterling refused evacuation until his men had been removed from the danger area. The ambulance had to make two trips through a hail of enemy fire. On its last trip, an antitank round slammed into the rear rack, but the medical personnel never faltered in their mission of mercy.

The 82d Reconnaissance Battalion had been ordered to protect the right flank of Combat Command B and if possible to contact the British on the Meuse River. Passing through Foy-Notre Dame, Company A, later joined by Company B, had an opportunity rare in warfare: they attacked and defeated their counterpart in the German army. Capt. James Hartford had been watching the village most of the morning. He could see vehicles approach, but could not tell where they were heading. Later he found that a sunken road was the reason. He told one of his platoon leaders to send one section into the town to determine what the Germans were doing. The platoon leader told Hartford that he would instead send the entire platoon but he immediately called for the entire company to join him. After knocking out an antitank gun, the key to the defense, Company B, 82d Reconnaissance Battalion, joined A Company in the battle for the town.

In the firefight, they captured almost 150 members of the reconnaissance battalion of the 2d Panzer Division, including the battalion commander. They destroyed or captured nineteen vehicles and one self-propelled gun. With this battle, the combat career of the German reconnaissance battalion was ended. While the 82d Reconnaissance Battalion contacted the British 29th Armored Brigade, their first meeting was not friendly. When a British tank advanced to meet the Americans, it was destroyed by the Americans. Col. Wheeler Merriam was talking with the British commander as the tank was destroyed. Merriam remembers that the English officer turned to him and said, "Well, your boys just browned off one of my boys."

Christmas Day became the nadir of the German attack. When White's two task forces joined at Celles, the enemy was "in the bag." The attack to the Meuse had been stopped, a fine Christmas present for the 2d Armored Division. Combat Command B now had to reduce the pocket, while preventing the arrival of enemy reinforcements and preventing a breakout by the trapped forces.

Capt. Francis A. Pfaff, commanding officer, A Company, 67th Armored Regiment, had established roadblocks, using his company and two medium tanks of I Company. During the night, artillery and mortars fired into the woods, keeping the enemy awake and hopefully forestalling any attempt at a breakout. However, about 2:30 P.M. on December 26, Staff Sergeant Robert L. Blakney reported that a strong enemy patrol was nearing the western flank outpost. Captain Pfaff went to the scene; the patrol was a two-company-strength infantry attack. Eight light tanks and two medium tanks immediately fired all their weapons. Pfaff dismounted from his tank, joining the melee by firing his pistol. He later admitted that it was virtually indirect fire.

Despite the bombardment, the enemy continued to advance; Pfaff ordered his men to fire canister. After several rounds, the enemy began to scream "Kamerad." More than 200 men surrendered; others tried to reach the woods. Again the tankers fired and about twenty Germans failed in their efforts. One prisoner was a Polish national, who after recovering his wits tried to talk to the Americans. Technician 4th Grade John J. Jankasz found that the prisoner wanted to return to the woods to talk some of his friends into surrendering. Pfaff gave the Pole thirty minutes and if he did not return, then he was still trapped. If he did return, perhaps taking the woods would not be as difficult. Pfaff told the prisoner that after thirty minutes he would shell the area with artillery and tank gun fire. The minutes dragged slowly; thirty minutes passed, then forty. As Pfaff was about to give the fire command, the Pole emerged from the woods, followed by eighty-eight comrades. Unfortunately, the most difficult task was still ahead for the tankers; they had to eliminate the pocket of Germans that had been surrounded the day before.

Clearing the woods and underbrush was an infantry assignment. Following a brief five-minute artillery preparation, the infantry quickly moved forward, supported by light tanks firing canister. Each dug-in position had to be individually reduced; stalled German vehicles became strongpoints. By evening the forest had been cleared, except for a small part of the Bois Coreux near Hubaille. The enemy lost a considerable amount of equipment: twenty-two tanks were captured or destroyed, along with four artillery pieces and forty-one other vehicles.

While clearing the woods, Combat Command B repelled two counterattacks from the south which were attempts to relieve the trapped German forces. The first, at 12:15 P.M., was a tank-infantry team and was stopped by the 1st Battalion, 67th Armored Regiment. The Germans pulled back, regrouped and reattacked. The Americans knew that the enemy tanks were heavier and that their antitank rounds would have little effect on the German vehicles. White went to the British 29th Armored Brigade and arranged for a flight of rocket-firing Typhoons to come to the aid of his combat command. Since no American radio had the same frequency as the British airplanes, White decided to lead the British aircraft with an American spotter Cub plane. The Typhoons destroyed seven of the enemy tanks, while the others fled. With that, the hopes of the trapped Germans faded.

At approximately 4:50 P.M., the remainder of the 2d Panzer Division attempted to break out of the trap but were repulsed. An additional fifty Germans found their way into the prisoner-of-war cages. Task Force B was divided into two sub-task forces and given two different missions. Task Force BA was to continue combing the woods, while Task Force BB was to seize and secure road junctions south and east of Verre, which guarded the routes from Hotton, Marche and Rochefort. The attack to clear the remaining enemy out of the woods began at 10:00 A.M. but the Germans strongly resisted. The woods and underbrush hampered the infantrymen, who realized they would make little progress without armor. The tanks moving only through draws, creeks and fills knocked out several antiaircraft guns. Then unexpectedly, the infantrymen, supported by the tanks, came upon a villa where they found almost 100 destroyed or abandoned vehicles. About 11:30 A.M. the remnants of the 2d Panzer had been cleared from the forest, and the sub-task force received another mission.

About noon, Task Force BB, approaching the crossroads near Verre, drew fire from enemy artillery but did not slow the march. Someone reported that a Panther tank was blocking the road, but the men did not find it; and by 4:30 P.M. Verre was secured without serious opposition. That night several weary American infantrymen found shelter from the weather in a house. The next morning, the startled visitors found seven

German soldiers who had also spent the night there and wanted to surrender.

Task Force A had been ordered to attack toward Rochefort and Houye to seize the high ground. They made excellent progress against surprisingly light opposition. For some, the brutal campaign took a sudden, brief and refreshing turn when the tankers seized the Chateau d'Ardennes, a playground for European nobility since 1867. Lt. Col. Harry Hillyard established his battalion command post in the hotel, which had electric lights, steam heat, a large dining hall, bathrooms, hot water and priceless paintings. The following day, General White arrived on an inspection tour and stayed for dinner, served by waiters in tuxedos in the elegant crystal dining room.

By evening on December 27, Combat Command B occupied positions along the Lesse River from Houye to east of Rochefort. That same evening, the 82d Reconnaissance Battalion relieved Combat Command B of responsibility for the area, with the tankers pulling back for maintenance and rest. About 4:00 P.M. the division received information that the 2d Panzer Division had been ordered to retreat to the southeast, destroying all equipment that could not be taken with them. During the day, the combat command discovered that the vehicles it had captured were without fuel.

On Christmas Day, while White and Combat Command B were surrounding the 2d Panzer Division in the Celles pocket, Combat Command A was ordered to capture Rochefort and Humain. Task Force A attacked in two columns but heavy fire from the Bois de St. Remy prevented further movement south. They consolidated their positions for the night. Lieutenant Culver was ordered to a spot where five roads came together. Though map reading was not one of his greatest talents, he was determined to establish the roadblock at the designated point. He figured the distance and told his driver to watch the odometer and to tell him when they had covered the prescribed mileage. He missed the actual distance by about twenty feet. Establishing the roadblock, they maintained it for the night. The enemy launched three counterattacks against the American positions but were repulsed each time.

Task Force B was attacked before it could start southward. A German, dressed in an American officer's uniform, approached the roadblock south of Buissonville and ordered the guards back to their bivouac area to prepare to move to a new area. Between 4:00 and 8:00 A.M., four German Mark V tanks coasted down the hill and took up firing positions about 800 yards from the American lines. The German attack began about 8:00. An American artillery forward observer, attempting to direct artillery fire, sent the wrong coordinates to the fire direction center and valuable time was lost correcting that error. Eventually, the tanks, half-tracks and tank destroyers began to fire, breaking up the German attack and inflicting heavy losses. The Reconnaissance Company of the 66th Armored trapped a German column near Verre, destroyed all fourteen vehicles and captured five American vehicles that the enemy had been using. The attack resumed and Task Force B captured Havrenne before dark. While scouting south of town, Capt. Henry H. Chatfield found five enemy tanks and two fuel trucks blocking a secondary road leading to the town. All available American weapons fired, destroying the enemy vehicles.

The major battle area in Combat Command A's zone was the town of Humain; later Brig. Gen. Sidney R. Hinds would say that the town was misnamed. Col. John C. MacDonald had been given the mission of protecting the left flank of Combat Command A, patrolling between Combat Commands A and B and capturing Humain. A reinforced troop of the 24th Cavalry Squadron attacked down the road from Jamodine and took the town about 2:30 A.M. The cavalrymen outposted the town and prepared to defend it. About 7:00 A.M. the Germans launched a strong attack which forced the Americans to pull back. They regrouped and launched an unsuccessful counterattack. At noon, a platoon of medium tanks was attached to the 4th Cavalry Group and the attack resumed in an hour; again the attackers could not dislodge the Germans. At 4:00 P.M. a third unsuccessful attack was attempted, this time from two directions. Afterward, General Collier visited MacDonald's command post and the tank platoon headquarters. He was told that the tank platoon leader did not want to attack down a road. Collier went to the scene, finding that he would be attacking into the face of several 88mm guns. He personally called the attack off and directed that it be readied for the next day. The Americans pulled back and encircled the town. While the Americans could not enter, the Germans could not get in or out.

The Christmas Day attacks had been successful for the 2d Armored Division. White had Celles surrounded, while Collier was defending against possible reinforcements. During the night, prisoners revealed that the Germans would have to use captured fuel or their attack would stall. Assessing the tactical situation, Harmon concluded that White's Combat Command B had matters well in hand but that Collier and Combat Command A had a serious problem. The difficulty was that Combat Command

A was being attacked by elements of two Panzer divisions, the 9th and 130th, which were supposed to aid the 2d Panzer's attack.

Harmon ordered Collier to assume a defensive posture, rather than trying to capture Humain, and to resume offensive operations on December 27. About 7:00 A.M., cavalry outposts alerted the 2d Armored that the Germans were preparing to attack along the Havrenne-Buissonville road. Harmon told Col. Carl Hutton, Division Artillery commander, to fire a time-on-target at Humain with all the 155mm and 8-inch howitzers within range. The artillery fire did not totally break up the attack, but it probably prevented German reinforcements from reaching Humain. At 7:50, the Germans launched the first of the day's three counterattacks against Combat Command A's lines. The first, against Havrenne, was composed of fifteen tanks and nearly a battalion of infantry. It was a bitter contest, with the Germans struggling to within 100 yards of the American positions before pulling back. In the battle the Americans suffered two damaged medium tanks but destroyed eight Mark Vs, four half-tracks and one self-propelled gun. One of these half-tracks contained a map which indicated that the Germans were to attack with two columns. That information permitted troops to shift to meet the second thrust, which occurred at 8:30. The Americans held their fire until the enemy was within point-blank range, then opened a withering fire that broke up the German formations and drove them off. The third counterattack was against Frandeux and, like the first two, it was repulsed with heavy losses to the Germans. After beating off these three attacks, the combat command continued to mop up their areas and planned to resume their own attack on the following day.

Humain was a thorn in the side of the 2d Armored Division and an entry point into the division's left flank. The cavalrymen reported that the enemy was attempting to reinforce the town and requested a time-on-target, which Hutton fired. For the rest of the day, the cavalrymen cleared the enemy whose formations had been broken by the artillery fire. While this was in progress, Col. Sidney Hinds's Combat Command Reserve was attached to Combat Command A and given the mission to capture Humain. His plan was a simple one: to encircle the town with tanks on the east, south and west, and attack with infantry from the north. To aid the attackers, Division Artillery shelled the town all night and fired a heavy one-hour preparation at 7:00 A.M. The artillery fire destroyed many houses and created much rubble, which aided the defenders. It required several hours for the tanks to get into position, but by 1:30 P.M. the infantry was in the town and had begun clearing the area. The infantrymen made slow but steady progress until they reached the crossroads near the center of town, where they were stopped by a heavy volume of mortar fire. By dusk on December 27, the road from Humain southward was in American hands, but about half of the town was still under German control.

During the night, the clearing operations continued with the Americans having to take each house. The Germans decided to make their last strong stand at a thick-walled chateau in an exposed area. To assault the position would cause heavy casualties. Hinds brought up the flame-throwing tanks from the Fife and Forfar Yeomanry, which moved into the open and aimed their blazing stream at a tree in full view of the enemy. The limbs burst into flames and the demonstration had the desired result, for in a few minutes the defenders, who had previously refused to surrender, marched out and the fighting stopped.

Meanwhile, the bulk of Combat Command A launched a three-pronged attack to seize possible crossings over the L'Homme and Lesse Rivers. Two columns west of Humain, meeting scattered but determined resistance, were on their objective by 6:00 P.M. The left column encountered heavy nebelwerfer fire from Rochefort and the chateau on the north edge of the town. That resistance was overcome and by dark the three columns had sealed the rivers to prevent any further enemy action north of them. Hinds was ordered to send some of his tanks south to help capture Rochefort. This attack started at 3:00 P.M. and met stiff resistance from the enemy, who were dug-in and obviously determined to fight. The defenders had another advantage as only a single road, passing through thick forests to the north, led into the town. Enemy infantry had already destroyed the lead vehicle and threatened to make that single lane a death trap. Hinds saw the danger and told Lt. Col. Lemuel Pope to gather his tanks and attack through the woods with every gun firing. Pope complied and the attack reached the high ground east of town.

On December 28, the division (with the exception of those units manning roadblocks, the 82d Reconnaissance Battalion and Division Artillery) was relieved by the 83d Infantry Division, the British 53d Division and the 4th Cavalry Group. The division reassembled at the same bivouac areas it had left just a week earlier. During the short stay, the men conducted maintenance, rested, opened Christmas packages and enjoyed a delayed Christmas dinner. By December 30, all elements of the division had been reassembled and began to make plans for the next phase of the Battle of the Bulge.

The VII Corps weekly intelligence summary said that the fight between the 2d Panzer Division and the 2d Armored Division was a fitting comparison of Allied and German armored might. Both were representative of their respective armored divisions. The 2d Armored had suffered 17 killed, 201 wounded and 26 missing. It had 7 light tanks and 28 medium tanks put out of action; 26 of the mediums were restored before the end of 1944. The 2d Panzer, which was thought to have 8,000 men and 100 tanks at the beginning of the battle, suffered losses proportionally higher than the Americans. It lost 82 tanks, 83 antitank and artillery pieces, 441 miscellaneous vehicles and 116 other type weapons, besides having 1,213 men captured and an estimated 550 killed. First Army sent a congratulatory note to Harmon, and Field Marshal Montgomery added in his own handwriting, "My very best congratulations to the 2d Armored Division."

The veteran division, which had been north of Aachen, Germany, when the Battle of the Bulge opened, conducted a classic road march to reach western Belgium before going into battle. It raced an enemy which had had several days' head start and was closing on the Meuse River. Had the Germans crossed the Meuse, the Allies' rear supply and communications areas would have been seriously threatened. The war might well have been prolonged. Initially the battle was fought to keep the enemy from moving north, but the crucial battles from December 25 to 27 were fought contrary to plans and perhaps contrary to the wishes of the army group and army commanders. Gen. Joseph Lawton Collins risked his career when he permitted Hell on Wheels to attack on Christmas Day. The 2d Armored met the enemy, stopped their attack and then began to push the remnants of the 2d Panzer Division back approximately ten miles. On the east flank, Collier and Combat Command A prevented further movement north and also prevented aid from reaching the German force fighting Combat Command B. The division now faced a serious challenge. It had effectively blunted the German spearhead, but the enemy still retained a salient in the American lines, which would have to be reduced before any thought could be given to continuing the offensive.

Chapter 17

THE BATTLES OF THE BULGE:
Reducing the Salient

The 2d Armored Division's attack to reach the area around Rochefort was only half of the Battle of the Bulge. In January, 1945, VII Corps was ordered to attack south to the town of Houffalize, where it was to link with converging elements of the Third Army and seal the enemy's salient in the Allied lines. The 2d Armored's attack over ice-coated roads, through fog and mist which created near zero visibility and through waist-deep snow drifts was the most difficult assignment the division had faced in its entire battle experience.

On December 28, 1944, the 2d Armored Division was pulled out of the line and given a few days to refit, conduct maintenance and rest. The men were treated to the Christmas dinners which most had missed. Since it was New Year, they had a dual treat of two turkey dinners. Headquarters Company, 67th Armored Regiment, had a party and dance with a few ladies present; not enough for each man to have his own partner, but their presence added to the gaiety of the occasion.

The Americans were in an advantageous position, enjoying superiority in men and equipment. However, if the German defenders were skill-

Above: Typical snowy road in the Ardennes.
Below left: Any building offered needed protection during the Ardennes action.
Below right: Steel tracks and slippery roads caused many accidents in the Ardennes.

ful, American efforts to close the salient would face serious problems. The 2d Armored was ordered to move to the Grandmenil area and to prepare for further operations. Despite the fact that the march covered less than half the distance of their December move, it was more dangerous and required more time because of the road conditions. The roads, typical of the Ardennes, were narrow with a high crown, usually paved and with steep grades which wound through sharp turns at the crest of the hills. The tanks and tank destroyers had particular difficulty. They were equipped with steel tracks which permitted forward movement. When they attempted to go around a stalled vehicles or to make a sharp turn, they often slid off into the ditch and had to be pulled out by wreckers or armored tank retrievers.

On New Year's Day, Harmon issued his attack order. The division was to advance at 8:30 A.M. on January 3 to seize the L'Ourthe River and to establish a bridgehead at Houffalize. The VII Corps assault was to be led by the 3d Armored Division on the left, with the 83d Infantry Division following, while the 2d Armored Division attacked on the right with the 84th Infantry Division following. The 84th Infantry Division's mission was to follow the attack, taking over the ground gained, and to block approaches to the L'Ourthe River from the southwest. The 2d Armored was to clear all enemy strongpoints from the line of departure to Houffalize. This order of method was a violation of armor theory and doctrine and delayed the tankers.

The intelligence summary which accompanied the order stated that the enemy attack had been contained but warned that German armored forces were still concentrated in the Hotton, Marche and Grandmenil areas. Included in this force were elements of the 12th SS, 2d SS Panzer, 130th Panzer Lehr, 9th Panzer, 560th Volks Grenadier and 116th Panzer Divisions and the Grossdeutschland Brigade. Additional evidence indicated the enemy still had a reserve force of more than six divisions which could be committed if necessary. This information, along with the weather conditions, caused General Harmon to warn war correspondents that the advance would be slow and painstaking. The weather restricted tank maneuverability and prevented air observation and tactical air support. For a while the weather threatened to postpone the attack but the division crossed the line of departure as scheduled, with five task forces of the combat commands abreast. Such a formation was dictated by the nature of their mission and by the below-freezing temperatures and driving snow. The inclement weather, which mandated American use of the roads, offered the greatest benefit to the German defenders.

Above: Infantrymen of the 41st Armored Infantry Regiment advance in the snow.
Below: In a half-track, men of the 2d Armored direct mortar fire at enemy strongpoints on the outskirts of Amonines.

The Ardennes area is hilly and heavily wooded, with deep, fast-moving streams, and dotted with small villages and numerous chateaus. The area of operations was bounded by excellent north-south and east-west highways, covered by thick snow and ice. Main roads could only be located by the fact that they were tree-lined. Hampering any cross-country movement were numerous fish ponds and hatcheries, dense woods, thick underbrush and many hills and valleys. To further complicate the situation, the area previously occupied by friendly troops had been covered with minefields which were either not plotted or were plotted erroneously. Sometimes these had not been reported to higher headquarters. When the Germans took the area, they emplaced plastic mines which did not register on mine detectors. These would be harmless unless the ice thawed or was worn thin by traffic. These areas had to be cleared or bypassed when encountered.

At 8:30 A.M. on January 3, Combat Command A attacked southward on the right flank of the division zone, using three task forces and four columns. Task Force A made excellent progress from Melines toward Trinal. Then as it reached the woods north of Trinal, it lost one medium tank to antitank fire but also captured twenty-five prisoners. The Americans secured the high ground to the west by noon. Ninety minutes later the attack resumed and the task force prepared to attack Beffe. The left column, which was to take Magoster and clear the forest between the columns, encountered stiff resistance in the woods, losing two medium tanks. However, it was able to take Magoster and fire on German vehicles retreating before the right column's attack. Beffe was taken by 4:00 P.M. and the forces consolidated their gains for the night.

Task Force B (the center column) was to take the high ground east of Magoster, attack Devantave and on order continue to Dochamps. After all that, the task force was to advance south along the Erezee-Hotton highway. The first segment of the assignment was accomplished in about thirty minutes; by 10:15 A.M. the objective had been organized for defense. Meanwhile, part of the task force, Company E, 66th Armored Regiment, had reached a point some 1,200 yards northwest of Devantave and reported ten enemy tanks in the town. The tankers called for tactical air support and took up firing positions. While the weather prevented air attacks, the supporting artillery shelled the town.

At 2:00 P.M., Task Force B was ordered to resume the attack to capture Devantave. As the attackers began to move forward, suddenly extremely heavy enemy tank and automatic weapons fire from the vicinity of Consy and intense artillery fire pinned the attackers to the ground. The enemy continued to rain fire onto the Americans and at 6:40 launched a combined tank-infantry counterattack from the woods west of Devantave. While these attackers were repulsed by tank and artillery fire, the Americans were unable to move forward. They consolidated their positions for the night.

The third task force, Task Force C, was to attack down the Amonines-Dochamps road. Its first objective, Amonines, was taken about 9:00 and the second, Fisenne, about 9:35. While the armored vehicles continued southward, the infantry started combing the area for enemy. The reconnaissance elements encountered a defended roadblock. Road conditions and approaching darkness prevented the tanks from leaving the road, so the task force pulled back to Fisenne to consolidate their gains for the day.

Combat Command B also attacked at 8:30 A.M. with two columns: Task Forces X and Y. On the right, Task Force Y was assigned the towns of Freyneux and Lamormenil. By 10:35 it reached a point about 300 yards north of Freyneux, before running into dug-in infantry and extremely heavy artillery, mortar and nebelwerfer fire. Company C, 67th Armored Regiment (the light tank company), charged the village and captured it with the supporting infantry immediately behind the tanks. After securing the town, the attack to take Lamormenil began. The other column of Task Force Y entered Lamormenil about 2:30 that afternoon. The Germans launched a tank-infantry counterattack which forced the task force to pull back about 100 yards, where it dug in to await the dawn. The Germans did not press their attack or harass the task force that night.

Task Force X, on the division's left flank, attacked south along the Grandmenil-Odeigne road but was slowed by enemy fire and adverse weather. Near the village of Corole, an enemy bazooka round hit Capt. Robert E. Lee's tank, exploding the ammunition and instantly killing the gallant captain and his crew. By the end of the day both combat commands had advanced between 2,000 yards and two miles. Their success was primarily attributed to surprise. Harmon called the corps commanding general, reporting that the roads were "regular toboggan slides." Collins told him to do the best he could. The heaviest losses were in the infantry, for the Germans apparently had developed a noiseless nebelwerfer, a fine area fire weapon. Infantry losses were the heaviest since the hedgerow battles of the Cotentin Peninsula.

The division's first day of attack caught the Germans by surprise. Some prisoners from the 3d SS Panzer Grenadier Regiment, 2d SS Panzer

Division, told the interrogators that they had been full of hope when the German attacks started on December 16. They had been impressed with the mass of arms and equipment that had been gathered for the attack. On Christmas Day the same division suffered heavy casualties and heard that the drive for the Meuse River bridges had been stopped by the Allies. The prisoners said that "this attack is more than we can take." Their appearance did not impress the division provost marshall, who thought that they were the "criminal type, ratty, young, and tough."

Collier's Combat Command A continued the attack on January 4, with Task Force A planning to capture Beffe. Still handicapped by the weather, it also met stiff enemy resistance. As two tanks from H Company, 66th Armor, moved to the high ground in support of the infantry attack, one was destroyed by German fire and the other pulled back. Company I of the regiment came to their aid and the attack resumed at 11:00 A.M. This time, Company B, 335th Infantry Regiment, 84th Infantry Division, spearheaded the assault and met little resistance. Beffe was cleared of snipers, roadblocks were established, and positions consolidated by 4:10.

Meanwhile, the left column of Task Force A remained near Magoster, driving the enemy from the immediate region. As the haze lifted, the Americans spotted seven German tanks in a valley about 800 yards to the southwest. A tank destroyer came forward to engage the enemy tanks but it was destroyed after firing a single shot. At 8:00 P.M. Lt. Col. Hugh O'Farrell, the task force commander, consolidated both columns at Beffe and sent a patrol to determine if Consy were held by the enemy. He had an unconfirmed report that the town and the road junction were clear. In fact, the enemy was in the hamlet, and in strength; the next day the battle to take it was bitter.

Task Force B planned to capture Devantave on January 4. The Germans attacked at 4:50 A.M., at 6:15 A.M. and at 8:30 P.M., attempting to drive them from the village. All three attacks were repulsed by artillery firing fuze VT8OE (POZIT) with deadly effect. The task force, resuming its attack at 3:35 P.M., ran into stiff resistance on the outskirts of town. After destroying four enemy tanks, it pulled back to the woods west of the objective to consolidate for the night. The men could hear the enemy digging in and improving their positions, but heard nothing else unusual.

Task Force C, commanded by Col. Hugh C. Parker, commanding officer of the 335th Infantry Regiment, 84th Infantry Division, continued to clear the enemy from the area around Amonines, then resumed its advance along the Amonines-Dochamps road. It encountered several roadblocks, the largest of which consisted of felled trees with 14 Teller mines attached. The Germans also had the barricade covered with mortars and small arms fire. With darkness setting in, the commander of the column decided to build its night defense around the enemy roadblock. During the day, Combat Command A had made slow but satisfactory progress, gaining about 2,000 yards in the face of determined resistance and abominable weather conditions.

In the left sector of the division zone, General White ordered Task Force Y of Combat Command B to attack and capture Lamormenil. Its advance was contested by small arms, artillery, mortar and antitank fire, as well as roadblocks. By 11:00 A.M. elements of the command had entered the edge of the town and by noon had forced the enemy troops out. Still, when the 3d Battalion, 333d Infantry Regiment, began moving into the town later in the day, the Germans from positions on the high ground west of the town laid heavy fire along the road which the infantrymen were using. The task force regrouped and attacked to take that high ground, but the determined resistance forced the men to halt and consolidate their positions for the night.

Task Force X continued to advance down the Le Batty-Odeigne road to take Odeigne and Dochamps. The two columns moved forward against heavy resistance, with the infantrymen suffering more than the tankers. Furthermore, the cold weather was taking its toll; Company C, 41st Armored Infantry Regiment, was reduced to twenty-two effective men. The Americans slowly moved ahead but the enemy limited their advance to about 1,200 yards. By the end of the day, one column was finally in position to attack Odeigne. The men were ordered in to defensive positions for the night and to prepare for the next day's action.

Combat Command Reserve, which had not been committed to the battle, had been placed on a thirty-minute alert when the fight opened. It was ordered to move to Le Batty to join Combat Command B and was renamed Task Force R. During the attack, conflicting reports were received at the division command post. One report said that the German infantry was well dug in and had plenty of ammunition. Another said that the German artillery was short of ammunition and fired at only known targets. Also it was reported that food was scarce and that the Germans had suffered heavier than anticipated casualties. Both reports may have been correct for they came from two different units, the 12th and the 560th Volks Grenadier Divisions.

The attack on January 5 was delayed for about an hour by weather conditions. Visibility was almost zero and the road conditions had not improved over the two previous days. Task Force B of Combat Command A did not advance but gave fire support to the attack of Task Force A. The latter, ordered to take Devantave and the hamlet of Consy, planned to capture Consy by using double enveloping columns. The approaches to both towns were hampered by felled trees, interspersed with mines and covered by artillery, mortar and small arms fire. The Germans, reinforced by tanks and infantry from Devantave, held back the Americans. After fighting all day, the task force had the town partially surrounded. The exhausted troops dug in and planned to resume the offensive the next day.

Task Force C made some progress against the same type opposition which was slowing the other task force of Combat Command A. At one point felled trees covered the road for a distance of about 150 yards. Among the trees were mines, and the whole roadblock was covered by automatic weapons, small arms, artillery and mortar fire. Since the tanks could not leave the road to bypass the blockade, the men again prepared defensive positions, using the German roadblock as the basis for their own positions.

Task Force R relieved Task Force Y, which then became the division reserve and moved to Estine. There, although they had little billeting space and conditions were crowded, for a moment the men were out of the snow and could enjoy a hot meal. They conducted maintenance and prepared to renew the attack if any task force met resistance it could not handle. Task Force R was now given the mission to take Dochamps and the high ground south of Lamormenil. Using two columns, Colonel Hinds advanced about 1,500 yards against mines and stiff enemy resistance before stopping about a half-mile from Dochamps. During the night, someone at division headquarters redrew the boundary between Combat Command A and Combat Command B, putting the town in the former's zone. The next morning, Task Force R bypassed the town and continued southward.

At 9:00 A.M. on January 5, Task Force X renewed its efforts to capture Odeigne, using a double envelopment from the northeast and west. In order for the tanks to attack from the west, they had to maneuver up a steep, winding road. The first two tanks made it to the top of the hill, but the third threw a track, effectively blocking the trail. At the rear of the column, three tanks bogged down, trapping the bulk of the force. To make an already serious situation worse, the enemy artillery and mortars started shelling the column. Despite the barrage tank retrievers rescued most of the vehicles. The two tanks that had reached the top of the hill encountered a new type of booby trap—trip wires attached to explosives and intended to catch the antennas of the tanks, then bring trees crashing down onto them. Fortunately, these traps were spotted and avoided by tying the antennas down.

The two tanks from the west column and the one approaching from the northeast were in position to attack the town. Approaching from the west, the tanks, with eight infantrymen from C Company, 41st Armored Infantry, raced through the town, firing wildly to give the impression of a larger force. The northeast force appeared; and by night, after overcoming a savage, determined defense, they controlled most of the town except for the south edge. The men consolidated their gains and prepared to renew the attack the next day.

On January 6, Task Force C led Combat Command A's attack to capture Consy. It attacked at 3:30 A.M., and for two hours the men struggled against an estimated infantry battalion reinforced with Mark V tanks. Task Force C then pulled back, and Task Force B renewed the attack at 8:30 A.M. The second assault met the same results as the first, so Task Force B decided to bypass Consy and proceed toward Devantave. Part of Task Force B entered the town at 11:00 and cleared it by noon, while the other part protected the flank. It then cut the road to Laid Prangeleux, and for the first time it seemed that enemy resistance was weakening.

However, Combat Command A had a new problem: Samree. Located on the high ground south of the Vielsalm-Laroche road and overlooking the approaches of Task Forces A and B, this was a crucial position; Combat Command A began considering how to take it following the capture of Dochamps. The Germans were equally aware of Samree's importance and were determined to hold it. The fight for this small town was to last for four days.

After capturing Odeigne on January 5, Task Force X, Combat Command B, attacked to clear the high ground to the southwest. Most of its opposition came from elements of the 560th Volks Grenadier Division. This German unit had recently been transferred from Norway where it had trained in dense woods and snow-covered hills—ideal practice for the action now being fought. The tank force infantry had considerable difficulty clearing the woods, having to maneuver through deep snow, thick forests and against an enemy skilled in this type of fighting. By evening, the enemy had been pushed back and the task force had made contact with the 3d Armored Division along the Manhay-Houffalize road.

At 8:30 A.M. on January 7, Task Force A, Combat Command A, continued the attack to capture the high ground southwest of Dochamps. The lead tanks ran into a minefield about 200 yards south of Croix du Laid Prangeleux. Since the terrain prevented the tanks' moving cross-country, the attack shifted to a southerly direction but was stopped by intense fire from a dug-in tank concealed in the snow. Heavy woods on both sides of the road prevented the task force medium tanks or tank destroyers from flanking the position. After consolidating for the night, a bazooka team inched forward to attempt to destroy the German tank. Dug-in infantry kept the Americans at bay. Division artillery tried to dislodge the tank, but that also failed. Finally Lt. Col. Hugh R. O'Farrell, the task force commander, had an artillery forward observer call for eight-inch howitzer fire. With the weapon's amazing accuracy and using an armor-piercing fuze, the forward observer was able to put an eight-inch shell inside the German tank and literally blow it to pieces.

Task Force C, meanwhile, had the assignment of capturing Dochamps. The terrain presented the same handicaps which had limited the other task forces. After overcoming three roadblocks and avoiding a minefield, the force entered Dochamps about 5:00 P.M. Mopping up the remnants of the defenders required most of the evening, but eventually the town was secured.

Hinds led Task Force R southward from Odeigne to take positions on the south side of the Bois d'Odeigne and across the Vielsalm-Laroche road. As the infantrymen moved through the woods, they encountered dug-in infantry with plenty of ammunition but only one antitank gun. After all possible weapons were brought to bear on the Germans, the attack momentarily picked up steam. It began to falter when the retreating enemy felled trees across the path of the attackers. By dark, the task force reached the south side of the woods and began to prepare defensive positions. To add to the men's misery, a severe, blowing snowstorm began at 6:00, lasting for five or six hours.

Task Force Y was relieved from division reserve and joined the attack south of Odeigne. Weather conditions posed a bigger problem than the enemy infantry, which had to be eliminated from the zone of operations. The woods were too thick for the tank units, forcing them to skirt the edge of the forest. Heavy antitank and tank fire prevented the tanks' joining their infantry. By nightfall the infantry had cut the Vielsalm-

Laroche road, the main supply and communications route from Samree. Combat Command B's three task forces cut this road at three points, effectively preventing reinforcements from arriving to aid the partially entrapped Germans.

At 8:30 A.M., White sent Task Force X south to sever the same highway which the other task forces were to cut. By 9:30 the 2d Battalion, 333d Infantry Regiment, covered by tank guns and meeting little or no opposition, secured its stretch of road. The tanks then moved forward to join them, reinforcing the roadblocks which were being emplaced. The infantry continued to clear the enemy for about 1,000 yards to the south and to place roadblocks on the roads and trails leading to the main route. At noon the 3d Armored Division contacted the task force and relieved it of its responsibility for the roadblocks. With the capture of the main road from Samree, the Germans suffered a severe blow. Now they had only one line of escape, supply and/or communications into and out of the Bulge.

The attack to capture Samree began in earnest on January 8. The combat commands were approaching from the north and the east. As the battle progressed, it became evident that the German 560th Volks Grenadier Division was fighting a delaying action, masterfully executed and aided by the adverse weather and terrain. It permitted the German army to withdraw a considerable amount of troops and equipment from the trap that was being built. Their one remaining escape route was through Houffalize—the division's final objective.

Task Force A, Combat Command A, moved about 1,200 yards toward Samree, but direct fire from tanks and antitank guns forced it to halt near Le Wate. Reconnaissance elements, seeking a route to enable the tanks or tank destroyers to advance, merely groped about trying to find the roads. Artillery fire was ineffective, for the forward observers could not see the targets. After limited gains, the task force dug in for the night. The new commanding officer of the 66th Armored Regiment, Col. Clayton J. Mansfield, former division chief of staff, went forward to get a firsthand view of the area around Samree. He was standing outside the tree line, when the fog and haze lifted momentarily. The Germans put an artillery airburst over his position, killing him instantly. General Collier told Harmon to give the regiment back to Lieutenant Colonel Stokes.

Task Force B, coordinating with Task Force A, attacked south from Dochamps in a flank attack on Samree. The tanks could not traverse the wooded terrain, so they skirted the edge of the woods west of Dochamps.

At that point they encountered one of the most well-positioned and deadly enemy emplacements of the war. The Germans had placed ten Tiger tanks at the edge of the woods, with the snow concealing them perfectly. As the lead American tank moved forward out of the fog and snow, it was immediately destroyed. The road, through a narrow defile, eliminated any possibility of maneuvering to flank the Germans. An attempt to rush their position with tanks or infantry would have been suicide. The task force pulled back and planned to attack over the open terrain west of Dochamps. The Germans had effectively prevented Combat Command A's attack.

Combat Command B was attempting to attack Samree from the east. Task Forces R and Y advanced abreast, but German resistance was as tenacious as any encountered in the war. Task Force R, on the south side of the Vielsalm-Laroche road, encountered a formidable roadblock. It was in rugged terrain and made up of felled trees, heavily mined and booby-trapped, and was covered with automatic weapons, dug-in infantry, artillery, mortars and log barricades. After two attacks, at 3:00 and 5:00 P.M., Hinds pulled his men back and dug in for the night. On the north side of the road, Task Force Y attacked to emplace a roadblock closer to Samree, but the troops became entangled in both friendly and enemy artillery fire and pulled back. The day's two attacks netted about 600 yards.

The weather, too, continued to take its toll. Hoping to give the tanks better traction, Harmon had ordered that steel tracks be changed to rubber ones, but the change was occurring slowly; he permitted only a few tanks at a time to be pulled out of the line. Most of the casualties among the men were now a result of exposure, frostbite, or trench foot. When these cases were brought to the battalion aid station, they were usually treated before wound cases. The men did not have snow pacs, but Hinds, having been reared in North Dakota, knew that thick felt socks provided good insulation inside rubber boots. He had his orderly make him a pair of socks from wool blankets, with soles consisting of seven layers. Then Hinds tested the idea himself. Worn over regular issue socks and inside GI overshoes, the makeshift footwear worked well. He took the idea to Harmon, who gave his approval; he even sent scouting parties to find blankets, enemy overcoats and any other wool items. Hinds sent his orderly to each company in the 41st Armored Infantry Regiment and to each unit in the division to show the men how to make the emergency snow pac. In about seven days most men had this improvised footwear.

Typically, as the Bulge concluded and the sock was not needed, a huge supply of snow pacs arrived from the United States. For their inventiveness, both Hinds and his orderly were awarded Bronze Stars.

The weather report for January 9 predicted snow flurries, heavy ground fog and limited visibility. When the fighting resumed on that day, the weather made the operation of armor extremely difficult, if not almost impossible. The snow drifts were nearly waist-deep on the men and almost turret-deep on the tanks. Task Forces A and B, of Combat Command A, attacked at 7:30 A.M. with the intention of capturing Samree. During the night, patrols had placed cinders over the snow for the tanks to rush forward and reduce the strong position which had held up the tanks of Task Force B. The tanks of Task Force A attacked and by 11:45 had flushed the Germans out of their positions and forced them to pull back to the town. Meanwhile the tanks and tank destroyers of Task Force A were brought forward and positioned so that they could fire on the town, only about a mile away.

Task Force B attacked down the Dochamps-Samree road, clearing the woods as it went. While moving through the woods east of Em de Benasse, they collided with retreating German infantry and two Mark IV tanks. After destroying one of the tanks by bazooka fire, the advance continued. At one point when the fog lifted, five Mark Vs were only 400 yards in front of the attackers. Since the infantry did not have tanks with them and could not get within bazooka range, the Germans escaped. By 9:25 P.M., Task Force B had pulled alongside Task Force A and consolidated for the night.

On the east flank of Samree, Combat Command B planned to renew the attack on January 9. Division artillery shelled the town all night, expending 12,514 rounds. The bombardment meant a sleepless night for the town's defenders. The town was defended by an estimated 300 infantry, reinforced by Mark V tanks. Capturing the town was a formidable task, but necessary in order to clear the enemy from the zone. As it had the previous day, Combat Command B attacked with two task forces abreast. Hinds led him command back to the German roadblock and began to reduce it slowly but systematically. Working under direct and heavy fire, the engineers and infantrymen removed first the mines and booby traps, then the logs and trees which were holding up the advance. By 5:00 P.M., with the roadblock overcome, the advance resumed until dark; then the command dug in, planning to renew the attack the following morning. The severe winter conditions continued to plague the

Americans as during the attack thirteen men were evacuated because of cold weather injuries and only three because of wounds or injuries suffered in battle.

At 8:30 A.M. Task Force Y attacked to install two roadblocks. It made good progress until blocked by strong antitank and tank fire from German positions near Chavrehez. The 3d Battalion, 67th Armored Regiment, reached the high ground overlooking the village and along with the 78th Armored Artillery Battalion (which fired the new POZIT fuze) killed enemy "by the hundreds." The American advance continued. By 6:00, when the command halted, it had emplaced the roadblocks and planned to attack the following day to capture Samree.

Just as Harmon had planned a decision day at Humain, January 10 was to be decision day at Samree. Four of the division's six task forces were to attack the town. During the night, a discussion was held to decide if Combat Command A would attack during darkness or wait until daylight. Since the infantry assigned to Task Force A had been reduced to understrength companies, it was decided to attack the following morning during darkness.

Samree, thought to be defended by 300 infantry, was actually held by several battalions and supported by twenty Mark V tanks.

The night of January 9, Hinds made plans for the final assault to capture Samree. One of his prime concerns was to have a cleared road to ease the advance on the city. Hinds knew that he had a 4.5-inch gun battalion attached to his regiment, but it was scheduled to be relieved the next morning. He also recognized the gun battalion had more ammunition than it could expend and that the Germans had emplaced TNT charges to fell trees and form large roadblocks. Hinds ordered the guns to keep his stretch of road under constant fire until he was ready to attack the next morning. He correctly reasoned that the Germans would not send men into the area to detonate the charges if the road were under constant fire. He called Maj. James F. Hollingsworth, commander of the 2d Battalion, 67th Armored Regiment, several times to check that everything was planned and ready for the next day. Hollingsworth kept assuring his commander that all was in order. Yet Hinds, cautious by nature and knowing that the weather was adversely affecting men and machines alike, decided to determine the situation for himself. Arriving at Hollingsworth's tank, Hinds beat on the sides for several minutes before the tank sergeant finally opened the hatch. He found that Hollingsworth had been hit. A German shell had hit the gun, forcing the breechblock back into the tanker's head, neck and shoulder. He was literally unconscious on his feet. No gas or ammunition had been delivered. Hinds found the battalion S-4 and told him to get the supplies to the men. The supply officer said that it would be difficult, but he managed to get enough for the attack to start on time.

The number of effective men and machines had been drastically reduced. Hinds moved to take the town with a battalion of tanks (three tanks), a company of the 17th Armored Engineers with a bulldozer and a battalion of infantry (forty-eight men). The task force encountered one roadblock. As the bulldozer moved forward to remove it, it hit a mine, which blew the trees and the bulldozer blade about forty feet in the air; but the enemy mine cleared the roadblock. The attack met stiff resistance from antitank and machine gun fire but made about 1,000 yards before turning southeast to clear the woods. There they flushed three enemy tanks; two escaped, but one was set afire by the 92d Armored Artillery Battalion which had been shelling the woods. By the end of the day, the task force occupied positions about 1,000 yards south of the Vielsalm-Laroche road.

At 7:30 A.M., the tanks of Task Force A launched an attack which caught the Germans by surprise, and fifteen minutes later it had reached the western part of the town. The following infantry quickly cleared the town, while the tanks continued southward, capturing the dominating high ground. Task Force B attacked at the same time and lost two tanks which overturned on the icy roads. By 9:00 it held the eastern part of Samree and then turned to take the high ground east of town. Few of the enemy infantry escaped, and all of the tanks were either captured or destroyed. By the afternoon, Samree had been captured and secured against counterattacks.

Samree was finally in American hands. After its capture and con-solidation, the Americans stopped for a day of rest and maintenance. Hot meals were brought to the men. Warming tents or heated buildings, available for one of the first times since the attack started, were good morale boosters. Another boost was the unique replacement depot es-tablished by General Harmon. Most of the casualties suffered frostbite or trench foot. For some reason, priorities had been distorted and the nones-sential items were unloaded before winter clothing. Some of the men were trying to hide minor disabilities, hoping to avoid being sent to a hospital and the consequent difficulty in rejoining their old units. Harmon set up a rest camp where the minor cases of frostbite, trench foot and combat fatigue could receive hot meals, medical alcohol and several days' rest before returning to their units. Eisenhower's headquarters ordered the practice stopped. Harmon somehow mislaid the order and failed to find it until the battle was concluded and the facility no longer needed.

Harmon described the caliber and character of his men. After Samree, captured in a heavy snowstorm, he visited the frontline soldiers. Harmon was depressed at having to order the men to renew the attack the following morning in the same kind of weather. He came upon two infantrymen; one clearing snow from the frozen ground, while the other was cutting pine boughs for their shelterless bed. One came over and saw that Harmon was blue with cold. The division commander, however, knew that he would sleep in a warm trailer that night, but the soldiers would have to sleep on the open ground. The soldier told him, rather reproachfully, that an old man like Harmon should not be out in the cold weather. The soldier had beaten him to the punch; he was cheering up the division commander, instead of the reverse.

With the capture of Samree, the division had accomplished half its mission. Now it had to take Houffalize and seal the ring around the enemy still west of that town, especially if the Third Army arrived at Houffalize about the same time as the attackers from the north. To accomplish this, Harmon reorganized the combat commands, assigning the 41st Armored Infantry to Combat Command A, while Combat Command B retained the 333d Infantry Regiment, 84th Infantry Division. At 8:00 A.M. on January 12, Combat Command A attacked and detected that the Germans were putting second-rate troops into the defense while withdrawing the 2d SS Panzer and 9th Panzer Divisions. Task Force A, commanded by Colonel Hinds, quickly seized the initial objective of Chavrehez and, after securing it, proceeded southward. Near Farm St. Jean, where the battalion commander and staff of the 2d Battalion, 1129th Infantry Regiment, were taken prisoner, the Hell-on-Wheelers also found a captured American mailbag. In it was a special delivery letter to Colonel Hinds from his wife and family. Combat Command A made about a mile before consolidating for the night.

Planning for its attack, the 333d Infantry Regiment sent patrols into the area south of the Laroche road and west of the Houffalize-Liege road. The patrol suffered heavy losses and its report was not good: the woods were thick and bounded with swamps; the tanks would be restricted to firebreaks which were defended by roadblocks covered by five tanks or self-propelled guns. With that bad news, Task Force Y attacked to capture

Les Tailles and Aux Censes. The initial attack, by infantry, was to clear the woods and protect the tanks as they negotiated the narrow trails. Finally the tanks were committed and joined the infantry, which had a difficult time clearing the enemy. They attacked the village at 3:40 P.M., completely occupying it by 6:00 and destroying one German tank in the process. Continuing Combat Command B's attack southward, at 10:40 A.M., Task Force X began its assault to take Petites Tailles. The town was defended by an estimated two infantry companies which were determined not to surrender. Petites Tailles, ordered taken by a frontal attack, was finally entered when I Company, 67th Armored Regiment, and a squad of Company B, 17th Armored Engineers, maneuvered through the 3d Armored Division's zone and attacked from the east. By 7:40 that evening, the village had been secured and the task forces linked at that point.

On January 13 both combat commands made better progress over the rugged terrain. While encountering some heavy resistance, they began to notice a decline in the enemy's will to fight. At 8:30 A.M., Task Force A attacked in two columns to clear the woods south of Em St. Jean. Moving through the trees, they encountered some light mortar fire and a few riflemen. They were held up at one point while the 17th Engineer Battalion built a forty-eight-foot bridge for the tanks. By the end of the day, the task force had made about 4,000 to 5,000 yards, reaching positions about 1½ miles north of Wibrin. Task Force B, however, met more severe resistance. Attacking south along the Wibrin road to clear the Bois de Wibrin, it met determined pockets of defenders which, had to be eliminated before they continued forward. But by the end of the day the woods had been screened and Task Force B had linked with Task Force A for the night.

Because swamps restricted the tanks to the narrow trails and the many felled trees restricted their forward movement, the engineers of Combat Command B worked all night clearing roadblocks of felled trees liberally sprinkled with mines and booby traps. Task Force X attacked at 8:00 A.M., securing Collas within two hours. After clearing the enemy from the village, the attack continued southward through the Petit Bois. Here, finding the enemy was a slow, time-consuming process, but by 8:45 P.M. the task force had passed through the woods and taken another village: Pisserotte, where the tankers stopped for the evening. Task Force Y, attacking at 8:00 A.M., was to seize the crossroads six miles north of Houffalize. Moving through thick woods and encountering dug-in infantry, artillery, mortar and antitank fire, the task force reached the west edge of Pisserotte by 5:00 P.M. However, friendly artillery fire kept the task force out of the village for a short time. By 8:45 P.M. it had been taken and secured.

The attackers began to make better progress when the German rear guard action, while still fanatical on occasion, generally began to lessen. Task Force A, Combat Command A, renewed its attack toward Houffalize at 8:30 A.M. on January 14. Its first task was the capture of two hills north of Avant Belhex. After that, it was to aid Task Force B's capture of Chevroumont and the high ground to the south, which overlooked Achouffe. Progress was satisfactory, except at Wibrin, where dug-in infantry and tanks on a hill south of town took the columns under fire, quickly destroying four medium tanks. In spite of their casualties, the tanks and infantry continued forward. Capt. James M. Burt maneuvered his H Company, 66th Armored, to a nearby hill where he could fire on the German tanks. This action permitted the infantry and tanks to enter the town and secure it without further interference. At 8:30 A.M., Task Force B attacked to seize Chevroumont and the high ground north of Petite Mormont. Meeting sporadic resistance, it was delayed while the engineers built a twenty-four-foot bridge over Rau de Valire. After advancing about three miles, the largest single day's gain, Combat Command A was about two to three miles north of Houffalize. It began planning for the final attack, which it hoped would require only one more day.

Combat Command B continued down the Houffalize road, keeping pace with Combat Command A. Task Force X launched a predawn attack to capture the hill north of Wilogne. Catching the Germans by surprise, the tanks were on their objective ten minutes later. The advance resumed southward at 8:00 A.M., through the woods of the Bois de Cedrogne— woods so thick the infantry had to lead the tanks through. After passing through the forest and meeting little resistance, the task force moved against the twin villages of Dinez and Wilogne, which were totally secured by 6:30 that night. During the day, the task force had had more difficulty with rugged terrain, thick trees and slippery roads than with the enemy.

The ring, which was tightening around Houffalize, became even tighter by the end of January 15. With little opposition, Task Force A entered Achouffe at 11:00 A.M. Here the advance stalled, while the engineers built a forty-five-foot bridge over the L'Ourthe River. When it was completed at 4:00 P.M., the attack resumed. By 8:30 the lead elements were 1,500 yards southeast of town and within a mile of Houffalize. During the night, infantry patrols entered Houffalize and reported that no enemy could be found. Task Force B made excellent gains of about 5,000 yards during the day. Attacking at 9:00 A.M., it quickly seized the high ground west of Achouffe by 10:30, then turned west to aid Task Force A's entry into the town. Company C, 17th Engineer Battalion, built a seventy-two-foot bridge over the Moulin River, and the attack continued southeastward at 5:40 P.M. Before stopping for the night, the task force reached the high ground north of Hazy, linked with Task Force A and prepared to attack to Houffalize the following day.

Combat Command B continued down the main road to Houffalize at 8:00 A.M. While trying to capture the ridge between Dinez and Fontenaille, Task Force Y met stubborn resistance from dug-in infantry and antitank guns. This was finally overcome and the advance continued toward Fontenaille at 1:00 P.M. After the town's capture, the attack continued and the village of Tauernaux was consolidated at 4:40. After dark, the task force sent patrols toward Houffalize to determine enemy dispositions. Task Force X, on the west side of the road to Houffalize, attacked and secured the ridgeline north of Mont, overrunning two dug-in tanks and their infantry support. By 1:35 that afternoon, they had taken the village. The terrain was becoming more suitable for armor; by 5:00 that evening, Hill 430, only a mile north of Houffalize, had been captured. After consolidating for the night, patrols moved forward to determine what enemy was located at Houffalize.

By the end of the day, the 2d Armored Division was only a mile from its final objective. Resistance had diminished considerably. The men knew the Germans had been committing their second- and third-rate troops, while making every effort to extract their better troops from the tightening noose.

January 16 was an eventful day for the 2d Armored. Combat Command A resumed its attack to enter Houffalize. Patrols were sent to the L'Ourthe River, while the tanks tried to enter from the west against infantry resistance. While the fighting was going on, Staff Sergeant Douglas Wood, a cameraman from the 165th Signal Photo Company, arrived at Wibrin. He knew that the 2d Armored Division was close to Houffalize and sensed that the linkup with the Third Army was imminent. He asked for and received permission to film the event. Lieutenant Colonel O'Farrell said that he was to be relieved by the 82d Reconnaissance Battalion and did not expect a historic meeting.

From the tank officer's position, Wood could look down on Houffalize and see Germans walking around on the highway south of the town.

The sergeant was about to return to Wibrin when members of Company F, 41st Armored Infantry, asked him to take some pictures of them. While he complied with their request, several Americans emerged from the nearby forest and said that they were a patrol from the 41st Armored Reconnaissance Squadron, 11th Armored Division. The patrol leader, Lt. Col. Miles Foy, commanding officer, 41st Armored Reconnaissance Squadron, wanted to be taken to an officer. Wood escorted him to O'Farrell's tank and called to O'Farrell, saying that a colonel from the 11th Armored Division wanted to see him. To both officers' surprise (they had been classmates at Fort Knox), their meeting was the linkup between the Third and First Armies which sealed the Bulge.

The division was ordered to hold a defensive line along the L'Ourthe River with a minimum of troops. The remainder of the division pulled back for rest and maintenance and attention to health needs. As the division was pulling back, the 66th Armored regimental surgeon was rushing to find General Collier. Unknown to even General Harmon, Collier had pneumonia. The doctor told Collier to prepare to get a massive shot of penicillin. Today, while telling the story, Collier laughs, saying that he believes the doctor used a horse syringe on him.

Harmon made his plans for defending the hard-won ground. A tank and infantry company were kept on alert for rapid deployment. Any evidence of a counterattack was to be reported to Harmon immediately. On January 19, the 4th Cavalry Group relieved the 2d Armored Division on the line, and the tankers moved to a new assembly area near Spirmont, Belgium, where they rested until February 2. Two days later they moved to positions around Margrat and Gulpen, Holland. The relocation was made in total secrecy, with markings painted out, patches covered or removed, and radio code names changed.

On January 19, Harmon wrote Gen. Omar N. Bradley that rumors were circulating that he was to be relieved of command of the 2d Armored Division and given command of a corps. Harmon said that his fondest wish was to lead the division in a victory parade in the United States, once the war was over. He told Bradley that if the rumors were correct, then he recommended that Brigadier General I.D. White be given command of the division. Harmon was ordered to assume command of XXII Corps and White assumed command of the division on January 19, 1945. With White's promotion, Hinds was relieved of the 41st Armored Infantry and took over Combat Command B. Lt. Col. Russell W. Jenna moved from division G-3 to take over the 41st Armored Infantry Regiment, while Lt. Col. Briard P. Johnson became the division G-3.

Major General Collins wrote Harmon that he and VII Corps, with pride and affection as well as regret, bid the division farewell, as it was again transferred back to XIX Corps. He hoped both units might meet again "in the final drive to Berlin." Harmon bade farewell to the division in a memorandum saying that the recent action of the 2d Armored Division "may well go down in history as the greatest contribution of the 2d Armored Division to the Allied cause." He was certain that the division's valor and perseverance against weather, terrain and enemy had shown the true greatness and spirit of the 2d Armored Division. As a token of affection for their division commander, the men of the 41st Armored Infantry, sent him a German battle flag they had captured. Harmon replied that he would always prize this gift from his frontline soldiers.

After the change of command and movement to different areas, the division settled into a routine of maintenance and training. To better understand the German weapons and tactics, captured bazookas and panzerfausts were demonstrated. German tanks were studied and used as targets on the antitank gunnery and artillery ranges. Later a warning was issued against firing high-velocity ammunition at the tank hulls, but bazookas and rifle grenades were still permitted. When replacements who had little more than infantry basic training arrived they started with the school of the soldier and progressed to squad, platoon and company training. Along with this, they were also instructed in the history and traditions of the division.

The battle of the eastern Ardennes, or the attack to eliminate the salient, was costly to both sides, but more so for the Germans. The 2d Armored met elements of the 2d SS Panzer, 116th SS Panzer and 560th Volks Grenadier Divisions. While there was no estimate of the killed, the Americans captured 1,742 prisoners; 1,150 were from the 560th Volks Grenadier Division. They destroyed 43 tanks, 8 self-propelled guns, 25 artillery pieces and 119 miscellaneous vehicles, as well as 15 American-made, German-used vehicles. The Americans had 121 killed, 63 missing, 484 wounded, 379 injured and 1,337 nonbattle casualties. The division lost 28 medium and 7 light tanks, 1 tank retriever and 2 tank destroyers.

There were striking comparisons between the December and January phases of the Battles of the Bulge. The distance covered was approximately the same, about thirteen miles. In December the battle to stop the German advance lasted six days, while in January fourteen days were required to oust the Germans from the salient. Battle conditions made the difference. Around Celles, Humain and Rochefort, the terrain was rela-

American troops entering Houffalize.

tively open, while the eastern Ardennes was rugged, heavily wooded and mountainous. The weather in December permitted air support, while not once in January did the poor visibility conditions permit air cover or support. In December, snow had just begun to fall; in January, it was deep enough to greatly impede both men and tanks.

The tactical orders contained crucial differences. In December Harmon was ordered to attack and destroy the enemy. In January this order was changed to an order of method: advance and clear the enemy from the zone. Further complicating the instructions, the 84th Infantry Division was ordered to cooperate with the 2d Armored. No provision was made for the infantry to clear bypassed pockets of resistance, but rather they were to take over ground already held by the tankers. Answering a letter from a Belgian officer as to why the division failed to reach Houffalize sooner and trap four German Panzer divisions west of that town, Harmon replied that "in all honesty we just weren't good enough to go faster under the conditions that we had to fight, and the Germans put up a very fine rear guard defense."

The Battle of the Bulge, on which Hitler had gambled so heavily, ended Germany's hope of winning the war. The German army, which had been given time to regroup several times before, was to get the same opportunity again. However, it would not have the men or equipment to fill the gaps when the attack came. The Battles of the Bulge had a sobering effect on the Americans. It stopped the overoptimism of November and December and forced them to realize that a major campaign would be necessary to occupy the enemy's homeland. Any thought that Germany would surrender to a static defensive army vanished when the first German soldier attacked on December 16, 1944. A nation which could launch such an attack still had the men and resources to conduct a prolonged war. That fact ended any hope that Germany was about to collapse.

Chapter 18

THE NEAR MISS

Before the German attack on December 16, Lt. Gen. William H. Simpson's Ninth Army had been making plans to attack across the Roer River toward the Rhine. Simpson loaned eight divisions to First Army to help stem the Ardennes attack. This naturally cancelled the Roer-Rhine operation. On February 3, 1945, the 2d Armored Division returned to the operational control of Ninth Army. With the return to Simpson, there was a noticeable increase in morale. The men trusted Simpson and appreciated his no-nonsense approach to the war. However, they were still under the authority of the British Twenty-first Army Group, an attachment that was to have a crucial and detrimental effect.

In early February, the division returned to the Aachen area to begin training for the attack across the Roer River. For almost a month, its personnel rested. The pass and leave policy was reinstituted. A group of the 142d Signal Company were befriended by a Dutch family in Waubach, Holland. The men pilfered supplies from the company kitchen and gave them to "good old Mom," who cooked food the like of which

Members of D Company, 41st Armored Infantry Regiment, pass through the destruction of Krefeld, Germany, on their way to the Rhine River.

the men had not tasted since leaving home. One night the woman offered the men a treat made from Dutch goods: it was burnt black and tasted awful. Not wanting to offend the hostess, the men ventured to say that it was good. Finally, Sgt. Russell S. Lamison asked what it was. The hostess replied that it was fried hog's blood. To the Dutch it was a treat; to the Americans it was revolting.

Hell on Wheels also had time to conduct needed maintenance and to train replacements. On George Washington's Birthday, an inspecting officer discovered that some men had never fired their basic weapons. An intensive program of firings began, in order to qualify them with their rifles, carbines, automatic rifles, submachine guns and pistols, as well as to familiarize them with all the regimental weapons. While the new arrivals were having weapons training, the air corps and ground troops experimented with the possibility of aerial resupply for the forward units, because most senior commanders anticipated a rapid advance. By the end of February, having had its losses of men and equipment made up, the division prepared to move. It was ready for what many thought might be their final attack. Hell on Wheels, taken off the secret list, repainted its bumper markings on vehicles and placed the patches back on the uniforms.

The plans for the attack across the Roer (Operation GRENADE) were made but were subject to change because of the ever-present danger of the Roer River dams. If the Ninth Army crossed the Roer and were cut off, it would have deadly consequences for the Allied efforts. The attack was scheduled but had to be postponed when the Germans destroyed the sluice gates, which raised the water level to above flood level. Simpson's chief engineer predicted when the water level would recede to its normal flow; the troops could only wait. During this interlude, the division learned that the Germans were employing a wooden antitank and personnel mine. Since these charges were not easily located with the regular metallic mine detectors, the division developed a new tool—the common pitchfork. It was ideal for locating and lifting the wooden charges. Consequently, Ninth Army bought about 3,000 of the new mine detectors, virtually the entire supply of the hardware stores of Belgium, Holland and Germany.

The men patiently waited for the attack. This was perfect tank country; the only obstacle to a rapid advance was the Nord Canal between the Roer River and the bridge over the Rhine River at Krefeld-Uerdingen. There were several small creeks parallel to the axis of the proposed advance, but they were not considered serious obstacles to the attackers. Aerial photographs made in November had shown that the enemy was constructing three defensive belts. The first, on the east bank of the Roer, consisted of infantry fire trenches, strongpoints, artillery positions, pillboxes and some antiaircraft positions, with an antitank ditch which was only about 25 percent completed. The second band of defensive works was a double row of infantry trenches extending from Ameln to Titz to Erkelenz. There were some antitank ditches here also, but they were small, only about 100 yards in length, and not connected. The final band was on the east bank of the Erft Canal, crossing at Gustorf, south of Garzweiler, to the south of Juchen, then to the Munchen-Gladbach area. Just prior to the February attack, new photos showed that the defensive trenches had fallen into disuse, their sides had caved in, and some were filled with water. The photographic interpreter concluded that the trenches were not usable; the order of battle personnel determined that the Germans did not have sufficient men to occupy the works. If the enemy had manned those trenches with determined troops, the attack would have faced serious problems.

The plans were made. XIX Corps would attack with the 29th and 30th Infantry Divisions to force open a bridgehead through which the exploiting force would be committed. If the defenses were strongly held, then the 83d Infantry Division would spearhead the attack. If the defenses were weakly held, then the 2d Armored Division would lead the corps and army efforts. That decision would be made by Simpson. The attack was to clear the area between the Roer River and the Erft-Rhine Rivers.

The 2d Armored Division, not exactly sure what its role was to be, prepared plans for three possible missions. Interestingly, they made them in the order in which they were actually executed. First was the attack to exploit the gains, if the infantry had easy going; second was to guard the corps and army flanks; third was to serve as a reserve force. Artillery blasted the opening for the initial infantry attack. Twenty or thirty battalions, lined up almost wheel to wheel, poured a heavy continuous barrage into the German lines, answered by only one or two rounds. 2d Lt. Frank L. Culver, D Company, 66th Armored Regiment, remembered that most of the enemy rounds were duds. At 3:30 A.M. on February 23, the infantry attacked. When the XIX Corps infantry divisions crossed the Roer River, they made faster gains than VII Corps on the south, creating a gap in the line. The 2d Armored, which had been placed on a four-hour alert, prepared to send one combat command to fill the gap.

During the afternoon of February 25, Combat Command B, now led by Colonel Hinds, was attached to the 30th Infantry Division and ordered to cross the Roer River at 9:30A.M. the following morning to protect the flanks of the infantrymen. To further confuse the enemy, the command was to maintain radio silence until it made enemy contact. For the next two days, Combat Command B primarily relieved the 30th Infantry as they captured successive towns. The tankers established five roadblocks in a defensive perimeter around the infantry's open right flank. However, Hinds's combat command did not have a totally passive mission. The 1st Battalion of the 67th Armored Regiment lost three tanks in a fire fight when the enemy counterattacked from Niederembt. The guns of C Company, 702d Tank Destroyer Battalion, drove the Germans away, damaging two tanks.

On February 27, as Simpson concluded that the Germans were offering minimal resistance, he decided to commit his "strong right arm"—Hell on Wheels—to the conflict. The XIX Corps issued its order: the 2d Armored Division would attack early the next morning to secure crossings over the Nord Canal and be prepared to pursue the enemy north, northeast or northwest. In the attack, the 2d Armored was to move to the center of the American advance, with the 29th Infantry Division on its left flank and the 30th Infantry Division on its right. Augmenting the division were two artillery battalions, the 65th Armored and the 696th and 258th Field Artillery Groups, made up of the 258th Artillery Battalion (155mm self-propelled guns), the 666th Field Artillery Battalion (155mm howitzers) and the 959th Field Artillery Battalion (4.5-inch guns). In addition, A Company, 739th Tank Battalion, (special mine exploder) and a flamethrower platoon of the 739th Tank Battalion were also attached. The 331st Infantry Regimental Combat Team, including the 908th Field Artillery Battalion from the 83d Infantry Division, was attached to the division and assigned to Combat Command B. During the night, prior to the attack, XIX Corps attached one battery of the 430th Antiaircraft Artillery Battalion (eight 40mm towed guns) and four quad .50 calibers mounted on half-tracks. The 40mm guns were assigned to the 258th Field Artillery Battalion, and the .50 calibers went to Division Trains. With these attachments, the 2d Armored Division again had more than twice the battle strength of a light armored division.

The intelligence annex described the Nord Canal as a drainage ditch about twenty feet wide, with gently sloping sides, and containing about 5½ feet of water. The railroad embankment on the north side of the canal was thought to be a possible obstacle.

Combat Command B, which had been protecting the right flank of the 30th Infantry Division, was replaced by the 113th Cavalry Group. Hinds's men began assembling near Kirchkerten to begin the attack the following day. They planned to attack up the Julich-Dusseldorf highway to Volkrath, where they would turn north, cross the Nord Canal and reach the Rhine near Bosinghoven. Hinds and Lt. Col.Clifton B. Batchelder stressed that they intended a fast-moving breakthrough operation. Both commanders wanted the tanks and infantry to move quickly and not get bogged down by defenders. During the night, Hinds talked to Col. G.A. West, division chief of staff, and asked if the division could arrange for the airborne divisions to schedule an attack on the east end of the Krefeld-Uerdingen Bridge, while he moved Combat Command B up to join forces with the paratroopers. The bridge was, according to Hinds, "like a sitting duck." However, the request was denied.

Possibly, nationalism or desires for personal aggrandizement figured in the decision. Simpson's Ninth Army was still under the operational control of Field Marshall Montgomery, who had planned the ill-executed airborne assault, MARKET GARDEN, at Arnhem. After the war, Hinds asked Lt. Gen. Robert F. Sink, who had helped him work out the problems of armor's linking with airborne troops at Fort Benning, if the airborne army really needed three weeks for planning a drop when they had done it in only two nights after work. Hinds vividly recalls the answer, "Nuts!" a good airborne expression.

Prior to the attack, Collier and Combat Command A thought that the most crucial area was around Juchen. It was a large bottleneck between Munchen-Gladbach and the Erft Canal, the logical place for a determined enemy to make a stand. Aerial photographs showed enemy anti-tank ditches and communications trenches across the high ground between the attackers and the Rhine River to the northeast. Besides a terrain analysis, the combat soldiers knew the enemy would be using buildings for defensive positions. The division personnel were reminded that the Germans marked their hospitals with a red square on a white circle. No troops were to attack buildings so marked.

The 2d Armored Division's attack began at 7:00A.M. on February 28, with Combat Command A on the left and Combat Command B on the right, paralleling the Erft River. It was to be a stop and start day, with a multitude of little villages taken, pockets of resistance overcome and some missed assignments. With Task Force Disney, the 1st Battalion, 67th Armored, leading Combat Command B's attack, the 2d Battalion "followed as if on a road march." The first settlement, Elfgen, was engulfed by a double envelopment, and the town, along with 111 prisoners, was secured by 8:25 A.M. Continuing east toward Elsen and Orken, they were intercepted by a German half-track crowded with infantry. The tanks of D Company, 67th Armored, raked it with .50 caliber machine gun fire. The advance then stalled when confronted with tank fire and dug-in infantry at Elsen. To remove this threat, B Company, 41st Armored Infantry Regiment, protected by the guns of D Company, 67th Armored Regiment, launched an attack to drive the enemy from the town. However, in the confusion of the battle, the infantry company commander missed his objective and instead cleared the nearby town of Orken. Meanwhile, a platoon from A Company, 41st Armored Infantry, and the tanks of D Company attacked Elsen, removing the enemy opposition, but not before the Germans destroyed two American medium tanks.

The tanks of G Company, 67th Armored, had thus far been following the attackers. Now moving toward Hemmerden, they drew direct fire from tanks or antitank guns and were delayed. The 2d Battalion of the 67th Armored, which had been following the assault waves, seized a crucial underpass west of Noithausen at 3:00 P.M. With A Company, 41st Armored Infantry, they attacked Hemmerden, which fell at 3:20 P.M. By this time, the spotty German resistance began to stiffen.

Meanwhile, the supply and maintenance section of A Company, 67th Armored, had a little battle of their own. The supply and fuel convoy was misdirected to Volkrath. On arrival, the platoon leader knocked on the door of a building he assumed was the headquarters of the 1st Battalion, 67th Armored Regiment. Six Germans answered the knock and promptly surrendered, while three others slipped out the back door. They were spotted by an alert staff sergeant, Walter G. Trusz, and in the ensuing fight one German was killed and two were wounded. Those at the front door made no effort to aid their countrymen. After the fight, the prisoners were placed on the hoods of the vehicles and taken to the rear.

Combat Command A attacked on the left of the division zone, with two task forces. Initially, Task Force A, commanded by Col. William M. Stokes, commanding officer, 66th Armored Regiment, led the advance, with Task Force B under Lt. Col. Hugh R. O'Farrell following. The column moved north from Garzweiler and made about 3,000 yards the first hour. D Company, 66th Armored, moving to take Priestrath, was accidentally fired on by Combat Command B, but captured the objective by

8:25 P.M.; it was the first of many small villages taken. The next serious threat to the column's advance was a railroad and overpass defended by dug-in infantry and antitank guns, plus a few tanks. However, the size of the attacking columns convinced the defenders to surrender without a fight. The civilians were then rounded up and held in the town, while the infantry searched the buildings for weapons and soldiers. While part of the column searched the houses, the remainder continued northward.

Task Force A continued its attack at 12:45, moving northeast toward Herberath. The advance was gaining some momentum, for by 4:40 P.M. three small villages had been captured. Outside of Wallrath the column began to receive 20mm antiaircraft artillery fire. The Americans quickly moved against the village, destroyed one gun and took 50 to 100 prisoners. In this small action, only one of many for the attackers, Lieutenant Culver was wounded. Infantry were riding on the back deck of his tanks. He had sent one scout ahead to check the side roads for German antitank guns or panzerfaust men. When his tank came to a hedge, he told the driver to go through it and then he felt a blinding yellow flash. Culver does not remember an explosion. He fell forward, hitting his head on the commander's hatch ring, deeply cutting his forehead. Blood was dripping over his gunner, who screamed that the tank had been hit and that Culver should get out so the crew could also. He tried to move but could not use his broken left arm. Finally the gunner pushed the tank commander out and the crew followed. The shell had hit the back deck, killing most of the infantrymen. Culver was evacuated to the aid station, then to the 48th Medical Battalion and to a hospital in England. After combing the area for stragglers and finding a hospital, the force consolidated on the north edge of the woods.

Major Herbert S. Long, commanding officer, 2d Battalion, 66th Armored Regiment, decided that now was the time to "hold the carrots in front of the jaded horses." The primary objective of Task Force A was the major road junction at Glehn. The battalion commander thought that it must be captured in spite of the approaching darkness. Without infantry support because there was not time to assemble them, he ordered A Company, 66th Armored Regiment, to attack and to cut the road between Glehn and Schlich. Just a few minutes before 7:00 P.M., the company commander, 1st Lt. John B. Roller, Jr., called to inform the battalion commander that the road was cut, that he had personally destroyed two bicyclists trying to flee Glehn and that he was working his way into the town.

While Roller was trying to enter the town, and he may have reached the outer edges, Major Long assembled E Company, 41st Armored Infantry, and sent them forward to support the tankers. Somehow the infantrymen got lost in the darkness and captured Scherfhausen, about 1,500 yards south of their target. However, during the night a combat infantry patrol and two tank destroyers entered Glehn and captured the bridge in the center of town which was needed for the next day's attack. To provide a ready reserve, the bulk of Task Force A was assembled in the open fields southeast of Schlich.

Task Force B followed Task Force A and, after passing through Juchen, was supposed to come abreast and to the left of it. Committed to battle at 12:30, Task Force B moved west of Juchen, turned north to attack Kelzenberg, which was cleared by 2:00. Next came a series of little towns: Wey, Hoppers and Nevenhoven, all secured by 4:30. The tankers captured seventy-five prisoners, who seemed to come out of the ground, waving their hands and wanting to be captured. Rapid progress indicated that the enemy line had been broken, but the terrain, softened by thawing snow and rain, slowed the advance. The attack continued northward. Schlich was captured by 8:30 P.M. despite the fact that G Company, 66th Armored, got lost in the dark and had difficulty finding the town. The task forces of Combat Command A assembled near Schlich, planning to renew their attack the following day to reach the Nord Canal.

Combat Command Reserve, commanded by Lt. Col. Russel W. Jenna, was to follow the advance of Combat Command A and to protect the division's left flank as the 29th Infantry Division moved toward Rheydt. While putting in a roadblock near Schaan, the reserve encountered bazooka and small arms fire. After a brief fight the Americans captured a 75mm self-propelled gun and twenty-one prisoners. Later, as the 29th Infantry Division moved alongside Combat Command R, the roadblock was manned by the infantrymen.

Moving quickly, the division had advanced about eight to ten miles by the end of the day. The artillery, in order to give prompt and close continuing support, leapfrogged its battalions forward. Some of the artillery units even had to fight to clear the enemy from their new areas before occupying them. The 78th Armored Artillery Battalion destroyed an 88mm gun by direct fire, while the 92d Armored Artillery Battalion overran and captured a four-gun 105mm battery. That night, February 28, White sent instructions to Hinds to use one battalion of the 331st Infantry Regiment to block possible counterattacks from Grevenbroich and to move the remainder of the regiment to positions from which they could capture Neuss. The two combat commands were to continue northward the next day, with Combat Command A seizing crossings over the Nord Canal by noon.

With only two hours' warning, Combat Command B started moving at 3:30, "barrelling down the highway to Volkrath, then turned north for Rockrath." At dawn, when the command began to draw enemy fire from Grefrath, the column deployed and returned the fire. At that time, the plan to attack Buttgen was suspended by Col. Paul A. Disney, commanding officer, 67th Armored Regiment, because a German counterattack from Kappellen toward Hemmerden posed a serious threat to the rear of the combat command and to the rear elements of the division. The air corps control officer, 1st Lt. Gerald P. Leibman, called for air support. Five flights of fighter-bombers broke up the tank assault and then attacked the woods near Birkhof, where they destroyed three more enemy tanks. Had the enemy waged a determined fight, it might have killed or captured General of the Army Dwight D. Eisenhower, who was visiting the Hell on Wheels command post at the time. Several tanks in the division's Maintenance Battalion were sent to repulse the attack, along with air corps fighter-bombers. After the fight, Eisenhower left the command post totally unaware of the danger.

After the German counterattack was repulsed, the 2d Battalion, 67th Armored, resumed its advance, drawing heavy fire from the woods west of Grefrath. Batchelder moved forward with three mortar half-tracks, but they were quickly destroyed. Pvts. Crawford Bragg and Melvin D. Gillespie stayed with their destroyed vehicle, manning the .50 caliber machine gun until enemy fire damaged it. They then started firing a .30 caliber machine gun until it too was destroyed and both men were wounded. They then removed the remaining .30 caliber machine gun and ammunition to a trench, where they continued to fire at the enemy. Finally, the 83d Infantry Division, which had by this time been committed to battle, rescued the two mortarmen. Though there were several witnesses, the men received only the Purple Heart for their part in the battle.

After the enemy had been stopped around Grefrath, the attack resumed to take Buttgen, despite enemy artillery and one Mark V tank. After clearing a path through the town, the column continued toward Holzbuttgen and the Nord Canal. Since reconnaissance units reported that the Germans had destroyed all the bridges in Combat Command B's zone, the engineers completed a forty-eight-foot treadway bridge over the canal by 5:20 P.M. The 2d Battalion of the 67th Armored Regiment crossed and assembled north of Kaarst, with the 1st Battalion following them.

On Combat Command B's right flank, the 331st Infantry Regimental Combat Team accomplished their assigned task of attacking and clearing Neuss. At noon the regiment was assigned to the 83d Infantry Division, which had been given the mission of capturing four bridges around Neuss and Oberkassel.

During the night of February 28, Combat Command A was ordered to proceed northward and seize crossings over the Nord Canal. As Task Force A moved from its assembly area near Schlich, it drew fire from the same tanks that had fired on Combat Command B from Weilerholfe and Buttgen. Weilerholfe, their first objective, was captured by 8:10 A.M. After fighter-bombers had destroyed three of the enemy tanks, the task force headed for the Nord Canal. Progressing about a quarter of a mile, the lead tanks of A Company, 66th Armored, and the infantry riding on them, came under 20mm antiaircraft artillery fire. The action of the Americans was aptly described by Maj. Cameron J. Warren, executive officer, 2d Battalion, 66th Armored. He reported that the enemy fire caused the "versatile M-24s to back up about as fast as they moved forward." For the next two hours artillery shelled the enemy who were delaying the task force's advance.

The German batteries, moreover, were not the only problem that A Company had that day. After leaving Weilerholfe, it was to capture Rottes. Somehow the company commander, 1st Lt. John B. Roller, Jr., started to assault the wrong town, Drisch. After learning of his mistake, he could not take corrective action because his radio had failed. Warren moved his tank to a position ahead of the others and motioned toward Rottes, but to no avail. Major Warren commented, "Not content with taking the objectives outlined, we have to go out of our way to take an extra town."

By 9:50 A.M., Task Force A began to draw fire from the bridge defense units at the Nord Canal. White wanted the combat command starting across by noon. After about 1½ hours of continuous but fruitless fire against the German defenders, a plan was devised to attack the bridge by a double envelopment. The bridge was crucial as it was considered the key to the task force's advance that day. Company A, 66th Armored Regiment, supported by infantry, attacked from the left while D Company, 66th Armored Regiment, attacked from the right. They captured the bridge intact and crossed with five minutes to spare.Once across, the attackers found four destroyed antitank guns, two Mark IV tanks, two 20mm antiaircraft guns, several machine guns and about twenty German soldiers waiting to surrender. After clearing the canal region, the column continued north to Osterath, which it overcame by 10:00 P.M. in spite of stiff opposition. After gaining about nine miles that day, the men got only a short rest.

At 7:00 A.M., Task Force B of Combat Command A attacked, hoping to seize a crossing over the Nord Canal by noon. Nearing the first objective, the road crossing at Kleinenbroich, the 3d Battalion, 66th Armored, used smoke for the first time. The German defenders were quickly captured and the advance moved through the woods near Eikerend, toward the crossroads to the northeast. From that location, they saw a German artillery column retreating to the north, parallel to their own route. The tankers spread out and fired on the Germans, hitting several vehicles. When a staff car started toward the bridge at sixty miles per hour, every weapon turned to fire at it. Just before reaching the bridge, it seemed to disintegrate.

The tankers reached the bridge, surprised the defenders and captured it intact. The engineers found that the Germans had explosives nearby, but they were not emplaced. The first vehicles crossed at 11:30 A.M. and continued the attack, while D Company, 66th Armored, and two squads of infantry from B Company, 41st Armored Infantry, remained on the south side of the canal to protect the bridge against possible counterattacks and to cut the main road to Munchen-Gladbach. To the north, the next town was Schiefbahn, which was to be captured by a double envelopment. The attack went smoothly and the town was in American hands by 5:00 P.M. After the town was secure, the soldiers seized the villages of Willich-Deppeskreuz. It took thirty minutes to eliminate the antitank fire from the two villages, but the tankers succeeded and rolled onward. By 10:00, Moosheide was taken and the day's gains were consolidated.

Early in the morning, Combat Command R was alerted for a possible German counterattack aimed at Hemmerden. Reconnaissance elements were sent to find suitable roads to the town. When air reconnaissance at 10:00 A.M. revealed no enemy, the alert was cancelled. At 12:30, Combat Command R was ordered to Kleinenbroich. It started moving, but soon rain limited visibility and made the soft ground even softer. Also the priority of movement, given to Combat Command A, forced the reserve to seek an alternate route. Shortly after starting, it had to stop for several hours and did not move again until about 4:00 P.M. When it did resume the advance and reached about 500 yards south of the Nord Canal, the reserve again had to pull off the road to permit artillery and supply vehicles to move forward to the assault echelons.

Part of Combat Command Reserve, Task Force Anderson, arrived at Schiefbahn in the late afternoon. Despite the fact that the town was in American hands, two company commanders were wounded by sniper fire. The task force prepared to resist possible German attacks. About 500 yards west of town, a platoon of infantry was posted to protect the tank destroyers. Company F, 66th Armored, and the 3d Platoon of G Company, 41st Armored Infantry, were sent south of town, while one platoon of F Company, 66th Armor, was to take positions to the west. However, it got lost and instead went north along the road to Willich. That proved to be a fortunate mistake; it may well have saved the platoon from annihilation.

Sometime between 5:30 and 7:00 that evening, a platoon leader reported to task force headquarters that the Germans were launching a strong counterattack with infantry supported by four or five Mark V tanks. The platoon leader reported that he could not find the American infantry which was supposed to be guarding the tanks of F Company. The tanks were eventually destroyed, but they slowed that part of the German attack by four to five hours. The last report that the headquarters received was that one man was alive and still firing all the tank guns.

At another roadblock, an inexperienced engineer officer was attacked. He pulled the roadblocking force back to the center of town, which permitted the Germans to approach with relative ease. By this time it was apparent that the German assault was not a single effort, but a series of attacks. The Americans could not yet determine where the bulk of the enemy was located.

Task Force Hawkins was alerted to move to the town to help repulse the approaching Germans. With its appearance, there were now elements of three task forces in the town and no unity of command. The Germans, an estimated infantry battalion supported by five or six tanks from the 130th Panzer Lehr Division, were trying to escape from the area around Munchen-Gladbach to the Rhine River. The German infantry was working closely with the German tanks. Entering the town, they reached the church serving as the command post of I Company, 41st Armored Infantry, before being pushed back. After a night of confused fighting, which ended about 4:00 A.M. on March 2, nine artillery battalions had fired in support of the defenders. However, the German artillery was also finding the range. The Germans pulled back after destroying five tanks and three half-tracks of I Company, 41st Armored Infantry. The Americans then regrouped without having lost an inch of ground. After dawn the task forces began to capture part of the enemy who had attacked Schiefbahn.

Because of stiffening resistance, the supply personnel were having difficulty reaching the assault troops. The supply route went through Schiefbahn, and while the attack was in progress the convoy pulled off the road to wait. Both ration trucks and a gas truck were destroyed. Company D, 41st Armored Infantry, received no fuel or ammunition until the following morning.

General Simpson decided to wait to see what the 2d Armored Division could do about crossing the Nord Canal before he shifted the boundary between the XIII and XIX Corps. However, he had taken the precaution of alerting both corps to a possible shift. This was important, for while the crossing of the canal won the battle, it was also important to inflict maximum losses on the enemy. Furthermore, there was also a possibility of capturing one of the Rhine River bridges intact. Simpson ordered the division to resume the attack during the night and to continue without stopping until they had a bridge or until all six spans (one at Neuss-Dusseldorf, one at Krefeld-Uerdingen and four from Duisburg northward) were destroyed. With those orders, White directed Combat Command A to cut the Krefeld-Uerdingen road, to block to the west and to continue the attack northward. Combat Command B, which was to get the 379th Infantry Regimental Combat Team from the 95th Infantry Division, was to attack and try to seize the Krefeld-Uerdingen Bridge.

At 1:30 A.M. on March 2, Combat Command A resumed its attack with Fischeln (inside the Krefeld city limits) as its objective. Companies E and F, 41st Armored Infantry Regiment, were to make their way up the Osterath-Krefeld road as far as possible, before tank elements were committed. Moving stealthily, the infantrymen captured some German sentries asleep at their posts and others asleep in their trenches. During the advance, the infantry battalion commander became concerned about his flanks and asked that a light tank platoon be assigned to the tail of each of his companies. However, about 4:00 A.M. Combat Command B entered Bovert, ending the concern about an exposed right flank. Twenty minutes later, reports were received that the infantry was in the southern part of Fischeln. At 6:02, they were reported to be one-third of the way through the town. Maj. Herbert Long, concerned about the slow progress, went into town to find the cause. He quickly saw that the infantrymen were doing a fine job, digging the Germans out of every basement and fire trench. He found that they had already taken about 200 prisoners, captured three self-propelled guns and ambushed four trucks loaded with troops. The final toll of 300 to 500 prisoners was accomplished with the loss of three Americans killed and eleven wounded.

Long sent A Company, 66th Armored, into Fischeln, following the 2d Battalion, 41st Armored Infantry. The tankers soon came under sniper and panzerfaust fire but reached the center of town. However, they could not advance further because of the "bowling alley," a 3,000-yard street into Krefeld with several German tanks parked on each side. Company E, 66th Armor, was committed with a platoon on each side of the road. Slowly, the German tanks began to pull back; by 11:45 A.M. the town had been cleared. Meanwhile, the 2d Battalion, 379th Infantry, was ordered to Fischeln to relieve the tankers, who became division reserve.

Task Force B, Combat Command A, assembled at Steinrath to aid Task Force A in its attack to capture Krefeld. While moving to the assembly area, they interrupted the attack of the 34th Tank Battalion of the 5th Armored Division. Gentlemanly, the 2d Armored held back to permit the Allies to continue their jobs. The men knew that the fight ahead would be a rough one, for the Germans might have hidden tanks behind every building. The Reconnaissance Company, 66th Armor, was assigned to the task force. One tank rounded a corner to find eight men of the Reconnaissance Company standing in front of a house with their hands raised in surrender. The tankers threw out smoke grenades, and in the confusion the prisoners escaped. The task force pulled back to regroup before starting again.

Pvt. Charles H. Coons, a rifleman in the Reconnaissance Company, 66th Armored Regiment, was helping clear Krefeld Oppum, when a burst of automatic weapons fire hit his squad leader and broke both his shoulders. The squad immediately scrambled for cover. Coons was unable to cross the open space to his wounded friend because of intense enemy fire. As darkness neared, he worked his way behind two enemy soldiers and killed them with a burst from his submachine gun. He carried the wounded corporal into a nearby house and gave him first aid. The enemy tossed a hand grenade into the room, but Coons threw it out before it exploded near an enemy machine gun crew. Again Coons fired with deadly effect. He then heard an enemy bazooka team maneuvering into position to fire at an American tank. For the third time he fired, killing three more Germans. Coons knew he had to get his corporal to aid, but he could not be moved without help. The area was still heavily infested with enemy soldiers. Hearing Germans enter the adjoining room, he pulled a rug over himself and the corporal, and they held their breath. The enemy was so close that the Americans could have reached out and touched them. After several anxious moments, the enemy left. The next morning, Coons found two civilians whom he forced to help carry the squad leader back to the aid station. He rejoined his squad later, at Vennikel, with yet another fight in progress.

Meeting increasing resistance, Task Force B moved through the 2d Battalion, 379th Infantry, to attack the road junction northwest of Bockum on the main Krefeld-Uerdingen highway. Although the area was heavily populated, the tankers were at the crossroads before they were aware of it. They cleared the road center and were then ordered to Viertelsheide. To capture that town, the tankers had to pass through an airfield near Verberg before heading north. Suddenly, they began to receive high-velocity direct fire from the area of their objective. They hid in ground depressions and made plans for sending infantry to scout the situation. Moments later, however, the commander of the 1st Battalion, 66th Armor, arrived with a medium tank company and an infantry company. The attacking mediums fired and moved in many directions at once; with this help the 2d Battalion, 379th Infantry, advanced and captured Vennikel and Berns. About this time, the 84th Infantry Division came alongside the left flank, firing on the 2d Armored Division, already under enemy fire. The task force went into defensive positions, permitting the 84th Infantry to pass and to stand as a defensive force while Combat Command B attempted one of its most spectacular efforts of the war.

On March 2, the first task of Combat Command Reserve was to secure Schiefbahn after the German attack. Two roadblocks were established and about thirty-five prisoners were taken. Other parts of the combat command reported the enemy had moved to the north after failing to capture the town. By midmorning, the Germans were no longer to be found and the flank was considered secure. Combat Command R was ordered to Willich to relieve Task Force B, Combat Command A, permitting that force to attack Krefeld-Oppum. With the relief of Combat Command R, their position was taken by the 82d Reconnaissance Battalion.

Task Force Hawkins of Combat Command R had an unusual experience. When it was preparing to follow Task Force B of Combat Command

A into the built-up area of Krefeld, a flight of P-47s circled the area for several minutes. The tankers had their aircraft panels displayed for identification purposes. Finally, the aircraft attacked, destroying a 155mm gun, killing an artillery battery commander and wounding several others. The planes carried British markings, but they lacked the characteristic bright luster of the P-47. Consequently, some witnesses suspected that the planes may have been rebuilt aircraft flown by German air force personnel. Regardless of this, at 3:45 the task force moved to the outskirts of Fischeln, where it came under the control of Combat Command B. It was ordered to attack and capture the southern edge of Bosinghoven. Occupying the town by 7:00, they were in position to participate in one of the war's biggest gambles.

On March 3, the final lines were drawn around the bridge at Uerdingen. Task Force Anderson (commanded now by Maj. Henry Zeien and later renamed for him) of Combat Command Reserve was attached to Combat Command A. It was to assist in capturing the small villages to the north of the Krefeld-Uerdingen road. Attacking in what the tankers called the "big-ass bird formation"—two platoons of tanks abreast (with infantry riding them), one platoon of tanks following, then a platoon of infantry in their half-tracks and the flank protected by tank destroyers—the force was to capture Kaldenhausen. Then came a maneuver which was "designed to confuse enemy and friendly troops." As Task Force Zeien started toward Kaldenhausen, a task force of Combat Command A was advancing to take Viertelsheide. They crossed one another's route without mishap.

After this confusion, the situation began to get serious for Zeien and his command. As they topped a rise in the ground, German 88mm fire hit two of the tanks. The infantry dismounted and began working their way forward to eliminate the antitank guns. They continued ahead but drew an increasingly heavy volume of fire. The Germans hit seven more tanks, igniting five. Fortunately, F Company, 66th Armored Regiment, which was down to six tanks, was replaced by I Company of the same regiment. The force dug in, planning to resume the attack the following morning.

Apparently every unit moving toward the Rhine had planned some gesture to show their contempt for the river. During the night of March 1, White called Hinds, giving him some information needed for coordination with nearby units. The most interesting portion of the message, intercepted and recorded because "this was division history in the making," said:

Div 6 (White) to CCB 6 (Hinds):
>   Want someone to throw a rock into that big ditch [Rhine]. It is very important.

CCB 6 to Div 6:
>   Yes. We will be close enough before daylight.

Div 6 to CCB 6:
>   Let us know as soon as you do. It will be quite a newsbreak for us. Understand?

CCB 6 to Div 6:
>   Will it be necessary to throw a rock into it?

Div 6 to CCB 6:
>   You can have someone peter easy easy in it, will be OK.

CCB 6 to Div 6:
>   OK. I'll peter easy easy in it myself.

Years later, Hinds, with a smile on his lips and a twinkle in his eye, proudly said, "I DID."

Sometime before midnight of March 1, Combat Command B's mission was changed. No longer was it to capture Neuss, but it was to attack northward in an attempt to capture the Uerdingen Bridge, cross the Rhine and seize a sizable bridgehead on the east bank. If successful, it would be a big step toward victory.

The concept first stunned and then stimulated the men, for "its very audacity lent it a promise of success in the face of a confused and beaten enemy." Achieving this goal would require round-the-clock assaults; the attackers could not be slowed by enemy action.

The advance, to accomplish perhaps the impossible, began at 12:20 A.M. on March 2 with the capture of Bovert and the nearby village of Ivansheide. Patrols were sent toward Strump where enemy tanks had been seen. After containing that town, the 1st Battalion, 67th Armor, with A Company, 41st Armored Infantry, continued northeastward toward Lank-Latum. The 2d Battalion, 67th Armor, moved on to Bosinghoven.

At the south end of Bovert, before the enemy retreated, there occurred one of those unusual events of war. Several tankers had been wounded and an ambulance crew ventured into the virtual no-man's-land to rescue them. As Pfc. Raymond Richardson was extracting the injured men from the tank, he was joined by "two bearded characters in gray-green uniforms, both of whom had pistols in their belts." Thinking that they wanted to surrender, Richardson reached for their weapons and almost had his arm broken. They helped him remove the wounded, place them on stretchers and carry them to the ambulance. Then the Germans drew their weapons, returned to their positions and resumed fighting. This was considered proof that not all Germans were brutal.

The attacks to clear Bosinghoven and Ossum met unexpectedly stiff resistance. Antitank and artillery fire from the woods between Bovert and the objective threatened to stop the column. Batchelder borrowed a tank company and sent it to the left flank with all its guns firing, but the Germans laid down a second smoke screen and escaped to the north. By a double envelopment, from the left and the right, the tanks entered the town, continuing to draw heavy fire. They reached the southern edge of Ossum, making some progress in clearing the left part of town, but enemy fire prevented movement on the right. Finally an infantry-tank attack carried the small village which had held the tankers up for several hours.

In spite of the determined enemy resistance, the men of the division were optimistic that the Uerdingen Bridge could be captured. At noon, division artillery was ordered to maintain harassing fire at both ends of the bridge to prevent German engineers from emplacing demolitions. At 4:35 P.M. White ordered the artillerymen to place a round on the enemy end of the bridge every thirty seconds, using VT fuzes. He told them he would be responsible for any overexpenditure of ammunition. Later in the evening, he ordered that a round be placed on both ends of the bridge and over the spans. The artillery battalions, besides firing in support of the attack, sank a ferryboat on the Rhine and destroyed two locomotives on the enemy side of the river. The 696th Armored Artillery Battalion, not to be outdone by the tankers or infantry, captured the town of Driest, along with three guns and about fifty prisoners.

The attack continued, and now tension and anticipation spread to XIX Corps. Gen. Raymond S. McLain stated that if the division secured the bridge, then the 379th Infantry Regiment was to remain attached and be sent across the river as quickly as the 95th Infantry Division could replace it. The infantry was to be followed by the bulk of Hinds's Combat Command B, while Combat Command A maintained roadblocks and then crossed to join Combat Command B. If the attempts were unsuccessful, then the infantry regiment would revert to the 95th Infantry Division and Combat Command A would continue to attack northward to the Rubrocks

Canal. Plans were made to attack the bridge at 2:00 A.M. on March 3, behind artillery fire and smoke. The men waited, anxiously hoping to capture one of the war's major prizes. If they could secure the bridge, then the heart of Germany would be opened to them.

While moving north on March 2, Hinds passed a company of DUKWs, amphibious 2½-ton trucks, which he wanted to use to sneak some infantry across the Rhine River as soon as the demolition wires were cut. He felt that an ''instantaneous sneak amphibious crossing before the slow-reacting guards were aware of what was happening'' would have been successful. He had also requested a paratrooper attack on the town of Mundelheim, on the east bank of the Rhine. Both the requests were refused. Supposedly, ''there was insufficient time to plan'' the airborne attack but the American Ninth Army was still under the tactical control of Montgomery's British Twenty-first Army Group. It is possible that the real reason for the refusal was that such plans did not fit into the fixed piece operations for which the field marshall was so famous. A first crossing by forces other than his own would rob him of glory and prestige. If that were correct, then the British were still disappointed, because Patton beat them across.

During the afternoon and evening, the attackers continued northward. The 1st Battalion, 67th Armored, attempting to move to Krefeld-Oppum, received intense antitank fire and could not move. Company G, 67th Armor, tried to flank the town on the left, but after moving 500 yards and losing two tanks, the effort stalled. The battalion's assault guns arrived and destroyed the enemy weapons, permitting the tankers to enter the town and clear it. After dark, the infantry arrived and defended the tanks while they refueled and planned to continue the attack.

That night Combat Command B launched a night attack to cut the road between Krefeld and Uerdingen. However, instead of now being in position to attack the bridge, the Americans first had to clear the built-up area on either side of the road. On the south flank, the combat command reached the approaches to the bridge about 8:00 A.M. On the north side, however, resistance mounted as three or four understrength battalions of the German First Parachute Army arrived at exactly the crucial moment to strengthen the defenses. Had they arrived only one hour later, the results might have been dramatically different. They were, according to Hinds, ''fine, young, Dutch SS men'' who fought tenaciously. The mission of clearing the north side of the bridge was given to the 1st Battalion, 379th

Infantry. It was a laborious, time-consuming process; the Germans defended from houses, pillboxes and dug-in positions which had to be individually eliminated. Finally, by 5:30 P.M. the approaches were clear.

The bridge was about 65 feet wide and 1,640 feet long, including the approaches, with a main span of 820 feet. Its road base was of asphalt, tar or some other flammable substance. When Hinds was notified that the approaches were clear, he quickly ordered K Company of the 379th Infantry across. He hoped that the infantry could capture the guards at the far end, while the engineers followed to remove the demolitions which were supposed to be buried in mine chambers on the west side of the river. The infantrymen had made about 100 yards and were actually over the water when they discovered the roadbed was impassable for tanks. They withdrew, securing the western end of the bridge.

While the infantry waited, an explosion rocked the bridge sometime between 8:00 and 8:30 P.M. Hinds immediately sent a patrol across to determine if the bridge were still suitable for infantry. At the west end, the explosion had dug a crater thirteen feet wide which prevented tanks' crossing to aid a renewed infantry assault. Hinds talked with Capt. George L. Youngblood, D Company, 17th Engineer Battalion, and told him to select his own men to check the bridge for demolitions and to cut every wire they could find. The thirteen volunteers advanced cautiously but found no explosives. Throughout the cloudy, moonless night, the patrol traveled on, reaching a point over dry land at the eastern end where a fire prevented their going any further. About 11:30 P.M., they reported back, confirming that the bridge was stable enough to support an infantry charge.

Hinds called division headquarters and talked to the chief of staff, Colonel G. A. West, telling him that he was about to order a battalion of troops across the bridge. West called Brigadier General I. D. White to report the conversation. White thought it was too late and he did not want to "sacrifice anything in vain." White feared having any troops caught on the bridge during daylight hours. However, he concluded that since Hinds was on the scene he knew the situation better. He added, "Tell him [Hinds] that I will back up his decision to the limit."

The decision was to send the 2d Battalion, 379th Infantry Regiment, and two companies of the 41st Armored Infantry Regiment across the bridge at 3:45 A.M. The armored infantrymen failed to arrive on time, so Hinds decided to send the 2d Battalion across alone. However, he let the battalion commander decide whether to send an advance patrol across first. A six-man patrol ventured across the bridge almost to the point Youngblood had reached and reported back that the explosion had left the bridge unusable even for foot troops. The mission was cancelled by the 379th Infantry regimental commander. At 7:00 A.M., the Germans decided the issue by destroying the bridge. The Germans had either replanted the charges or had moved two or three trucks loaded with explosives onto the span and detonated them. On March 4, White gathered all nineteen men of the patrols at division headquarters, where he pinned Silver Stars on them. Not one man of the two patrols had even been wounded, in spite of having been subjected to intense artillery fire.

With the bridge literally destroyed in their faces, the division spent March 4 clearing their zone of enemy remnants. The next day, they were relieved of this duty by elements of the 95th Infantry Division. For the next three weeks most of the men underwent a period of rest, vehicle maintenance and training. Ironically, Hell on Wheels established its headquarters in the very building in which Field Marshall Walther Model, commander of German Army Group B, planned the Battle of the Bulge.

During this time of rest and maintenance, the men had daily recreation in the form of movies and softball and baseball games. Apparently some members of the 82d Reconnaissance Battalion thought that the ball games were too tame, for one night seven men commandeered two jeeps and began crashing through roadblocks and shooting up the area. The spree, which lasted about eight hours, and was reported to corps headquarters, had apparently begun with a drinking session. The matter was turned over to the inspector general for his consideration.

The citizens of Hasselt, Belgium, decided to honor the 2d Armored Division for liberating them. On March 24-25, Major General I. D. White, representing the division, received a green silk flag from the people as a token of their appreciation. Today, the flag is proudly displayed in the Hell on Wheels Museum at Fort Hood, Texas. In telling Harmon of the ceremony, White wrote, "There is no doubt about the 2d Armored's being the U.S. Army as far as they are concerned." All elements of the division were represented. The honor guard from A Company, 82d Reconnaissance Battalion, was the first American unit to enter the town.

The Cologne Plain attack, or Operation GRENADE, was a success by any standard; the enemy suffered about 900 killed and 2,500 prisoners, with 37 tanks destroyed or captured, along with 225 guns. About 150

Above: The Adolf Hitler Bridge destroyed in the face of the 2d Armored Division.
Below (L to R): Col. Sidney R. Hinds, Brig. Gen. John H. Collier and Col. Gustavus A. West receive the croix de guerre.

German towns were liberated over an area of about 140 square miles. To accomplish this, the 2d Armored lost 90 killed (including the attached units), 286 wounded or injured, with 38 missing.

The attack was directed against the Rhine River. Apparently Montgomery, when planning the attack, failed to consider two possibilities. First, if the bridges over the Rhine had been destroyed before the attack, then a sizable portion of the German army would have been defeated west of the river. When it became apparent that the Adolph Hitler Bridge could be captured by "Roosevelt's Butchers," no encouragement was forthcoming from anyone except the senior American commanders. Simpson and Hinds agreed that the operations stopped on the wrong side of the river. Whether seizing the bridge would have hastened the end of the conflict is a matter of speculation, but the Ninth Army was now positioned to attack the heart of the industrial Ruhr, the main source of German war materials.

Chapter 19

THE RACE FOR BERLIN

In the latter part of March, 1945, the Allies were on the Rhine River, the last major barrier to an uninterrupted advance to the interior of Germany. Considering the zones of attack, the American Ninth Army was in position to move almost directly eastward and seize the biggest prize of the war—Berlin. Within the Ninth Army, the XIX Corps had the most direct route to the German capital. Spearheading the attack of XIX Corps was, as usual, the 2d Armored Division. The advance was to be conducted in several phases: surrounding the Ruhr, attacking through the Teutoburger Wald, moving to cross the Elbe River, and entering Berlin.

SHAEF (Supreme Headquarters Allied Expeditionary Force) planners felt that Berlin was too far from Normandy. They wanted the major American efforts directed at the heart of Germany. According to their thinking, the goal should be the Ruhr industrial area: a small triangle of some thirty-five miles along the Rhine River, from Wesel to Dusseldorf, and extending nearly sixty miles inland. The land between the Lippe and Ruhr Rivers covered approximately 6,000 square miles and contained 2,500 factories, as well as iron and coal mines—the basis of the German

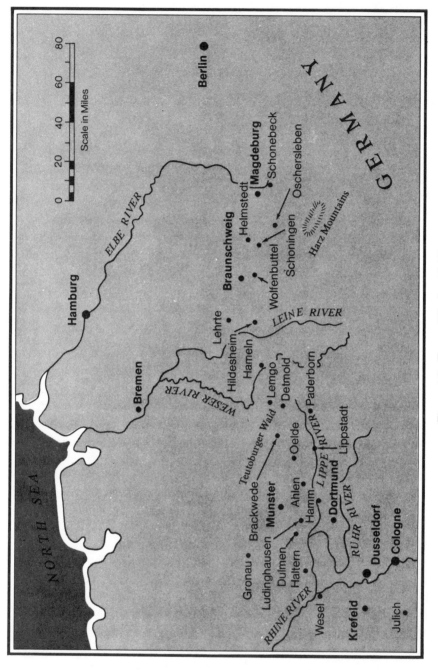

Figure 10. Toward Berlin, 1945.

steel, synthetic oil and chemical industries. The capture of the Ruhr, the foundation of the German war machine, would force the Nazis out of the war. To remove the Ruhr from German control was the final phase of Operation OVERLORD.

Elements of Ninth Army crossed the Rhine on March 24, 1945. That same day, Company E of the 17th Armored Engineer Battalion fulfilled one of Gen. George S. Patton's prophecies by building a 1,152-foot treadway bridge in seven hours, eight hours ahead of schedule. In two days the assault forces created a bridgehead twenty-five miles in length and six miles deep. Beginning at 1:00 A.M. on March 28, the 2d Armored was ordered to cross the Rhine on two bridges, pass through elements of the 30th Infantry Division and cross the Lippe River. There they were to move through the 17th Airborne Division and turn eastward, exploiting the breakthrough created by the XVIII Airborne Corps. White concluded Field Order Number 4 with the warning that the division was to be prepared to continue to "advance on Berlin generally along the autobahn."

For some unexplained reason, plans were suddenly changed and the attack delayed until 6:00 A.M. on March 30. Combat Command A was to cut communications routes east of Hamm and to secure crossings over the Dortmund-Ems Canal, while on the south flank Combat Command B was to attack toward Beckum, seizing the crucial roadnet in that area. Reconnaissance patrols were to scout along the autobahn, after which the commands were to advance toward Berlin. Prior to crossing the Rhine, the division G-3, Lt. Col. Briard P. Johnson, drew plans for the attack on the German capital. The enthusiasm for the assault filtered down to the men. They attacked with more spirit and energy than in any previous action. The men were well aware that this campaign might be the finale of the long, bitter war.

Moving to their attack positions near the Haltern-Dulmen line, the division had an experience which fully showed that the enemy was in disarray. Lt. Col. Wheeler Merriam, commanding officer, 82d Reconnaissance Battalion, had stopped alongside a railroad track to report his position, when a German train passed his location. He reported that fact to White who called the 92d Armored Artillery. The American salvos quickly cut the train in half. The stunned prisoners believed that the enemy was still on the west bank. They had no idea that the Americans were on the east bank, much less that they had gained so much territory.

About 9:00 P.M. on March 29, Brig. Gen. Sidney R. Hinds started his reconnaissance elements eastward. They met resistance about seven miles east of Haltern and about two miles west of Ludinghausen on the Dortmund-Ems Canal. After making contact with the enemy, Combat Command B separated into two columns and moved to clear the resistance it had met. Scouts found a bridge still standing over the canal, and D Company, 17th Armored Engineers, was sent to secure it. Just as the engineers arrived, the Germans destroyed the bridge, injuring several men. The scouts immediately began looking for any other spans not destroyed. The reconnaissance elements found two underpasses blocked by oil drums filled with dirt and defended by infantry, artillery and anti-tank guns. After a stiff but brief fight, the tunnels were secured and the combat command passed under the Dortmund-Ems Canal, saving valuable time. Once across, the area was cleared of resistance, and a bridge was constructed and in operation by 5:30. The attackers refueled, resupplied and rolled onward.

The division began its now traditional round-the-clock attacks. The tankers met the first determined resistance at Herbern, defended by about 200 dug-in infantry, supported by antitank weapons. The 1st Battalion, 67th Armor, and the 3d Battalion, 41st Armored Infantry, deployed and took the defenders under fire. As the infantrymen started forward, they were pinned down by small arms fire. Colonel Batchelder went forward, reorganized the stalled troops and resumed the advance "with more caution and considerably less speed." The defenders were routed by mortar fire, which killed fifty Germans and caused another ninety to surrender. These casualties were officer candidate school cadets who "were well on the way to commissions until the mortars delivered their valedictory."

After this brief but bitter fight, which characterized the advance, the Americans continued their attack. Nearing Ahlen, the column was met by a civilian delegation which surrendered the town to the 2d Armored, for it was a hospital town garrisoned by about 3,000 patients and their medical attendants. As German police guided the column through the streets, many of the townspeople stood and cheered. For them, the war was over.

Outside Ahlen, Combat Command B's assault troops paused to refuel and eat. While having dinner at a gasthaus in Ahlen, someone at the table suggested that Hinds call ahead to make reservations at Beckum. The communications officer somehow managed to get the German commander on the phone and the prisoner-of-war interrogator demanded that the town surrender in the name of humanity. The entire staff table was roaring with laughter because they thought it was an act for the evening's entertainment. Hinds's offer was refused, so he told the German commander that his men and tanks would be on the edge of Beckum at midnight. If one shot were fired, then the town would be leveled. To fulfill his promise but not having intended to move so quickly, Hinds now had to get Combat Command B to Beckum. When the command arrived and entered the town, it found that the German military had pulled out and left the civilians to their fate. The act of "bravado," as Hinds said, "and a sort of enjoying the war attitude" enabled the combat command to execute a classic double envelopment, which may have contributed to shortening the war by many days.

Meanwhile outside of Ahlen, as the threats were being exchanged, a German troop train was passing through the town trying to escape eastward. While the military police platoon was eating at the depot, the train pulled in and for a few moments confusion reigned supreme. The military police fired at the cars, while the Germans tried to lower their 20mm antiaircraft weapons to fire at the Americans. Nearby, two batteries of the 92d Armored Artillery faced in the opposite direction. The cannoneers immediately turned their vehicles around to bring the 105mm howitzers to bear on the train. One gunner was so surprised at the train's presence that he missed his first two shots. The artillery quickly found the range and destroyed the train. After capturing the Germans, the Americans found that the train was carrying over a million antipersonnel mines.

At 1:50 A.M. on April 1, Hinds was ordered to change the direction of the main attack and move to Lippstadt. There he was to intercept a strong enemy force trying to escape from the Ruhr. The combat command's right column had become entangled in stiff resistance after moving through Beckum; the left column had been ordered to move to secure passes through the Teutoburger Wald. The left column changed directions and objectives and overran all enemy opposition heading for Lippstadt. The attack went slowly during the night but gained speed in the day.

Just as the 3d Battalion, 41st Armored Infantry, arrived, a large German column was attempting to break out of the trap. Lt. Col. Arthur J. Anderson, the battalion commander, asked Hinds for reinforcements and was told that "he was the reinforcements and to lay it on them." Hinds confessed that he then held his breath for a while. Realizing the tremendous significance of Lippstadt, during the heavy fighting Gen. Raymond S. McLain, XIX Corps commander, arrived to verify that Combat Command B had reached its objective. The corps commander felt that he had

American tankers roll through captured Ahlen, while German civilians line the streets.

to verify personally Combat Command B's arrival before he reported it to Ninth Army headquarters. Hinds then committed "his reserve," his own tank and armored car, to escort the corps commander back about five miles to a place of some safety. At 3:45 P.M., after repulsing several German escape attempts, the 2d and 3d Armored Divisions joined hands at Lippstadt, sealing the Ruhr pocket and trapping some 350,000 Germans, more than the Russians had captured at Stalingrad. Sealing the pocket also denied the Germans huge quantities of munitions. With the arrival of the 3d Armored Division came word that its commander, Maj. Gen. Maurice Rose, a former Hell-on-Wheeler, had been killed outside Paderborn, while leading his column.

The linkup, on Easter Sunday, also April Fool's Day, brought a few minutes' respite, but soon the 2d Armored was relieved by elements of the 30th Infantry Division. The tankers turned their attention to the east where they had to get through the Teutoburger Wald to enter the German plain. The first effort was at the pass near Haustebeck, where the 2d Battalion, 67th Armored Regiment, encountered stiff resistance. It attempted to move north to the pass near Detmold, which was defended by about 200 troops from the German tank school at the town. The terrain was such that the road could easily be defended and could not be bypassed. The tanks and tank destroyers tried until dark to force the roadblock but were unsuccessful.

Combat Command A had a totally different and distinct mission from that of Combat Command B. Gen. John H. Collier and his men were to secure crossings over the Dortmund-Ems Canal and then to cut the communications links east of Hamm. Afterwards they were to be prepared to continue the attack eastward for Berlin. Collier's command made good time until he found that the bridges over the canal had been destroyed. The leading infantry from G Company, 377th Infantry Regiment, 95th Infantry Division, quickly found a barge which they turned sideways and used as a temporary bridge. Enemy machine guns opened fire on the men trying to establish the 800-yard-deep bridgehead, but the mortars of the 2d Armored Division quickly silenced the defenders. The engineers came forward and built a treadway bridge for the tanks and other vehicles. Once across, they continued the attack eastward. The southern task force, Task Force A, moved north and crossed the bridge. After clearing the Dortmund-Ems Canal, Task Force A continued to gain ground against intermittent small arms fire and over poor roads. By nightfall, the task force had made some thirty miles against sporadic resistance.

At Rinkerode, they encountered some Hitler Jugend [Hitler youth organization to train and indoctrinate German youth in Nazism, mobilized in the later phase of the war] who appeared to be between fourteen and seventeen years old. After a stiff fight and losing one tank to panzerfaust fire, the men cut the Hamm-Munster railroad and then the Cologne-Berlin autobahn near Oelde by 7:15 P.M. Ahead lay the Teutoburger Wald.

Task Force B resumed its march, halting near Ascheberg to refuel and to permit the men a hasty meal. After resuming, they encountered an enemy column and destroyed it in a sharp fight. The Germans began to slow the advance with well-prepared roadblocks defended by dug-in infantry, but the Americans reached Drensteinfurt about dawn. As the lead vehicle neared the town, it was destroyed by enemy fire and the column quickly deployed for a double envelopment. The fight began about 9:00 A.M. and by 10:00 the civilians were beginning to show white flags. The defenders, however, were officer candidates and were less willing to surrender. During the battle some of the buildings were set on fire, forcing the defenders to flee to the nearby woods, where they were either killed or captured.

After securing the town, the column continued eastward against spotty opposition which was largely bypassed for the following infantry to clear. Near Oelde, the tankers fired on an eastward-bound train, destroying the locomotive and two lead cars. More than fifty soldiers tried to escape, but they were rounded up and the undamaged cars immobilized. That night the task force stopped for a few hours near Stromberg, some twenty miles east of Drensteinfurt. The Teutoburger Wald lay ahead.

The most direct route to Berlin was through the Teutoburger Wald, a heavily wooded and relatively uninhabited low mountain range that resembled the terrain of the eastern Ardennes. Since ancient times it had served as an effective barrier against invading armies. In 9 A.D., the German chieftain Arminius led his hoards against three Roman legions—the XVIIth, the XVIIIth and the XIXth—and defeated them. If the division were superstitious (for they were a part of the XIX Corps), they did not show it.

On the same day that Combat Command B was linking up with the 3d Armored Division at Lippstadt, Combat Command A was attacking in three columns to secure three passes through the Teutoburger Wald—the first natural barrier encountered by the division since crossing the Dortmund-Ems Canal. The columns were Task Forces A, B and R. Near Oelde, Collier divided Task Force A, creating Task Force Warren, composed of D Company, 66th Armored Regiment; E Company, 377th Infantry Regiment; A Battery, 65th Armored Artillery Battalion; and a section of A Company, 702d Tank Destroyer Battalion. Task Force Warren was to secure the north pass through the Teutoburger Wald, to prevent the Germans from defending the defile and to block the escape of the Germans trapped in the Ruhr pocket. The Americans moved out at 6:10 P.M., barrelling down the autobahn as fast as the tank could move, bypassing a large enemy force at Brackwede. The column held its fire to achieve maximum surprise, and many enemy vehicles moved half the length of the column before realizing that it was a hostile force. Some German soldiers even tried to hitch rides on the tanks. The speeding Americans also passed civilian cars, even a horse and buggy in which two German soldiers were riding with a girl. They also went through an underpass while a three-car German reconnaissance unit passed overhead. Coming upon a roadblock after dark, three men of the force were told by the German sergeant in charge to be alert because the Americans were heading in their direction. The men of Task Force Warren realized that they were achieving the desired surprise. The German who had issued the warning was killed before he could alert his forces.

The rapid advance ended about 8:00 P.M., near Wilhelmsdorf, when intense panzerfaust fire stopped the column. The armored vehicles moved off the road while the infantrymen worked their way forward to clear a 2½-mile stretch of highway. By early morning, Task Force Warren had reached the foothills of the Teutoburger Wald, and later that morning they attacked Lamershagen. The enemy resisted with all types of weapons. The terrain was such that the tanks could not give protective fire to the infantrymen, who finally cleared the town after bitter house-to-house fighting.

To take full advantage of the shock and surprise generated by Warren's advance, Collier created a second special task force, Task Force Zeien. It was to pass through Warren and secure crossings over the Weser River about forty miles east of the Teutoburger Wald. Yet because of the determined resistance met by Warren and the other two task forces, Zeien's scheduled attack was delayed.

The center pass through the Teutoburger Wald in Combat Command A's zone was through the town of Oerlinghausen. Attacking at 8:30 A.M. from positions near Oelde, Task Force R moved eastward, securing Schloss Holte by 3:00 P.M. A few miles to the northeast, they entered the villages of Dalbke and Lipperreihe without a fight. The approaches to

Oerlinghausen were heavily wooded and when the force reached a point about 100 yards from the town, they found that it was defended by heavy machine guns and 20mm antiaircraft fire. They managed to clear the pass west of town, but panzerfaust and automatic weapons fire kept the men out of the town itself. Forward movement stopped until darkness, when I Company, 377th Infantry Regiment, circled four miles to reach the south edge of town. At dawn, three infantry companies attacked. The enemy infantry (reported to be a combat team of former paratroopers) maintained their determined stand, fighting from each house and basement until late in the evening.

The next day the Germans launched two counterattacks which twice forced the American infantrymen out of town. Finally, the task force tanks slipped around and cut the Lage road, threatening the enemy's rear. By 8:30 P.M. the village was secured and the task force was relieved by elements of the 117th Infantry Regiment, 30th Infantry Division. On April 4, Task Force R followed Task Force A to Lage, acting now as Combat Command A reserve.

Task Force B was assigned the south pass, the road leading to Detmold and Augustdorf. Attacking at 3:15 A.M., April 1, they made approximately five miles before meeting enemy resistance at Stukenbrock. After scattering the small delaying force, they moved about two more miles before ambushing a German supply convoy passing through Rietberg. F Company, 377th Infantry Regiment, entered the town and captured a German supply column which was loaded with gasoline and rations. By 2:00 P.M., Rietberg was secured and the attack continued eastward. Three hours later the Americans were stopped by fire from Augustdorf (17 miles north of Rietberg) and from the woods surrounding the approaches to the town. Attacking with infantry, the task force entered the western edge of the city by 9:30 P.M. After fighting all night on April 1, the infantrymen cleared the houses of defenders. However, when attempting to continue their advance, they encountered stiff opposition from dug-in infantry, tanks and antitank fire at the northeast edge of town.

At 7:00 A.M., April 2, the Germans launched a counterattack which was turned back. They attacked again at 10:00, with an estimated battalion. By using artillery fire, which burst at tree-top height, Task Force B inflicted heavy losses and repulsed the second assault. Because it was now apparent that getting through the Teutoburger Wald was an infantry task, the 119th Infantry Regiment of the 30th Infantry Division was assigned to the combat command. By the end of April 3, all the enemy had been cleared from the pass, except for those still holding out in Pivitsheide. On April 4, Task Force B broke through the pass onto the German plain, capturing Detmold by 6:30 P.M.

Task Force A had been slowed by the destroyed bridges on the Berlin-Cologne autobahn and had overcome heavy resistance from dug-in infantry and panzerfausts at Lamershagen and Wilhelmsdorf. After those bitter firefights, they were placed in combat command reserve until 1:00 P.M. on April 3, when they were committed to move against Lage and Lemgo. Lage was captured with little resistance. Lt. Col. Hugh O'Farrell moved his task force to positions for the assault on Lemgo. Suddenly the burgomaster came out to ask if the town would be given an opportunity to surrender. O'Farrell gave him thirty minutes to persuade the defenders to cease hostilities; after that, he would subject the town to an artillery barrage prior to sending the tanks and infantry forward. The time passed; O'Farrell waited an additional five minutes, but there was no hint of surrender. O'Farrell then ordered the promised attack. After taking the village, the Americans found that the burgomaster had been hanged by the fanatical SS defenders. Some twenty-five years later, the burgomaster's son contacted the Department of the Army, asking for aid in locating the commander of the task force which captured Lemgo. The department located O'Farrell, who wrote the son that his father had been acting in the best interests of his town and humanity and was certainly no traitor. As a memorial, the town named its new elementary school after the dead burgomaster.

The task force secured the town and in the process liberated a large winery, where "everybody got stinkin' drunk": Germans, Russians, Poles (freed prisoners) and Americans. While the attack troops took the winery, the 142d Signal Company captured a supply depot containing mainly office supplies but also a welcome bonus: officers' liquor supplies. For about an hour, according to Sgt. Russell S. Lamison, the officers and men played tug-of-liquor-cases, with each man trying for a favorite. Finally the military police placed the area off limits; for days afterwards the Signal Company was a "well-oiled unit." Smiling now, Lamison adds, "Had there been an attack the first evening, we might have lost the war." After sobering the men, Task Force A raced thirty miles to secure crossings over the Weser River near Hameln, of Pied Piper fame. Now the tune was being played by the Hell-on-Wheelers, musicians of Mars.

After capturing Lippstadt, Combat Command B was ordered to turn its attention to the passes through the Teutoburger Wald, south of Combat

Command A's area. The 2d Battalion, 67th Armored Regiment, eliminated the resistance at Waldburch after a brisk fight. Overcoming more opposition at Hustenbeck, they continued the advance for Detmold. The stiffest opposition of the day was at Hiddesen, where SS and dismounted panzer forces fanatically defended a roadblock. The enemy defenders prevented any advance during daylight. That night the 120th Infantry Regiment, 30th Infantry Division, replaced the tankers who then moved south to take advantage of the recently secured pass at Berlebeck. A small task force was sent to attack the Germans at Detmold in the rear, while the bulk of Combat Command B continued its movement.

Movement through the Berlebeck Forest was slow, primarily because of roadblocks covered by infantry manning automatic weapons and panzerfausts. However, after creeping through the forest, the men secured the town of Berlebeck by 7:00 in the evening. Reconnaissance elements pushed onward to Fromhausen, where they encountered strong small arms and automatic weapons fire. Due to the approaching darkness, the attack was delayed until the following day, when Fromhausen was taken by 3:00 P.M. With it secured, the division had broken through the last terrain obstacle for an approach to the Elbe River and ultimately Berlin.

After crashing through the forest, the next town was Bad Meinberg, which surrendered after 1st Lt. Arthur Hadley and his famous "talking tank" went into action. Hadley was a psychological warfare officer who had mounted a loudspeaker on his tank which broadcast surrender appeals to townsmen and soldiers alike. One day some tankers asked him to what he attributed his success. His reply: "I just have that uninhibited, repulsive Yale charm which, coupled with a magnetic and very irritating voice, drives them to surrender to shut me up." Whatever the reason, Hadley convinced several towns to surrender, speeding the division's advance.

On April 4, General Simpson, commanding general, Ninth Army (now controlled by the American Twelfth Army Group) detailed future plans. Part of Ninth Army was to eliminate the Ruhr pocket, while the bulk of the army was to advance rapidly eastward, maintaining contact with the British Twenty-first Army Group. Those forces moving eastward were to "exploit any opportunity for seizing a bridgehead over the ELBE River and be prepared to continue the advance to the east on BERLIN, or to the northeast."

Once through the Teutoburger Wald, the division headed east in full accord with the commander's directives. The men had sensed that the collapse of Germany was imminent after crossing the Rhine. Now, moving onto the German plain, they only wondered when that collapse would occur. On the afternoon of April 4, Combat Command A reached the Weser River, with Combat Command B pulling alongside it the next day. By about 4:00 A.M. on April 5, reconnaissance units of Combat Command A neared the vehicular bridge over the Weser at Hameln. When the lead vehicle was about thirty to forty yards from it, someone dashed from a nearby house, fired several shots, and the bridge was destroyed. The railroad bridge to the south met the same fate. Aerial reconnaissance showed that all bridges in the division's zone had been destroyed. At 10:00 A.M., Collier ordered the 119th Infantry Regiment to cross the river in assault boats and to secure a bridgehead near Ohr. The engineers quickly built a 384-foot bridge and Task Force B started across by 3:40 that afternoon. On the west bank of the river, while part of the combat command cleared the zone of enemy opposition, the bridgehead was quickly enlarged to about three miles deep and four miles long.

Most of Combat Command A crossed the Weser River on April 5. They were at first given the mission to clear the eastern part of Hameln, but unexpectedly were ordered to seize Eldgasen. The command started moving about noon. South of Dorpe, the 14th Armored Artillery Battalion bogged down on a gravel road. Meanwhile the main body had come under savage fire while moving through a narrow pass. Instead of trying to force the enemy out during the failing light, they decided to coil for the night.

The following morning the attack resumed at 2:00 A.M., with the immediate capture of Eldgasen and the rapid seizure of several other little villages. Twelve hours later, they captured a bridge over the Leine River north of Sarstedt. When the tanks and their infantry passengers from E Company, 119th Infantry Regiment, started across, someone spotted a burning fuze which was attached to about 1,200 pounds of explosives; the tank commander told the infantrymen to cut the wire. Sgt. Wilhelm O. Jordan leaped from the tank and instinctively jerked out the fuze. Simultaneously the sensitive detonating cap exploded in his hand, blowing off two fingers. The sergeant's heroic action saved many lives as well as the bridge. Thereafter, the attack continued until the fall of Sarstedt at 5:15 P.M.

Having broken through the Teutoburger Wald, Combat Command B headed for the Weser River. Passing through Bad Meinberg without opposition, they stopped southwest of Blomberg to resupply the tanks.

The infantry moved into the town and quickly captured it. The task force planned to attack Bad Pyrmont from three directions, but the initial vigorous resistance faded as artillery shelled the positions which had been hastily prepared in a potato field. Later, when asked why the defenders did not fight from within the buildings, the burgomaster said that he chased them out of town—''if they wanted to get a last minute Iron Cross they could do it in the potato field, not in his burg.''

After the unopposed entry into Bad Pyrmont, the advance to the Weser River continued. Air corps reconnaissance reported that no enemy could be located along the route of attack, but all the bridges had been destroyed. Part of Hinds's command had moved to Ohr and crossed on the bridge built by Combat Command A. The next day, most of the combat command crossed the river, resuming the attack eastward at 6:00 A.M. They made excellent progress against scattered resistance until they came to the Leine River. Crossing at Gronau about 10:30 A.M., they continued eastward to Bartelde, where they turned northeast to capture a pass through the Diekholzen Forest.

The 1st Battalion, 41st Armored Infantry Regiment, crossed the Innerste River, cut the roads east of Hildesheim and effectively isolated that town. The 67th Armored Regiment encountered dug-in infantry and panzerfausts which delayed the column for several hours. After driving the enemy back, the column continued its movement, securing a crossing over the Innerste River south of Hildesheim. The 1st Battalion, 67th Armored, also moved to take the city and cut the roads to the east. Hadley and his talking tank were with them. He moved to the edge of town, warning that 100 dive-bombers would attack if the Germans failed to surrender. While many Germans were surrendering to the tank, a flight of German fighter-bombers suddenly appeared and seemed to stiffen the fading German morale. Hadley, not to be outdone, told the prisoners that he would be back for them and fought his way back to American lines. Later, the 1st Battalion, 67th Armored Regiment, moved back into the city and secured it.

White was ordered to suspend offensive operations at 6:00 P.M. and to prepare to meet possible counterattacks from the east or north. The halt permitted other armies to come abreast of the Ninth Army, which at that time was spearheading the drive across Germany.

On April 8, a day of rest and maintenance, the division made limited objective attacks to secure better positions for resuming the advance eastward. Combat Command B secured the pass near Bodenstein and a crossing over the Innerste near Baddekenstedt. A small force of Combat

Command A was ordered to secure a bridge site over the Zweigcanal west of Harsum. Attacking at 4:30 P.M., the supporting artillery was firing a time-on-target, when the civilians ran up white flags. The town was quickly secured and the engineers began building a bridge to aid the command's attack to Lehrte the next morning. This assault was to support the 5th Armored Division's attack on Hannover.

At 7:00 A.M. on April 9, Combat Command A attacked to protect the flanks of the 5th Armored Division. North of Hildesheim, it overran an airfield, capturing eighty-three damaged planes. At Gretenberg, General McLain cancelled the support mission, because the 5th Armored Division was moving across Combat Command A's front. Near 5:00 that afternoon, Collier's men were relieved by the 125th Cavalry Group and moved to assembly areas to prepare for the planned attack eastward.

When the drive through Germany resumed, the 2d Armored was to secure a bridgehead across the Elbe River (more than 100 miles east of its current position) and to assist the 30th and 83d Infantry Divisions. White ordered the division to attack at dawn on April 10, using four columns, with Combat Command A on the left and Combat Command B on the right. The 82d Reconnaissance Battalion was to lead the advance, with a reconnaissance company ahead of each combat command. If they encountered any resistance, they were to eliminate it or contain it with minimum force, while alerting the combat commands. Thus, with a bare twenty-four hours for maintenance and rest, the men resumed the attack.

On the afternoon of April 9, the tankers moved to assembly areas, ready to attack eastward the following day. Combat Command B sent patrols to secure passes and bridges, so that its forward movement would not be delayed when dawn arrived. Attacking at 9:00 A.M. on April 10, in what many soldiers considered the final operation of the war, the right column of Combat Command B met little opposition until it was west of Lewe. There the tankers took enemy antitank guns under fire and speedily eliminated them. By evening the column had stopped east of Gross-Dohren.

The advance surprised many Germans. When the left column of Combat Command B stopped a train, the engineer confessed he had not realized that Americans were within fifty miles of Wulferstedt. Roaring through several towns, they saw busses and trollies still operating. Upon seeing the tankers, many civilians threw their packages in every direction as they ran for cover. On the east edge of Salzgitter the column met the most determined resistance it had encountered since the Teutoburger Wald. A battery of eight 88mm guns defended a formidable roadblock, but the column's artillery finally overcame it. By 7:00 P.M., they had seized a bridge over the Oker River before consolidating for the night.

While Combat Command B made about twenty miles, Combat Command A had more difficulty. It had to operate in a heavily industrialized area of Braunschweig and Immendorf. On the north flank of the advance, Task Force A moved against stiff artillery fire to about eight miles southwest of Braunschweig. Many thought it was the heaviest fire since crossing the Rhine. Task Force B, on the south flank, met initially strong opposition from the defensive belt of dual-purpose antiaircraft guns which defended the Hermann Goering steel works. An effective flanking attack and artillery finally silenced the guns, with sixty-seven destroyed or captured. The steelworks were in American hands by 8:00 P.M. When the attack continued, elements of the combat command had to stay near the two cities to prevent looting and rioting caused by the liberation of the forced laborers and prisoners-of-war.

Meanwhile, Combat Command B was having the finest day in its history, perhaps the best day of any armored unit during the war. At 6:30 A.M., the left column attacked from Schladen, destroyed an enemy truck convoy thirty minutes later and continued eastward, meeting almost no opposition. After refueling, the march resumed. The first stiff fight was at Oschersleben, where enemy panzerfaust fire destroyed a self-propelled howitzer of the 92d Armored Artillery Battalion. The artillerymen lowered their cannons and machine guns and fired at every possible defensive position as they moved through the town.

Meanwhile, outside the town, the enemy quickly formed a new defensive line after a platoon of D Company, 67th Armored Regiment, passed by them. Instead of becoming frightened, the troops continued on to the airport, where they shot down two planes and captured seventeen FW-109s on the ground. A tank destroyer with the platoon shot down a third plane as the Germans were attempting to land. Finally, after a half-hour artillery fight, the German defenders faded away and the march continued. At 4:05 P.M., Hinds requested that the division schedule an airborne attack for daylight on April 12, against the Elbe bridge in its zone. The airborne drop was denied because the paratroopers were assisting Montgomery in his battle to clear Holland, Denmark and northern Germany. Hinds requested and received ten DUKWs, 2½-ton amphibious cargo trucks.

The 1st Platoon, C Company, 82d Reconnaissance Battalion, was leading the left column but not making its usual rapid advance. It kept getting tangled in the lead tank elements. When Lt. Col. Wheeler Merriam asked why the platoon was being held up, he learned that it had run off its maps. Merriam gave the needed maps to his adjutant, 1st Lt. Harold Douglass and told him to give them to the platoon leader. The adjutant had hoped to get into the fight, so he drove down the road in his armored car, waving for the platoon to follow. Barrelling through Ottersleben, the reconnaissance personnel fired their weapons, scaring the civilian population and surprising the military, some of whom were taking a leisurely stroll. Douglass led the platoon to the airport, where they shot up twenty-five parked planes and two which were attempting to land. About that time, the local forces regrouped and panzerfaust and 20mm antiaircraft guns began to fire on the intruders. Douglass realized that the situation was serious and radioed for help. The 1st Battalion, 67th Armored, and the artillery responded, but the Germans stopped them at the west edge of town. After dark, the platoon escaped, losing two half-tracks and two jeeps. The column was now at Magdeburg, having advanced fifty-two miles in thirteen hours.

At 6:30 A.M., the right column of Combat Command B, led by Col. Paul A. Disney, attacked from positions near Gross Dohren. It made almost unopposed progress until it reached Anderluch where it encountered a 1,700-man German column marching alongside the road. The Germans quickly surrendered. After securing the prisoners, the advance continued to Klein Oschersleben, where there was a two-hour stop to reservice the vehicles. At 5:00 P.M., the march resumed; three hours later 2d Armored Division headquarters was electrified by a message from Disney: "We're on the Elbe."

When the lead tanks topped a rise overlooking Schonebeck, Maj. James Hollingsworth saw the bridge was still standing and that the Germans were using it to evacuate their own armor. He wanted to capture the span before the Germans could destroy it. The major tried unsuccessfully to attach one tank company to the tail of the fleeing enemy force, hoping it could get across before they became aware of the ploy. Once alerted, the enemy fanatically defended the bridge and all its approaches. Because the approaches were mined and covered by small arms fire, the Americans did not rush ahead. The next morning, the Germans destroyed the bridge. However, White knew that Hinds was making plans to locate a suitable crossing site and to bring up the 17th Armored Engineer Battalion to build a bridge.

To ease pressure on a possible bridging operation, the 2d Armored

Division tried to negotiate a surrender with the German commander and the burgomaster of Magdeburg. When the talks failed, the decision was made to go ahead and attempt a bridging operation, despite German control of the city. Attempting to pressure the defenders, White requested air support from fighter-bombers, but there is no evidence of an air corps attack. He also directed divisional artillery to shell the autobahn bridge with POZIT fuze and to bombard the town. Combat Command A was then ordered to move to the Elbe and to surround Magdeburg, preventing ground troops from attacking south along the west bank. At 6:15 A.M., Task Force A attacked from its positions near Wolfenbuttel, making fairly good progress until it tried to leave Helmstedt. There the enemy covered the roads with small arms and panzerfaust fire. The task force infantry had a slow, time-consuming chore in removing the opposition, but the advance continued until by night it was northwest of Magdeburg. Task Force B met intense fire from antitank guns located on the east bank of the Elbe, but it did not have as difficult a time as Task Force A. After calming a civil disturbance at Olvenstedt, it consolidated positions there for the night. Both task forces were in position, blocking roads north and west of Magdeburg.

Combat Command Reserve moved to surround the south and southwest portions of the city. Early in the afternoon, Col. G. A. West warned the combat command not to become involved in a "cat and dog fight," but rather to be in position to assist Combat Command B in forcing a river crossing. By late in the day on April 12, both combat commands had effectively isolated Magdeburg. Now Combat Command B could attempt a river crossing—a dangerous task, but one which the 2d Armored had accomplished many times before.

Earlier that day, Combat Command B had combed the west bank of the Elbe River, eliminating enemy opposition and seeking a suitable bridging site. The location had to meet two requirements: it had to be in the division zone, and it had to be established as quickly as possible. Three alternatives were found: on old wagon ferry site in Westerhausen, the barge-loading site north of Schonebeck, or a place south of the destroyed bridge at Schonebeck. Since Westerhausen had been cleared and fighting was still raging at Schonebeck, the wagon ferry site was chosen. First, the infantry would cross to establish the bridgehead, then the engineers would build a bridge for the heavy equipment.

Because the infantry battalions had been fighting all day, time was required to assemble the assault troops. Instead of attacking at 6:00 as planned, or at 7:00 as directed by White, the first wave did not start across until 9:00. Most of the two leading battalions (1st and 3d Battalions, 41st Armored Infantry) reached the opposite shore by 11:00 P.M. The 3d Battalion of the 119th Infantry Regiment followed to be the reserve. Apparently no thought was given to sending antitank weapons across; the bridge would be built and tanks and tank destroyers would be available very early the following day. The initial objectives were secured and defensive positions prepared.

At 10:45, in total darkness, the engineers began the bridge. Originally, they had hoped to use a searchlight to create artificial moonlight, but the cloudless night made that impossible. By 5:30 A.M., when the bridge was about half completed and sufficient pontoons had been prepared to finish it, the Germans started shelling the bridge and both banks with heavy and extremely accurate artillery fire. Within an hour the fire lifted; but most of the pontoons on the bank and in the water had been destroyed. The American artillery retaliated, attempting to silence the enemy guns. Smoke pots were set up, and the engineers renewed their efforts. However, the Germans then increased their fire. Again the American artillery attempted to silence the German guns, while the engineers tried for a third time to get the bridge across the river. Again German artillery responded with an increase in tempo, stopping work for the third time. In the afternoon, the bridge work resumed and reached to within twenty-five feet of the west bank, when the German fire started again, destroying floats and the bridge's eastern part. Work stopped for the fourth time.

While the engineers suffered under the enemy fire which could not be silenced, the infantry on the east bank saw little action. Late in the day, plans were made to shift the bridgehead south, closer to Schonebeck, now cleared of enemy resistance. The Americans hoped that this move would place the bridge out of sight of the enemy artillery observers.

The first day's operations at the bridgehead had been memorable for General Hinds. A reporter came to the Elbe and asked how he got the word across to the men. Hinds replied that it was done in the usual manner: radio, messengers, liaison and personnel visits. The reporter hinted that he had news which might warrant some extraordinary means of communication. Hinds exclaimed, "Don't tell me the war is over and we haven't heard of it?" "No," the reporter answered, "the president is dead." That fact was to have an effect unforeseen by either participant in the conversation; the death of Franklin D. Roosevelt may have been the deciding factor in Eisenhower's decision to stop on the Elbe.

At 9:00 P.M. on April 13, the three infantry battalions executed a maneuver not in the "Leavenworth book" (school solution): reversing a bridgehead on a hostile shore without tank or heavy weapons support. The men, who had been in almost constant operations since early on April 11, were nearly collapsing from fatigue. However, they did get the new bridgehead established and some defensive positions prepared before dawn on April 14. While the men were moving, White and Hinds were preparing for the possibility that the men would have to be withdrawn from the east bank. The 83d Infantry Division had established a bridgehead downstream at Barby, and 2d Armored hoped to use it to send tanks across to aid the infantrymen in the Schonebeck bridgehead, if necessary, and if time permitted.

Sometime between 5:00 and 6:00 A.M., several hundred German infantrymen, supported by tanks and self-propelled guns, attacked the 2d Armored's bridgehead. The Americans, who had no antitank weapons except bazookas, were quickly overrun in the outer perimeter. Using the American prisoners as shields, the German tanks stayed out of bazooka range, methodically firing down the line of American foxholes. Division artillery fired heavily and broke up the counterattack before the enemy reached the final perimeter. The survivors of the two overrun battalions pulled back to the final perimeter, awaiting instructions. At 10:18, Hinds believed that the situation was improving in spite of the engineers' difficulty in establishing a ferry.

About this time, Colonel Disney, who was on the east bank commanding the action, was wounded. The executive officer of the 67th Armored Regiment, Lt. Col. Francis H. Barnes, was with Disney. Barnes called Hinds, telling him that the task force commander had been wounded and that he would take command of the regiment. Barnes was ordered back to the west bank. On his return he drew continuous fire and upon landing encountered more artillery and direct fire from antitank weapons. Barnes is convinced that the enemy was monitoring the radio nets.

Soon optimism quickly began to fade. At 10:50, the commanding officer of the 3d Battalion, 41st Armored Infantry, Col. Arthur Anderson, reported that he thought that he had lost his battalion. At 11:10, the division reported to XIX Corps that the situation was "pretty bad," they might have lost the "3/41 AIR complete." Possibly two of the companies were with the 3d Battalion, 119th Infantry Regiment, which was reported to be heavily engaged. At 12:15, corps headquarters was again informed that they might have lost an infantry battalion, and they requested all possible air support: "We have never asked for air support urgently before but we need it now." The request was turned down. The XIX Corps assistant G-3 for air later said, "We had practically no planes to give them for support. They just were not available because the air strips had not been moved forward with the same rapidity as the advance of the armor and infantry. There were captured enemy bases in the area, and it seems as though it would have been a simple job to move the fields forward, but it was not done. On the day the 2d Armored was forced to withdraw, it was perfect for flying, clear and unlimited visibility."

The engineers made a final effort to complete the bridge. While the 17th Armored Engineer Battalion had been working on the span, the 82d Engineer Battalion was trying to reinstall the ferry. German artillery, however, forced the engineers to abandon their efforts. Without antitank weapons and after investigating the situation for himself, Hinds decided that the position was untenable. About 1:30 P.M., he gave the order to evacuate the bridgehead. He had already discussed the possibility of abandoning the east bank and had White's approval to do what he considered necessary. The withdrawal was orderly and a tribute to the men's training and discipline.

First out were the riflemen, protected by machine gunners and bazooka men. The DUKWs, now reduced to three, served as water taxis, bringing back Americans and Germans alike. During the withdrawal, the number of DUKWs was further reduced to one, but it continued to perform successfully. Some soldiers ventured to swim the river.

Late in the afternoon a Cub plane of the 78th Armored Artillery Battalion, flying over the east bank, reported that 1st Lt. Louis W. Perry and about sixty men of the 3d Battalion, 119th Infantry, were trapped in a basement and planning to break for the river. The artillery fired a heavy, accurate barrage and smoke screen to aid them. All night, men straggled back, with the final count not as bad as had been feared. The bridgehead was never totally withdrawn, for approximately one company, supported by artillery and tank guns, stayed on the east bank protecting the ferry head as long as the division was on the Elbe.

Meanwhile, White had gone to the command post of the 83rd Infantry Division at Barby to get their consent to use their bridge to send across Combat Command R. He wanted the command to attack north to ease the pressure on Combat Command B. After White had been informed about the withdrawal order, he changed the orders to Col. Russel W. Jenna, directing him to help secure the left flank of the 83rd Infantry's bridgehead, pending further instructions. White recommended to McLain that the combat command be attached to the infantry division, which it was. During its stay on the east bank, it had helped to break up several enemy counterattacks and then to enlarge the bridgehead.

Simpson planned to spearhead the attack on Berlin with the 2d Armored Division, flanked by the 30th Infantry Division on the north and the 83d Infantry Division on the south. A day after XIX Corps attacked, it was to be followed by XIII Corps on the north. McLain had ordered the 35th Infantry Division to contain Magdeburg and the remainder of the corps to attack late in the afternoon of April 15. But fate intervened. Simpson reported to Bradley's headquarters, where he learned that the Ninth Army had been ordered to stop at the Elbe. Simpson personally delivered the order to the 2d Armored Division, where it was received with stunned surprise. Many, then and now, have felt that had the division been allowed to attack, it would have been at the outskirts of Berlin within twenty-four hours. For the 2d Armored Division, the race for Berlin ended at the Elbe River and in bitter disappointment—for the moment.

By midnight of April 16, the 30th Infantry Division reported that it had failed to negotiate the surrender of Magdeburg. A ground attack was ordered, preceded by a heavy air strike intended to deflate German morale enough to cause them to surrender. The air strike occurred as planned, with the ground assault by the 30th Infantry and Combat Command A of the 2d Armored, beginning at 2:45 P.M. The German civilians helped by pointing out buildings in which defenders were hiding. In return, the Americans promised not to destroy the informant's house. Every effort was made to keep that promise, but occasionally an errant shell landed where it had not been aimed. After about twenty-four hours, the town surrendered and the fighting stopped. For the next few days, the division continued to comb the area for stragglers and bypassed pockets of resistance. Then, on April 19, came the good news that the 2d Armored Division was to move back to an area around Wolfenbuttel, Immendorf and Braunschweig.

On April 20, the division moved, alerted to the possibility that the Germans might try to escape to the Harz Mountains. Combat Command B's dawn patrol found about 100 vehicles entering the Konigslutter Forest about a mile north of Schoningen. The exits were quickly sealed and Hadley's talking tank began to broadcast surrender requests, while an infantry clearing force captured a few prisoners. One of the first captives said that he was the driver for Major General Unrein and Lieutenant

General Becker. Hadley's tank assured the generals that if they surrendered they could ride to the prisoner-of-war compound in a plush sedan, which, according to General Hinds, was "oversized and underpowered." The German generals refused the offer. When Unrein was later captured, he had the privilege of riding to the prisoner-of-war cage standing in the back of a truck. Later Becker was also captured, while attempting to escape disguised as a forester and riding a bicycle.

In the dash across Germany, the 2d Armored Division overran a 3,000-square-mile area, capturing 45,022 prisoners and 80 Nazi party and Security Agency personnel. It destroyed or captured 48 tanks, 255 antitank or artillery pieces, 579 vehicles, 18 trains, 265 airplanes, 5 airports and 205 hospitals. While establishing such a fine record, the division suffered 81 killed, 153 missing and 401 wounded and lost 7 medium tanks, 6 light tanks and 9 half-tracks. In his special order of the day, White observed that Magdeburg fell two years and six months after the division had sailed from the United States. He added, "We are finally across the Elbe and the war is finally and irrevocably lost. No unit had written a brighter chapter in the history of this war."

As an occupying force, the 2d Armored Division's primary duty was the security of its area. It assumed a role in the military government with a few but exacting rules. There was a curfew, which permitted civilian movement from 7:00 A.M. to 6:00 P.M., and a blackout, and no civilian was permitted to use binoculars or cameras. The troops were also restricted. No civilian property was to be taken; if it were, then the accused would face a charge of looting.

When commenting on military government, Brig. Gen. Sidney R. Hinds said, "After all, [Gen. George S.] Patton was doing at his high level exactly what we, at several echelons lower, were doing, without any official authority whatever, to try to bring some order out of the war chaos, by putting the most able German officials immediately in temporary charge, pending the arrival of the Allied military government crews; get things going and back to normal, and to the devil with denazification at that point. By that time there were few Nazis around anyway." Hinds was right when he observed, "Patton's modus operandi proved correct, while the proposed [Hans J.] Morganthau 'Potato Field' economy proved asinine, if not downright foolish."

The first responsibility of the local government was to restore public utilities, then to provide citizen labor details to remove the rubble and for other cleanup. Direct orders were issued to the Germans, telling them what was required and where and when the work was to be done. The officers were told that no questions were to be asked and no excuses were to be accepted.

Once local government had been established, the next mission was the collection, segregation and evacuation of displaced persons and prisoners-of-war. Perhaps with some indication of the future, Combat Command B was ordered to move all western displaced persons and prisoners west of the international boundary before April 27. German women who claimed to be engaged or married to western displaced persons would be permitted to move with them. Underlined for emphasis, this fact was "not to be advertised." During this phase of activities, the division moved more than 30,000 persons.

In May the division received several choice bits of information. Near midnight on May 1, it overheard the BBC report that Hitler was dead. Several days later, it learned that German officials had surrendered at 1:41 A.M. on May 7; all active operations were to cease at 12:01 A.M. on May 9. The first people to receive the surrender message were the enlisted men in the message center of the 142d Signal Company. Sgt. Cleo Norris had "liberated" a case of Scotch, saving it for the end of the war. The message came in code, which was to be decoded only by an officer. The duty officer was asleep when the message center team received it; he had told the men to decode any incoming messages and then to get it to the addressee. The decoding sergeant saw enough to realize the import of the message; he told Norris that for a bottle he could have the same information. Norris replied that the Scotch was for the end of the war. The decoder answered that the end had come.

On May 12, the division was relieved of its occupation duty to establish a staging area for troops destined for duty in the German capital. While the Hell-on-Wheelers were performing occupation duty, the Belgian government awarded the division its croix de guerre. It was the first time that a foreign military force received the award. The mass citation resulted from the division's being the first Allied troops to enter the country and freeing many cities from the Nazi grip. Later, Hell on Wheels blunted the German spearhead just three miles short of the Meuse River, during the Battles of the Bulge, and helped close the enemy salient at Houffalize. The award ceremony was impressive; all the division and attached units troops, the 195th Antiaircraft Artillery Battalion and the 702d Tank Destroyer Battalion, stood in the review. Flags and guidons snapped in the breeze, aircraft flew overhead, and the men paraded for the dignitaries.

Sometime, while in the Bienrode area, the division learned that it had been selected to be the first American division to enter and guard the American sector of Berlin. Many veterans feel that the division was selected because of its outstanding battle record. Others add that the airborne divisions could not have withstood possible Russian harrassment. The tankers had their full complement of equipment, while the paratroopers had their rifles and little else. The disappointment about the halt at the Elbe passed, and the men worked long hours to get their equipment and vehicles into presentable condition. During this time, Gen. I. D. White was relieved of command and returned to the United States to take command of the Cavalry School at Fort Riley, Kansas. Gen. John H. Collier became the division commander; Col. Carl Hutton assumed command of Combat Command A.

On July 1, the advance party departed for Berlin, while the main body followed two days later. The first Hell-on-Wheeler to enter the center of town was Pfc. Harvey Natches. He drove his jeep down Unter den Linden with Associated Press correspondent Daniel De Luce as a passenger. Russian women traffic police officers saluted smartly as the 2d Armored Division soldier drove past lines of citizens. The third crossing of the Elbe proved to be almost as difficult as the previous two. The Russians, apparently not wanting the Americans to bring armor into the city, had built a small load carrying bridge, but with a Scotch bribe and an extra ninety-mile road march the tankers entered the city. On the Americans' national birthday, following a forty-eight-gun salute, the Stars and Stripes were raised over the defeated German capital.

During their stay, until August 9, 1945, the division served as occupation troops and also as honor guard for Pres. Harry S. Truman at the Potsdam Conference. During the high-level discussions, the division conducted a review for the governmental leaders. Instead of the troops' moving by a reviewing stand, the tanks and all other vehicles were lined up, using a theodolite, and a movable reviewing stand passed the tankers. One reviewer, Gen. George S. Patton, had tears in his eyes as he passed the division he had trained and commanded. In conversations with 2d Armored Division officers, General Patton said that he wished that he had had the division with him so that they could have "really gone to town."

The war was over for Hell on Wheels. While at Fort Benning, Colonel Barnes had told General White that he wanted to come home as soon as the war was over. He did not want to enter Berlin because it was just another bombed city. White, after tallying the points for rotation, granted the request. After rotating out of Berlin, high-point men were sent

Above: Hell on Wheels marches into Berlin.
Below: Pres. Harry S. Truman presents the Presidential Unit Citation to the 17th Armored Engineer Battalion.

home, while volunteers, low-pointers and replacements manned the division. It settled into a routine of occupation duty and training, a routine which was to last until late December when the division was alerted for shipment back to the United States—three years and two months after sailing from the navy yards at Newport, New York and Hampton Roads.

Chapter 20

A BACKWARD GLANCE

Throughout history man has attempted to devise better weapons with which to impose his will on his enemy. He has experimented with many vehicles to increase mobility, which would permit an attacker to position himself on the flanks or in the rear of his foe. Once the attacker has gained this advantage, he is usually able to cause confusion and disrupt vital supply and communications routes which are necessary for controlling an army. The ancients used chariots and later cavalry for this purpose. Leonardo da Vinci devised a tanklike vehicle which mounted a cannon inside a protective covering and was propelled by horses. As time progressed, battlefield movement was reserved for cavalry, while the infantry usually attacked over open ground against entrenchments, a technique which reached its maximum employment during World War I.

During the industrial revolution of the late nineteenth and early twentieth centuries, the internal combustion engine was developed, which was to make revolutionary changes in warfare. With the engine, man developed the airplane, which permitted a new look at the battlefield.

At the same time, trucks were used to move large bodies of troops rapidly to various sectors of the battlefield for offensive or defensive purposes. In World War I, all the necessary factors—entrenchments, massed artillery, automatic weapons, barbed wire and no-man's-lands—were present and forced a new concept in warfare. To break the almost three-year stalemate, the tank, crude and slow, was introduced. It proved successful when measured in terms of efficiency and reliability of the time. Since it was a new weapon, its use was dictated by both necessity and traditional concepts. It was to be an infantry support weapon, reducing strongpoints which prevented or delayed an infantry attack.

With the American Tank Corps's return to the United States following the war, it fell victim to historical traditions, to a new spirit of international disarmament and to bitter feuding between the service branches. The tank, since it was slow and because it had been an infantry support weapon, was given to the infantry and labored there for two decades. A few far-sighted officers sought to make the tank into a powerful offensive weapon, but they were told to hold to branch lines or face disciplinary action. Given those two possibilities, most chose to remain silent or to discuss forbidden matters within a circle of well-chosen friends. At times, these men risked their careers to advocate the creation of a tank unit which would employ tactics designed to increase battlefield mobility and to cause panic among the enemy.

The changing international situation had a tremendous effect on the evolution of armor in the United States Army. In the late 1920s, Great Britain developed an armored force and demonstrated it to foreign visitors. The American secretary of war witnessed the demonstration, and when he returned to the United States, he directed that the army begin to develop a similar force. Attempting to comply with the secretary's direction, the army encountered resistance from the chiefs of cavalry and infantry, as well as a federal statute which gave tanks to the infantry. This controversy delayed development of armored vehicles and tactics for the next twelve to fifteen years.

During the late 1920s and early 1930s, armor leaders received their training through a skillful evasion of the federal statute which detailed tanks to the infantry. When the Mechanized Force was created, it served as a laboratory for the training of armor leaders and the development of tactics. This was a crucial period in armor evolution, for many wanted to see the experiment fail. However, it was successful, and when the Armored Force was created in 1940, a second evasion of the 1920 statute, the leaders who had served with the Mechanized Force emerged to take command of the armored divisions and regiments.

Armor historians point to the 1930s as the period when cavalry tactics were adapted for the tank. Infantry maintained that the tank was merely another weapon with which the foot soldier could better carry out his assignments. A closer examination reveals that both cavalry and infantry were correct. The tactics of deep thrusts, penetrations, wide turning movements and exploitation of enemy flanks and rear areas were the traditional role of cavalry. However, once committed to battle, tanks usually advanced at a much slower rate, which resembled the support role which infantry had advocated. Thus, instead of being one or the other, armor tactics were the skillful blending of both cavalry and infantry.

Far-sighted theorists of the 1920s and 1930s knew that successful armor warfare would require more than tanks. Armor had to develop the team concept, including the addition of artillery, antiaircraft protection, engineers, infantry and chemical troops. During the experimentation, Adna Chaffee, Daniel Van Voorhis and others foresaw that airplanes would also be needed to perform reconnaissance and attack missions. Their beliefs were totally justified when the Germans attacked and quickly defeated their neighboring nations.

The 2d Armored Division was activated during controversy at the War Department. Some, especially the chiefs of cavalry and infantry, denied that such a force was needed and asserted that in reality it already existed within their own areas of responsibility. Gen. George C. Marshall denied such a contention, implying that the two branch chiefs had had an opportunity to create such a force, but they had been reluctant to do so. Others at the War Department, primarily those whose branches had traditionally been support branches, readily endorsed the plan and suggested organizational improvements. Later some of the suggestions were to be incorporated.

Activated by Brig. Gen. Charles L. Scott, the men of the 2d Armored Division were pushed to achieve a state of combat readiness before the end of 1940. This was difficult, if not impossible, because of the shortage of men and equipment. Scott started the division on its way to becoming a battle-ready force, but soon he was assigned to replace the dying Adna Chaffee as 1st Armored Corps commander. Succeeding Scott was perhaps the most famous commander of the division, Maj. Gen. George S. Patton, Jr. He followed the model outlined by Scott and led the division to achieve even higher standards. Training emphasized keeping the men alive while inflicting maximum damage on the enemy. Patton, a firm believer in publicity, led the division on an extended road march and in three peacetime maneuvers. While the press made the division, its exploits and its colorful commander famous on these maneuvers, critics said that the division would not do as well in combat. When Patton left the division in 1942, he had a trained, battle-ready force, which was polished and honed by his successors. One officer's wife, Mrs. Sidney R. (Regina) Hinds, said that because of the division's training she never doubted that her husband would return alive. That tribute was all that any division commander could ask.

Once committed to battle, the 2d Armored Division showed that armor doctrine had been founded on solid ground. Most interestingly, when permitted to exploit gains or holes which the infantry created, as in Sicily, its advance was rapid. The men showed that, contrary to the critics, they could make long sustained marches and attacks against an enemy. After each battle, the division trained, incorporating those ideas learned from experience and from observers who witnessed other forces in combat. The division learned a new technique: attacking under overhead artillery fire. The remainder of its skills were those that had been imparted at Fort Benning or during the maneuvers.

The 2d Armored Division owed its success to several factors: training, which created a will for the offensive; continuity of command; and organization. At no time did the division avoid a fight, unless specifically ordered to do so. Even so, the men had several engagements which might have slowed a less determined division. The most serious struggles faced came after D day at Vire, Mortain, Barenton, through the Siegfried line, the closing to the Roer River and the bitter struggle through the Battles of the Bulge. The division's offensive spirit remained undaunted. At times, the division was slowed to a snail's pace in these actions, but the men continued to inch forward against formidable opposition. Then, with a few days of rest and maintenance, they continued to attack.

The 2d Armored Division commanders—Generals Scott, Patton, Crittenberger, Harmon, Kingman, Gaffey, Brooks, White and Collier—all desired to fight the enemy. Disregarding individual personalities and judging the generals on tactical ability, the historian finds that they were all well qualified to command the division. With the exceptions of Harmon and Brooks, the division commanders were promoted to that assignment from within the division. Commanders at all levels demonstrated a concern for the welfare of their men. The men in the ranks were well aware of that concern and appreciated it.

Organizationally, the heavy division structure was the primary factor in the 2d Armored Division's success. With two armored regiments and an armored infantry regiment, the division was able to maintain itself, in spite of heavy losses. When huge attachments were added, usually an infantry regiment and five to seven artillery battalions, the 2d Armored Division had a combat strength more than twice that of the light divisions, which had only three tank and three infantry battalions. No less an authority on armor warfare than General Patton knew that there was no comparison between the light division and the 2d Armored Division with its powerful attachments.

The 2d Armored Division usually planned only one or two days ahead when operating against the enemy. Flexibility, one of the primary characteristics of armor, permitted the division commander to shape the combat teams which were employed. With the division's organization and the usual attachment of an additional infantry regiment, the division commander could create three equal-strength combat teams. Employing mission orders, which gave an objective and zone of attack, also emphasized flexibility and permitted the best utilization of armor. When the division received an assignment of method, it was usually slowed and suffered higher losses of men and material.

The history of the 2d Armored Division reveals that it came into existence during controversy, that it trained rigorously and that it became a battle-ready division only after more than two years. As it moved through the war, it impressed friend and foe alike. Perhaps one of the greatest compliments it received was during the Battle of the Bulge, when a captured German general asked how many 2d Armored Divisions the Americans had. He added that the last German intelligence reports had placed the division north of Aachen. Apparently the enemy failed to consider that the tankers could move the distance involved and be ready for a major fight.

Many students of behavior, then and now, have feared that when battle-hardened veterans of the 2d Armored Division were returned to society they would not be able to adjust to a quieter life. What was not considered was that the soldier was a civilian at heart, simply doing his duty. As soldiers, they did kill and delighted in seeing the ''master race'' fight for discarded cigarettes; the same men fed the Sicilian and German children, often denying themselves to do so.

The 2d Armored Division is justly proud of its history, written across two continents, through blazing sun, rain, fog and snow. Its professional performances revealed an aggressive determination and desire to be a great combat team. Attacking across mud and through snow, it has written its story in blood, sweat and tears. Bravery was the only accepted standard; often deeds of valor were rewarded with less than the merited decoration. For thirty months, the division fought, and its battle history reveals that once it started toward greatness, it continued until it had attained that status. The 2d Armored Division epitomized armor warfare during World War II and demonstrated convincingly that it was second to none.

Afterword

by Gen. George S. Patton

All of us, and there are tens of thousands, who have been privileged to serve in Hell on Wheels owe a great debt of gratitude to Donald Houston for compiling this splendid story of our division. As one of its peacetime commanders, I am especially pleased to see the division's wartime exploits gathered into a single work. This distinguished historian and educator has literally "put it all together," recording our history professionally and accurately. If it is true—and I think it is—that what is past is prologue, Houston's study will make a significant contribution to future battlefield success.

Don Houston records the past forthrightly and faithfully. The people he writes about—those who etched the Hell on Wheels story before and during World War II—have passed from the army's active ranks. Yet their names remain with us, the great fighting men who met the awesome responsibility of forging and fighting this distinguished combat division. The names of Harmon, White, Brooks, Collier, Hinds, Rose, Merriam, O'Farrell and Hollingsworth are synonymous with the 2d Armored.

But there were others, the lesser known: those of lower ranks who did their full duty. Through the author's efforts in military research, we now know something more of Whittington, Corpron, Prawdzik (the eternal first sergeant), Bennie Boatright, Burt and Robert Lee. They too contributed to our sacred tradition. Here I mention but a few. One could fill dozens of pages with the names of those this volume honors.

And then there were those others—the old, old veterans, the pioneers of armor. Although not members of the 2d Armored Division, their influence on its development is felt even today. They were the founding fathers who worked to mold our combat expertise during those uncertain days of World War I. We proudly remember such as John J. Pershing, S. D. Rockenbach, Joe Viner, Elgin Braine, Compton, English and the colorful Sereno Brett. They coined the old Tank Corps motto, "Treat 'em Rough," now all but forgotten by an army that sometimes lets valuable traditions pass from view.

All of these soldiers ride with us today. At each ceremony, field exercise or maneuver, their spirit, enthusiasm and professionalism join us in the turrets of the five tank battalions of the 66th and 67th Armored Regiments. Their enduring influence is felt by all.

435

I am confident both groups would thrill, as we do, to the strains of the "2d Armored Division March," written in 1941 by my late mother, Beatrice Ayer Patton. Veterans of World War I would recognize within the musical score the tune of "Glorious," that war's tank corps song. Those old soldiers who joined in Georgia in 1940 would similarly recognize some of the strains of "Dixie," a song not only synonymous with the deep South, but also marking the division's birthplace.

Now all of that is past. Don Houston has told the tale for all to read and absorb. The future lies ahead, and it is to that future that "we sons of today" must turn our gaze. The record, the reputation for professional perfection, gallantry and dedication, has been firmly established by our predecessors.

And what is the mission for us who carry on? Today's army simply calls it "combat readiness." But the mission is more complex. I like to think of it as the professional, moral, spiritual, mental and material capability to carry out the military objectives of the United States of America without fail, always and every time, probably against heavy odds, in the toughest conditions of weather and terrain, anywhere in the world. This is our interpretation of readiness in its most comprehensive meaning. This is where we stand—ready to fight and ready to die if the need arises. No soldier who marches beneath the shadow of our colors can expect to contribute less. Historically, it is the elite regular to whom our nation has turned in times of peril. She will continue to do so in the future.

Hell on Wheels today will not deny history. It is ready for the country's call to arms. It will do its full duty.

GEORGE S. PATTON
Major General, USA

Appendix I

Division Commanders

Scott, Charles L.	July 15, 1940–November 3, 1940
Patton, George S., Jr.	November 3, 1940–January 18, 1942
Crittenberger, Willis D.	January 18, 1942–July 31, 1942
Harmon, Ernest N.	July 31, 1942–April 6, 1943
Kingman, Allen F.	April 6, 1943–May 5, 1943
Gaffey, Hugh J.	May 5, 1943–March 17, 1944
Brooks, Edward H.	March 17, 1944–September 12, 1944
Harmon, Ernest N.	September 12, 1944–January 19, 1945
White, I. D.	January 19, 1945–June 8, 1945
Collier, John H.	June 8, 1945–September 4, 1945
Devine, John M.	September 4, 1945–March 24, 1946
Leonard, John W.	March 24, 1946–October 10, 1946
Hobbs, Leland S.	October 10, 1946–August 25, 1947
Christiansen, James G.	September 27, 1947–June 25, 1949
Smith, Albert C.	June 26, 1949–October 31, 1950
Palmer, Williston B.	November 1, 1950–November 23, 1951
Gailey, Charles K., Jr.	November 24, 1951–March 23, 1952
Read, George W., Jr.	April 3, 1952–August 15, 1953
Doan, Leander L.	August 16, 1953–January 19, 1955
Ruffner, Clark	January 20, 1955–April 5, 1956
Babcock, Conrad S., Jr.	April 5, 1956–May 31, 1957
Johnson, Wilhelm P.	June 1, 1957–October 29, 1958
Wheeler, Earle G.	October 30, 1958–March 11, 1960
Farrand, Edward G.	April 1, 1960–June 30, 1961
Wright, William H. S.	July 1, 1961–February 12, 1963
Burba, Edwin H.	February 13, 1963–August 28, 1964
Mather, George R.	September 3, 1964–July 1, 1965
Kelly, John E.	July 22, 1965–June 5, 1967
McChristian, Joseph A.	July 3, 1967–July 20, 1969
Shea, Leonard C.	July 22, 1969–October 31, 1969
Coats, Wendell J.	November 1, 1969–August 29, 1971
Cantley, George G.	August 30, 1971–July 13, 1973
Fair, Robert L.	July 16, 1973–August 4, 1975
Patton, George S.	August 5, 1975–

Appendix II

Division Awards

Medal of Honor	2
Distinguished Service Cross	23
Distinguished Service Medal	7
Silver Star	2,302
Legion of Merit	30
Distinguished Flying Cross	3
Soldier's Medal	189
Bronze Star	6,404
Air Medal	378
Distinguished Unit Citation	13
Belgian Croix de Guerre	Entire division

Appendix III

Statistics

2d Armored Division plus attachments 702d Tank Destroyer and 195th Anti-aircraft Artillery Battalions

Battle days	238
Killed in action	1,160
Missing	253
Captured	55
Wounded	4,410
Injured, nonbattle	952
Died, nonbattle	259
Returned to duty	3,063

Bibliographical Essay

Interviews

The most important sources of material were the personal interviews with those involved with the 2d Armored Division. Gen. Jacob L. Devers, former commanding general of the Armored Force, and Gen. William H. Simpson, former commanding general, Ninth Army, provided the overall view of the division. Former division commanders John H. Collier, Willis D. Crittenberger, Ernest N. Harmon, Allen F. Kingman and I. D. White provided the perspective which only they could offer. It is important to remember that Collier, Crittenberger, Kingman and White had led units of the division before assuming its command. Thus their reflections often start with battalion, regimental or brigade level. Former staff officers Maj. Gen. Lawrence R. Dewey, Maj. Gen. Robert W. Grow and Maj. Gen. Harold R. Peckham helped to tell how the division surmounted its earlier problems. Both Dewey and Peckham served in battalions before moving to their staff assignments. Sidney R. Hinds, a regimental S-3, battalion commander, regimental commander and combat commander, was a Benning-to-Berliner and told the story from many points along that line. His wife, Regina, offered a woman's view not often expressed. Battalion and company commanders and platoon leaders contributed their thoughts. This group included James M. Burt, Donald A. Chace, James Hartford, Hugh O'Farrell, Fred Smith and John K. Waters. Brig. Gen. Wheeler Merriam, commanding officer of the 82d Reconnaissance Battalion in Europe was able to fill in many gaps. Battalion Sgt. Maj. Victor S. Prawdzik provided his unique insight.

Correspondence

During the research period, many letters were sent to members of the 2d Armored Division Association. Their replies are included at the appropriate places in the manuscript. Often, the respondents directed the author to new sources of information. Col. Francis H. Barnes's taped letter was particularly valuable, while Dr. T. D. Boaz, Jr., contributed his ship's newspapers. Louis Clark and James S. Crawford gave the enlisted man's view, while Frank L. Culver's taped message told of a "virgin second lieutenant" and his role in the division. Donald D. Dimock was a medic. Lewis H. Dorsett was a junior officer in the supply battalion; his notebook is most informative about the size of the division and the amounts of fuel and oil needed to move Hell on Wheels. Gerald M. Emig, Lt. Gen. Hugh M. Exton and John E. Flahaven pointed to other materials. Arden Gatzke told of a young tanker's life. Herman F. Gonyea contributed photographs while Gen. Paul D. Harkins spoke of his staff duty. Brig. Gen. Sidney R. Hinds was a constant correspondent who was ever-ready to answer any question or direct me to someone who could. Albert J. Isacks related the experiences of a new member to the division when it was in England. Maj. Gen. Briard P. Johnson gave freely of his time and detailed knowledge to help with the manuscript. He also provided maps for the book. Neil R. Jones loaned parts of an unpublished manuscript. George K. Kattas, Phillip Lamb and Russell S. Lamison all gave enlisted men's points of view. Col. Herbert S. Long was generous with his recollections while Alex Migdon furnished a manuscript of his activities. Charles Frederick Morse helped with a maintenance man's view; Frank K. O'Nail furnished photographs. William M. Page recalled the division's early days; Dr. Norris H. Perkins contributed many pages of letters and recollections, as did his wife. Samuel W. Tackitt drove some 400 miles to bring me a tape which he had compiled. Ralph L. Reints, Thomas M. Strickland and Aloysius Villmer all told of the enlisted men. Gen. I. D. White read the manuscript and gave some helpful suggestions; Col. John S. Wier, commanding officer of the 48th Medical Battalion, helped regarding the formation of the battalion and its use in combat. Chaplain Urban J. Wurm loaned his insightful diary.

Manuscript Collections

The greatest collection of military materials is the United States Army Military History Research Collection at Carlisle Barracks, Pennsylvania. It contains the Omar N. Bradley papers which shed much light on the European theater of operations. Also extremely valuable are Brig. Gen. Bradford G. Chynoweth's papers, which reveal the frustrations of an armor enthusiast who could not convert senior commanders. Maj. Gen. Charles Corlett's papers contain an unpublished manuscript which praises the 2d Armored Division. Lt. Gen. Willis D. Crittenberger's papers shed light on the division's early days from the point of view of the armored brigade commander and then division commander. Gen. Alvin C. Gillem's papers are illuminating because of his position on the Infantry Board and because of some divisional materials not in the division records. Ernest N. Harmon's papers, which follow his military career from West Point to his retirement, are most helpful for his tenure as division commander. John P. Lucas's papers contain his diary which is the single most useful item. Brig. Gen. Sidney R. Hinds's papers contain his thoughts about the evolution of armor and the 2d Armored Division. His pictorial ''War Book'' follows the division from Fort Benning, Georgia, to Berlin, Germany.

Several persons still retain their papers. Included in this group is Maj. Gen. Robert W. Grow. Most useful is his diary and an unpublished manuscript, "The Ten Lean Years," an insightful narrative of armor's growing pains in the 1930s. Daniel O. Magnussen's papers are most useful in attempting to understand Maurice Rose. John K. Waters's papers are helpful in seeing the division from a company commander's point of view.

Gen. I. D. White and Maj. Gen. Briard P. Johnson have donated their papers to their alma mater, Norwich University, North Field, Vermont. Both collections contain materials about the 82d Reconnaissance Battalion, 67th Armored Regiment, Combat Command B, and the division, especially for the war years. Johnson's also contain information about the postwar division.

Maj. Gen. Charles L. Scott's papers in the Library of Congress are classified. Containing references to his days as division commander and his corps command era they are especially useful concerning his time in North Africa with the British.

The two most important archival collections are Record Group 337, Records of the Army Ground Forces; and Record Group 407, Combat and Administrative Records of the 2d Armored Division, both of which are in the National Archives, Washington, D.C. Records of the Army Ground Forces detail the maneuvers and critiques by the various commanders. The divisional records fill approximately forty-two cubic feet. They contain the after-action reports, the G-2 and G-3 records and logs, orders and maps of the division and its component elements. Sadly lacking however is a roster of those who served with the division.

The Office of the Chief of Military History, now called the Center for Military History, is rich with materials about the campaigns of the 2d Armored Division. Most often, however, these manuscripts indicate neither author nor preparation date. "The Attack on Fedala and its Defenses" narrates the difficulties of amphibious landings against somewhat determined defenses; "Attack on Mehdia and the Port Lyautey Airdome" does the same for the northernmost landing of the Western Task Force. Franklin Ferriss, captain and military historian in Europe, wrote "Operation of Task Force Stokes, 16–18 September 1944," (December, 1944) about the clearing of the triangle in the crossing of the Albert Canal. Lt. Frank Houcek's "Elbe Operation" detailed the race for the Elbe River and the problems faced once the division was on the Elbe. Lt. Irving Levine in "The Rhine River Operation, 28 February to 5 March (1945)" tells of that move, while his "The 2d Armored Division: Rhine-Elbe Operations" treats that part of the war. "The Last Offensive," by Charles B. MacDonald covers the main battle for the defeat of Germany from the end of the Bulge to the American entry into Berlin. Royce L. Thompson authored three studies: "American Intelligence on the German Counteroffensive: November–15 December 1944," (two volumes); "Employment of VT Fuzes in the Ardennes Campaign, European Theater of Operations, 16 December 1944–January 1945''; and "European Theater of Operations Command Gasoline Status, August–September 1944."

Service schools were useful sources of information. Many students were required to make a detailed study of some aspect of the war. Col. Paul A. Disney studied the "Operations of the 82d Reconnaissance Battalion in the Sicilian Campaign, July 10–22, 1943: Personal Experiences of Battalion Commander," (1946–1947) while a student at the Command and General Staff College's School of Combined Arms at Fort Leavenworth, Kansas. Advanced students at the Armor School, Fort Knox, Kentucky, made studies of various phases of the Hell on Wheels operations. John M. Barnum and Committee 6 studied "The Armored Division in the Double Envelopment: 2d Armored Division in the Mortain Counterattack" (1949). Howard E. Bressler authored "2d Armored Division in the Ardennes" (1948). Linden K. Cannon and Committee 5 describe the painfully slow attack to the Roer River in their report, "Hell on Wheels in the Drive to the Roer" (1949). Albert R. Cupello and Committee 12 made a detailed study of "Armored Encirclement of the Ruhr" (1949), concentrating on both the 2d and 3d Armored Divisions. William E. Dressler and Committee 3 in "Armor Under Adverse Conditions: 2d and 3d Armored Divisions in the Ardennes Campaign" (1949) reach the same conclusions as Dressler. Adolph J. Gondek and Committee 17 worked on the "Operations of Cavalry Reconnaissance Squadron Integral to the Armored Division" (1950) and concluded that the attack of the 82d Reconnaissance across Germany was a classic use of a reconnaissance battalion. Glenn T. Pillsbury and Committee 3 described the "Employment of 2d Armored Division in Operation COBRA, 25 July–1 August 1944" (1949–1950). Charles F. Ryan and Committee 4 detailed the "2d Armored Division in the Sicilian Campaign" (1950). Jack F. Wilhm and Committee 25 investigated "Armor in the Invasion of North Africa" (1949–1950) with a critical eye to the role of armor in amphibious operations.

Two master of arts theses were most useful: Timothy Nenninger, "The Development of American Armor 1917–1940," University of Wisconsin (1968); and George Macon Shuffer, Jr., "Development of the U.S. Armored Force: Its Doctrine and Tactics, 1916–1940," University of Maryland (1959). Both detail the painfully slow growth of the Armored Force.

Published Materials

The *Congressional Record* for 1941 and 1945 contains references to the 2d Armored Division, while *The Statutes at Large of the United States of America from May, 1919, to March, 1921* contains the law which gave the tanks to the infantry. The House of Representatives and subcommittees of the House held hearings on the national defense. Hearings before the Committee on Military

Affairs, House of Representatives, Sixty-ninth Congress, resulted in the publication of "Historical Documents Relating to the Reorganization Plans of the War Department and to the Present National Defense" (1927) which contains the testimony of General of the Armies John J. Pershing, who recommended that tanks be assigned to infantry. The House of Representatives Committee on Appropriations heard testimony for the creation of an Armored Force in 1941; the following year, the subcommittee of the House Committee on Appropriations heard testimony from Maj. Gen. John K. Herr who opposed an Armored Force.

Additional governmental publications include the annual reports of the War Department for 1917–1940. They detail the painfully slow growth of armor for the period. In 1934, the War Department published *Defense Against Mechanized Units*. Four years later, it reissued *Defense Against Mechanized Units* because of the progress made in antitank weapons. *The New Army of the United States* (1941) by the War Department was a guide for newsmen. In 1948, the War Department published *The Medal of Honor of the United States Army* giving the citations of the winners to that date.

The chief of cavalry printed *Cavalry Weapons: Special Text Number 160* (1934) stressing that armored vehicles were almost invulnerable to antitank weapons. In 1937, the chief of cavalry issued *Cavalry Marches and Camps: Special Text Number 161* which detailed the problems of marching horse and mechanized units. The chief of infantry issued *Tank Operations: Special Text Number 14* (no date), a correspondence course stressing that tanks were infantry support weapons. The Infantry School issued *Notes on Tank Marksmanship* (1936–1937) and *Tank Combat Principles* (1939–1940), again stressing that tanks were infantry support weapons.

The twenty-five-volume *World War Records, First Division, AEF, Regular* (1928) contains a detailed plan for the use of tanks in the support of infantry. The First United States Army *Report of Operations 20 October 1943–1 August 1944*, seven volumes (1944), covers the early landings and operations of the 2d Armored Division. The subsequent publication, *Report of Operations 1 August 1944–22 February 1945*, four volumes, continues the report until the 2d Armored Division became part of the Ninth Army. The Twelfth Army Group's fourteen-volume *Report of Operations (Final After-Action Report) 12th Army Group* (1948) supplements the other large unit records.

Unit histories are important both as a guide and a source of information. E. A. Trahan's *A History of the Second United States Armored Division* (1946) is primarily a reproduction of division after-action reports. *History of the 67th Armored Regiment* (1945) edited by Briard P. Johnson is both a history of that regiment and of Combat Command B, 2d Armored Division. Morton Eustis's *War Letters of Morton Eustis to His Mother* (1945) is an outstanding source for the thoughts of a platoon leader in the 82d Reconnaissance Battalion. Unfortunately, Eustis was killed near Domfront, France, in August, 1945.

Several other unit histories were also of immense value. Robert S. Allen's *Lucky Forward: The History of Patton's Third U.S. Army* (1947) is helpful for the formation of that army. *Conquer: The Story of Ninth Army 1944–1945* (1947) details Ninth Army operations in which the 2d Armored Division played a leading role. Thomas L. Crystal, Jr.'s *Breaching the Siegfried Line* (1945) details the attack by XIX Corps to reach the Roer River. Joseph H. Ewing, *29 Let's Go: A History of the 29th Infantry Division* (1948), is extremely valuable because the 29th Infantry Division was a corps partner with the 2d Armored Division. George M. Fuermann and F. Edward Cranz, *Ninety-Fifth Infantry Division History 1918–1946* (1947), cover the attachment of a regiment from that division to Hell on Wheels. Robert L. Hewitt in *Work Horse of the Western Front: The Story of the 30th Infantry Division* (1946) elucidates the role of another corps partner of the 2d Infantry Division. George F. Howe, *The Battle History of the 1st Armored Division: "Old Ironsides"* (1954), deals with the early days of the Armored Force. H. R. Knickerbocker and Jack Thompson, *Danger Forward: The Story of the First Division in World War II* (1947), cover the attachment of various elements of that division to the 2d Armored Division. Joseph B. Mittelman, *Eight Stars to Victory: A History of the Veteran Ninth U.S. Infantry Division* (1948), is helpful in providing information on the landing at Port Lyautey. Guy Nelson, *Thunderbird: A History of the 45th Infantry Division* (1970), discusses the prewar maneuvers. Donald G. Taggart, editor, *History of the Third Infantry Division in World War II* (1947), is an important source concerning the landing at Licata.

The Department of the Army's Office of the Chief of Military History (now the Center for Military History) series, *United States Army in World War II*, was the most important secondary work consulted. Martin Blumenson's *Breakout and Pursuit* (1961) covers the attack at St. Lo and the chase of the German army to the Siegfried line. Hugh M. Cole's *The Ardennes: Battle of the Bulge* (1965) is perhaps the best work on that battle. Blanche D. Coll, Jean E. Keith and Herbert H. Rosenthal in *The Corps of Engineers: Troops and Equipment* (1958) write about the organization and training of armored engineers. Albert N. Garland and Howard McGaw Smyth, *Sicily and the Surrender of Italy* (1965), continues the legend that the navy, not the 2d Armored Division, stopped the German tank attack at Gela. Kent Roberts Greenfield, Robert R. Palmer and Bell I. Wiley, *The Organization of Ground Combat Troops* (1947), is a useful source for the early days of training and preparation for war. Gordon A. Harrison, *Cross-Channel Attack* (1951), provides an important account of the invasion of Europe. George F. Howe, *Northwest Africa: Seizing the Initiative in the West* (1957), covers the attack and seizure of North Africa. Richard M. Leighton and Robert W. Cookley in *Global Logistics and Strategy 1940–1943* (1955) detail the problems of raising and equipping a large military force in a short time. Charles B. MacDonald, *The Siegfried Line Campaign* (1963), covers a bloody chapter in the 2d Armored

Division history. Maurice Matloff and Edwin M. Snell, *Strategic Planning for Coalition Warfare* (1953), discuss the problems of multinational forces. Maurice Matloff's *Strategic Planning for Coalition Warfare 1943–1944* (1959), a continuation of the previous title, states the problems succinctly and intelligently. Lida Mayo's *The Ordnance Department: On Beachhead and Battlefront* (1968) details the problems of the Ordnance Department in supplying the necessary weapons to the combat soldier. Robert R. Palmer, Bell I. Wiley and William R. Keast, *The Procurement and Training of Ground Combat Troops* (1948), is useful for the early maneuver era. George Raynor Thompson, Dixie R. Harris, Pauline M. Oakes and Dulany Terrett, *The Signal Corps: The Test* (1957), relates the challenge and success of the Signal Corps in providing communications equipment. Marcel Vigneras, *Rearming the French* (1957), covers that aspect of the 2d Armored Division's activities.

Two important works, Wesley Frank Cravens and James Lea Cate, *The Army Air Force in World War II*, seven volumes (1949), and Samuel Eliot Morison's fifteen-volume *History of United States Naval Operations in World War II* (1947), detail the operations of both branches. They serve as a valuable supplement to the *United States Army in World War II*.

Works by participants were useful to gain insight to the various operations of the 2d Armored Division. Field Marshal Earl Alexander of Tunis wrote *The Alexander Memoirs 1940–1945* (1961), which provides the British view of the American soldier from first impressions to their gallant role in Europe. Stephen E. Ambrose, *The Supreme Commander: The War Years of Dwight D. Eisenhower* (1969), is a must to understand the strategy of the Supreme Commander. Omar N. Bradley, *A Soldier's Story* (1951), gives a closer look at operations in Europe.

My Three Years With Eisenhower (1946) by Harry C. Butcher, Eisenhower's naval aide, recounts the activities surrounding the Supreme Commander. Mark W. Clark's *Calculated Risk* (1950) is a valuable account of the invasion of North Africa and Italy. Dwight D. Eisenhower's *At Ease: Stories I Tell to Friends* (1967), *Crusade in Europe* (1948) and the five-volume *The Papers of Dwight David Eisenhower* (1970, edited by Alfred D. Chandler, are extremely important sources regarding all aspects of the 2d Armored Division history. Ernest N. Harmon's *Combat Commander* (1970) is a valuable autobiography. John K. Herr and Edward S. Wallace, *The Story of the U.S. Cavalry* (1953), details the controversy surrounding armor during the late 1930s. Joseph Patrick Hobbs, *Dear General: Eisenhower's Wartime Letters to Marshall* (1971), gives an overview of the war in Europe. George S. Patton, Jr.'s *War As I Knew It* (1947) provides a glimpse of the general's experiences. Erwin Rommel, *The Rommel Papers*, edited by B. H. Liddell Hart (1953), is a useful account from the German perspective. Lucian Truscott's *Command Missions: A Personal Story* (1954) gives rewarding insights into that fighting commander's views.

Wesley W. Yale, I. D. White and Hasso E. von Mantauffel, *Alternative to Armageddon* (1970), draws on the 2d Armored Division's experiences to suggest that static warfare is costly and that mobility should be the answer in future conflicts.

Gen. George S. Patton, Jr., is closely associated with Hell on Wheels. Fred Ayer, Jr.'s *Before the Colors Fade* (1964) tells of the early days of the division. Editor Martin Blumenson's *The Patton Papers*, two volumes (1972 and 1974), are indespensible for the early era of armor and the division. Oscar W. Koch's *G-2: Intelligence for Patton* (1971) is informative about the planning of the invasion of North Africa. Other useful Patton biographies include: Alden Hatch, *George Patton* (1950); Harry Semmes, *Portrait of Patton* (1955), *Warrior: The Story of General George S. Patton* (1967); James Wellard, *General George S. Patton, Jr.: Man Under Mars* (1946); Charles Whiting, *Patton* (1970); and William Bancroft Mellor, *Patton: Fighting Man* (1946).

Other helpful secondary works include Martin Blumenson's *The Duel for France* (1963), *Kasserine Pass* (1967) and *Sicily, Whose Victory?* (1969). John S. D. Eisenhower's *The Bitter Woods* (1969) gives some information on the action on the northern flank of the Bulge. Peter Elstob's *Hitler's Last Offensive* (1971) is a detailed account of the German Ardennes offensive. Mildred Hanson Gillie, *Forging the Thunderbolt* (1947), is both a biography of Adna Chaffee and a description of the evolution of armor. W. G. F. Jackson, *The Battle for Italy* (1967), is useful for the invasion of Sicily. David Mason's *Breakout-Drive to the Seine* (1969) is a general account of the attack to cut the German escape routes from France. Forrest C. Pogue's two volumes, *George C. Marshall: Education of a General 1880–1939* (1963) and *George C. Marshall: Ordeal and Hope 1939–1942* (1965), narrate the problems faced by the chief of staff in meeting the demands of a world war. Cornelius Ryan's *The Last Battle* (1966) is an outstanding work on the attack across Germany. His *A Bridge Too Far* (1974) depicts the problems of lack of prior planning and the faultless execution of an attack. John Toland, *The Last 100 Days* (1967), covers the final drive across Germany.

Periodical Literature

Newspapers were valuable for the day-to-day operations of the division. *The Columbus* (Georgia) *Ledger* was the hometown newspaper of the division. *The Commercial Appeal* (Memphis, Tennessee) helped with the Tennessee maneuvers, as did *The Nashville* (Tennessee) *Banner*. The invaluable *New York Times* covered the major aspects of the division's history from its activation to the present day. *The Dallas* (Texas) *Morning News, The Shreveport* (Louisiana) *Times,* and *The Times-Picayune* (New Orleans, Louisiana) were helpful for the Louisiana maneuvers. *The Stars and Stripes, The Armored News* and *Le Tomahawk* were the major military newspapers consulted.

Professional military journals proved extremely helpful. They contained important articles, often by participants in the development of armor theory, battles, maneuvers or training activities. Hanson W. Baldwin, "Great Decisions," *Infantry Journal* (1947), considers the crucial decision of Gen. J. Lawton Collins to permit the 2d Armored Division to attack and defeat the Germans at Celles. Frederick M. Barrows, "Streamlining the Offence: The Evolution of the Panzer Division and its Place in Blitzkrieg," *Military Review* (1942), was a prophecy of American armor based on the German experiment. "The Battle of Bridges," *The Cavalry Journal* (1942), presents the problems of the 2d Armored Division in the Louisiana maneuvers. C. C. Benson, "Mechanization-Aloft and Alow," *The Cavalry Journal* (1929), concerns the influence of mechanization on military units. K. S. Bradford, "Modern United States Cavalry," *The Military Engineer* (1940), praises the development of the armored divisions. "Tank Combat Principles," *Infantry Journal* (1925), is a far-sighted article about the role of tanks in combat. Russell Brooks, "Casablanca: The French Side of the Fence," *United States Naval Institute Proceedings* (1951), implies that the combat assault may not have been necessary had the Allies been more open with the French. "The Cavalry Maneuvers at Fort Riley, Kansas, 1934," *The Cavalry Journal* (1934), discusses the first joint maneuvers of horse and mechanized cavalry units. Adna R. Chaffee, "The Seventh Cavalry Brigade in the First Army Maneuvers," *The Cavalry Journal* (1939), details the training of infantry and cavalry units as partners in offensive and defensive operations. John K. Christmas, "The Mechanization of Armies," *The Military Engineer* (1929), foresaw the mobile armies of World War II. John K. Christmas, "The New Light Tank Makes a 144-Mile Road March," *Infantry Journal* (1929), discusses the experimental mechanized force. Bradford G. Chynoweth, "Cavalry Tanks," *The Cavalry Journal* (1921), urged the cavalry to adopt tanks, while his article, "Tank Infantry," *Infantry Journal* (1921), suggested that infantrymen be trained in cavalry tactics. Harley Cope, "Play Ball, Navy," *United States Naval Institute Proceedings* (1943), discussed the invasion of North Africa from the navy viewpoint. Willis D. Crittenberger, "2d Armored Division Tanks at Battle of Alamein," *Armor* (1959), tells the role of the tanks at the Battle of Alamein. Paul A. Disney, "Reconnaissance Units Training Test, 2d Armored Division," *The Cavalry Journal* (1941), describes the tests which all reconnaissance units were required to take.

Hugh M. Exton, "The 2d Armored Division in Operation COBRA," *Military Review* (1947), is an armored artillery battalion commander's view of that battle. His article, "From Morocco to Berlin," *The Field Artillery Journal* (1948), draws on his unique experiences. J. F. C. Fuller, "Tactics and Mechanization," *Infantry Journal* (1927), is perhaps the best article concerning the internecine conflict. Michael J. L. Greene, "Contact at Houffalize," *Armored Cavalry Journal* (1949), outlines the linkup of the 2d Armored Division and Third Army to close the Bulge. A. T. Hadley, "The 'Propaganda' Tank," *Armor* (1951), discussed the merits of the famous talking tank. L. S. Hobbs, "Breaching the Siegfried Line," *Military Review* (1946), outlines the ways and means the XIX Corps penetrated the famous German defensive line. Harold G. Holt, "The 1st Armored Car Troop," *The Cavalry Journal* (1928), details the organization and training of the armored car unit. William S. Hutchinson, "Use of the 4.2-Inch Chemical Mortar in the Invasion of Sicily," *Military Review* (1943), tells that for the first time the heavy mortar was used as a fire support weapon with outstanding results. John H. Johnson, "Tanks in the Jungles," *Infantry Journal* (1925), narrates the use of tanks to support training in Panama. Oscar W. Koch, "2d Armored Division Maneuver in Tennessee," *The Cavalry Journal* (1941), reviews the division. Henry Cabot Lodge, Jr., "The Enemy in Africa," *The Cavalry Journal* (1942), is an introduction for 2d Armored Division personnel to combat while supporting the British.

"Mechanized Force Becomes Cavalry," *The Cavalry Journal* (1931), praises the decision to maintain a tank force in cavalry. "Mechanizing the Army," *The Military Engineer* (1928), urges the adoption of mechanized means for all arms and services. Alfred E. McKenney, "The New Benning," *Infantry Journal* (1941), discusses the problems of an army post when the military enlarges. F. M. Fuller's "2d Armored Division Combat Loading," *Armored Cavalry Journal* (1947), tells of the loading of the division for the invasions of North Africa, Sicily and Normandy. Leonard H. Nason, "The Fight at Mt. Carmel," *The Cavalry Journal* (1941), is a battalion executive officer's view of the maneuver. John C. Neff, "Race to the Elbe," *Infantry Journal* (1947), outlines the larger view of the final attack in Germany. Bruce Palmer, "Mechanized Cavalry in the Second Army Maneuvers," *The Cavalry Journal* (1936), demonstrates that mechanized forces could outmaneuver foot troops; however, the generals failed to agree. Howard P. Persons, Jr., "St. Lo Breakthrough," *Military Review* (1948), details that battle. "The Second Armored Division Grows Up," *The Cavalry Journal* (1941), narrates the division's first year. "17th Engineers Demonstrate New Bridge," *The Military Engineer* (1942), is a useful account concerning the new treadway bridges used during the maneuvers. Nathan A. Smith, "The Theory of Mechanization," *Infantry Journal* (1935), bitterly attacks those who did not see the value of tanks in an army. William H. Speidel, "The Tank School," *Infantry Journal* (1925), discusses the organization and training received at the tank school.

E. A. Trahan, "Armor in the Bulge," *Armored Cavalry Journal* (1948), discusses the 2d Armored Division in the Bulge from the division G-2 point of view; his article, "Speed: Essence of Armor," *Armored Cavalry Journal* (1947), discusses the 2d Armored Division's attack through the Siegfried line. I. D. White, "Reconnaissance Battalion, Armored Division," *The Cavalry Journal* (1941), is a detailed discussion of how a reconnaissance force is to be used in an armored division. K. B. Edmunds, "Tactics of a Mechanized Force: A Prophecy," *The Cavalry Journal* (1930), well describes how armored forces were actually used in combat.

The popular news journals are helpful in explaining how the division was employed in Europe and during the maneuvers. Often the writers were on the scene. Included in this group are *Newsweek, Time* and *The United States News*. Other useful but less well known publications include *The American Magazine, The American Mercury, The Christian Science Monitor Magazine Section, Collier's, Current History, Current History and Forum, Fortune, Life, The Literary Digest, The Nation, The New Republic, New York Times Magazine, Popular Mechanics Magazine, Popular Science Monthly, The Saturday Evening Post* and *The Scientific American*.

Finally, two historical publications, Benjamin Franklin Cooling, "The Tennessee Maneuvers, June, 1941," *Tennessee Historical Quarterly* (1965), and G. Patrick Murrey, "The Louisiana Maneuvers: Practice for War," *Louisiana History* (1972), discuss aspects of Hell on Wheels history.

Index